HABITS OF INEQUALITY

LORNE TEPPERMAN
NINA GHEIHMAN

OXFORD
UNIVERSITY PRESS

OXFORD
UNIVERSITY PRESS

Oxford University Press is a department of the University of Oxford.
It furthers the University's objective of excellence in research, scholarship,
and education by publishing worldwide. Oxford is a registered trade mark
of Oxford University Press in the UK and in certain other countries.

Published in Canada by
Oxford University Press
8 Sampson Mews, Suite 204,
Don Mills, Ontario M3C 0H5 Canada

www.oupcanada.com

Library and Archives Canada Cataloguing in Publication

Tepperman, Lorne, 1943–
Habits of inequality / Lorne Tepperman, Nina Gheihman.

Includes bibliographical references.
ISBN 978-0-19-544794-1

1. Equality. 2. Equality—Canada. I. Gheihman, Nina II. Title.

HM821.T46 2013   305   C2013-901939-1

Cover image: Ugurhan Betin/iStockphoto

Printed and bound in the United States of America

1 2 3 4 — 16 15 14 13

Contents

Heaven on Earth

———————•◆•———————

Man is the creature of circumstances.
Robert Owen, English social reformer

Perched on the banks of the Wabash River, on the western border of Indiana, sits a small town with a population of less than one thousand. Nestled in rolling hills and covered with a forest of maple trees, the town of New Harmony still offers remnants of the wilderness it was before its discovery by an English visionary and pioneering social reformer. Unexpectedly, this patch of nature would become the setting for a utopian social experiment, a bold move to better the human condition and then, in the end, return to insignificance.

The visionary Robert Owen was born on May 14, 1771 in Wales to parents of humble origin. He was an exceptional student, but his schooling was cut short when, at ten years of age, his parents apprenticed him to a London textile merchant. Fortunately, Owen's employer allowed him access to the employer's library, and soon Owen began to spend five hours a day reading. He spent the rest of his time working and saved most of what he earned. After learning management skills as the superintendent of a factory in Manchester, at age twenty Owen became partner in a cotton mill and soon developed interests in other industrial enterprises.

As a manager, Owen was disturbed by the degrading conditions the workers faced, toiling endlessly under strict factory discipline and living on the edge of survival. The condition of the child workers especially saddened him. Denied an education and constantly exposed to harsh living and working conditions, these young people—the future of England as Owen saw them—led cruel lives.

Owen resolved to focus his personal efforts on bettering the lives of working men, women, and children.

Only a few years later, Owen got the opportunity to put his principles into practice when he married the daughter of the owner of a large factory in New Lanark, Scotland. As manager (and part owner) of this cotton mill, Owen promptly began his experiments in work reform. He raised the workers' wages and never cut them, even when the company experienced economic difficulties. He improved working conditions, gave the workers homes and other necessities, maintained strict standards of cleanliness in the workplace, and set up schools for both the child workers and their parents. He even offered his workers sick leave with pay, a benefit previously unheard of.

So remarkable were these reforms that soon reformers from around Europe began to study Owen's ideas. From all over, people travelled to New Lanark to see for themselves Owen's progressive policies at work. Yet, despite a growing number of admirers, critics attacked Owen from all sides. They were sure that offering workers such comforts would make them lazy and, in the end, destroy the factory's profitability. However, history proved otherwise. Owen's initiatives benefited the workers and also profited the owners, with the mills making more money than ever before. The factories showed in practice that Owen's conviction that a person's good character did not depend on personality or biology, but rather on social circumstance, was indeed correct.

For the next three decades, the social experiment continued, and Owen's faith in the possibility of better lives for his workers persisted. In fact, his faith grew, fed by the experimental successes at New Lanark and elsewhere. Encouraged by this success, Owen wished to repeat his experiment on more fertile soil. Viewing Great Britain as a society steeped in a harsh history of class divisions, Owen turned westward toward America, the so-called land of opportunity. There, he hoped to extend the possibilities for human improvement through social co-operation.

On a cold December 4, 1824, at fifty-three years of age but as energetic about his ideals as ever, Owen arrived in the United

States. His goal was to buy land where he could build a community that eventually would become New Harmony. The land he bought comprised twelve thousand hectares and would soon be dotted with farms, orchards, vineyards, a church, small houses, and factories. This new setting was perfect for a unique social experiment—one more ambitious than ever tried before.

Owen set up the new town within a few months and invited people to apply for the eight hundred available spaces. The opportunity attracted people looking for equality—men and women from all walks of life. Together, they soon built a community contemporaries called the Athens of the West, referring to the equality of citizens in the ancient Greek city state.[1] Owen proclaimed it was

> a system founded on the external laws of nature, and derived from facts and experience only . . . found on full examination, by competent minds, to be the least visionary and the most easy of practice of all systems which have been proposed in ancient or modern times to improve the character and to insure the happiness of the human race.[2]

Within just a year, New Harmony had become a new centre of experiment and change in America. Everyone contributed their time and labour and shared the fruits of their work. In New Harmony, people were bound to the community as a whole, rather than to each other as individuals or family members. Here, ordinary people were taking revolutionary steps, far ahead of their time in risk and sophistication.

Beginning with a blank slate, Owen developed educational and instructional programs for everyone, from infant to adult, based on views he expressed in *The Book of the New Moral World*. Owen's community became a centre for progressive thinking, complete with the scientific exploration of ecosystems, lectures on women's rights, and open discussions of abolition. From this new harmonious community, Owen and his followers banished what they considered a trinity of evils—traditional religion, conventional marriage, and private property. They saw all social inequalities as rooted mainly in the inequalities of property and wealth.

It is no wonder that many historians today see Owen as one of the world's first socialist philosophers, though he was never formally trained in philosophy. But Owen was even more than a philosopher. In New Harmony, he and his followers had put their beliefs into practice and built a new kind of human community—a community built on social equality.

As months passed, however, it became clear that the community was not functioning entirely according to plan. Robert Dale Owen, Owen's son, later described the population of New Harmony as follows: "It is a heterogeneous collection of radicals, enthusiastic devotees to principle, honest latitudinarians, and lazy theorists, with a sprinkling of undisciplined sharpers thrown in."[3] Historians, in retrospect, agree with the analysis Robert's son offered, pointing to the idealism of the community members. They were all freethinkers, willing to dream but many unwilling to work. In short, the community's work did not get done. Locked away in this isolated place and subject to the limitations of a simple material existence, people lost their idealism. Soon, their creative thoughts and stimulating debates turned to bitter quarrels.

One central problem was the division of labour within the community. It was an egalitarian division, in which all were treated equally regardless of their talents, and for this reason it was inefficient. As well, an excess of labour was expended to enforce equality. For example, all goods in the community were collected centrally before being distributed equally. Yet this centralized distribution often introduced new problems. One member recalls, "even salads were deposited in the store to be handed out, making 10,000 unnecessary steps, and causing them to come to the table in a wilted, dead state."[4]

Within two years many community members had lost their enthusiasm for the project and Owen had lost popular support for his vision, even among those closest to him. For a while, Owen refused to accept the failure of his experiment; however, he could not continue this pretence once people began to leave the community in large numbers. Understandably, Owen was also upset by unsuccessful efforts to reorganize the system—for example, by the failure of seven constitutions drafted over the short period of the community's existence and the failure of businesses that were to provide for the community's needs. Disappointed by what was an undeniable failure, Owen blamed the community members, saying that many of them were poor human material for the experiment. In this way, he came to undermine his original, optimistic conception of human nature.

Owen was perhaps the first, but not the last, to discover the dangers of a command economy. Comparable efforts to equalize property through legislation and a command economy—for example, in anarchist Spain, communist Russia, and the socialist Israeli kibbutzim during the twentieth century—met with different fates, but none survive intact. Yet, despite continued failures to invent and practice equality, the ideal of equality itself persists even today. The present book is an effort to understand why Canadians continue to fail at the effort of equality and why they continue to strive for it nonetheless. It is also a book about the attainability of imperfect equality—a goal that perhaps Robert Owen would have supported in the end.

Acknowledgements

In writing this book, we have been helped by the co-operation and guidance of our publisher at Oxford University Press, David Stover. David has always urged us forward; yet he has also understood our reasons for recurrent delays. Also, he has given us useful criticism at every stage of the (lengthy) writing process. We hope the book in your hands finally justifies David's patience and encouragement. We are also grateful to Katie Scott of OUP, who commissioned reviews and advised us how to respond to them, and to copy editor Marion Blake for her efforts to clarify our work and make sure we justified everything we said with correct references.

We are also indebted to a group of undergraduate students who, working as research assistants, helped with the research part, persevering even in the face of undefined tasks and high expectations. In alphabetical order, we thank Walt Dick, Laurel Falconi, Anita Feher, Caitlin Hamblin, Tina Hsu, Michael Jeanette, George Kazolis, Jessie MacDonald, Krystyna Maitland, Iana Nedvijenkio, Samantha Sarkozi, Ashley Sewrattan, Cristina Tucciarone, Laura Upenieks, Noelle Van Raes, Laura Wong, and Sandra Zhou. Thanks especially to Nikki Meredith who helped edit the book in the final push toward completion.

On a personal level, Nina wants to thank those closest to her— Boris, Natalia, Galina, Svetlana, Serghei, and Martin, who came into her life just as this book did. Their love and support helped her enormously to complete the work on this book. Lorne thanks his Aunt Toby and Uncle Oscar for their lifelong battle to make Canadian society more just and equal, and for setting an example.

Lorne Tepperman and Nina Gheihman,
University of Toronto
February 2013

The Inequality Myth

—•◆•—

"If men define situations as real, they are real in their consequences."
W.I. Thomas and D.S. Thomas, American sociologists

The Game of Life

One of the oldest board games still in common use was invented in 1860 by a man named Milton Bradley. A successful lithographer, Bradley initially earned his fame with a portrait of his contemporary, a clean-shaven president Abraham Lincoln. Unfortunately for Bradley, Lincoln grew a beard soon after, and this became a crucial part of Lincoln's iconic image. People quickly lost interest in Bradley's former bestseller, and sales plummeted accordingly.

Bradley then decided to invest in an unlikely new product: a board game he called the "Checkered Game of Life," to be played on a red and ivory checkerboard. In this now-familiar game, players moved around the board from a starting point suitably named infancy; if they succeeded, they could end on a square titled happy old age. Players successfully completed the game by passing lightly over squares named after risky life-states: crime, politics, Cupid, honour, college, Congress, idleness, and so on. The game was an immediate hit, selling forty-five thousand copies in the first year; its popularity remained steady for a whole century.

In 1960, a redesigned version of the game by Reuben Klamer was reintroduced as most of us know it today, that is, as the modern Game of Life. An international success, people now refer to the game by a variety of names: El camino de la vida, Destins, Gra w życie, Igra života, Jogo da Vida, Jugar a vivir, Levensweg, Reis Läbi

Elu, Spiel des Lebens, Traguardi, Triumf, and Vain elämää, among others. Given its lasting, widespread popularity, this game shows that most of us strive for survival and success, making these goals just as universal as the quest for equality.

Today, it is hard to find someone who *hasn't* played Bradley's Game of Life at least once. A popular staple in many households, the game remains exciting because most of us can relate it to our own lives. We all play the real game of life every day by making choices that, in some ways, determine our fate. Just as in the game, every choice we make in real life takes us a step closer to one outcome, but further from another. These choices start early, usually in our teens when we elect the business path or the college route, and as we grapple with whether and when to get married. And the choices continue until we retire—sometimes unintentionally—to the Poor Farm or Millionaire Acres. As real-life players in this game, we all want to finish life in comfort and good social standing. At the very least, most of us try to avoid destitution, imprisonment, sickness, and rejection.

Over time, Bradley's Game of Life has been updated repeatedly to reflect changes in the broader economic and cultural milieux. The income a player could earn, for example, was raised to reflect rising real-life prices. Life Tiles were also added to represent new kinds of life accomplishments. As of 1992, players could receive rewards for making socially useful decisions such as recycling, learning CPR, and saying "no" to drugs. In many respects, this continued refinement made the game more realistic. But does the Game of Life really reflect the world in which we live?

In some ways, it does: we all try to avoid certain obstacles and attain certain goals, and we all have to make (sometimes difficult) choices to achieve each of these ends. Yet in many other respects, real life is not like this game at all. One important difference is that many of our real life choices are not made consciously or freely. Another related difference is that each of us starts off with different choices to make and different resources to make them. As sociologists say, everyone is born with different life chances.

Originally introduced by sociologist Max Weber in his analysis of class inequality, the term *life chances* was quickly adopted by others in the field.[1] The phrase is effective because it recognizes the chancy or probabilistic nature of real life—just like the rolling of dice that determines players' chances in the Game of Life. Weber's term has been particularly useful in research on social mobility, which studies why and how some people get ahead in life, while others do not.

When we are born, our game of life depends most importantly on our social and economic background. In turn, this socio-economic starting point depends on our parents' class status. Once we take these background factors into account, we can readily see that every child has a different set of life chances from the child next door—or (more likely) on the other side of the railroad tracks. These include a different set of chances for gaining education, wealth, power, prestige, good health, and other life prizes.

To return to the differences between Bradley's game and reality, the Game of Life is premised on the charming but socially unrealistic idea that everyone starts out on equal footing. The game also assumes that players will be offered different opportunities—like higher or lower income, for example—on an arbitrary basis, according to the roll of the dice. However, these outcomes are not purely chance-based in real life; instead, the chances of winning big at the game of (real) life are slender and shared amongst a select few. While a completely level playing field does not exist anywhere, societies do differ in terms of the degree of fairness they offer their members.

In other words, people who are born into rich, powerful, or famous families will likely live their lives under these conditions. Likewise, people from poor, disadvantaged, and unknown families are likely to finish their lives as such. These outcomes are not irrevocable. As sociological research has shown repeatedly, some people in industrial societies do overcome the odds against them, rising from rags to riches, poverty and powerlessness to wealth and power—but these cases are undeniably rare. As such, life outcomes are rarely a matter of pure chance: each of us plays this game with a stacked deck, loaded dice, and a tilted roulette wheel.

Sociology, the field we work in, explores how this real game of life works and tries to explain why most people won't win. After reading this book, you will know more about the odds you have stacked against you and about some of the strategies people use in their efforts to overcome these odds. You will also learn about the ways people respond to failure when the strategies they have chosen don't work in the way they wanted. Most importantly, you will learn about the dangerous side of this unequal game we are all playing and the high social costs exacted from each of us as individual players, and from our society as a whole.

What Is Inequality?

When we meet people for the first time, we often ask, "What do you do?" Our curiosity about how people spend their days shows that our perception of others is closely tied to how they make a living. By asking people this question we are trying to learn how well they are playing their game of life. We then use the answers to compare ourselves with others—to see who has been more successful in the game of life and who has made better life choices so far. These differences between people, in turn, form the foundations for important social inequalities.

Inequality describes the state of being unequal or uneven. In social terms, inequality is also about receiving more or less of life's rewards, and is therefore about hierarchical (that is, better–worse) differences between any two people. In comparing one person to another, we may see that one is richer, the other poorer; one is powerful, the other powerless; one is respected, the other disrespected; one is socially included, the other excluded; one is safe, the other is endangered; and so on, through a long list of socially important differences.

We know from personal experience that there are many natural inequalities between people. By this we mean that some people are tall, others short; some beautiful, others plain looking; some smart, others less so. As sociologists, we are interested in how these natural inequalities become social inequalities and in the social consequences that stem from this process. In particular, sociologists are interested in:

- how people *dramatize* or *perform* inequalities;
- how people *view* inequalities;
- how people *explain* inequalities;
- how people *justify* inequalities; and
- how people *invent* or *construct* inequalities.

As a familiar example, consider the performance of inequalities around physical beauty. People tend to favour others whom they consider to be beautiful (rather than plain looking or ugly). We know this from personal observation and from the constant bombardment of media images designed to promote consumerism by making us feel comparatively ugly. These images bleed into our everyday lives and influence the way we see other people and ourselves. So we are all aware of the difference between beauty and ugliness, but how does this translate into a form of inequality? That is, how do different societies reward beauty or punish plainness? Also, to what extent do different societies privilege and reward beauty versus other personal qualities like intelligence, strength, or reliability, for example? Why do some societies reward beauty—especially in women—more highly than they reward, say, intelligence? And in opposition, what are the unwelcome consequences of a plain appearance (let alone unsightliness), and how do these consequences vary from one society to another? Finally, it also makes sense to question why our society puts such a large emphasis on physical appearance, and how differences in physical attractiveness lead to inequalities.

In trying to answer these questions, we suggest that inequalities in appearance have long-term impacts, as do other inequalities. Unattractive people, as defined by both their own self-perception and the views of others, often suffer mental and physical health problems that are associated with secondary life consequences. How and why these processes happen will become clearer throughout the course of this book.

Another characteristic of inequality is that it often has additive and even multiplative effects, so people with two or more disadvantageous qualities are worse off than people with only one. For example, plain-looking, unintelligent people are doubly disadvantaged in our society—unless, of course, they are born rich. More interestingly, these disadvantages can interact with one another multiplicatively in a process that sociologists call *intersectionality*. The results of this process are worse than we might expect from the mere summation of two undesired traits. Intersectionality, therefore, makes it impossible to predict the effects of inequality by simply adding together individual disadvantages. However, it does force us to specify the conditions under which we might expect a particular characteristic (such as gender or race) to cause the greatest disadvantage.

In fact, a better name for this phenomenon would be *conditionality*, since it is centrally concerned with the conditions under which particular traits or characteristics produce significant disadvantage. Being a woman, for example, is not always disadvantageous; there are conditions under which lower social class can be more disadvantageous. This becomes clear when we think about the sometimes troubled relationship between white professional women and their poorly paid, less-educated, and often non-white nannies and cleaning ladies. Both the employer and employee are women in this instance; it is the differences of class and race (rather than gender) that are important in defining the life-chances of each woman and the relations between them.

Intersectionality originated as a feminist concept associated with the work of law professor Kimberlé Crenshaw.[2] To give a more concrete definition than the one we have been working with, the theory of intersectionality proposes that various biological and social categories such as gender, race, class, ability, and sexual orientation interact on multiple levels to produce systematic social inequality. By this reckoning, the traditional categories used to study oppression within society, such as racism, sexism, and homophobia, for example, do not act independently of one another. Instead, these conditions interact to create unique forms of discrimination and disadvantage.

This idea of intersectionality gained prominence in the late 1960s and early 1970s in connection with the multiracial, multiclass feminist movement that challenged the idea that gender alone determined women's lives. Instead, feminists proposed that it is the combination of gender with race and class—perhaps even with sexual orientation and geographic location—that determines the course of a person's life. So it makes a difference if someone is rich or poor, young or old, married or single, white or racialized, educated or uneducated, native-born or immigrant, socially connected or isolated, and so on. Each type of person will have different life experiences depending on which of these oppositional categories they fall under.

In the mid-twentieth century, a sociologist named Gerhard Lenski confirmed the importance of intersectionality while introducing a concept he called status consistency.[3] Imagine Arnold, a middle-aged worker who is of high status because he gets paid well, but is of low status because he failed to receive even a high school diploma. As you can imagine, these conflicting social positions have both positive and negative influences on Arnold's social status. Consider a more current example: Janice has a PhD in moral philosophy, but she is unable to get a job that capitalizes on her education. As a result, she works two part-time jobs, serving coffee at Starbucks and shelving sweaters in Banana Republic. The important question we need to address is: how do these status inconsistencies affect the way Arnold and Janice live their lives?

Some, following the work of sociologist Gerhard Lenski, have shown that status inconsistency has consequences that we cannot predict by merely adding or averaging the so-called dimensions of social status alone. Some evidence suggests that people who are status inconsistent feel uncomfortable about their situation: Janice, for example, probably feels under-rewarded, while Arnold might feel over-rewarded. Perhaps because of this discomfort, status inconsistent people have been found to adopt radical political stances against consistently higher status groups. For example, highly educated but status inconsistent women like Janice are more likely to be liberal or politically radical than highly educated women who do not struggle with issues related to status inconsistency. Ultimately then, Janice is more likely to be politically radical than her sister Sarah, who trained and became employed as a social worker.

All of this is to say that sociologists cannot readily predict a person's life chances by merely averaging individual advantages and disadvantages. The complexity of people's lives, with so many characteristics affecting their social position—both consistently and inconsistently—makes this kind of simple calculation impossible. In particular, the concept of intersectionality poses a problem for us in that it implies that disadvantage comes in different combinations. As a result, disadvantaged individuals—such as women, racial minorities, or poor people—may find it hard to share a common identity and band together to take political action. Their lives differ too significantly in important ways to make such action possible.

However, this complexity does not mean that everyone's life is unique and that sociologists cannot draw general conclusions about inequality. Clearly, if we were incapable of coming to these kinds of conclusions, we would not be writing this book. The mere existence of the study of sociology proves that we are able and willing to generalize about life, disadvantage, and inequality. In fact, our very goal as sociologists is to make theories that are valid in general, rather than in relation to particular people and circumstances. Accordingly, some individuals will have experiences that don't fit with our theories, but this doesn't make our theories any less applicable to the general population.

But why should we bother? Does it matter if some of the differences between people translate into inequalities? Sociologists think that it does matter, especially because people, and the broader societies in which they live, have developed what we call habits of inequality. We will argue in this book that modern industrial societies—Canada included—make a habit of turning natural differences into social differences and, in turn, into social inequalities.

The differences that give rise to inequalities go well beyond the differences in physical attractiveness we discussed earlier. We all know that people are compared across dimensions such as class (which includes education, income, and job status), gender, race, age, sexuality, and so on. And throughout our book, we will demonstrate that people in modern industrial societies (once again, including Canada) share a set of processes around which people perform social inequality—processes that include exploitation, domination, racialization, and victimization, among others. As we will see, these processes are enacted in a variety of venues, including the economy, the state, religious institutions, and popular culture. Further, these processes take a variety of forms and spread through a variety of social mechanisms, many of which are invisible.

Like all bad habits, those related to inequality negatively affect our everyday lives. Wherever you look, you will see Canadians turning differences into inequalities, whether these are between the rich and the poor, men and women, immigrants and native-borns, Caucasians or racialized people, young people and older people, and so on. Usually, these constructed inequalities carry moral distinctions, or ideas of better and worse, and these distinctions are at the root of our problems. Namely, the people on the bottom end of these comparisons always experience negative consequences, including those on moral and psychological, as well as social and economic, levels.

In grappling with these consequences of inequality, we began to wonder if differences between people can exist without inequalities. In other words: is inequality an inherent and inevitable result of the characteristics that differentiate people? Through our study of inequality in other countries, we have learned that the answer to this question is no: differences do not necessitate inequality. We now know this because some of the countries we examined make less of a habit of inequality than Canada does. The people in these other countries are less likely to dramatize differences as inequalities, and less likely to view differences in terms of the good versus bad dichotomy we've been discussing. In addition, stronger limits are enforced within these countries on the range of permissible inequality. As we will see, these qualities are evident in all of the countries at the uppermost end of the Human Development Index (HDI)—countries like Sweden, Finland, Norway, Denmark, Iceland, and New Zealand, for example. These countries prove that people can be different, but remain equal, because they do not frame differences as better or worse. While the countries we have listed are particularly good at this, we want to form some judgments in the following chapters about where Canada stands in this regard.

Even though we have been suggesting that other countries are doing a better job than we are, there are also countries that are doing far worse than Canada—countries where the habits of inequality are even more marked and ingrained. The United States is one example, as we will be discussing further, but there are many others as well. Most of them are lower down on the HDI than the countries we mentioned above. So, while Canada is doing better than many countries, we are also doing far worse than others. Exploring our standing relative to other countries in this way is useful because it gives us a goal to aim for—not a dream of perfection, but an attainable goal.

Perhaps that is what Robert Owen was trying to achieve at New Harmony. The goal of his social experiment, as in many other imagined utopias throughout history, was to build a fair and prosperous society in the face of the seemingly unshakeable inequality that surrounds us. This goal, which has captured the academic interest of many sociologists, is also the goal of many people who are not sociologists. In fact, the majority of Canadians appear to care about the kind of society we live in and see social inequality as a problem yet to be solved. As such, this book will try to explain why Canadians have this bad habit of inequality in the first place. We also intend to address the costs of this habit, both for each of us on a personal level, as well as for our society as a whole. By showing you the negative effects of inequality, and by explaining how this inequality arises and operates, we hope to take a small first step toward solving the problem.

Views about Inequality

Inequality exists everywhere, and people have said a lot about the topic over the years. Some of their views may be mistaken or based solely on personal experience, as opposed to being rooted in actual fact. Yet, one theme that comes through fairly consistently in these discussions is that some measure of inequality is normal, natural, and inevitable. What's more, some people believe that inequality is far from unfair; in line with this thinking, efforts to reduce or eliminate inequality would be unfair as well as unsuccessful. So, people tend to hold strong, passionate, and often bitter views on inequality.

As sociologists W.I. Thomas and D.S. Thomas once famously remarked, "If men define situations as real, they are real in their consequences." So if people believe, for example, that social inequality is evil, this belief becomes part of our reality and effectively influences our views and behaviour as a result. For example, such beliefs can lead people to take action, which in turn can have social effects like legislation or policy modifications. In fact, much of human history has been driven by beliefs about justice and injustice, fairness and unfairness, equality and inequality. Likewise, people's beliefs about class, race, gender, sexuality, and various other topics all shape the social organization of inequality, as we will see in this book. These beliefs, however vague or abstract, therefore play a considerable role in shaping the society in which we live.

Evidently then, sociologists not only study objective social problems, where the harm done is clearly evident: problems like homelessness, racial violence, and malnutrition, for example. We also study people's subjective beliefs and the social consequences of these beliefs. Such subjective realities are no less important than objective ones, but they are harder to measure since they are often products of private thought and contemplation, which are much less visible than their objective counterparts. This virtual invisibility of beliefs makes sociology and the other social sciences more elusive than branches of the physical sciences, like chemistry. Atoms do not think and take action based on their thoughts, and atoms do not have the free will that would allow them to do so. But because humans do, explaining and predicting human behaviour is more complicated.

As sociologists then, we need to carefully consider people's thoughts and beliefs, as well as the objective situations in which they find themselves. The subjective aspects of social problems—that is, the sense of unfairness that people feel about being poor, discriminated against, or victimized by domestic violence, for example—reflect our capacity for emotional reaction as human beings. In turn, these feelings can lead people to take action in the hopes that they can make a better life for themselves. But these actions, in addition to potentially altering their own lives, often change those of others.

These subjective responses frequently lead to what sociologists call the social construction of human problems. The process of constructing a social problem usually involves the search for villains to blame, the creation of a moral panic, pursuing a crusade for better behaviour, demanding improved laws, and sometimes initiating full-blown social movements that put the problem on the political agenda. The most effective means by which to create this kind of movement is to engage in claims-making—a process by which people try to capture public attention and mobilize opinion around particular problems and their possible solutions.

So, our view of something as a social problem is determined by changes in actual (measurable) reality and by changes in our perceptions of reality. By bringing together both objective and subjective elements, we can define inequality as a social problem characterized by

- visible, measurable features that threaten people's well-being; and
- strong beliefs in inequality as a social problem that warrants collective, remedial action.

That's Not Fair!

Before taking the trouble to study and explain its causes and effects, we need to know why we think inequality is a social problem. To begin, we would like to quote French philosopher Jean-Jacques Rousseau, who offered the first theory about social inequality over two hundred years ago. According to Rousseau, social inequality involves some kind of privilege, by which we normally mean, "a right, advantage, favour, or immunity specially granted to . . . a certain individual, group, or class, and withheld from certain others or all others."[4] Rousseau is suggesting that society provides some people with more privileges than others; this unevenness is not natural, but rather socially contrived. Further, this imbalance may force some people to respect and obey other, more privileged, people.

Rousseau goes on to ask whether there are any circumstances under which this unequal distribution of privilege is justified. In response, he suggests that social inequality must be proportional in order for it to be just; disproportionate inequality or privilege, by mutual exclusion, is unjust. In Rousseau's words, "moral [that is, social] inequality, authorized only by positive right [that is, human law], is contrary to natural right, *whenever it is not combined in the same proportion with physical inequality*"[5] (emphasis added). To paraphrase, any privilege or inequality that does not clearly arise out of a natural difference is contrary to the laws of nature. In other words, social inequality is unjust if it exceeds natural inequality.

Rousseau's theory is attractive in one respect, though unattractive in another. On the negative side, it asks us to imagine a natural law against which we can judge human laws. Most of us would agree that it is impossible to identify natural laws, so we do not even try to do so. The closest anyone comes to framing such natural laws today is perhaps seen in evolutionary psychology. There, some researchers still ask about the likely survival value of certain human behaviours or preferences. Sociologists rarely do this, however, as we recognize the huge cultural variation in social arrangements throughout history. From this perspective, every imaginable activity has survival value in some circumstances, but not in others.

On the positive side, Rousseau correctly identifies why most people care about social inequality: unjustifiable privilege is unfair. We all appear to have some general sense of what is fair and unfair, even though we may disagree with each other at the margins. Whenever we see someone receiving unjust privileges, or if we are deprived of just rewards, we experience a strong emotional response to this moral breach—we typically get irritated, angry, and even outraged. Whether this response is universal we cannot say, but it is certainly Canadian. So, in modern terms, Rousseau is saying that we know when unjustified privilege has gone too far, and we reject it. What's more, this response to inequality is not unique to modern-day Canada; Rousseau's views have been supported throughout history and across many different nations, helping to ignite the French Revolution in 1789 and the Russian Revolution in 1917.

For our purposes, we will be using a more up-to-date sociological definition of social inequality. By this, we mean the unequal (and usually unjustifiable) privileges, rewards, or opportunities that different people receive within a given society. Put simply, people mean fairness when they say equality and unfairness when they say inequality. Equal treatment can therefore mean identical treatment, but it can also mean comparable or similar treatment. Ultimately though, being treated equally means being treated in a fair and justifiable way.

Whether we judge equality in terms of equality before the law, equality of occupational opportunity, or equality of economic outcome, we expect an equal process to be fair. That said, inequality might be a constant feature of the human condition, since people in large, modern societies do not seem to be able to escape privilege and unfairness. In trying to understand why this is so, we will be discussing many different theories and concepts. We will see, through this process, that some of these theories focus on a single factor to explain inequality, such as capitalism or patriarchy. Our main argument, however, is that there are many important factors to consider in explaining inequality, all of which are linked with and dependent upon each other.

By reviewing each of these factors, we are essentially trying to answer the question: is inequality unavoidable? According to economic liberals today, the answer is yes, inequality is the price we have to pay for dynamic economic growth under capitalism. Throughout the twentieth century, communist states tried to reduce these economic inequalities through a rejection of capitalism. However, these experiments ultimately failed, merely creating different, equally abusive forms of inequality. In the end, new politically based inequalities were created that were even harsher and less fair in some respects than the class inequalities they replaced.

These experiments collapsed around 1990 under the weight of social discontent. No one was prepared to defend them anymore. Given this historic experience, what degree of equality can we truly aim to attain? What can people realistically hope for in their search for fairness? From a liberal standpoint, the collapse of communism justifies any amount of inequality, no matter how extreme. Few people today continue to believe that perfect equality can be achieved through communism or socialism. Some even believe that these approaches have proven that social inequality is inevitable.

We do not share these views, and our book is dedicated to explaining why social equality is a realistic goal. As one of many examples, recent brain imaging research shows that humans might be naturally inclined to believe in equality.[6] A team of researchers from California and Ireland carried out what is called functional magnetic resonance imaging (fMRIs) on participants who were engaged in money-transfer imaging. The researchers found that reward centres in the brain respond more positively when a poor person gets a financial reward than when a rich person does; this holds true whether the study participant is poor or rich. This study suggests that we have some kind of inherent tendency to favour a balance of the economic scales—that is, to favour equality. However, this is only one experiment, taken out of its social and cultural context. As sociologists, we want to consider what inequalities are justifiable, and what equalities are humanly attainable, all within specific contexts. We also want to consider various types of unfairness and the different ways through which they can be remedied.

Throughout this book then, we will argue that inequality still makes a difference, just as it did in Rousseau's time: social inequality has important consequences for crime and justice, war and peace, and of course, the everyday game of life. We will also see that the disadvantage stemming from social inequality is usually inherited. That is, our society maintains a large underclass in which disadvantage is transferred from one generation to the next, from parents to blameless children and grandchildren. What's more, those who inherit this disadvantaged status have little hope of escape, and will likely live their entire lives in this condition. We will see, in addition, that the global spread of capitalism, besides encouraging economic growth, disperses and preserves social inequality to a previously unknown degree. But most importantly, we hope to explore what can be done to stop this cycle. To this end, consider the dilemma faced by Ms. Jones.

Ms. Jones's Class

Imagine you are an elementary school teacher like Ms. Jones, who must decide how to divide her time in helping her fourth grade students learn to read. How can she be fair while going about this task? Sociologist Christopher Jencks[7] suggests five approaches: democratic equality, moralistic justice, weak humane justice, strong humane justice, and utilitarianism. Most obviously, Ms. Jones might choose to give five minutes of help a day to every student in the class. In doing so, she would have chosen what Jencks calls the democratic equality approach. Or, noticing that some students appear to be making bigger-than-average efforts to improve their reading, Ms. Jones might choose to give them more of her time, thereby choosing moralistic justice.

Yet, Ms. Jones knows the desire to learn may vary among children from different social and economic backgrounds. For example, some of her students have parents who offer a great deal of encouragement and who constantly read and discuss books with them. Others, in contrast, never read or discuss books with their families, and their parents do not explicitly encourage learning. To compensate for these discrepancies, Ms. Jones might choose to give more of her time to students from less-advantaged backgrounds, since they have the most difficulties to overcome. In doing so, she would choose what Jencks calls weak humane justice. Or, Ms. Jones might choose strong humane justice, giving more time to any student who has been shortchanged by life in any way. This approach would involve, for example, giving extra help to students with physical disabilities or abusive parents. Finally, Ms. Jones might take the practical (and non-moralistic) route Jencks calls utilitarianism, giving more time to the best readers and less time to the worst ones. Her reasoning might be that, based on tests and research, the best readers are most likely to benefit from each additional minute of her attention.

If you were Ms. Jones, which principle of fair allocation would you choose? Obviously, there is no single right answer. People debate these kinds of problems in public life all the time, and only when we have to make such choices ourselves does it become clear how difficult fairness is to implement. Currently, the dominant academic view of justice is probably based on philosopher John Rawls's difference principle.[8]

The Rawls principle asserts that the unequal distribution of scarce goods—like power, money, health care, and so on—is justifiable only when it increases the advantage of the least advantaged groups in society. In other words, equality is the default position, unless inequality will serve to improve the status of the disadvantaged. This sounds a little like what we call affirmative action or employment equity in certain domains, where schools or companies establish quotas for different groups to ensure sufficient representation. It also sounds like Ms. Jones's strong humane justice approach.

This principle of fairness is different from the one put forward by Rousseau, because it makes need the criterion for all decisions.

That is, the Rawls principle suggests that sharing should not undermine the position of people who are already needy. Allocation, by this standard, should not increase inequality, but preserve or reduce it. In choosing a course of action then, Rawls asks us to imagine that you are at the bottom of the social ladder, lacking any knowledge about your future, your talents, or your skills. Achieving social justice from this standpoint will require you—the most deprived—to choose in your own best interest. In this state of deprivation, you make your decisions behind a veil of ignorance. And since you are unlikely to choose against your own best interests, you will equalize the distribution of social goods.

As an example, imagine that you are no longer Ms. Jones, but Sally Smith, her ten-year-old student. Despite being the worst reader in the class, Ms. Jones puts you in charge of assigning help with reading. Assume, in line with Rawls's thinking, that you will do this with your own interests in mind. Accordingly, you will maximize the well-being of the least advantaged students in the classroom, since you want to avoid making your own situation any worse. If we all imagine ourselves in the position of the least advantaged person in society, we will act (rationally) in the most just and equitable ways. This is not because we are benevolent saints, but because we do not want to make our own position any worse than it is already.

Outside academia, Rawls's approach is not well known. Far more familiar in our society is the notion of equality as rewarding people according to their merit. If justice consists of giving people what they deserve, but people's abilities, skills, and investments of time are unequal, then justice would seem to call for unequal outcomes. However, this meritocratic approach forces us to ask what forms the basis of merit and which personal qualities we can justly reward. For example, should we reward people for being beautiful? For their height? For their shoe size? Besides, who can rightly claim credit for their own merit? Can you ethically demand a reward for having been born smart or pretty? And how can we distinguish between those attributes for which a person can claim credit, and those which are his or hers merely by chance? Consider IQ or sports skills like strength and speed. Surely, these qualities are affected at least as much by chance as they are by design. Even beauty requires a fair amount of time and work to cultivate.

We need to distinguish between these different types of features because justice may not be served by rewarding chance qualities. How does society benefit if we reward people for being beautiful, or even for being smart? What if they are beautiful but mean? Or intelligent but wicked? Even a quality like the ability to work hard is a chance attribute, since it can be a result of body chemistry, childhood socialization, or early role models. As such, being a hard worker may not be a morally proper basis for reward. The main point here is that we do not deserve praise for results we did not achieve by ourselves. Why should we be rewarded for having been born into a wonderful family, while someone else is punished for having been born into an awful family?

Sociologists have grappled with this question in the so-called functional theory of stratification, credited to sociologists Kingsley Davis and Wilbert Moore.[9] They argue that, in all human societies, some positions (for example, brain surgeons and nuclear physicists) have more functional importance than others (such as car sales people and hairdressers). People who hold these more important jobs typically need special skills to perform adequately. However, the needed skills are scarce because talent is rare and training is costly. (Think about it: are you choosy about who performs brain surgery on you? Or would you be choosier about who sells you a car?)

Because people who can hold these important jobs are rare, society will have to persuade those with the necessary aptitude to learn these special skills. To this end, adequate rewards need to be offered to induce the right people to spend long hours in classrooms and laboratories, to endure late nights studying for tests, and to tolerate the other (perhaps less rewarding) circumstances necessary to acquire the skills they need. These rewards often involve money and high social status or prestige. This fact, in turn, suggests that social inequality is unavoidable: as long as different skills are valued differently and require different amounts of aptitude, effort, and investment, we will need to offer people different rewards for what they do. And we will do so because, in the end, inequality benefits all of society by helping to turn out "useful" people, like brain surgeons. In this sense, inequality allows society to survive, which is why we find inequality everywhere, in every society throughout history. This argument suggests that without inequality, a society would perish! We would have a glut of hairdressers, but no brain surgeons, since no one would put in such extreme effort only to be rewarded in the same way as someone who had exerted minimal effort.

This is a persuasive theory, at first glance, because it seems to be consistent with our everyday experience. A lot of us also believe in the functional theory of stratification because it is endorsed by people who are seen as fair, just leaders. However, this theory is not without flaws. First, it ignores the inheritance of wealth and status. People who inherit their money and prestige from their parents do not necessarily have skills that contribute to the survival of society, or to social well-being of any kind. Further, these people haven't been required to exert themselves to develop useful skills. Consider Prince Charles or momentary celebrity Paris Hilton as examples: what kind of social contributions do these two make? What justifies the privileges they enjoy, as Jean-Jacques Rousseau might ask?

A second flaw is that functional theory ignores class conflict, gender conflict, and other disagreements about society's most important roles. Who says a Wall Street lawyer is more socially valuable than a car mechanic, or that a doctor is more socially valuable than a nurse? There is widespread agreement about the relative value of, say, doctors and car mechanics, but even that agreement is not universal. We also need to consider how much of this agreement is genuine and how much is due to false consciousness or the manipulation of our thinking by powerful groups? The Canadian Medical Association is a more powerful lobby for rewards and respect than a Canadian Car Mechanics Association (which doesn't exist).

Third, functional theory fails to explain a wide range of anomalies: for example, why leading figures in organized crime, sports, and entertainment are rewarded with high wages and social prominence. Are these people important for the survival of society, relative to less-rewarded nurses, social workers, and teachers? Equally, how do we explain the low rate of rewards for parenting, nursing, teaching, and eldercare? Surely, our society could not survive very well without these poorly rewarded activities.

In reality, the functional theory does a poor job of accounting for many types of inequalities. Consider the following tongue-in-cheek typology of social players in the Game of Life:

The Shakers
These members of society create change and benefit from it. Examples include Bill Gates and David Suzuki. As a group, they conform to the functional theory of stratification.

The Royals
These people do nothing of social value, but they benefit nonetheless. Paris Hilton and Prince Charles serve as examples. They do not conform to the functional theory of stratification.

The Saints
These meritorious members of society create change even if they do not benefit from it, such as Nelson Mandela and Mother Teresa. They do not conform to the functional theory of stratification.

The Pawns
This vast group, composing the majority of the population, does most of the work to keep society running but remains largely unrecognized and unrewarded. They do not conform to the functional theory of stratification either.

Contrary to what functional theory proposes, a select few members of society are rewarded far too much, while the majority are rewarded far too little. Some do great good, and some do great harm—and yet doing harm does not seem to preclude the acquisition of wealth, arguably the most sought-after reward. Pawns—collectively undervalued, historically replaceable people—are in fact the driving force of history, yet they are ignored, under-rewarded, and often even abused by the powerful. Given our understanding of this, it is unclear why Canadians accept the functional theory of stratification, which so obviously fails to describe their own firsthand experience. Probably, this is because the functional theory is a fairy tale about fair rewards, and people love to believe in happy endings. However, the latest economic recession, starting in 2008 and only gradually ending, is surely the consequence, in large measure, of market failure—something that functional theory fails to account for in its description of getting ahead.

Many people also accept evident inequalities because they believe they have a good chance of moving up the social ladder. They may have no pie today but will (possibly) have pie tomorrow, if only they work hard enough. Some of us accept the inequality of condition—a wide difference between rich and poor, for example—because we believe that equality of opportunity exists.

This leads us to ask what kinds of opportunities are available to ordinary people and what kinds society should make available. A complete answer to this question would require a thorough discussion of social mobility—the topic of many sociological studies. Research shows that in industrial societies, many middle-class people (and their children) are socially mobile. In other words, equal numbers of middle-class people move up and down the social ladder throughout their lifetimes, depending on the state of the economy. However, people born very rich rarely move down the social ladder, while people born very poor rarely move up it. Education is the single best resource you can use to improve your status if you are poor or middle-class. But education, in turn, is predicted by the social class into which we are born: people born rich get more (or better) education, and they get more out of this education.

With this in mind, how should Canadian society increase social opportunities in a fair way? Should we offer open-entry, free university education, thereby committing the same amount of money to everyone's education, regardless of their abilities? Or, should the talented get more opportunities than the less-talented, perhaps in the form of more tuition support? Should we base all entrance scholarships on ability, not need, even if that means privileging middle- and upper-class children? Notice that we are facing the same moral issues that Ms. Jones and her fourth-grade readers struggled with.

In the end, we may be mistaken when we think that social mobility based on equal opportunity can solve the problems stemming from social inequality. Economist Friedrich Hayek[10] has proposed that we can never expect competitive market outcomes—such as the outcome of an equal-opportunity struggle for educational success—to reflect merit. After all, luck plays too large a part in determining who gets what: some people are born smarter than others or have more prosperous, literate, and supportive families, for example. However, as Hayek suggests, that does not mean we should completely reject markets as a mechanism for allocating rewards. Markets are valuable because they efficiently direct scarce resources to the places that bring the greatest return—however unjustly. In the end, the market will produce adequately trained brain surgeons, car salespeople, and sports celebrities. This process may not be fair, but it will be efficient and effective.

Further, Hayek proposes that the poor are better off with this unequal distribution of rewards than they would be under any other circumstances. This is because the market increases productivity, as we saw in our example of the struggle for upward mobility. This system makes everybody try just a little bit harder; the resulting productivity ends up benefitting those who have the least, through taxation and wealth redistribution. In the end, competitive struggle is better for everyone, even if it is particularly better for some.

As you might imagine, views about the functional theory of stratification, social mobility, and market competition vary according to people's political outlook. Liberals, for example, endorse the value of equal opportunity and deem inequalities of outcome legitimate if they reflect genuine differences in merit. From a liberal point of view, everyone should have the same initial opportunity to become a concert pianist or brain surgeon; if people with real talent are the only ones who succeed, that is just fine. However, liberals have trouble agreeing on the conditions that are needed to ensure that each of us does, in fact, start off with this equality of opportunity. They also have trouble defining what constitutes merit. Some hold an extreme libertarian position, arguing that people are entitled to do whatever they choose, with whatever resources they have acquired legitimately, and that this is more important than equal opportunity. Meanwhile, traditional conservatives regard hierarchy—that is, inequality—as being good for societies. They see it as a source of social discipline, rewarding those who have worked hard while punishing those who have not. Some conservatives think inequality is unavoidable, or perhaps a necessary part of any civilized society. Others respect tradition, and because they see inequality as traditional, they correspondingly view it as being acceptable.

Sociologists, for our part, have tried to avoid such doctrinaire political and ideological debates. For us, the debate about inequality is meant to be empirical and descriptive, not moral and prescriptive. Despite these intentions, sociologists have leaned to the left in our political orientation. Many sociological studies have looked at welfare policies, the family, education, and earnings in an attempt to uncover popular views about fairness in the distribution of advantage and disadvantage. As a result, many of us have taken the stance of the social critic, pointing out failures and hypocrisies in our social policy.

Lady Justice

Most modern societies claim to strive for justice, so all of the social sciences have examined the concept at some length. In fact, justice is a central moral concern for all of us, even outside of academia, since we are all preoccupied with fairness. So, to some degree, we are all concerned with justice—we want to believe that people (eventually) get what they deserve. In line with this thinking, M.J. Lerner and Carolyn Simmons put forward the just-world hypothesis, a theory that states that we all need to believe that we live in a fair world.[11] They suggest that in order to maintain this delusion, we use many psychological strategies to convince ourselves that good things happen to good people and that bad people get the punishment they deserve.

Lerner proposed that this belief is the result of normal childhood development. At a certain point, children stop trying to gratify their immediate desires and begin to work toward future rewards. This change happens through the creation of a personal contract with the parent, in which the child starts to feel deserving of certain rewards by virtue of having put in the necessary work.[12]

But given the vast amount of inequality in the world, how can belief in the personal contract be maintained? It only makes sense to delay our gratification today if we can be certain that we will get what we deserve tomorrow. In effect, this means believing that tomorrow's rewards will be even better than today's. Holding this belief, of course, is only possible if we conclude that *all* people get what they deserve. And to believe this, we must generalize our personal contracts, using them to explain other people's circumstances. So, if we believe that we will be rewarded for good behaviour, we also have to believe that other people will get punished for their bad behaviour.

It is hard—maybe even impossible—to retain a pure belief in a just world. Yet, because we want to believe that things will work out for us if we are good enough, or if we work hard enough, we often blame innocent victims for their circumstances. In order to maintain our personal contracts and a sense of justice, we need to explain victims' suffering by believing they brought it on themselves.

Of course, reality is more subtle than we have been making it out to be. In the short term, when people encounter an innocent victim, they acknowledge that his or her suffering is undeserved, and correspondingly react with compassion. But this only occurs when they expect that the victim's suffering can be alleviated. When presented with the same victim, along with the expectation that his or her suffering cannot be alleviated, people use a variety of techniques to make the victim's condition seem deserved. These strategies can include impugning the victim's character, and suggesting that their own poor choices were the ultimate cause of their suffering.[13]

These reactions are common in our society. For example, many of us believe that people on welfare choose not to work. Similarly, victims of sexual assault are often blamed for their suffering if they wear provocative clothing. Both instances reveal a tendency to hold people responsible for their unfavourable conditions. But whether we are aiding or blaming the victim, our beliefs stem from a concern with justice: ultimately, we are trying to either right wrongs or to make them appear deserved. People are thus always, consciously or unconsciously, concerned with the justice of inequality.

Like equality, justice is a difficult concept to define. We can distinguish at least four different kinds of social justice: equity or fair exchange, distributive justice, procedural justice, and retributive justice or fair compensation. Equity or fair exchange mandates the equivalence of outputs to inputs for all of the parties involved. An example of this type of justice would be that someone who works very hard should get a pay raise. By this reasoning, if everyone works hard, everyone should get a pay raise, and if no one works hard, well, everyone continues to get paid the same amount (or, perhaps, gets fired). That is only fair and just.

Second, there is distributive justice: a fair allocation of resources, rights, and obligations across an entire category of contenders. What people get out of a process should reflect what they put in, compared to other people. The simple rule behind distributive justice is that people who do more should get more. A similar rule is that people who bring more to the table—more talent, skill, energy, or commitment, for example—should take more away. As such, distributive justice allows for unequal outcomes, so long as they are justified by unequal inputs. This idea may be close to what

Rousseau had in mind when he spoke about privileges justified by natural inequalities.

Third is procedural justice, which guarantees that fair procedures will always be followed in allocating rewards, even if these fair procedures result in unequal outcomes. So, for example, a judge's guarantee that she will follow the law in the same way, with the same procedures for everyone, does not guarantee that everyone will get the same outcome. However, it strikes us as fair nonetheless. Defendants who are judged in the same way cannot complain that the judge was biased against them, even if they do not get the decision they hoped for. Thus, procedural justice is equivalent to the rule of law as modern people understand it.

Fourth is retributive justice or just compensation. The main arguments here are that people who do harm should be punished appropriately, and that people who have been victimized should be compensated appropriately. So, for example, people who cheat on a test should get a zero; people who steal money should return the money; and people who break a window should repair the window. Ultimately, the point of just compensation is to ensure that victims are suitably compensated and, if possible, to reverse wrongdoings.

Sociologists have always been interested in the ways people react to unfair treatment. Today, sociologists also study people's feelings of frustration, anger, and resentment when they witness injustice or are victimized by injustice. Recent research shows[14] that witnesses react more negatively to occurrences of procedural injustice than to any other kind, especially when someone in authority commits the injustice. As Rousseau argued, we may hate to see people receiving unfair advantages, but we hate it even more when people in power dole out these privileges.

This can happen in many ways. Consider, for example, a worker who deserves a promotion for a job well done, but whose boss decides not to grant this deserved benefit, choosing instead a close friend for the promotion. In this instance, the other workers are likely to feel some mix of frustration and resentment toward their boss's actions. The boss has the authority—that is, the right and the power—to make this choice; yet the choice is seen as unfair. Since it was based on favouritism rather than merit, the decision is procedurally unjust. As a result, the other workers see their boss's unfair decision as inappropriate or perhaps as an abuse of power, even though they were not directly affected by the decision.

That said, the same research shows that people are less outraged by procedural injustice when they have no expectation of procedural justice—that is, when they expect decisions to be made in a biased fashion. To use our previous example, the workers would probably be less outraged if the boss promoted his son-in-law—an understandable choice, though unjust—than if he promoted someone merely because that person was Irish, or handsome (qualities the boss unaccountably admired). Likewise, they would be less outraged if they had always experienced biased decision-making, as one regularly experiences in political systems that run on patronage. At least these leaders make no pretense of fairness, so people's expectations cannot be violated.

As these varied situations suggest, people's ideas about fairness and justice are often nuanced and unconscious. However, as a general rule, those of us who believe that things will work out for people who deserve it will enjoy high levels of life satisfaction, positive mood, and the confidence to overcome difficult situations.[15] In contrast, people who do not believe, or only weakly believe, that the world is just toward them score lower on scales of psychological well-being and often display symptoms of depression, anxiety, and paranoia.[16]

Yet the just-world theory may not accurately reflect the way things work in reality. If strong beliefs in a just world are unwarranted, they may be comparable to opiates, as Karl Marx described religious belief. Much like religious non-believers, people with weak just-world beliefs feel less included in their community than those with strong beliefs. As a result, they often display antisocial behaviours, including abuse, withdrawal, and sabotage.[17] On the other hand, research shows that just-world believers are often seen as more socially attractive and valuable than people who display weak beliefs, possibly because they seem more positive and optimistic.[18] In other words, a belief in a just world tends to promote conformity and social inclusion.

But even though conformity and cohesion are good in themselves, do these positive effects of the just-world belief make up for the negative ones, such as victim blaming? And how are we to live comfortably knowing that no matter what they do, some people will never get what they deserve?

The answer is that we don't live with this conflict: it is impossible to truly believe in a just world while also recognizing that some people will never be rewarded (or punished) as they should be. Strong believers in a just world simply ignore evidence of unfairness, actively disregarding the fact that the world is not always just so that they can continue to adhere to their beliefs.[19] They do not want to think that they, or people like them, could be complicit in terrible injustices, so they blame victims when the real perpetrators are part of their own social group.[20]

If the just-world hypothesis is valid—and research suggests it is—then most people believe that things are the way they should be in the world. These beliefs have serious implications for how we think about inequality. Namely, most people think that unequal treatment is fair and deserved. These beliefs therefore have implications for what we think can or needs to be done about inequality; if the majority of people feel that inequality is fair, the majority of people also think that nothing should be done to reduce it.

However, just as individuals vary in their embrace of these beliefs, so do societies. That's why societies differ in their approaches to and acceptance of their habits of inequality. In other words, people are treated more equally within some societies, and some societies are less tolerant of inequality, depending on the extent to which they embrace just-world beliefs. This variation proves that we Canadians can aspire to reduce unequal treatment, because other societies have shown that greater equality is possible and even functional. Because both individual and society-wide beliefs in a just world have such important implications, we will return to this hypothesis in the last chapter.

But we don't want to focus only on hypotheses; rather, practical and attainable goals for increasing equality in Canada will be the focus of our book. You might have already figured out that sociology is the study of the possible. As sociologists, we do not compare real societies with ideal or utopian societies like Robert Owen's New Harmony or Marx's communist society. We compare them with other real societies, since only real societies can give us a practical sense of what is possible. In other words, we sociologists base our arguments on those aspects of reality that can be measured and recorded so that other sociologists can test our findings with new studies.

In contrast, people used to judge social problems based on religious criteria. In many societies, such as our neighbouring United States, this tendency to moralize about social life is still evident. We can even see this kind of religious perspective on social problems in Canada: as late as the 1950s, for example, many Canadians worried about premarital sex, considering it to be sinful and immoral. We are less likely to worry about premarital sex today, however, and are more likely to worry about other issues, like the state of the environment. In addition, physical and mental health have very recently become important concerns for many citizens, including academics, politicians, policy-makers, social activists, and others.

Part of the reason for this shift of focus is that people today feel entitled to a safe, healthy life of their own choosing; they demand choice to a degree that was uncommon in the past. Today, we recognize that health and safety—not morality—are good indicators of social well-being. So, in this book, we will keep coming back to issues of health and safety, because related measures (like illness, crime, addiction, victimization, and destruction, among others) point to how well a society is providing for its people. If we see that inequality produces these harmful results, detracting from our health and safety, it will be easy to see that inequality exerts a harmful influence on society. And if inequality does, in fact, have these damaging effects, it is a social problem we need to take seriously. Given our varied backgrounds, we may not be able to agree on whether or what kind of god exists, so we cannot depend on religious or moral criteria to determine whether inequality is good or bad. However, we can all agree that we would prefer to live safe, happy, long lives. Evaluating inequality on these terms will allow us to come to the most universally applicable conclusions.

In trying to figure out whether people are differentiated by important inequalities, we need to empirically measure these inequalities and their effects. Remember, there can be differences without inequalities, but there cannot be inequalities without differences. As such, the starting point for any sociological analysis of inequality is to recognize and measure the differences between people. We must then try to understand how these differences are discovered or invented—in other words, how they have been socially constructed as inequalities.

PART 1
Habits of Inequality

CHAPTER 1

Exploitation

————— ◆ —————

*"The history of all hitherto existing society
is the history of class struggles."*
Karl Marx

Lucky Number

The paths people follow through life are often made clear when they're still young. Several cultural examples show that we tend to leave little room for change past a certain age. Consider the well-known Jesuit maxim: "Give me a child until he is seven, and I will give you the man."[1] Inspired by this maxim, in 1964 the documentary *Seven Up* was aired on the United Kingdom television show *World in Action* and received worldwide distribution and screening in cinemas. The concept consisted of the director Michael Apted following fourteen British children—ten boys and four girls—over the course of their lives. Every seven years, the series presents new footage of these fourteen subjects juxtaposed with material from the previous films.

Apted chose his false celebrities purposefully: they were meant to represent segments of British society, differentiated by class. Because of their different class origins, the children, adolescents, and then adults lead vastly different lives on-screen, reflecting each of their different backgrounds. In effect, Apted was inventing something like our current idea of reality television—but his version was very class-focused. He could have called his series *How Class Matters*.

You might think that his seven-year-old subjects wouldn't be too different from each other, except for some superficial personality differences. Some might be shyer, while others could be more outspoken, but in the end, children are just children, right? Apted proved the opposite to be true, providing support for the Jesuit quotation by noting extraordinarily obvious differences between the upper- and lower-class children in his sample even at only seven years of age.

In his first film, Apted starts us out at the top of the social ladder. He introduces us to John, Andrew, and Charles first, showing them sitting together on a comfortable couch at their exclusive boarding school. The product of privilege, these three boys look like miniature adults, already sporting school uniforms—crisp white shirts, ties, wool sweaters, and tweed jackets. At merely seven-years old, Apted shows them discussing weighty matters. They could be taken for their parents:

> ANDREW: I read the *Financial Times*.
> JOHN: I read the *Observer* and the *Times*.
> CHARLES: (to John) What do you like about it?
> JOHN: Well I like . . . I usually look at the headlines and then read about . . . about it.
> ANDREW: I like my newspaper because I've got shares in it and . . . know every day what the shares are . . . but on Mondays they don't move up so I don't look at it.

Apted dubs these boys the "Three Wise Men." They amuse us because they're having these seemingly adult discussions, but they also astonish us with how learned they already seem—and how snobby they are. Already, at seven-years old, these Wise Men have made a good start at being what the British comedy troup Monty Python famously called upper-class twits. Even if they are merely copying what their parents or other adults say and do, it's clear that they take themselves seriously and expect others to do the same. And, importantly for us, these seven-year-olds seem to have their futures neatly planned out: when Apted questions them about the education they hope to attain, each boy describes the top British universities, Oxford and Cambridge.

Apted then compares these boys to three boys from humbler backgrounds. Neil and Peter are both middle-class boys from the Liverpool suburbs; Paul grew up in an orphanage. In response to Apted's questions about their future plans, the three boys reply:

NEIL: I don't, I don't figure I need to go to university, cause I'm not going to be a teacher.

PETER: I don't think you ought to go to university if you want to be an astronaut.

PAUL: (looking confused) What does university mean?

Clearly, the class lines that divide them make for some stark contrasts between each set of seven-year-olds.

At fourteen, in the next episode, the children are questioned about their career plans. Class differences are highlighted perhaps even more obviously at this stage. The upper-class boys are already able to foresee a comfortable and privileged future for themselves. John, one of these aloof "Wise Men," states confidently: "I think I will follow a legal career." And sure enough, he goes on to become a lawyer. The lower-class boys respond differently. Tony, wanting (but failing) to become a jockey, ends up as a taxi driver. Simon, meanwhile who also grew up in an orphanage, says, "I'll just walk around and see what I can find." Neil decides that instead of being an astronaut like he wanted to be at seven, he will try to become a coach driver.

Even just these snippets give us a pretty good idea of how the British class system works—specifically, how it influences education, aspirations, and life experience. At only seven years of age, the course these children will take through life has already become clear. The latest episode of the documentary covers the interviewees when they are in their fities and plans unfold largely as expected. The upper-class boys go on to costly private schools and the best universities, as they (and their parents) planned. The working-class boys end up in state schools, and their futures as Apted states, remain as uncertain as they had described it when they were seven. While it's true that some of the interviewees encounter a few surprises along the way, the social class into which they were born largely shapes the clothes they wear, their body language, the way they talk, their education, and finally, what they spend their lives doing.

The same has been found to hold true for our own class system. In 1978, Canadian sociologists Bernd Baldus and Verna Tribe interviewed 108 local school children ages eleven and under to learn about their ideas on inequality. They found that, by the age of eleven, children can already recognize the signs of inequality, such as how people dress and talk, and the kinds of cars they drive. More interesting still, these children had already formed (or adopted) moral judgments about inequality. These included accounts about why some people are rich, with some suggesting that "they deserve it." In opposition, some kids explained why people are poor by arguing that "they didn't work hard enough." So, even young children recognize class inequality as a significant aspect of social life, and they too seem to endorse the ever-popular belief that virtue is rewarded.

But what do all of these studies tell us about social class, one of the most historic forms of social inequality and one that is still prevalent today? In this chapter, we argue that classes and class inequalities are inevitably linked to exploitation. This is because economic differences are often turned into economic inequalities by powerful, wealthy classes who exploit less powerful, less wealthy classes. And through this process, the rich and powerful make themselves even richer and more powerful.

In order for this exploitation to occur, however, economic differences need to be framed in terms of class differences: the rich need to define themselves as the upper class, while simultaneously naming the poor as the lower class. This process of class differentiation is important because it produces different lives for people of different sorts or backgrounds. But it also produces an ideological system that justifies economic inequalities by making cultural and even moral distinctions between people of different classes. Because of this way of thinking, people in every society and civilization throughout history have become divided along class lines.

As simple and obvious as these concepts may seem today, we owe this interpretation of history to the first sociologist who studied inequality systematically: Karl Marx.

The Winning Side of History

Karl Marx—the first serious student of social class—was born in 1818 to wealthy parents in Prussia (part of present-day Germany). He studied in Bonn and Berlin, where he began to read political philosophy and to associate with other young, politically progressive students. In 1843, he married and moved to Paris. A charismatic young man, Marx tended toward grand theories and generalizations. Joshua Muravchik, author of *Heaven on Earth: The Rise and Fall of Socialism*, puts it this way: "Where others saw meaning, Marx could see meaning within a meaning, behind a meaning, and then a bigger meaning."[2]

Marx's radical socialist colleagues were essentially in awe of him. Many recognized that he would inspire change, and some went as far as to describe him as the prophet who could aid the miserable working classes. But Marx was no political leader; he spent most of his time alone, reading, thinking, and writing in the British Museum. He was an ideas man, not an activist, although he did encourage others to take action. He also had little patience with other people's contributions, and often refused to consider them entirely. Nevertheless, one day, an article by another German, Friedrich Engels, caught his eye.

Engels was also born to wealthy Prussian parents, in 1820. Manfred Stegar, author of *The Quest for Evolutionary Socialism*, describes Engels as "a bit of a rebel. He was the typical frat boy in many ways. He was very interested in the military . . . sports . . . pubs . . . and women, but he was also an intellectual. He was in many ways the kind of person you would immediately recognize as a leader and as somebody people would congregate around."[3] In

1842, while he was still a student, Engels began to openly discuss his strong belief in communism, effectively rebelling against his privileged background. Unsurprisingly, Engels's father became concerned about the radical crowd with whom Engels spent his time. In an attempt to separate him from this group, he sent Friedrich to work in a branch of the family factory in Manchester, England.

Soon after his arrival, and contrary to his father's wishes, Engels began to study how working-class families in Manchester lived and were treated. He eventually published his research in 1845 in a book called *The Condition of the Working Class in England*.[4] But even his initial observations revealed that English industrial workers were deprived, or even destitute; they were experiencing conditions just as bad as those in today's least developed countries. Yet Engels saw an upside: all of this misery would provide fertile soil for revolution and, thereby, the path to a better society. He believed that before long, workers would reject capitalism and find the strength to overthrow the factory owners who exploited them so extensively. Engels began to put these early ideas into writing, and Marx, who edited a radical socialist publication, came across them. The two began corresponding, and in the summer of 1844, they met for the first time in Paris, initiating what would become a long intellectual partnership.

Engels's writings on the working class formed the basis for what later became known as Marxism. Marx was the more intellectually flamboyant of the two, and it suited Engels to encourage his friend's intellectual genius. This (partially) explains why the philosophy is called Marxism, not Engelism. Together, they joined the Communist League, and in 1848, when the League decided to put its ideas into writing, they agreed to compose the *Manifesto of the Communist Party*.[5]

The pamphlet that was produced through their joint effort would become one of the most influential publications of all time. It opens with the now-familiar passage:

> The history of all hitherto existing society is the history of class
> struggles. Freeman and slave, patrician and plebeian, lord and

serf, guild-master and journeyman, in a word, oppressor and oppressed. . . . Our epoch, the epoch of the bourgeoisie, possesses, however, this distinctive feature: It has simplified class antagonisms. Society as a whole is more and more splitting up into two great hostile camps, into two great classes directly facing each other—bourgeoisie and proletariat.[6]

In addition to its content, the timing of the pamphlet's publication links it to revolution. The year of its publication, 1848, was marked by upheavals across Europe, from England in the west to Russia in the east. The breadth of social unrest showed just how agitated the working class already was; yet, the revolutionary uprisings of 1848 failed to achieve their goal, for reasons that Marx and Engels would think about a great deal. What's more, the next decade saw a fierce counter-revolutionary backlash that forced Marx and Engels to move to London, which was safer and more politically stable at the time. There, Marx's evolving views continued to win him both admiration and persecution, especially after the Paris Commune in 1870, another revolutionary effort that tried to put socialist ideas into practice, but ultimately failed to survive.

Despite these failures, Marx and Engels remained convinced that revolution and the fall of capitalism were inevitable. Their conviction is evident in the *Communist Manifesto*, which offers a compelling theory of history—in effect, a prediction of the success that socialism would eventually enjoy. Their work asserts that throughout history there has always been a struggle between the oppressed classes and those who oppress them. However, they argue that capitalism changed the nature of that struggle, making the relationship between bourgeoisie and proletariat markedly different from anything that came before, and marking it as the last historic struggle between these two groups.

In their words, "by bourgeoisie is meant the class of modern capitalists, owners of the means of social production and employers of wage labour. By proletariat, the class of modern wage labourers who, having no means of production of their own, are reduced to selling their labour power in order to live."[7] The struggle between these two new classes would be, they predicted, the final struggle; Marx and Engels saw capitalism as the last mode of production because it carries the seeds of its own destruction. They claimed that capitalism cannot survive without constantly increasing profits. This means capitalism must constantly make the production process more efficient, pay ever-lower wages, and control the workers ever more closely, in order to extort the maximum possible profit. To survive then, capitalism always has to expand, but by expanding, it creates an increasingly larger and ever more destitute working class that will eventually revolt.

A workers' revolution, then, is as certain as the growth and fall of capitalism. And, according to Marx and Engels, this revolution will give rise to a new society like no other—one with no state and no private property. In this post-revolutionary society, people will contribute according to their ability, receive according to their need, and fulfill their creative potential. These new people might farm in the morning and write poetry at night, as Marx famously mused. While some of these ideas are similar to those put forward by utopians like Robert Owen, Marx and Engels differentiated themselves by calling this imagined, post-revolutionary way of life communism.

In hindsight, since the collapse of Soviet communism, many have mocked the idea. Most people argue that capitalism has prevailed, thereby proving Marx's theories wrong. Even during the heyday of Soviet communism, many observers had remained skeptical and derisive, and within the Soviet Union itself, many people with first-hand experience pointed out its flaws. For example, a famous Soviet joke goes: "Communism isn't the same as capitalism at all. Under capitalism, some men oppress all the rest. Under communism, it's the other way around."

Still, communism in Russia and elsewhere was important in several ways. First and most importantly, it pressured capitalists in other countries to accept a variety of forms of democratic socialism. As a result, some non-communist countries took progressive measures in regard to work conditions in the nineteenth century. Many more emerged only in the twentieth century with the threat of more severe egalitarian measures. Second, communism was like a beacon for the working classes, giving them confidence in their historic mission, and legitimating their goals of improved wages and working conditions. Though some of these gains have been eroded in the last few decades through so-called globalization, they would have been even smaller if the working classes hadn't had the example of communism to confirm that their struggle would inevitably succeed.

By looking at some of Marx and Engels's thoughts on capitalism and the class system, we can gain a better understanding of how these systems work today in their infinitely more complex forms. They argue that in most industrial societies, capitalism divides the population into two opposing classes, with a class being defined as a group of people who have the same relation to the means of production. By this, they are referring to the materials needed to produce goods: capital, property, machinery, and other resources. Under the capitalist system, workers are provided with access to this machinery and capital, and they produce goods in exchange for a wage.

But the wages are often low, sometimes even at the subsistence level, meaning that they are only enough to keep the worker alive and productive. Because there are usually more workers than jobs, people become desperate for any work at all, regardless of the wage; this explains why people are willing to accept such low pay. For their part, upper-class capitalists know that continued unemployment, even in times of prosperity, ensures that a reserve army of labour will be available in case extra hands are needed. The bourgeoisie thus have virtually unlimited access to labour, and they know it; they can pay the lowest wages they like, because they will easily be able to find another worker to replace one who refuses their offer. And in turn, the mere threat of unemployment (and the associated poverty) guarantees that workers and their union representatives will comply with the capitalists' wishes.

This set of economic arrangements means the bourgeoisie can rule and exploit the proletariat, or working class. Because they must sell their labour in exchange for the money they need to survive, the working class has only three choices: they can work for the capitalists, more or less on the conditions they dictate; they can form unions and try to change the conditions set by the capitalists; or they can revolt, overthrow the capitalists, and create a new, egalitarian, classless society. However, the working class was least likely to choose the third option; even though compliance may be bitter, it seemed safer, surer, and easier than organizing a revolution.

The means of production mediates this dynamic between the capitalists and the proletariat. In every society, according to Marx, the means of production determines differences in social position: who is in power and who is not. However, as the technologies of production change over time—for example, from horticulture to farming to industrial work—the means of production also change. In turn, the forms of ownership and control practices change. Even forms of exploitation change, requiring forms and strategies of conflict to change as well. In the end, these ever-evolving means of production cause constant shifts in power relations.

According to this theory, class conflict is an inescapable feature of any society beyond the smallest and least developed, such as hunter-gatherer societies (which still exist today, although they are gradually being swallowed up into the larger and more dominant societies around them). But capitalist industrial societies are particularly prone to class conflict, since the interests of the bourgeoisie and the workers are so fundamentally opposed: lower wages and worse working conditions for the proletariat mean higher profits for capitalists, and any concessions by the capitalists to the workers mean lower profits.

Further, people often remain divided along class lines for generations. Having been born into the proletarian class, workers rarely have the chance to improve their situation. They cannot further their education or improve themselves in any other way because they are forced to work for capitalists in order to survive. As a result, they live off of subsistence wages, and are always exhausted from their routine and endless hours of work. According to Marx, the only way to change this situation is for working-class people to recognize how similar their economic experiences are. This means seeing their common relationship to the means of production and looking past their religious, ethnic, linguistic, cultural, and gender differences, among others. Marx called this awareness of similarity class consciousness, and identified it as essential to both mobilization and revolution. If workers do not see their common fate— that is, their common economic situation—they cannot control or change the class system.

Marx distinguishes between two types of class awareness: a class that is aware in itself and one that is aware for itself. The latter is aware that they have a common relation to the means of production and that they are capable of mobilizing to pursue their own interests. The question for Marx is, how does a class in itself become a class for itself? Usually, what prevents the transition between these two types of awareness is false consciousness—a belief in the ideologies perpetuated by the dominant capitalist class that blame people for their own troubles, rather than the system as a whole. To oppose and overthrow capitalism, workers need to develop a revolutionary class-consciousness and believe that they are on the winning side of history. As Marx and Engels declare in the *Manifesto*: "Workers of the world unite! You have nothing to lose but your chains."[8]

A Whole Lot More for a Whole Lot Less

Why do socialists still talk about Engels's and Marx's work today? After all, no worldwide class revolution has unfolded, and no classless industrial societies have been established. Marx and Engels put little faith in using peaceful methods (like unionization and the ballot box) to drive significant change—but this is precisely what happened.

History has shown that what we call "democratic socialism," comprising small improvements and timely social reforms, has dealt with many of the working-class concerns that Marx and Engels put forward. And though a new and more complex breed of capitalism is spreading through globalization, a revolution by the working class still seems unlikely. Workers, after all, are divided by other factors—such as geography, culture, language, religion, and values—that make them unlikely to come together as a single revolutionary group. Even provocations such as the Great Depression of the 1930s and the world recession that began in 2008 have failed to set off a class revolution. So, despite Marx and Engels's predictions, capitalism has survived. It has endured thanks to a combination of protection by Western governments, and to the war-making that has yielded profits, increased productivity, and a boost to employment rates. In effect, capitalism has been considered too big to fail.

In addition, our modern version of capitalism has introduced factors designed to appease the working class; welfare measures, consumerism, and promises of upward mobility for the lucky few have recently started to placate workers. Since the mid-twentieth century, Western workers (especially in the US and Canada) have lost their class-consciousness and shifted their focus to identity politics, which have more to do with other types of inequalities we will discuss later on—inequalities based on race, sexuality, and even age. And gradually, as unionized manufacturing jobs have been lost to overseas workers, Canadian and American workers have lost their political voice. Today, few of these workers have read *The Communist Manifesto*, know what it says, or put any trust in its message.

Today's working class therefore remains unlikely to revolt, since it lacks the necessary class-consciousness. But, as Marx recognized, the development of such class-consciousness has always posed a huge challenge. Successful mobilization requires successful organization—that is, a developed capacity for a group of people to behave as a collective actor. Protest and revolution need tight organization and loyal membership: everyone must share the risks and dangers. This means expelling so-called free riders, or people who want the benefits of class protest without facing the dangers and potential costs. It also means that class-based organizations, such as trade unions, need to be able to mobilize their members behind strong leaders. These leaders, for their part, must ensure that the group exercises self-control (not self-expression), and works toward collective interests (not individual ones). In these ways, class mobilization forces people to blindly trust union and party leaders; to value equality over liberty; and to work toward long-term, instead of short-term, goals.

Workers will only agree to this kind of self-sacrifice if they have an ominous, repellent enemy—something that all of them can agree to detest. In Marxian theory, that enemy is exploitation. By this, we mean the control and use of an economic resource—be it capital, property, or technology—to profit at the expense of the workers. Marx, however, based his theory of exploitation on what he called the "labour theory of value," which focuses on the forced extraction of surplus value from workers. It is this labour theory of value that allows capitalists to exploit and benefit from the poverty of the workers.

From the workers' standpoint, this exploitation is unfair and dehumanizing; it makes life unsatisfying by making work unsatisfying. From the capitalists' standpoint, however, exploitation (and the profit it yields) is the very reason investors put their money at risk. Investors in production control a unique commodity that, when used, creates more value than it costs. This commodity is labour power. In capitalist societies, workers—who lack access to or control over the means of production—are forced to sell their labour power to whoever owns the means of production. The trick for capitalists is to maximize profits by paying workers low wages in exchange for their labour power, while charging consumers high prices for the products this labour power yields. But, as a result of this process, workers are forced to survive from paycheck to paycheck, and meal to meal. Viewed this way, surplus value is the difference between the wages a worker receives and the value of the product he produces.

The idea that labour is the supreme source of all wealth was not a unique Marxian contribution. Rather, this was a common belief shared by most early political economists. As one example, Adam Smith proposed that if workers owned their own means of production, goods would be priced in proportion to the labour needed to produce them. However, later neo-classical economists backed away from the theory of surplus value because it was too abstract; no one could measure the surplus value workers were producing.

Today, the notion of surplus value remains widely rejected. Mainstream economists, and even many Marxists, recognize its technical defects. One obvious problem is that the costs of subsistence vary historically and culturally, so we have not been able to solidly define how much labour time is necessary for survival. Despite flaws such as this, the theory originally provided a new perspective on society in general and on the system of private property in particular.

Marx's original theory thus used the term exploitation to refer to economic unfairness, including notions of disadvantage, trickery, greed, and dehumanization. Today, most sociologists use the term exploitation in a more general sense, following Max Weber, another founder of sociology. Among modern sociologists, exploitation means profiting unjustly from the labor of others. (For a detailed discussion of current thinking, see the work of Erik Olin Wright.[9])

In Wright's analysis, there are three principles or criteria of exploitation: inverse interdependence, exclusion, and appropriation. First, inverse interdependence means that the material well-being of the controlling group depends on the material deprivation of the controlled group. By this reasoning, wealth is a zero-sum game, and for capitalists to win wealth, workers have to forego it. Second, exclusion means that the exploited group must be barred from accessing the resources they need to survive (like land, housing, water, health, or credit), except through paid labour. In effect, capitalists have to starve workers into submission in order to gain their surplus value. Finally, appropriation means that exploiters take the profits made by the labour of the exploited. To do this, they must control the operation of the state and legal system, as well as the economy.

In other words, the first of these principles says that exploitation occurs when the material welfare of one class depends on the material deprivation of another. So, for the capitalist class to thrive, it must deprive the working class of some material wealth. Next, the exclusion principle shows how this inverse interdependence of capitalists and workers, revealed in the first principle, relies on workers being excluded from access to necessary resources. This exclusion usually depends on some form of legal property rights. Third and finally, the appropriation principle reveals that creating and attaining surplus value is the goal of the entire system, since the capitalist class cannot survive without this surplus value. And because appropriation is a principle of exploitation, the capitalist class is equally incapable of surviving without exploiting the working class.

These are important ideas, but Marxist theory today is not the same as it was a century ago. This is partially because newly emerging means of production lead to new forms of exploitation and in turn new forms of resistance by the working class. Exploitation and people's responses to it are therefore always changing, making it difficult for any related theory to stay precisely relevant throughout history. Further, socialism and communism are no longer theoretical ideas that need to be tried out in real life; they have been tested, though some have argued that they haven't received a fair or thorough trial. So, while we recognize that Marx's original theories have been revised or replaced, his ideas remain some of the most helpful in developing our understanding of class inequality and conflict. Therefore we will continue to explore his thoughts in the hope of expanding upon them, thereby drawing some conclusions that may be more applicable to today's capitalist societies.

The Problem of Alienation

It's clear that Marx believes capitalism is bad for workers. But why does he think so, specifically? One reason is what he called alienation. According to Marx, exploitation and the general unfairness of a capitalist society make people feel unappreciated, undervalued, and worthless. It is this general feeling of isolation and meaning-lessness that has come to be defined as alienation.

For Marx, there were four types of alienation a worker experiences under capitalism. First, the worker becomes alienated from the product of his or her labour. Instead of being used by the worker upon completion, the product is taken and sold by the capitalist, who then enjoys the profit. Often, this process makes products completely unaffordable for the workers who originally made (or helped to make) them. Second, since the product of the worker's labour is taken away, capitalism makes the work itself meaningless—an activity over which the worker has no control and no autonomy. The capitalist decides what the worker will do, and how long he or she will do it; as a result, there is little chance for creativity or innovation. Third, capitalism alienates workers from their own sense of humanity—from the very feeling of being human. The worker is made to feel like a robot, going through the motions in order to earn the needed paycheque. Finally, in relation to this third point, the worker also comes to feel alienated from other workers, especially because they are often treated like replaceable commodities rather than human beings. Because they are forced to compete with one another for jobs, workers usually find it difficult to develop meaningful and authentic relationships with each other. In these ways, capitalism may even encourage self-hate and misanthropy.

These ideas about alienation, like those surrounding exploitation, proved useful for twentieth-century sociologists who adopted Marx's theory. A clear testament to his legacy is the theoretical orientation that still bears his name, Marxism, and all the work that has emerged from it. Some of this work is called Marxist, meaning that it follows Marx's classic theories. Other work is sometimes dubbed neo-Marxist, meaning that it is a reinterpretation or reworking of those classic theories.

In the mid-twentieth century, one of these neo-Marxist works explored how capitalism and alienation had evolved since Marx's time. This book was *Labor and Monopoly Capital*, written by Harry Braverman and published in 1974.[10] After working for years as a coppersmith and in various related trades, Braverman was able to provide an insider's perspective on working-class experience. As a skilled crafts worker, he saw firsthand how craftwork was transformed by capitalism—a transformation that eventually shaped his union activism and writing career. His work in all of these areas helped him see that, despite important technological advances, the human experience of work was never going to improve under capitalism.

Braverman's book explores the development of capitalist production over the last two centuries. He proposes that modern work, while demanding ever-higher levels of education and expertise, has become increasingly mindless, bureaucratic, and alienating. It has been degraded by capitalists seeking to increase their control over the labour process by separating execution from design—or handwork from headwork. Thus, increasingly, the workplace has been divided economically and intellectually, with one class of people acting as robots, merely operating machinery, and another class acting as experts and managers. Given this division of roles, management's goal is not to humanize work—despite claims that are occasionally made to the contrary. Rather, management aims to lower labour costs while increasing profits and global competitiveness.

When Braverman wrote this book, most people still believed the world was getting better and better. Many thought that machines would eventually do all the work, and the biggest problem would be figuring out how to use newfound leisure time. However, this optimism proved to be unjustified; leisure has certainly not become a social problem, and for many workers, technological advances have made work even more meaningless, underpaid, and exploitative. In the end, Braverman's argument for the ever-increasing mindlessness of work seems to have been correct.

Our current situation also supports his ideas on the exploitative nature of capitalism. Especially for third-world workers who toil in conditions similar to those seen during the Industrial Revolution, global capitalism has meant exploitation. But even in Canada, many of the jobs that were considered white-collar and middle-class during Braverman's time are now becoming more repetitive and unfulfilling than before. Some positions today, for example, simply require monotonous data entry into a computer file. Ultimately, these changes to employment opportunities are meant to increase profits. One managerial strategy used to this end is often disguised as "job enlargement" or "reorganization." Essentially, staff reductions are made to cut costs, forcing remaining workers to be more efficient. Fewer people therefore produce the same output, reducing the money that goes toward wages, thereby yielding greater profits. Another management strategy creates the illusion of employee decision-making that gives workers a chance to participate by choosing between fixed, insignificant alternatives. These strategies are often framed as helping to humanize work by creating an interesting, fast-paced environment in which there is never a dull moment.

Thus, capitalism's separation of skill from knowledge, or handwork from headwork, degrades the meaning of work. It also creates two different types of workers. On the one side, a few highly skilled, highly trained people, whose time is infinitely valuable, do the brainwork. On the other, a mass of indistinct workers, whose time is judged to be worthless, tend the machines. And as these machines become ever more intelligent, their human tenders become more and more expendable—more easily controlled, ignored, or fired.

All of these ideas are closely linked to Marx's notion of alienation, a theory that was becoming increasingly popular around the time when Braverman's book was published. Though Marx and other European philosophers had first addressed it a century earlier, the theory of alienation had remained below the surface, receiving little scholarly attention. Thanks in part to a revived interest in classical sociological theory, sociologist Melvin Seeman resurrected the idea in 1959 by combining the insights of Marx, Emile Durkheim, and Sigmund Freud.[11] His goal was to develop a multi-sided concept of alienation that could unify contemporary social, psychological, and political discourses around inequality.

Seeman's reconceptualization identified the following six dimensions of alienation. He also used the survey statements we discuss below to measure how prevalent these dimensions were in his own society.

> *Powerlessness:* A sense of little control over events, measured with statements such as "nothing I do makes a difference" and "you can't fight city hall."

> *Normlessness:* A sense of the incomprehensibility of personal and social affairs, measured with statements such as "being 'good' just won't cut it anymore" and "nice guys finish last."

> *Meaninglessness:* Achieving goals through socially unapproved means, measured with statements such as "I can't make sense of it all anymore" and "what's it all about?"

> *Cultural Estrangement:* The rejection of commonly held values and standards, measured with statements such as "my culture's values aren't mine" and "what is success, anyway?"

> *Self-Estrangement:* Engagement in activities that are not intrinsically rewarding, measured with statements such as "my work doesn't mean anything to me" and "what I learn in school isn't relevant."

> *Social Isolation:* A sense of exclusion or rejection, measured with statements such as "I'm alone," "I don't fit in," and "no one visits me anymore."

Seeman's work initiated a flurry of research on alienation that lasted for about two decades; then social scientists largely deserted the theory again. However, this is not because alienation disappeared under a new form of capitalism. Many researchers continue to study and discuss this problem of alienation, but they do so using different terms. Some research continues to focus on people's lonely lifestyles, such as sociologist Robert D. Putnam's recent book,

Bowling Alone.[12] Others have called attention to low voter turnout and diminished confidence in public institutions. In addition, studies of consumerism, addiction, and religious fundamentalism consistently find a trend toward people's continued, desperate search for meaning. And research on the so-called impostor syndrome addresses a newer version of Marx's concept of self-estrangement. According to these studies, it seems that alienation has continued to be a problem in capitalist societies, just as exploitation has.

On the other hand, many people today seem to deny or ignore feelings of alienation. We mentioned earlier that people often prettify the world by claiming that it is just and fair. This same thought process leads many of us to define our workplaces as fulfilling and non-alienating. Accordingly, and contrary to what Marx would have expected, most people today say they like working. Many also claim to have found meaning in their work: whatever the job, they make a game of finding this meaning by gossiping, flirting, debating politics, and ridiculing management. Perhaps because of such games, many people like their work so much that they are reluctant to retire, now that compulsory retirement has been abolished in Canada. These experiences do not sound like alienating ones.

Sociological research confirms these suggestions, showing that most people find their work rewarding precisely because it *is* social—not isolating, or alienating in the Marxian sense. People enjoy and value the informal relationships they develop at work, suggesting that working (or at least keeping busy in the company of others) may be a natural human need. The problem with work emerges when it becomes exploitative, when people are expected to work hard under bad conditions like long hours, little pay, or little respect. This is when work—something that should be meaningful and fulfilling—becomes robotic and dehumanizing.

A Lifelong Debate

There is no denying that Marx's theories were revolutionary. Both in his time and in ours his ideas have been incredibly influential, to the point that they formed the basis for an entire socialist empire—the so-called Communist Bloc of nations, centred on the USSR and China—in the twentieth century.

In retrospect, however, Marx's economic theory seems too simplistic for today's world, and even perhaps even for his own. For Marx, all of social and cultural life—even the books we read, the prayers we chant, and the beliefs we hold about family and marriage—are just mere reflections of economic life. Economic relations are thus the structure of society, while social-cultural relations are merely the superstructure over this economic foundation. In principle, Marx denies that ideas and beliefs can shape social and cultural life, except to the most superficial degree. This is where his otherwise promising theory goes wrong.

It is in this respect that Marx differs most from Max Weber, another founder of sociology whom we mentioned earlier. Born in Erfurt, Germany, Weber was the son of a wealthy and worldly businessman and politician and a mother who had been raised in strict Calvinist orthodoxy. These biographical facts would later influence Weber's intellectual development. In particular, he believed that by adopting the Calvinist Protestant emphasis on hard work and thrift, he would be able to overcome a natural tendency toward laziness and self-indulgence. This combination of his mother's religious beliefs and his father's business and political acumen encouraged Weber to work hard and to embrace learning passionately.

His hard work appears to have paid off. Weber was hired as a professor immediately after finishing his studies. During several productive years, he wrote on an incredibly wide range of subjects that spanned geographies and epochs. However, Weber suffered a series of personal challenges during the last two decades of his life, including the death of his father and, subsequently, several nervous breakdowns. Despite these interruptions to his work, he is still considered to be among the most influential thinkers in social science. He made substantial contributions to an array of scholarly disciplines, including politics, science, religion, law, formal organization, and economics, among others. In sociology, his conception of power has been especially influential.

Even though Weber was only nineteen when Marx died Weber's biographers have often said that these two scholars appear to be in debate with one another in terms of their ideas on class and power. Weber undoubtedly considered Marx to be brilliant, but he had a big problem with Marx's belief that ideas were not as important as material reality. Unlike Marx, Weber considered ideas—whether they were political, economic, or religious—to be just as important as economic relations.

This belief formed the basis of Weber's most influential work on the topic, *The Protestant Ethic and the Spirit of Capitalism*.[13] In this book, Weber proposes that religious ideas played a key role in the development of capitalism in the West, thereby also explaining why the East developed differently. He argues that values associated with ascetic Protestantism and especially Calvinism—like the emphasis on hard work, sobriety, and frugality, all of which Weber himself held dear—stimulated and supported the development of capitalism, bureaucracy, and the Western rational-legal state.

For Weber, capitalism is not a purely material phenomenon, as Marx claimed. Instead, he argues that capitalism rests on certain key ideas, some of which cannot be solely explained by relations of production. These include religious ideas; for example, capitalist relations of production reflect uniquely Protestant beliefs about working hard and striving for success. This explains, according to Weber, why the most sophisticated forms of capitalism arose in northwestern Europe and not in India, China, ancient Israel, or the Roman Catholic Mediterranean areas of Europe. Weber's earlier work on comparative religion supports this thesis, providing evidence based on a deep analysis of faiths both within and beyond European borders.

Weber also extended Marx's definition of class, incorporating some non-economic aspects of social life. Remember that, for Marx, a class is a group of people who share a certain relationship to the means of production, be it as capitalist-owners or powerless wage-labourers. For Weber, on the other hand, class position is not only about economic relations of ownership, but it is also about education and skills, making it more broadly a social position. So, Weber would define a class as a group of people with similar economic interests, opportunities, and conditions, whose material well-being is significantly affected by their education and skills. This is a more nuanced definition than the one Marx provided, as it takes into account the complexities of modern economic life.

Weber's definition may therefore be more easily applicable to the Canadian class system. Just by looking around us, we can understand that classes in our society aren't like neat layers in a cake—they are more like those in an Italian sandwich. In the sandwich we can see a more or less distinct top and bottom (the bread), and many different ingredients inside that are essentially separated by type (lettuce, tomatoes, cheese, salami, and so on). However, these layers aren't of the same height and consistency, nor are they neatly arranged. At certain points, they overlap and become indistinct, while at other points, they remain fairly well differentiated.

So, as our analogy suggests, making class distinctions may not be as simple and clear-cut as Marx seems to have believed. He was correct in arguing that social class is fundamentally linked to the work people do, but he seems to have been less correct in his argument that this work-status connection is only mediated by people's relation to the means of production. The link is more complex than that, because people in a similar relation to the means of production may differ widely in their earnings, the nature of the work they do (for example, whether they do headwork or handwork, as Braverman discussed), and the amount of power and authority they wield. A self-employed business worker, for instance, is a different kind of capitalist than the larger-than-life factory owner Marx imagined.

This is where Weber's definition becomes helpful. In the Weberian sense, class is determined by people's market position in the economy—that is, by how much money and status they gain from their occupation—not by their relation to the means of production.

Weber also expanded on Marx's ideas of class formation. In addition to the processes of exploitation and class-consciousness that Marx put forward, Weber saw that classes form through exclusion. By this, he meant that classes fight to keep their distinctions and privileges, often subdividing into smaller status groups, or sets of people with a shared social position with similar ideas of prestige, esteem, and honour. Viewed another way, class is a special kind of status group organized around a variety of social differences, such as religion, ethnicity, nationality, regional location, or even race. The chief feature of a status group just like that of a class is the practice of drawing boundaries between insiders and outsiders. So, for example, members of a certain status group may build a country club open only to select (that is, socially similar) members, preventing everyone else from playing golf or tennis or from socializing with the elite.

Status groups can also be made up of professionals in the same field, who regulate entry into their profession and protect their authority to train, certify, and manage practitioners. In this sense, Marx's version of a class would only be one type of status group—one that uses control of the means of production to include and exclude people, to reward them, or exploit them. Marx also believed that people could only gain power or control over others, by owning the means of production—hence the dominance of class in his analysis. On the other hand, Weber argued that people can also gain power by entering high-status groups and influential political parties. They would therefore be just as capable of dominating others as people with economic control, like the capitalists Marx described.

In today's post-industrial societies, Weber's analysis is the more useful because it is more subtle and comprehensive. Also, it deals with present-day realities more effectively than Marxian analysis, which is firmly rooted in early nineteenth-century capitalism. Today, for example, it is no longer necessary to own a business to control the means of production; it is only necessary to manage the organization or influence its board of directors. The control of productive capital began to pass from owners to managers a century ago, in a process economist James Burnham influentially called the managerial revolution.[14] By taking this change into account,

Weber's conception of class more accurately reflects our experiences than Marx's does.

Weber's analysis is also more applicable because today's working class is international, due to multinational ownership and global competition. This is what we call the globalization of work: an advanced version of economic imperialism heralded by Marx and Lenin in their writings on capitalism. Globalization has made the mass mobilization of workers in any given country even more difficult because jobs can always be shipped overseas if the local workers demand higher wages or more job security.

For Weber, control over distribution is just as important as ownership or control over production. This fits well with our post-industrial, globalized economy, in which ownership of the means of production may be concentrated, dispersed, hidden, or socialized. Further, the stock market is a large player in our present-day economy, as is the government. And both the market and the government stand in a complex relationship to Marx's bourgeoisie and proletariat. It is less clear today than it was in Marx's time who's in control, how or why jobs are destroyed or created, and what can be done to increase the well-being of the average Canadian worker.

Nowhere is this complexity more evident than in the rapidly growing service sector. Here, incomes are diverse, ranging from six- or seven-figure annual incomes for managers and professionals to four-figure pay for salespeople and burger flippers. This wide differentiation in the so-called service class reflects the growth of a few highly skilled and well-paid job categories at the upper end of the pay continuum and the proliferation of unskilled or semi-skilled, poorly paid jobs at the lower end.

Polo, Pointe, and Privilege

> *"Class is an aura of confidence that is being sure without being cocky. Class has nothing to do with money. Class never becomes intimidated. It is self-discipline and self-knowledge. It's the sure-footedness that comes with having proved you can meet life."*
> Ann Landers, advice columnist

In the 1990s, a sociologist named Annette Lareau carried out an intriguing study on parenting practices.[15] She wanted to know why parents have different parenting philosophies—that is, why they raise their children in different ways. To do this, she looked over a large number of families, and then chose twelve for close observation. She and her assistants spent several weeks visiting each of the families for hours at a time, going with them to soccer games, doctor's appointments, parent–teacher nights, and sitting in on their home lives. In this way, the researchers collected mountains of data on their participants.

Lareau and her team expected to see many different types of parenting strategies during their observations—for example, helicopter parents who hover over their children's every move, versus mellow parents who let their children learn through their own mistakes; zealous parents who schedule every hour of their children's lives, versus parents who just let their children be. The researchers also wondered if there were racial differences in the ways people parented, perhaps due to different cultural expectations. What they found, however, were only two opposed parenting philosophies, divided by class, and not racial, lines.

The working-class parents in Lareau's sample practiced a parenting strategy she called the accomplishment of natural growth. By contrast, the middle- and upper-class parents practiced what Lareau called concerted cultivation. To simplify, consider this analogy: if children were trees and parents were gardeners, working-class gardeners would let their trees grow naturally, without trimming them or otherwise trying to control their growth. Middle-class gardeners, on the other hand, would tend to their trees regularly and rigorously, making sure they received the right amounts of certain specific resources like soil, water, and sunlight, and that they were avoiding the proximity of weeds.

In a concrete sense, the working-class parents let their children develop freely; they let them play outside with neighbourhood children, and they let them play the games that the children themselves chose. In contrast, the middle-class parents raised their children according to what seem like educational blueprints, providing enriching activities such as ballet, piano, or tennis lessons. Often the middle-class children participated in all three of these activities, in addition to several others. Middle-class parents in this study therefore limited their children's freedom to spend time in a way the parents deemed wasteful.

These class-based differences in parenting practices cut across race, religion, and other attributes. So class, according to this study, is the key to understanding parenting styles. The Williams family offers a good example: Alexander Williams is a middle-class black boy whose life perfectly illustrates concerted cultivation. His mother continually stresses the importance of exposing him to new and different experiences that will build his confidence and expertise. Commenting on Alexander's music training in particular, his father says:

> I don't know baroque from classical—but he does. How can that not be a benefit in later life? I'm convinced that this rich experience will make him a better person, a better citizen, a better husband, a better father—certainly a better student.[16]

Through all of their extra-curricular lessons and classes, middle-class children gain a certain kind of cultural advantage over working-class children—how to dance, play an instrument, or play tennis, for example. Beyond that, they also develop a sense of entitlement. By participating in organized events where they meet a large number and variety of people with advantaged backgrounds, these children come to feel a sense of specialness. As Lareau explains in the book she wrote based on this research:

> From this [concerted cultivation], a robust sense of entitlement takes root in the children. This sense of entitlement plays an especially important role in institutional settings, where middle-class children learn to question adults and address them as relative equals.[17]

In her book, Lareau offers several examples to illustrate this sense of entitlement. To continue with our discussion of the Williams family, Alex's mother rehearses him while they are on their way to a doctor's appointment, ensuring he knows what to say to the doctor to make sure the visit is useful and efficient. Sure enough, Alex is assertive during his appointment and asks all of the questions he intended, plus a few others when he doesn't understand what the doctor has said. By helping him develop his conversational skills, his parents are making sure that Alex will be ready to speak and argue effectively in adult institutional realms. When he gets to university, the workplace, and beyond, Alex will already feel comfortable addressing people in positions of authority as relative equals, and in making sure his needs are satisfied. These intangible skills are precisely what most people need today to achieve what we conventionally call success in the world of managerial and professional work. As such, middle-class parents pass along attributes that will help their children grow into and flourish as middle- to upper-class adults.

We can link Lareau's work on what might be called the culture of privilege to research by earlier sociologists, especially Thorstein Veblen and Pierre Bourdieu. At the turn of the twentieth century, Veblen published a notorious book called *The Theory of the Leisure Class*.[18] In it, he critiqued the conspicuous consumption of the upper-class members of his time, whom he described as living a life of ease and leisure, as though everyday were a holiday. Reading this book a century later feels like déjà vu, since many of Veblen's arguments still seem to apply to the upper classes today—to the socialites, minor celebrities, and Paris Hiltons of the world.

Veblen proposed that the symbolic nature of social prestige, with its emphasis on rapidly changing fads and fashions, encourages a wasteful, needless consumption of time and goods. However, he acknowledged that this wasteful consumption also serves a social purpose: it reaffirms the status and power of groups that can afford to live in such a privileged manner. Through conspicuous (and wasteful) consumption, privileged groups ensure their own stability and purposely distinguish themselves from less wealthy individuals. For example, wealthy people often adorn their lawns with costly, time-consuming topiary because such vegetation provides evidence of surplus financial security and labour power. According to Veblen then, the upper classes knowingly and purposely use conspicuous consumption patterns to distinguish themselves from the lower classes.

Half a century later, Pierre Bourdieu pointed out that classes (and especially upper classes) pass on their taste for certain interests and hobbies from one generation to another, along with their wealth and property.[19] The children of privileged families are therefore raised to have what is considered good taste in our society—for food, clothing, music, and leisure activities—since having good taste is the mark of their privilege.

Bourdieu referred to this refined taste as cultural capital.[20] More broadly, we can think of cultural capital as the generalized skill set that people inherit and can use in different forms and institutional settings. Some of these skills might include knowledge of high culture, such as classical music, fine wine, and art history. In this sense, people are excluded from the upper class by their inability to display the skills and experiences we expect from this exclusive community.

As Veblen pointed out earlier, the upper classes favour skills that are acquired through great expense and trouble—skills like ballet dancing, horseback riding, skiing, and scuba diving. Poorer people often do not have access to these kinds of activities, so those who can participate in them are distinguished as wealthier members of the upper classes. As some of these activities become more easily accessible, they are stricken from the upper-class list of desirable tastes and attributes. So, once poorer people have the chance to engage in such activities, blurring class lines, richer people no longer want to take part. In this way, the upper classes are constantly distinguishing themselves from the lower classes through their choice of leisure activities.

In addition to this kind of inclusion and exclusion, Bourdieu suggests that our tastes are shaped by our life experiences and circumstances, which he calls our *habitus*. Habitus is both a product of our social position and also reinforces it: our habitus reinforces our social position through generations as we inherit tastes from the people around us (especially our families). This concept suggests that at both ends of the social ladder, class status is inherited. The children of upper- and middle-class people inherit property, cultural capital, and what has been called social capital or the social connections (acquaintances, friendships, and relationships) that people form from going to the same schools and working in the same companies. On the other hand, the children of poor people inherit poverty, disadvantage, and poor life chances, as we saw with Michael Apted's documentary *Seven Up.*

Habitus contributes to this inheritance of class markers, but our legal system also plays a role: the laws governing property and inheritance help to guarantee the security of wealth as it passes through family hands across generations. Beyond that, upper- and middle-class parents guarantee their children an education and varied forms of social capital, both of which help these children to attain the well-paying jobs and social status that will keep them in the upper- or middle-classes. As a result, stable social classes form and maintain themselves over time, creating class subcultures, class awareness, class-consciousness, and the potential for class mobilization. Social and cultural factors, such as taste, education, cultural capital, social connections, and self-confidence contribute to perpetuating poverty and ensuring it continues from one generation to the next, since poverty is merely the absence of this financial, social, and cultural capital.

Ladder of Inequality

When people talk about inequality, they usually mean class, status, income, or some other form of economic inequality. But does class- or status-based economic inequality still matter? Some sociologists believe that the differences between social classes are no longer relevant because people do not think about these differences any more, or because differences in material rewards are small for most people. For example, some working-class jobs are well paid, while some middle-class jobs are poorly paid, complicating the hierarchical relationship between the two and (perhaps) encouraging people to focus on other problems. In line with this thinking, political scientist Ronald Inglehart claims that identity politics and issues like the environment, peace, and terrorism have replaced class politics in importance, because baby boomers—the largest single voting bloc today—grew up in relative postwar plenty.

Despite these claims, current evidence suggests that class inequality does still matter, especially because class inequalities are widening. As Marx noted, class-based inequality changes over time. One example that confirms his belief is the hollowing out of the middle class that we have seen in the last twenty years, caused by the loss of well-paid unionized jobs. Today, with the shrinking of the unionized manufacturing sector, life in the working class—even life in the middle class—is very different than it once was, with more unemployment, more under-employment, more self-employment, more precarious employment, and more time pressure. These changes are related to the weakening or virtual disappearance of unions in many domains of work.

These differences in work life are also related to what sociologist Edna Bonacich has called the split labour market.[21] Her original theory attempts to explain labour market segmentation according to race or ethnicity in terms of market considerations, not individualized attitudes of prejudice. Accordingly, Bonacich argues that ethnic antagonism may not be a cause of labour market discrimination, so much as a consequence of it. When two or more ethnically distinct groups of workers compete for the same jobs, the employer will typically hire workers from the group that is significantly cheaper. This is simply because employers—especially profit-minded capitalists—prefer to hire cheaper workers. Following this preference, they create an antagonism between higher- and lower-priced groups, since cheaper labour threatens more expensive workers.

Remember, these differences in the cost of labour are sociological, not the result of personal preference or psychological prejudice. And yet these actions may lead to psychological and political outcomes, such as an opposition by native-born, unionized workers against immigrant workers from poorer countries. The result is not only prejudice and political conflict within the working class, but also a split labour market that limits lower-priced, now stigmatized workers to specific occupations, or even excludes them from the labour market entirely.

Consequently, a three-tier system emerges in which the participants have different and even conflicting motives. First, the capitalists want a cheap and passive work force, so they can compete most profitably with other businesses. As a result, the higher paid—usually native-born, white, and male—workers feel threatened and want to exclude the cheaper labour from their unions, their jobs, and their country. However, the poorly paid, often immigrant, non-white, female, and much younger or much older workers still want jobs and a foothold in the labour market. Often, employers use this latter group as scabs to break or threaten to break strikes. Though they are typically unskilled, these cheap labourers are usually easy to train, and training them may be cheaper than relocating the work overseas. Thus while the former, more highly paid, male workers may be exploited and manipulated by their capitalist employers, the latter group of female, poorly paid workers arguably experience this to an even greater degree.

This three-tier system brings us to the problem of pay inequality. Research has found that the level of income inequality in a country is an indicator of other inequalities and social problems. British scholars Richard Wilkinson and Kate Pickett in particular have done a lot of work on this topic.[22] In 2007, they provided a summary of previously published evidence, all of which suggests that many problems typically associated with relative deprivation are more prevalent in more unequal societies. Wilkinson and Pickett were able to come to this conclusion by using income inequality as an indicator of a more generalized socio-economic inequality within these societies.

Based on their research and that of many other scholars, we have found that the number of issues associated with income inequality is astounding. Some of these include morbidity and mortality, obesity, teenage pregnancy rates, mental illness, low social capital, low levels of trust, racism, hostility, and homicide. Each of these issues taken on its own is problematic, but listed in combination, the extent of these problems becomes even more worrisome. All this is to say that we have a lot of very good evidence pointing to the fact that income inequality is problematic on a number of levels.

In the following chapters, we will take this initial evidence on income inequality even further and ask whether we should also be worried about other types of inequality. Of course, there is no fully reliable measure for gender, racial, or sexual inequality, as there is for income inequality (we will discuss the Gini Index, which measures income inequality, in a later chapter). This makes measuring every other type of inequality that much more challenging. That said, we believe that indicators like the unequal division of labour in the household, employment discrimination, and the illegalization of gay marriage can be used as evidence for the existence of these other types of inequalities. Nonetheless, we still stress the importance of income (and class) inequality, since this is the type of inequality most studied and best measured in our society today.

So, even though people don't talk about it as they used to, class inequality still matters. Whether they know it or not, people are still members of a social class, and they still suffer the consequences. True, class-consciousness is weak today, unions are losing their influence, and contrary to what Marx predicted, many people like their jobs, even if they are exploited. While some may think that these factors prove that class inequality is unimportant today, we believe that its influence on the wide range of other social problems we've mentioned make class and economic inequality hugely troublesome. In fact, people suffer from inequality of any and every kind, whether they know it or not. In the next chapter, we will talk about gender inequality—a type of inequality that people discuss far more often than class or economic inequality, especially since the rise of the feminist movement.

CHAPTER 2

Domination

———— ◆ • ————

"Woman's virtue is man's greatest invention."
Cornelia Otis Skinner, American author and actress

Gathering Up a Storm

On Saturday, May 21, 2011, the *Toronto Star* published an unusual article[1] on a curious subject: an allegedly genderless baby named Storm. There's nothing ambiguous about Storm's genitalia, but Storm's parents, Kathy Witterick and David Stocker, have decided that when the time is right, Storm will choose his/her gender independently. They are not telling anyone whether their baby is a boy or girl. No one knows, except for Storm's brothers Jazz (five years old) and Kio (two years old); a close family friend; and the two midwives who helped to deliver the baby in a birthing pool on New Year's Day.

In total then, only seven people know the sex of the baby, and it will stay that way until Storm decides to adopt a particular gender identity. "If you really want to get to know someone, you don't ask what's between their legs," says the father, justifying this controversial choice.[2] Stocker and Witterick say they thought long and hard about their decision. The difficult part is constantly answering other people's queries, most of all from the people closest to them. When Storm was born, the couple sent an email to friends and family, saying:

> We've decided not to share Storm's sex for now—a tribute to freedom and choice in place of limitation, a stand up to what the world could become in Storm's lifetime (a more progressive place?).[3]

According to the *Star* article by Jayme Poisson, "Witterick and Stocker believe they are giving their children the freedom to choose who they want to be, unconstrained by social norms about males and females."[4] However, friends and relatives have been critical and largely unaccepting of the couple's decision, arguing that they are imposing their own values on their children. Storm's grandparents were more sympathetic but said they still felt uncomfortable having to explain the gender-free baby idea to others. One of the public's biggest complaints is that genderless children will become confused about their identities as they grow up, and that their failure to conform will make them easy targets for bullies.

In her defence, Witterick writes: "In fact, in not telling the gender of my precious baby, I am saying to the world, 'Please can you just let Storm discover for him/herself what s(he) wants to be?!'"[5] Surrounded by overbearing parents who sign their children up for endless classes and lessons, Stocker and Witterick want to let their kids make decisions for themselves. They believe parents are being selfish if they try to make their children's choices for them, such as what toys to play with, how to arrange their hair, or what clothes to wear.

Their child Jazz, for instance, has currently decided he wants to grow his hair in three braids—two at the sides and one at the back with bangs in front. His favourite colour is pink, so he wears a pink stud in one ear and paints his nails with sparkly polish. Brother Kio keeps his curly blond hair chin-length, and prefers purple over Jazz's pink. Not surprisingly, both boys are often mistaken for little girls. But their parents do not correct the mistake, since they believe their children can decide whether to tell others or to let it pass. In short, they encourage their children to discover themselves—to be whoever they want to be, regardless of society's conventional gender roles.

Fittingly, Stocker teaches at an alternative school west of Dufferin Grove Park in Toronto. Here, he sprinkles his lessons with progressive ideas about class, race, and gender. The family has also travelled extensively, living with local families in Cuba to learn about the revolution and visiting Mexico to speak with a revolutionary group. Witterick, currently a stay-at-home parent, has given workshops to teachers on violence prevention and has organized breast-feeding support groups.

Both Witterick and Stocker grew up in liberal families and carry on the liberal tradition in their Toronto home. Strong believers in community, they sleep together with their children on two mattresses pushed together (co-sleeping). Witterick also practices un-schooling, a version of home-schooling based on the belief that learning should be driven by a child's curiosity. Under this system, children learn by asking questions when they are curious about the world, not by reading textbooks and writing tests. No report cards are issued.

In fact, the parents let their children direct their own learning. Though Jazz was old enough to go to school last September, he chose to stay home. Worried that people might fixate on his gender and his choices of dress and behaviour, he chose to avoid this by skipping school. To explain his views on this matter, he has written a booklet under his pseudonym, Gender Explorer, that reads in part, "Help girls do boy things. Help boys do girl things. Let your kid be whoever they are!"[6]

The decision to keep baby Storm genderless for the time being was inspired by a book Stocker found in his school library called *X: A Fabulous Child's Story* by Lois Gould.[7] Published in 1978, the book is about a child who leads a happy and well-adjusted life without a specified gender identity, urging other children to lead gender-free lives. The book inspired these parents: "It became so compelling it was like, how could we not?" says Witterick.[8] And despite their frustration about frequent criticism, the parents believe that they are making a statement for freedom and progress with Storm. They believe Storm, released from the bonds of gender, will be an inspiration to others, just like X.

For Witterick and Stocker, any criticisms and hardships Storm may face in the future are outweighed by the freedom to choose, a freedom they thoroughly support. In their view, every obstacle can be overcome with love and support:

When faced with inevitable judgment by others, which child stands tall (and sticks up for others)—the one facing teasing despite desperately trying to fit in, or the one with a strong sense of self and at least two "go-to" adults who love them unconditionally. . . . Everyone keeps asking us, "When will this end?" . . . And we always turn the question back. Yeah, when will this end? When will we live in a world where people can make choices to be whoever they are?[9]

The Other

Regardless of whether we agree with Witterick and Stocker's choice, their decision raises intriguing gender-related questions. They remind sociologists that gender, in the end, is socially constructed—not given by nature.[10] Storm has a *sex*, determined by his or her biology, but that does not mean Storm automatically has a *gender*. This highlights the important difference between what sociologists call sex and what they, and we, call gender. This chapter focuses on the latter.

By sex, sociologists mean biological characteristics that make a person biologically male or female. Most (though not all) people fit unambiguously into one category or another, and with the biological distinctions comes a wave of physical characteristics—the ebb and flow of particular hormones, for example. By gender, however, sociologists mean the expectations of behaviour and appearance that people describe as masculine and feminine, which are conventionally associated with a person's biology.

Gender, most sociologists argue today, is a social performance that dramatizes biological differences. We know this is a socially staged performance because different societies do the performance in different ways. Social performances around gender vary from one society to another, just like the class performances we have already discussed, and the ethnic performances we will discuss in the next chapter. So, from a sociologist's point of view, there is no point focusing on supposed essential features of maleness or femaleness; our interest is in reviewing the experiences of people who perform the male or female role in Canadian society today.

In our society, as Witterick and Stocker surely know and as their children will discover, gender matters. Life is different for men and women, and much of that difference is socially constructed. Of course, there are important biological differences between men and women—most notably, women can bear children and men cannot. However, the significance of that difference varies from one society to another, and with declining birthrates it is becoming less significant.

Of greater interest to sociologists is the fact that, until now, in most societies throughout history, women and men have been treated unequally. The experience of womanhood has largely been a lesson in inequality—in how it is to be less than men. In 1949, a French philosopher and feminist famously proclaimed, "One is not born, but rather becomes, a woman."[11] Simone de Beauvoir, the writer of these words, was the long-term partner of philosopher Jean-Paul Sartre. In the introduction to her book *The Second Sex*, she explains she set out to write the book after receiving a sudden insight.[12] One day, she realized she could not understand herself without first saying "I am a woman"—that is, without confronting her gender. But why, she asks, must a woman (usually) acknowledge her gender to understand her life, while a man would not do so (at least, not in her time)? What Beauvoir means, and spends the book arguing, is that men are considered the neutral, the default, or the basis to which women are compared. One cannot explain being a woman without explaining it in relation to what it means to be a man. In making this argument, Beauvoir asserted that gender differences, and the inequalities they create for women, are oppressive, unnatural, and socially constructed.

Social construction, as we have already hinted, is the process that makes differences seem large or small, important or unimportant. In this case, it does so by imaginatively assigning different social roles to different sexes. So, for example, a society may assign men the role of protector and women the role of procreator. But present-day societies vary in this regard: in some societies, the differences between men and women are dramatized by the social conventions we know as gender norms—men are permitted to be bold and blustery, women to be passive and emotional, for example. In Canada, the staged differences between men and women are less marked today than a generation ago. In school or at work today, we ridicule emotional meltdowns by women and grandiose posturing by men, since we now realize these are not biologically necessary behaviours—they are merely dramatizations of gender.

Still, stereotypical beliefs about men and women, masculinity and femininity, remain and continue to shape our relations. Men and women view themselves and view one another as dramatically different. Often, women are inclined to ridicule men for their outspoken efforts to gain and keep power. Often, men are inclined to recognize and admire women's more hidden power. As well, both recognize that relations between men and women are often coloured by sexual desire and intrigue. So, the relations between men and women are often about the struggle for power, in which sexual access and information control are important elements.

Despite what may be women's greater subtlety in the wielding of power (though of course, this is probably a gender construction as well), in this chapter we will see that men use socially constructed gender differences to justify the domination of women by men. Both the economic system and the biological facts of reproduction help to produce gender inequalities, but neither would lead to the domination of women by men without social constructions—that is, these realities do not alone explain gender inequality. Gender ideology legitimates the domination of women by making cultural distinctions between the sexes that appear timeless, universal, and essential. These cultural distinctions lock women, as well as men, into narrow, limiting conceptions of masculinity and femininity.

Beauvoir used existentialist terminology to describe this situation. She said that society has defined men as the Subject and women as the Other. By this she means that owing to their reproductive function in society, women historically did not play a publicly influential role and thus stood outside the public sphere. As such, women were defined as the Other by men, who have historically played a public political and economic role. This relation has made men the Subject; they have defined the characteristics of women, the subordinate Other, as necessary and innate. Over the course of history, this relationship has been institutionalized and developed into so-called patriarchal societies.

The default position in most traditional societies, then, is that men are considered the norm—they define the situation unless contrary information is provided. We can see this inequality even in the traditional use of masculine words—for example, in the use of mankind to refer to all of humanity and the use of his (in most languages) whenever gender is unspecified. Beauvoir proposes that precisely this kind of reasoning leaves women in a subordinate position by default. Men, then, are constructed to be in power, while women are always "defined and differentiated with reference to man."[13]

In short, Beauvoir asserts that women are subordinated to men merely by virtue of their gender. This subordination has seeped in to all of society's institutions, so that it is hardly noticeable to most people.

To Love, Cherish, and to Obey

I [woman] take thee [man]
For my wedded husband
To have and to hold
From this day forward
For better for worse
For richer for poorer
In sickness and in health
To love, cherish, and to obey
Til death do us part.

Solemnization of Matrimony

Consider the marriage vows in the Protestant liturgy. The married life of a woman is to begin with her promise to "love, cherish, and to obey" her husband—a promise that is traditionally not reciprocated by the husband. This is not mere piety. In traditional marriages, and perhaps even in modern ones, men enforce this promise on their wives.

This is a major finding in sociologist Meg Luxton's book *More than a Labour of Love: Three Generations of Women's Work in the Home*, a study of homemakers in a small northern Canadian mining town.[14] Flin Flon, Manitoba, is a single industry, primary resource city with a population of ten thousand. Situated more than five hundred miles north of Winnipeg, life in Flin Flon is controlled by its economic core—the Hudson Bay Mining and Smelting Company Ltd. Perched on the top of a muddy hill, "the Company," as Luxton calls it, overlooks the small houses below it. These company-owned homes house the company's employees and their families; here, the working men spend most of their hours between factory shifts. But for their wives, the work is never done.

In keeping house and caring for their husbands and children, the women do work that is undervalued, unpaid, and unending.

> It's looking after your family and what could be more important? You don't have anyone standing over you so you get to do what you want, sort of. But you don't get paid, so you're dependent on your husband, and you have to be there all the time, and there's always something needs doing. I feel so confused because it should be so good and it never is. —Generation II woman (born 1930)[15]

Over fourteen months in the 1970s, Luxton observed the lives of these working-class women and men; she also interviewed one hundred women about their activities within the household. What she found was that feminism had not yet reached Flin Flon. In social and cultural ways, Flin Flon in the 1970s was the same mining town it had been fifty years earlier. The Company was still the main employer of the Flin Flon men. Most families still followed the traditional form, with a male breadwinner husband and a female homemaker wife—the model that had emerged with early industrial capitalism more than a century earlier. In Flin Flon as elsewhere, paid work maintained and shaped family life, and men—rarely women—did the paid work. So, people still lived as they had in decades past; the lives Luxton witnessed provided a unique glimpse into lives one or two generations earlier.

Many outsiders—perhaps even the homemakers themselves—would consider the work women do in this community to be just a labour of love—productive work performed out of care for others, without payment or recognition. Yet Luxton understands that work is work, whether love is involved or not, and beneath the pieties, Flin Flon's women are treated unfairly. She interviewed three generations of these women and found that what they do requires hard labour, meets the demands of others, and makes it possible for the family to function. But because the work is carried out within the home, it is unpaid, and because it is done for the family, it requires an intense emotional investment. One woman says,

> I never really thought about it before. It's just what I do every day. It's a bit startling to try and think about it as something more than me just living my life. But it is important to ask why I do things the way I do and especially how what I do is like what other women do. —Generation III woman (born 1951)[16]

These women are carrying out the tasks of what Luxton and other sociologists call social reproduction—work that ensures the development and continuity of the family. This work includes bearing and rearing children, preparing meals, doing housework, and dealing with the family's emotional issues. Because the work is domestic and goes on without discussion, it seems natural and non-negotiable. Some women feel as though they are completely free to make their own life choices, yet, in many ways, their lives have come pre-packaged. As they accept the local package on offer, other choices disappear from the horizon. Most women follow the same life course as their mothers and grandmothers, with predictable steps and experiences. They grow up, date several potential marriage partners, marry and settle down, produce children, and then become dutiful housewives. In following the same pattern from generation to generation, they all accept the duties that come with the package, however daunting some of them may be.

Luxton, as an outsider, is free to delve into the moral underpinnings of these women's lives and the work they do on a daily basis. She is able to question the fundamental differences between their work and their husbands'—the so-called gendered division of labour—and to situate the women's work in a broader historical, social, and economic context. The husband's work is easily described: as a paid job; his work is central to the family economy and therefore, to family life. For this reason, the husband's needs are always first to be satisfied; meals, family time, and women's leisure are all organized around his schedule. Because the women are economically dependent on their husbands, they have little if any decision-making power within the household. They must organize their lives to satisfy their husbands' needs. Doing this means more than housework and child care; it also includes providing emotional support for husbands and children, shopping, paying bills, and organizing family schedules.

In doing all this work, women preserve their families, literally keeping them alive. And, as Luxton points out, they are also preserving the larger capitalist system that has arranged their lives in this fashion.

> I send my husband off to work each day and my kids off to school. It's women like me keep the whole system running. Weren't for us, the men wouldn't work and there wouldn't be no kids to grow up, would there? —Generation II woman (born 1927)[17]

Despite its importance for the family and for capitalism, women's work often goes unnoticed; usually, it is taken for granted. The husband comes home tired and hungry from his shift at the Company, expecting to find steaming meat and potatoes ready on the table. He may imagine his wife is doing nothing at all during the day. After all, she gets to stay home the whole time. Besides, he thinks that if her work were important, it would be paid—like his work.

In this culture and beyond, men's wage work is seen as more important than women's domestic work, which is always organized around the needs of wage work.

> Those changing shifts are awful. It's a constant reminder that his work comes first, over any other needs this family might have. We can never get ourselves organized into regular pattern because our lives are always being turned upside down. —Generation III woman (born 1947)[18]

But while his work ends with the whistle, her work never stops. Luxton begins her book with a proverb reminding us that "a man works from sun to sun. A woman's work is never done."[19] Even when her children are asleep and her husband is at work, the woman is forever responsible for the family's well-being, often busy making sure that everything is ready for the next set of events. As well, she shoulders the responsibility for what sociologist Arlie Hochschild has called emotion work or emotional labour. Emotion work, like other work that women do, is hard work. It means preserving an atmosphere of warmth and comfort, while providing satisfaction and completing tasks quietly and efficiently. Women in this community are trained to recognize and care for the needs of others, even if it means denying their own needs.

For the women of Flin Flon, emotional work also includes satisfying husbands' sexual demands. According to Luxton, sex in this context is also more than a labour of love—it is a duty, a type of work, and a way of greasing the domestic wheels so Mr. Breadwinner, happy and fulfilled, can keep bringing home the needed dollars. Sex is a duty for married women, but even single women are expected to provide sexual services to their dates. That's the unspoken gender bargain in Flin Flon. If they break this rule, they risk missing marriage offers. On this theme, a sixteen-year-old girl comments:

Boys always expect you to go all the way. And if you won't, then they go find someone else who will. Andy [her eighteen-year-old boyfriend of six months] said that it wasn't worth his while taking me out all the time, spending his money on me, if I didn't come across. —Generation III woman (born 1962)[20]

Not surprisingly, then, the women of Flin Flon also report suffering domestic violence, both physical and psychological. Boyfriends and then husbands are always pressuring them to do what the man pleases, and because of their limited skills and limited local opportunities, the girls and women have little choice. Many wives confide that they feel distant from their husbands; their partnership is more about economic dependence and social expectations than about love and respect. In this rigidly gendered setting, women have little chance of self-fulfillment or self-assertion.

Luxton's book obviously focuses on the lives of women, but it also recognizes that men in this single-industry community face tremendous pressures too: the class-based pressures of the workplace. The community itself is a patriarchal system that dominates women's lives socially and psychologically. It is also a paternalistic capitalist system that dominates men's lives socially and psychologically. Men are the direct pawns in this system of capitalist inequality, while women—wives, mothers, and daughters—are the indirect pawns.

While women are solely responsible for the care of the family, men are solely responsible for financially supporting the family. Therefore, the men stay in unfulfilling, difficult, and even dangerous jobs, and both the men and women stay in what often prove to be difficult, stressful marriages. Flin Flon is not a happy place. But the men and women do not share their unhappiness. In these patriarchal homes, women and men continue to lead lonely, largely separate lives. Neither men nor women in these households have much power in society as a whole, but most of the familial power is in the hands of men. The women—the Other—have household labour on their minds.

The Opposite of Self-Actualization

The first sociologist to take housework seriously was Ann Oakley, when she published *The Sociology of Housework*.[21] Oakley's own life illustrates the female condition in our society—at least, what it used to be. Born in London, England, in 1944, Oakley attended the University of Oxford, becoming one of the first students to major in sociology there. After graduating, she took time off to marry and have children. Then, after the birth of her third child, in 1968, Oakley decided to pursue doctoral studies. After graduating, she looked for academic work but was unsuccessful in finding it. Instead, she held various part-time jobs while writing both fiction and non-fiction books on sociological topics. Eventually, she wrote a major work on a topic about which she had come to know a great deal.

The Sociology of Housework is Oakley's most famous book and was the first academic work to think about housework as real, unpaid work. It came before Luxton's study of Flin Flon, and well before many other studies considered to be feminist classics, including Arlie Hochschild's *The Second Shift*.[22] In her book, Oakley pointed out that housework is legitimate, difficult, and worthwhile work, not just a labour of love. As Luxton's work would do later, Oakley's book drew needed attention to domestic inequality and its link to a variety of real-life dilemmas—especially the conflict between family life and paid work.

Oakley's research for the book was based on interviews with a small sample of working- and middle-class homemakers. Though the sample was small, the responses were consistent: both the working- and middle-class women reported a similar (high degree of) identification with their household role. That is, they defined themselves mainly as homemakers.

However, both working- and middle-class women found housework unpleasant, expressing similar negative attitudes toward it. These homemakers were caught in a permanent conflict. In spite of their dislike for housework, their lives were centrally organized around homemaking. The women felt they had authority and status only within their own household, though even here they might have less authority than their husband and children. Most of the women had reluctantly come to terms with the monotony, isolation, and low social status of their domestic lives. They viewed their lives as normal, inevitable, and the natural order of things.

It was this very acquiescence that Oakley found so problematic. By settling into the hated housewife role, women had legitimated their own subjugation. Like kidnapped people who begin to take the point of view of their kidnappers (the so-called Stockholm Syndrome), these women had become complicit in the drudgery of their lives. Beliefs about the proper role of women had disempowered and imprisoned them, especially under conditions of motherhood. All the while, the women could never be satisfied doing housework. As Oakley states, "Housework is work directly opposed to the possibility of human self-actualization."[23] By this Oakley means that by its nature, housework cannot be satisfying: it is cyclical (you have to keep cooking, washing, and cleaning endlessly); its products are intangible (a healthy, clean, and well-fed family); and it goes unnoticed except when it is not done.

Yet despite their unhappiness with housework and motherwork, women felt morally and socially obliged to continue playing this fundamentally alienating, frustrating, and self-destroying role. Women socialized by a patriarchal gender ideology accepted voluntary servitude as wives and mothers. Here are a few of Oakley's musings, in her own straightforward words:

> Society has a tremendous stake in insisting on a woman's natural fitness for the career of mother: the alternatives are all too expensive.[24]

> Families are nothing other than the idolatry of duty.[25]

> There are always women who will take men on their own terms. If I were a man, I wouldn't bother to change while there are women like that around.[26]

Not everyone agreed with Oakley's views. In a contemporary review of her book on housework, Judith Hammond wrote that Oakley "narrowed and distorted the picture of housewifery into that of a thankless joyless task."[27] This, Hammond claimed, was because of a small, unrepresentative sample. Perhaps it was also due in part to prejudices and personal experiences on Oakley's own part. Other studies found that many women are less negative about their domestic experience. However, we cannot disagree that Oakley rightly called sociologists' attention to the neglected topic of housework. Because of her insights, we are more aware of its relation to gender inequality and for the need to explore this problem systematically, without prejudice. Both Luxton's and Oakley's work has also taught us that gender is all around us, in the most ordinary and commonplace forms.

In recent years, the household division of labour has continued to change. Some works on the topic include Arlie Hochschild's classic *The Second Shift*, mentioned previously, as well as Canadian Katherine Marshall's "The Family Work Week"[28] and Peter Burton and Shelley Phipps' "Families, Time, and Well-Being in Canada."[29] They show that, in the last two decades, more and more Canadian families— including those with less education and lower incomes—have shifted to a two-earner model in which both men and women work in the labour market (and yet women often still do a larger share of household labour). While some may think this has to do with greater gender equality, it is also a change that is largely due to the growth of income inequality in Canada over the same period. Incomes at the top of the distribution have increased significantly since the mid-1990s, making unnecessary any significant increases in total family hours of paid work. However, family incomes for those in the middle have stagnated despite a rising cost of living and two income-earning parents. The result has been a significant increase in the number of paid hours worked per week by both partners. Burton and Phipps report, "between 1994 and 2006 . . . average family hours of weekly paid work rose from 61.6 to 67.9 hours for the middle decile, but fell from 76.7 to 74.4 hours for those in the top 10 percent."[30]

In turn, this has meant that inequality of well-being among families with children has increased even more quickly than income inequality, and this, in turn, has caused an increase in stress and anxiety. The authors find that subjective feelings of stress due to too many demands and too little time have also shifted down the income scale, as most families put in more hours of paid work, and have less time to spend with their children and in other activities.

In addition, despite more awareness on the part of men, gender inequalities at home remain between husbands and wives in the division of labour. In recent years, while it is true that women have been doing less housework than in the past, this is mainly because they have less time to do housework due to their paid work and not because men are doing their fair share. On average, women still do more hours of household work than men do, even if they are working full-time.

Also, when children arrive, most couples put away their progressive, gender-neutral ideas temporarily, if not permanently.[31] Wives stay home, taking on the main child care responsibility, and couples fall into traditional, patriarchal patterns. The husband, however well intentioned, continues to work full-time, earning a higher salary than his wife could earn part-time, and at home he gets to enjoy leisure denied to the wife.

What Classical Sociology Has to Say

Although the classical sociologists did not write much about gender directly (with the exception of Friedrich Engels), they do still have a lot of insight to offer into the processes underlying gender inequality. Max Weber, in particular, wrote at length about domination, the particular process of inequality that we argue underlies gender relations. By domination, sociologists mean rule by either coercion or by legitimate authority, and as both Luxton's and Oakley's books show us, women are subordinated—and thus dominated—under the capitalistic economic system of our society.

Dominant people or groups exercise power over others by brute force or through the acceptance of their power as legitimate.

So, at its core, domination is about compulsion and persuasion. To simplify, Weber defines domination as "the probability that certain specific commands (or all commands) will be obeyed by a given group of persons."[32] This process is not always based on relations to the means of production: in fact, it usually is not. So, we are moving away from Marxian analysis with the study of domination.

Also, though compulsion is often a part of the process, Weber notes, "Every genuine form of domination implies a minimum of *voluntary* (or willing) compliance, that is, an *interest* (based on ulterior motives or genuine acceptance) in obedience."[33] Weber then provides some examples of such dominance—parent-child relationships, employer-employee relationships, teacher-student relationships, and political rule that is accepted and obeyed.

Dominance, according to Weber, is a power relationship that involves four key elements. First, it implies voluntary compliance or obedience—people are not forced to obey at gunpoint, but do so more or less voluntarily. Second, people obey because they have an interest in doing so, or at least think that they have such an interest. Usually, they expect to benefit in some way. Third, those who comply believe in the legitimacy of the actions of the dominant individual or group. Fourth and finally, obedience is not haphazard or brief, but part of a sustained relationship of dominance and subordination, so that regular patterns of inequality are established. Said another way, dominance is part of the institutionalization— the stable establishment—of an unequal social relationship. When it continues for a long period, domination becomes structured and expected, part of the power structure of a society.

Weber's definition, focusing on willing compliance, gives us a useful way to examine all unequal relationships that become regularized or institutionalized. Employer-employee or other types of relationships characterized by domination often involve compulsion—at least, financial compulsion; the use of force is not normally an aspect of this. Most of the time, subordinates obey because they implicitly and resignedly accept their subordination.

For various reasons, the relations between men and women follow routinized patterns of dominance (by men), and rebellion against or subversion of dominance (by women). Traditional relations between husbands and wives may demand as much compliance and obedience as affection, as Luxton's study of Flin Flon shows. Wives may comply with their husbands' wishes because they believe they have a traditional obligation to do so, or because they think they will benefit from doing so. They may appear to believe in the legitimacy of their husbands' actions and the sanctity of the (unequal) marital relationship.

Over time, the traditional gendered marital inequality creates a permanent pattern of dominance and subordination in the home and the larger community. We see this kind of development among traditional (fundamentalist) Muslims, Jews, and Christians. To say this is not to deny that some husbands use compulsion to secure obedience—many husbands abuse their wives, using coercive violence to maintain their power where traditional sources of legitimacy are lacking. However, what strikes us about Weber's theory is that it calls attention to the relative rarity of violence and force in most relationships, including relations between men and women. Where violence and force are used, our legal system treats this as a crime. So, usually, legitimate domination—not force or the threat of force—accounts for most of gendered subordination in our society.

But how do men (for example, husbands) gain the legitimacy to dominate women (for example, wives)? Weber says that people grant a given power arrangement legitimacy when they consider it valid. Often, in granting legitimacy, they evaluate the relationship in terms of its fairness or necessity. Thus, they assess its moral grounding since moral grounding gives the dominant person power and eliminates the need for coercion. Said another way, powerful people eliminate the need for force if they can make subordinates feel they ought to obey and that a failure to obey is immoral, sick, or abnormal. In traditional societies, husbands rely on these kinds of ideologies, often religion-based, in order to dominate their wives.

As a result, the word of a husband is given the weight of the word of a supreme deity.

In many societies throughout history, the term patriarchy has served to describe such a legitimating ideology. Patriarchy, literally meaning "rule of the father," is a term originally used to describe societies based on the authority of male household heads over all subordinates—wives, children, and other dependents. This household authority gave men the right in traditional law to dispose, as they saw fit, of all family property and to command obedience from their household members.

Today, patriarchy has come to mean male domination of any kind. Some feminist research has described a variety of gender inequalities (such as gendered differences in the distribution of household work and in paid employment opportunities) as patriarchal inequalities, and often this usage is warranted. Many present-day women continue to treat their father or husband as the unquestioned household head whose word is law. They may be accustomed to doing so, been taught it is right to do so, or fear the physical and economic consequences of failing to do so. The practice of taking the senior adult male of a household as the family head implicitly assumes male dominance in the society. Classifying a whole household according to the characteristics of its male head ignores the rights and contributions of other family members. Further, it assumes the interests of the household head are the same as those of the other family members. It paints the wife and children, whatever their ages, as mere servants and dependents of the household head.

It is also worth noting that many of the major world religions, including Judaism, Christianity, and Islam, are patriarchal, in the sense that they view men and women differently and give greater social, domestic, and sacramental authority to men than women. In the households of people who practice these same religions in their traditional (or fundamentalist) forms, violence against women is particularly common, as compared with secular or less-traditional households, leading to the conclusion that traditional religion serves to justify, condone, or at least ignore such violence.

Today, however, with more two-earner families and less child-bearing, few women are willing to view men as the breadwinner and the "head of household." Canadian and American women have the legal tools to challenge and escape domineering men, though they sometimes lack the economic resources to survive on their own. This means that traditional ideologies about gendered subordination have had to change. Biblical rules ordering wives to obey their husbands, as in the traditional matrimonial vows, are no longer sufficient to ensure that wives obey their husbands.

In modern societies, the ways in which we instill habits of compliance are subtler. As the well-known sociologist Michel Foucault[34] has proposed, people are taught that compliance with authority is normal and people who repeatedly oppose authority are made to appear abnormal and sick. In this scientific age, scientific notions of normality are used as sources of legitimation, in place of traditional assertions that point to God. Today people are taught to look for and accept the fact of normal, essential differences between men and women. Women are still criticized if they behave in masculine ways, which usually means independently or aggressively, as we saw at the beginning of the chapter. This is because they are behaving abnormally, not immorally.

Over the past century, Western women have faced this problem repeatedly in their struggles to overturn male domination and gain equal treatment in society. There has been a crisis of legitimacy around traditional notions of gender and gender inequality, and women have been unwilling—in ever larger numbers—to accept willingly the traditional privileges granted to men. Like other subordinate people we discuss in this book, they have begun to lose the custom of thinking hierarchically, or the taste for accepting domination. In modern societies, the ideology of citizenship is an ethical principle that can apply to a variety of inequalities. In general, it gives widely varying people the same legal, political, and social rights—for example, equality before the law, right to property, access to freedom of speech, financial resources through social welfare, and the right to vote.

It is probably because the notion of citizenship is so important that the early feminist movement was mainly concerned with suffrage. By gaining the right to vote, women could hope to become full citizens, eventually shaping government policy around issues important to women. Full citizenship—legal, political, and social—has been a long time coming to women. The first feminist theorist, Mary Wollstonecraft, writing in the late eighteenth century, drew attention to gender inequality and the disabilities women faced in her time—fifty years before Marx first set pen to paper about class inequality. Women's problems of subordination and abuse are still being resolved, but we are certainly further along today.

Guns, Games, and God

Unlike income inequality, gender inequality has no universally agreed-on measure. However, there are several places we can look to find indicators of gender inequality in our own society and in others.

We have already noted the extent to which women are held solely responsible for the work of social reproduction, whether they can choose their marriage partners freely, and whether they can divorce if they are unsatisfied with their marriage, and we will shortly consider how society views female victims of domestic abuse and rape. Yet another important indicator is women's participation in the labour force, and how much women earn relative to men for identical or similar work.

We've all heard the claim that women earn seventy-seven cents for every dollar earned by a man. But if that is true, asks Warren Farrell, why would anyone ever hire a man? In *Why Men Earn More*, Farrell effectively lays to rest many of the myths around male-female pay inequality.[35] A statement like that one is supposed to show the disparity in earnings—the pay gap—between genders. But a woman and a man who hold the same job, have the same credentials and experience, and work the same hours will normally receive the same pay. Though gendered discrimination was common only a few decades ago, that kind of discrimination is illegal and uncommon today. Yet people, and especially the media, keep citing this phrase, to the confusion of most audiences.

This misleading statistic is often calculated by comparing the average salaries of all men to the average salaries of all women in the labour market. Doing this fails to take into account important differences in occupation, education, hours worked, and other differences that are relevant to jobs and careers. For the most part, differences in earnings between men and women are due to the different choices men and women have made educationally and occupationally. In turn, these different choices reflect differences in the priorities placed on life goals. Women typically give higher priority to family life than men do, for example. But that is not the whole story.

Farrell proposes that, in choosing a career, men prioritize earnings above everything else. Women prioritize interest, fulfillment, safety, flexibility, and the opportunity for work-life balance. Take physicians as an example: everyone knows physicians make a good living, but precisely how much doctors earn depends on their specialization. Women physicians choose pediatrics, psychiatry, and family practice—practices with regular hours that put a high emphasis on interpersonal skills. Men physicians choose fields like surgery and emergency care that demand more years of education and less predictable hours. In short, women doctors usually choose to work in fields that are compatible with a personal life. But this choice of fields will inevitably mean lower earnings than in the fields chosen by male physicians.[36]

Then there is the fact that most women take time off to have children and raise a family in the midst of paid work. This decision also carries costs in the labour market, and many women do not realize the likely extent of this cost. For couples in which the husband earns more, it seems to make sense economically for the woman to stay home while the children are young and for the man to increase his working hours. (However, research on same-sex partnerships has shown a different kind of economic rationale that has other advantages.)

In doing this, men invest time in building their careers while women undermine their career trajectory. Often, they have a lot of trouble finding suitable work again when they return to working full time. They may also get stuck in the "mommy track" of their profession—that is, in less economically significant sub-fields such as human resources. Even women who climb to the top of the ladder in that specific field may be left out of personal meetings where the important business is transacted.

It seems there are only two ways for changes to occur. The first involves policy: specifically, setting up programs that help women to balance work and family life. Such programs would provide good quality, subsidized, affordable, licenced, and educational daycare centres for women who require them. This is the option chosen by the province of Quebec, which has more progressive child and family policies than the rest of Canada. However, doing this means overhauling the economic system, at least to some extent.

Alternatively, we can put the onus on women to choose fields that bring higher pay—traditionally male-dominated fields such as business and engineering. This would mean women turning aside from fields such as education, journalism, and social work—fields that traditionally pay lower wages than male-dominated occupations requiring the same amount of skill and education. As journalist Ashley Herzog, author of *Feminism vs. Women,* writes:

> What women's studies majors who lament about the pay gap do not realize is that they are contributing to it. . . . If women's studies majors are so outraged by the pay gap, maybe they should all drop out and enroll in the College of Engineering. That act alone would do more to close the pay gap than blaming sexism.[37]

But this is not to deny the continued existence of workplace discrimination against women. With industrialization and the bureaucratization of office work, gender inequalities in work-places have surely declined, but they have not disappeared entirely. Many women still voice suspicions of a glass ceiling at work. Some employers still promote men over women who are more competent. Where a glass ceiling exists, women can have considerable success at work but only up to a certain point. Women remain highly underrepresented at the highest levels of business, academia, and government. The question is, why?

In 2009, the *Economist* put Rosie the Riveter on the cover with the caption "We did it!" Wearing navy blue worker's overalls, a red and white polka dot bandana, and showing off her muscle with an intent stare, Rosie is a cultural icon of World War II, showing what women could and should work for their country. In 2009, women became half of the workforce across all industries. But as Nicki Gilmour of *The Glass Hammer*, an award-winning blog, writes, "We can interpret that in two ways: either as a positive advancement for women as they can have economic freedom by earning their own wage or that women have to work to support themselves and their families."[38]

Gilmour analyzes the job statistics and finds that women still make up less than 13 percent of board members in the US. Only 50 percent of women with an MBA continue to work after they have children, and (perhaps for this reason) women run only 2 percent of Fortune 500 companies. More and longer participation by talented women in the labour market would be a huge boost for the GDP, but women tend (more than men) to drop out of the competition. And as Gilmour puts it, women are the least represented in the three male-dominated spheres: the military, sports, and religion (or as we might say, the 3 Gs—Guns, Games, and God).

Women can bring many valuable skills to the workplace, and companies stand to gain by hiring women. If only they made it easier for their female employees to handle both work and family life, more women would come and stay. Instead, most companies expect women to act like their male colleagues and, by evaluating them on this basis, many companies miss the point of hiring women at all.

Research shows that in general, heterogeneous groups outperform homogeneous groups, and gender diversity pays off. In fact, any kind of diversity in a group invites differing opinions and allows for opportunities of discussion and debate. This increases the chances of finding a better solution to the issue in the end.[39]

Women are especially useful in a diverse mix. A recent study by organizational psychologist Anita Woolley and colleagues, reported in the *Globe and Mail*, showed that groups function better when they include members with social sensitivity—a trait typically found in women.[40] How smart the group is, then, depends on the amount of social skills its members possess and therefore the proportion of women in the group. The researchers found that this effect was linear—that is, the more women, the smarter the group.

Of course, men have social skills too, but women have been socialized to pick up non-verbal cues on other people's faces, understand what other people are feeling, and then to draw out those feelings so the person experiencing them can recognize and discuss them. By contrast, groups with members who act in traditionally male ways—dominating the conversation, for example—tend to be less collectively intelligent, even if one or two members are individually quite intelligent. So, employers and companies need to stop expecting that women will behave like men on the job and start accepting the unique skills women possess that make them valuable members of the work environment.

On top of the lack of structure to accommodate women and their needs in the workplace, one of the biggest problems facing women in the labour force is that many gender myths still abound in our society. Elisabeth Kelan, author of *Performing Gender at Work*,[41] outlines three persistent gender myths that have an influence on women's ability to perform in the labour force:[42]

> *Gender Myth 1:* Gender discrimination is passé.
> After decades of legislation to ensure equal treatment of men and women, there is still strong disparity between men and women in

the workplace. However, many people seem to assume the gender issue is solved, which has led to a phenomenon called gender fatigue. A more subtle form of gender discrimination continues.

Gender Myth 2: Merit, talent, and skill are objective categories.
We often assume merit, talent, and skill are objective categories that tell us something about how individual employees perform. However, these categories are more biased than we think. For instance, social skills are often valued differently in men and women. Therefore, these skills have a strong gender dimension with an enormous impact on performance evaluations.

Gender Myth 3: Career stories are gender-neutral.
It is often assumed that how you tell your career story has little to do with gender. The career trajectories of men and women often are not dissimilar, but how men and women talk about their careers is different. Women often talk about their careers as being due to coincidence, while men talk about their careers as an outcome of rationally planned action. We often want to hear the career stories men offer because they are more closely linked to the ideal of the driven individual.

A common complaint by women in the workplace is that men seem to think women are less successful in business because they are timid, afraid to show leadership, or inclined to avoid conflict. Other men say women are not serious about business. However, research consistently shows that these are mistaken beliefs. Most women who leave the business world do not do so because of work-life issues but because the workplace environment subtly denigrates their abilities.[43]

This research builds indirectly on a classic study by sociologist Rosabeth Kanter, whose book *Men and Women of the Corporation* posed an early challenge to the stereotypical beliefs about why women did not participate in the workforce as fully as men.[44] Kanter is successful herself: she is a Harvard Business School professor and well-known business consultant. She has also written numerous books and articles on organizational issues, especially around the value of diversity. Her 1977 book is based on research conducted while she acted as a consultant with the organization she studied. In her research, she discovered that women's lack of organizational success cannot be explained by essential differences between men and women; instead, it has larger structural causes.

Kanter's book challenges many of our assumptions about the traditional system of merit and reward within organizations. The common belief is that women's opportunities are limited because women act differently from men; for example, they are too timid, shy, or likely to avoid conflict. Kanter turns this reasoning on its head and shows that it is precisely because women have less opportunity for promotion that they are forced to act like women: subservient, devious, seemingly unambitious. When men and women have the same opportunities, both act in the same way, Kanter finds. Whether they are men or women, people who experience blocked opportunities, powerlessness, and tokenism display less-than-average ambition and productivity; this is a result of holding weak, dead-end positions.

Kanter also shows that all the women connected with large organizations—whether as executives, secretaries, or even wives—are in a similar bind. For example, female secretaries, however ambitious and talented, are tied to the fortunes of their male bosses. (Think of the all-knowing secretary Joan in the popular television series *Mad Men!*) Their earnings rise and fall directly with those of the boss, regardless of the women's own efforts and talents. Similarly, the wives of organizational executives, also often ambitious and talented themselves, are tied to their spouses' fortunes. Both secretaries and wives are powerless, yet heavily dependent on the fates of the men to whom they are linked. Because of this powerlessness, they are obliged to act in a typical female fashion. Their seemingly typical female performances—deferential, passive, devious, seductive, and so on—support the male view that women, by nature, are poor executive material.

Kanter generalizes from this finding to hypothesize that people—any people—who are in a numerical minority will feel restricted in what they can do and, for this reason alone, they will try to stay out of sight. They will also feel incredibly stressed, and the more outnumbered they are, the more stressed they will feel. As their numbers increase, however, they will engage more vigorously in organizational matters. The interaction and communication across (in this case, gender) boundaries will increase and normalize. Men will become more familiar with women's actual abilities, for example. Women will feel less need to hide their talents and more willing to compete aggressively.

However, adding a few token women to an organization will not bring about a significant increase in choices for women, nor allow women to flourish. Women have to be numerous enough to be taken for granted, so that gender fades into the background, no more relevant than hair colour or shoe size. Kanter's tokenism theory is useful because we can apply it beyond the sociology of gender. In fact, we can use it to study any organizational setting that contains different kinds of people, whether men or women, racialized workers or white workers, anglophones or francophones, immigrants or native-borns, and so on. In every case, Kanter feels it is to the organization's advantage to make the best possible use of its human capital—the educated and willing potential employees. More diversity in organizations will mean more equality in society; just as importantly, it will also increase productivity. The diversity decision will prove to make good business sense.

However, achieving diversity is often hard to do. External relations with clients and other firms in the industry may hinder an organization's ability to change. As well, organizations often copy one another and remain locked into patterns set up at another time or place. No less importantly, large organizations also have internal environments that resist change; for example, islands of vested interest and their own culture. The large frogs in these small ponds will often resist change, fearing that they will lose power.

Being a Woman around the World

In her book, Beauvoir proposed that all women in all societies have been subjugated historically, and continue to be. Despite Beauvoir's claim of the universality of gender inequality, it is also apparent that gender inequality does not exist at the same level in different societies—especially today, over half a century after the publication of her book.

Societies are complex systems that operate according to unique combinations of culture, belief, wealth, education level, and degree of religiosity. Gender, which is socially constructed, therefore has different meanings in different societies. In some societies, being a woman means strong inequalities of power. In others, being a woman is secondary to other characteristics that constitute the person and may be more consequential, such as class.

How a society treats women is dependent on the social attitudes toward gender. Cross-cultural analyses of gender inequality provide evidence of the variations of gender attitudes. Consider the analysis by Amina Yaqin who studied the dolls that different cultures use to socialize girls on gender attitudes:[45]

> North American girls have Barbie. She has large blue eyes, long blond hair, long slim legs, and a large chest. She is fun loving and sweet. She has a huge closet, with plenty of different outfits to choose from, ranging from bikinis to party dresses. She has a boyfriend Ken, with whom she has an off-on relationship. In her spare time she loves shopping, partying, going to the beach, playing with her pets, and driving around in her many cars.

> Middle Eastern girls have Fulla. She is young, thin, with a small chest. She is loving, caring, respectful to her mother and father, does not lie, and embodies a modest Muslim woman. She wears an abaya (thin, all enveloping-cloak) and has a wide range of headscarves to choose from. She does not have a boyfriend.

Her favourite activities include saying her prayers as the sun rises, baking a cake to surprise her friends, and reading a book before bedtime.

A society's culture, and the surrounding belief systems and attitudes associated with it, play a large role in determining where a country falls on the gender inequality continuum. Researchers Simon Duncan and Birgit Pfau-Effinger refer to societies as masculine or feminine, and whether they are one or the other sets out the script for how gender relations are played out.[46]

Feminine societies are considered the most egalitarian with high levels of gender equality. Though not exactly gender utopias, they are nevertheless the closest representation of gender equality that a society has achieved thus far. According to these researchers, only the Scandinavian countries can truly be called feminine societies. Though things are still gendered there, women's spheres have expanded to encompass traditionally male roles, activities, and objects, thereby giving women substantial influence and room for action in society.

On the other hand, strict divisions of gender roles dictate masculine societies. Synonymous with patriarchy, these societies are characterized by strong gender inequalities since they follow the traditional mindsets of male entitlement and female inferiority.[47] Stereotypical traits reflecting this mindset include assertiveness and strength for men, modesty and tenderness for women. Most Middle Eastern, African, and some South Asian countries are considered masculine. Countries such as the United States, Italy, and Ireland are also masculine. Canada is among the countries that fall in the middle of the masculinity scale. Western European countries have the lowest levels of masculinity and, not surprisingly, more gender equality.

At the extreme masculine end of this continuum is *machismo*, a cult of exaggerated masculinity.[48] In this kind of culture, men are socialized to assert power and control over women, to showcase male virility and sexuality, and to uphold male honour at all costs.

The inherent inferiority of women and the belief that men have the right to control women guide the manner in which gender relations are played out. For instance, women in Latin American communities can hold one of two roles: Madonna or whore.[49] The Madonna is representative of the veneration men have for motherhood and the female virtues of chastity and nurturance. Women who do not perform womanhood in this way are dubbed whores.

These differences in the level of gender inequality across societies are reflected in specific ways, one of which is the solution societies have created (or failed to create) for the problem of the incompatiblity of work and family lives. That is, countries have developed different models for fulfilling the needs of the separate private and public spheres in our society, and these involve certain gender roles then normalized in that society. Some social norms and policies place women predominantly in the private sphere of the household (doing housework, child care, or eldercare); others encourage them to enter the public sphere of the labour market.

These differences can even be seen in developed countries. According to Duncan and Pfau-Effinger,[50] countries like Japan operate under a traditional model, in which work is seen exclusively as a male domain and the household as a female domain. Countries like the UK and Germany operate under a housewife model, in which women are encouraged to enter the labour force until they get married/have children, after which it is seen as socially appropriate to stay in the home to raise them. Countries like the US, Canada, and France operate under a dual model, in which women are encouraged to take on two roles simultaneously: they participate in the labour force and also accomplish household duties.

Finally, Scandinavian countries operate under the equality model, which assigns both men and women an equal amount of work in the labour force and in the household. With their equality model, Scandinavian countries enact the most gender equality in the workforce through policy and attitudes. The benefits are evident in other domains: women hold more positions of authority in the public sphere, enjoy greater sexual freedom, better contraception, better child care, and more political activism by women and unions. So, equalities, like inequalities, come hand in hand.

As Sjoberg (2010: 40–41) notes,

> industrialized countries in the post-war period have gradually moved toward gender equality . . . [but] there are still large cross-national differences regarding gender equality in family-oriented institutions. In the 1950s, all OECD countries were characterized by the predominance of a male breadwinner model, which basically meant that the father went out to work while the mother stayed home to look after the children. However, since then the Nordic countries . . . have gradually moved toward a dual-earner model, where social and family polices can be viewed as being explicitly aimed at . . . allowing a working mother, and thus a dual-income family.[52]

In fact, in Scandinavian countries the female employment (that is, participation) rates are a few percentage points over male participation rates, due to the large number of women employees in the public sector.[53] In comparison, only 60 percent of women in Canada participate in the labour force.[54] In the United States, nineteenth-century ideologies of women belonging in the home still permeate gender attitudes toward women. Only a little more than 50 percent believe that women should be allowed to work indefinitely.[55]

As well, even women who do work often occupy lower-prestige and lower-paying jobs than men.[56] That is true even where men and women are hired within the same profession. One big reason for this is the male culture of the workplace, which becomes more rampant among the top sector of companies. The old boys' network tries its best to keep its masculine identity, leading to the exclusion of women from many higher positions.

A major consequence of the economic inequality between men and women is that women are at a greater risk of encountering financial troubles in their lifetime than men. As the research makes clear, that is because women's financial situations depend on many factors that they cannot control. It is also because, when women do make choices, sometimes those choices place them at an economic disadvantage. If a man is successful financially, he will likely be more stable than a woman whose finances depend on whether she marries, whether and how many children she has, whether she separates or divorces, how long her husband lives, and so on. All these factors affect men to some extent, but they sometimes have cataclysmic effects on women.

In Canada, many more women than men face poverty after divorce, especially if they have custody of the children. Twenty-five percent of Canadian women have low incomes the year they break up with their partner, compared to only ten percent of men. As well, one in ten women live in poverty in the year after their breakup.[57] As custodial parents, divorced women have more (child-related) expenses than their husbands; if they have to stay home to take care of preschoolers, they have no employment income with which to pay those expenses. In this situation, many women drift into welfare dependence.

Women are also more likely than men to face poverty in later life. On average, women live longer than men. Yet, they are less likely to have a job-related pension because they are more likely to have held precarious jobs, such as those which are part-time, temporary, provide lower incomes, fewer benefits, less prestige, and a lack of unionized support. In fact, women are more likely than men to remain in these jobs for their whole life. More than 50 percent of employed Canadian men work in the least precarious jobs, while 70 percent of women work in the most precarious ones.[58] Along similar lines, a report from the YWCA notes that "women account for 70 percent of part-time employees and two-thirds of Canadians working for minimum wage." So, on average, women only amass two-thirds of what men do throughout their lives.[59]

Even when they enter traditionally male-dominated occupations, women sometimes find their credentials devalued by what sociologists have called the proletarianization of professions. The large-scale entry of women into areas like pharmacy and law tends to drive down the prestige and income of those occupations. On the other hand, when large numbers of men enter a profession traditionally dominated by women, the opposite seems to happen. Prestige and income rise, as has been evident in teaching and social work. How about this phenomenon as evidence of gender inequality in our society?

Differences in gender inequality across societies are also evident in other societal domains besides work and occupations—for example, in the way people get married. Feminine and progressively masculine countries (most European countries, the US and Canada, and select Asian countries) show high levels of gender equality regarding marriage.[60] In these (mostly Western) countries, people can choose whom they want to marry based on their own personal criteria.

By contrast, in mostly Eastern societies that practice individual choice marriage, people have more collective interests when choosing a partner. They can choose their partners independently (often based on qualities of loyalty and commitment) but afterwards, they must also present them to their family and peer groups for approval. The response of these groups has a large influence on whether or not the two people get married.

The most gender-unequal form of marriage is forced marriage. A forced marriage is one that is arranged without the full consent of both partners.[61] Women are the victims in most instances of forced marriage. A forced marriage consists of either a woman being pressured (physically, emotionally, or financially) into a marriage she does not want and which she cannot ever leave, or of people being linked to others in childhood. Forced marriages are considered subcategories of arranged marriages since in most arranged marriages the individual has a right to veto the parents' choices, thereby gaining some freedom in the decision-making process.[62]

Forced marriages are most common in Muslim and Middle Eastern countries.[63] This should come as no surprise since these also tend to be the most masculine countries in the world, with the strongest patriarchal attitudes and the most gender inequality.

A dowry is also often part of the marriage bargain, and also represents gender inequality. A dowry is the payment a bride's family makes to the husband as compensation for marrying their daughter.[64] Dowry exchange practices are evident to some degree in the majority of South Asian marriages, even though they have been legally banned. Dowries are highly gender unequal because they make women sources of economic potential for men.[65] They also increase the risk of violence toward women, both from their own and their husband's families, if the dowry is seen as inadequate or if the full payment is not properly made.[66]

To a smaller extent, forced marriage can also be found in Western countries inside some immigrant populations, in some Orthodox Jewish communities, in Chinese immigrant communities, and in some Christian groups such as the Mormons. All Western countries have criminalized forced marriage since it violates the UN Universal Declaration of Human Rights. In these countries, in addition to few if any forced marriages, there is also greater freedom to divorce for both partners. Within these societies divorce is seen as a normalized element in a couple's relationship, with women, as well as men, having the right to exit a relationship that is not working.

High levels of social support by the government give women the economic freedom to live independently and to raise children. The highest divorce rates are found in Sweden, where over half of marriages end in divorce.[67] The US and Canada also have high divorce rates, with almost half of all marriages ending in divorce.[68] But with low levels of government support, over 60 percent of single mothers live below the poverty line, unlike in Sweden.[69] Social policies that favour marriage make divorce economically risky for women, especially women with children to support.

Related to marriage is domestic violence, which represents gender inequality in its most severe form. There is a strong division between countries in which domestic violence is socially acceptable and countries in which domestic violence is considered a crime or, at best, a social anomaly. The most patriarchal countries are typically the ones in which domestic violence is a socially acceptable act. In those societies, women are not given equal status as human beings and are subjugated to male control. Therefore, if husbands and fathers choose to harm the women they own, it is not criminalized by the state.

For example, in 2002 the Indian Protection from Domestic Violence Act went as far as to justify the occasional beating of a wife, and to protect the husband in the matter.[70] Legal and parliamentary institutions reinforce the patriarchal system that exists in the country, since the law does not look at domestic violence as a human rights violation. As a result, violence toward women is common, and women are not offered any means to protect themselves. In fact, in these overly patriarchal cultures, women are often told that it is their duty to bear their husband's actions without any resistance.[71]

Domestic violence is different in Western countries, where it is seen as a criminal act that violates the norms of individual human rights. Domestic violence is also a matter solely between a husband and his wife, and does not include the husband's family members. All Western countries legally condemn domestic violence, but countries differ in the level of state assistance abused women are offered. Anglo-Saxon nations like the US, Canada, the UK, and Australia have governments that take a very laissez-faire approach in handling domestic violence victims.[72]

Scandinavian countries like Sweden take the opposite approach to dealing with domestic violence. In Sweden, the government is highly involved in ensuring gender equality; dependence on the state is viewed as necessary.[73] The state essentially becomes the accuser, absolving the victim from having to do the accusing. Women are also given comprehensive social assistance, which makes the act of leaving an abusive partner a lot less risky.

In fact, research shows that depending on how equal or unequal a society is, people in that society view victims—such as victims of marital violence—differently. In societies with more gender inequality, people respond to victims as either men or women, that is in a gendered way. Depending on the gender of the victim, people have different reactions to what occurred, which highlights the expectations, assumptions, and stereotypes that underlie gender relations in these societies. Since women have historically been dominated by men, most of the research on the effects of just-world beliefs on gender has involved women—typically, victims of rape and domestic abuse. Studies have shown that, regardless of one's reaction to a victim of rape or domestic abuse, the reaction is ultimately concerned with protecting the perceiver's sense of justice.

Research has found that, perhaps surprisingly, people typically blame the victims of domestic abuse and exonerate the predators when no reason for the attack is given.[74] However, when participants are given any reason for the attack, they tend to blame the perpetrator and pity the victim. Likewise, in studies conducted on the perception of rape victims, if no reason is given for the attack, participants typically blame the victim (for example, for not being aware of the situation, or for being promiscuous).[75]

These reactions stem from a concern with one's own personal safety: in order to feel safe, people need to believe that good behaviour is an indication that one deserves, and will receive, positive outcomes and fair treatment.[76] As we mentioned earlier, people need to believe that bad things only happen to people who deserve them, in order to maintain the personal contract that gives them the confidence to pursue future goals. So, when it appears that something bad has happened to someone who doesn't deserve it, most people will find a way to make the situation appear deserved.

What's even more intriguing is that the physical beauty of female victims plays a large role in people's perception of that victim. One study found that people rate the death of a woman as more tragic and unfair, and blamed perpetrators more, when she was physically attractive.[77] Further, when participants were told that a female victim suffered a great deal, they often tended to (falsely) remember that they had been told she was unattractive. It appears that physical appearance, which is extremely important for women in many societies, has been equated to their moral goodness. Since people want to believe that good people suffer less than bad people (because good people would not deserve to suffer), it is clear that beautiful women are often perceived as being good.

The impact of gender stereotyping also has serious and harmful consequences for male victims. Given the existence of certain myths (such as the myth that men always desire sex), male rape victims (some of whom are gay) who come forward about their attacks are often themselves blamed, face stigmatization, or are not taken seriously.[78] People in societies characterized by less gender equality and more gender stereotyping blame male rape victims more than people in countries that challenge gender norms. But, given the limited amount of information on male rape victims, they are at a disadvantage in the majority of societies. This dearth of research may be a result of the limited number of male rape victims who step forward after an attack, as they fear being labelled as weak, inadequate, or gay.[79]

Men and women with strong just-world beliefs also react differently to incidences of domestic abuse or rape. Typically, men react negatively toward both male and female victims, whereas women empathize with victims.[80] Researchers have speculated that women react with empathy because of an identification with the victim and a primeval reaction to protect themselves. Men blame the victims because they are more likely to presume the victim consented; perhaps they are also more likely to identify with the perpetrator.[81]

Thus, as we have seen in this chapter, women lead lives that are similar to men's lives, but still encounter many more barriers and constraints. Some of these constraints are the result of inequalities based in class relations, while others are a result of cultural ideologies. But as research from Scandinavia shows, most are rooted in the structure of our state, and how much effort it makes to help women bridge the private and public spheres of our society. Canada still has a lot of work to do here; it can start with providing good quality, affordable daycare.

In the next chapter, we will discuss racial and ethnic inequalities, and racialization. In doing so, we will see many of the same patterns about women applied to racialized minorities.

CHAPTER 3

Racialization

———— • ◆ • ————

*"The problem of the twentieth century is the
problem of the colour line."*
W.E.B. Du Bois, American sociologist and activist

A Mile in Another's Moccasins

Over the years, some classic experiments have shown that you
can change people's behaviour—even their thinking—by changing
their social roles. Consider the famous psychological experiment
at Stanford by Philip Zimbardo, which split college students into
two groups.[1] One group of randomly chosen students was told to
play the role of prisoners, and the other group was to play the role
of jailers in a mock prison. After a brief time in their respective
roles, these players were going well beyond what they had been
asked to do to play their part. The jailers were behaving in authoritarian, aggressive, and hostile ways toward their prisoners, and the
prisoners were resisting vigorously. Each set of students quickly
developed loyalty for their own group and strongly resented the
group playing the opposite role. This finding leads us to wonder,
could you develop racial hatred in the same way, by assigning
people randomly to one or another racial group? Consider this
example, which began with the shooting of American civil rights
leader Martin Luther King Jr.

On April 5, 1968, a student in Jane Elliott's third grade class in
Riceville, Iowa, asked: "They shot a king last night, Mrs. Elliott. Why
did they shoot that king?" The day before, King had been assassin-
ated while standing on a motel balcony in Memphis, Tennessee.

That night, as she heard about the incident on the evening news, Mrs. Elliott became upset by the ignorance of white male commentators. Without realizing it, they showed a remarkable lack of sympathy for the black community. One white reporter, pointing a microphone at a local black leader asked, "When our leader [John F. Kennedy] was killed several years ago, his widow held us together. Who's going to control your people?" Hearing this kind of talk, Mrs. Elliott knew it was time to bring the lessons she had been teaching her students about racism to the next level. If grown men could display such ignorance and bigotry, how could she help to make sure young children reacted to the tragedy more conscientiously?

Earlier on, Mrs. Elliott had depicted Martin Luther King Jr. as a role model for her students—their Hero of the Month in February—and she knew words would not be enough to explain his violent death to them. Though everyone can imagine being treated like an inferior, few know what it feels like or is to imagine the kinds of psychological, emotional, and social effects this treatment might have. Inspired by the Aboriginal saying "oh, Great Spirit, keep me from ever judging a man until I have walked a mile in his moccasins," the next day Mrs. Elliott arrived to class with a purpose in mind and fabric collars in hand.

Mrs. Elliott began the day by asking the children what they thought brotherhood means. Then she asked them whether some people in society are not treated like our brothers; here, the children singled out black and Aboriginal people. "Why do we not treat them like our brothers?" she asked. Predictably, the children answered: "Because they're of a different colour."

Even though the children were answering the questions suitably, Mrs. Elliot felt certain they had no clear understanding of discrimination from personal experience. In the late sixties, Riceville was a small farming town with an all-white, all-Christian population of less than one thousand people. Most of the children in her classroom had only seen black people on television, and all they knew of them was what they had heard adults say. Many had already learned the typical stereotypes about laziness, unemployment, and violence associated with black people in the US. Mrs. Elliott wanted to tap into, and expose, precisely these prejudices.

In the sunny classroom of this small town school, with little pairs of eyes turned toward her, Mrs. Elliott told the children that it would be interesting to see what would happen if people were judged not by the colour of their skin, but instead the colour of their eyes. The blue-eyed children will go first, she says, and will act as if they are better than the brown-eyed children. The brown-eyed children, then, will wear fabric collars so that people could tell their eye colour from far away.

After instructing all the brown-eyed children to put on the fabric collars she had brought, Mrs. Elliott then handed out certain privileges to the blue-eyed children. She granted blue-eyed children five extra minutes for recess, second helpings at lunch, free access to the water fountain, and access to a new play park. Meanwhile, she ordered the brown-eyed children to remain indoors while the blue-eyed children played outside. The brown-eyed children were also limited to one helping of food at lunchtime, and ordered to use paper cups so they didn't contaminate the water fountain for the blue-eyed people. Most important, they were forbidden to play with their former friends, who were now to be viewed as their blue-eyed superiors. The brown-eyed people were now not good enough to play with the blue-eyed people.

At first, some of the brown-eyed children protested, defending themselves. However, Mrs. Elliott used several tactics to convince them of their inferiority. To prove that blue-eyed children were superior, she used pseudo-scientific explanations. For example, she stated that the melanin responsible for making blue eyes was also linked to higher intelligence and better learning ability.

To support her argument, she singled out some students as examples. During a lesson that morning, for example, one little girl was not ready to read at the same time as everyone else. "Is everyone ready?" asked Mrs. Elliott, noticing her. "Everyone but Laurie! Well, she's brown-eyed. You begin to notice today that we spend a great deal of time waiting around for brown-eyed people." The children quickly picked up on this lesson. Later that day, as Mrs. Elliott searched for a yardstick, one little boy piped up: "We keep it on your desk, Mrs. Elliott, so that you can use it if the brown-eyed people get out of hand."

Though Mrs. Elliott had first explained the exercise to the children, she was surprised by the results. She "watched what had been marvelous, cooperative, wonderful, thoughtful children turn into nasty, vicious, discriminating little third graders in the space of fifteen minutes. Immediately, I [had] created a microcosm of society in my classroom." By recess that afternoon, the brown-eyed children were already feeling hurt and bewildered by the exercise, and betrayed by their teacher. They expressed their suffering at being treated as inferiors:

> It seemed like when we were down on the bottom, everything bad was happening to us.

> The way they treated you, you felt like you didn't even want to try to do anything.

> It seemed like Mrs. Elliott was taking our best friends away from us.

After recess, Mrs. Elliott learned there had been a fight between two of the boys. One child punched another in the gut for calling him a name—"Brown eyes." The boy in question had always had brown eyes, and yet suddenly, this fact was the basis for an insult. Another classmate finally realized, "Oh, that's the same way as when other people call black people niggers." The brown-eyed boy had punched the blue-eyed boy, who had been his best friend the day before, then admitted with a shake of his head that using violence had not stopped the name-calling. Nor did he feel better after having done it.

The next day, Mrs. Elliott reversed the exercise, saying, "Yesterday I told you that brown-eyed people aren't as good as blue-eyed people. That wasn't true. I lied to you yesterday." "Oh boy, here we go again," one boy said as he rolled his eyes. "The truth is, brown-eyed people are better than blue-eyed people." Squeals of laughter and smiles are now appeared on the faces of the brown-eyed children, and even more so when Mrs. Elliott recited the privileges that they were to enjoy. They were permitted to take off their collars and put them on fellow blue-eyed students, which they all did with great enthusiasm, despite what they had endured the day before.

All that day the brown-eyed children mocked the blue-eyed children and took advantage of their newfound privilege. However, they did not do so as severely as the blue-eyed children had the day before when they were superior. The brown-eyed children already had first-hand experience with the inferiority treatment and they did not like it.

The exercise brought about obvious changes in behaviour and attitude. What's more, it even changed the children's learning ability. Over years of repeating this exercise, Mrs. Elliott measured incredible changes in the children's aptitude. Each year, she gave the children four tests—one two weeks before the exercise, two on each day of the exercise, and another two weeks after the exercise. Consistently, Mrs. Elliott found the children did better on the day that they were part of the superior group. In many cases, they did far better than they had two weeks earlier. Equally important, they tested at a higher level for the rest of the year, after having gone through the exercise.

Mrs. Elliott sent the results to Stanford University for analysis, and the reviewers there agreed that these test results were remarkable. The children's measured intelligence changed depending on whether they were being treated like superiors or inferiors, all within the span of twenty-four hours. Knowing that you are superior, it seems, improves your performance and well-being; the opposite happens to inferiors.

In the four decades since Mrs. Elliott first introduced this exercise in her classroom, she has become a pioneer in what is now known as diversity training. The exercise has been tried everywhere, in classrooms, workplaces, and even prisons. Some have criticized

Mrs. Elliott's approach for being harsh and even psychologically damaging, but she doesn't mind. She has been hired by countless corporations to give workshops and lectures on what it's like to suffer discrimination. And documentaries such as the PBS *A Class Divided*, in which the above classroom interaction was recorded, have shown the public her controversial approach.[2]

Debates continue about the ethics behind her experiment, and people who have participated in it have mixed feelings about it. Most of those who went through it recall it vividly, even today. They say that those two days of inferiority and superiority had profoundly affected their lives and taught them how to treat their fellow human beings properly. Others, by contrast, have said the experiment was hard to endure and they wouldn't want their own children going through it.

But that, really, is the point of the exercise. Mrs. Elliot proposes that we do not know the feeling of inferiority until we go through such an experience. Even then, we only get a glimpse of what it is like to live one's entire life under a cloud of prejudice and unequal treatment. The more people who know this feeling, the better off we are, she says. Yet, when asked if she would like the exercise to be used more widely, Elliot responds with a definite "No." Instead, and characteristically so, she would like to see the need for the exercise disappear.

Drawing the Colour Line

What Mrs. Elliott tried to teach her children with the blue eyes– brown eyes experiment is the arbitrary nature of the differences that divide humans. Before the experiment, Mrs. Elliott's students lived in harmony. No one paid attention to eye colour any more than to height or shoe size. However, once Mrs. Elliott introduced this distinction, real differences started to emerge. The students began pointing fingers at each other, finding justifications for superiority and inferiority among themselves ("Brown eyes!").

This exercise, then, shows the social construction of differences based on race and ethnicity. This is not very different from the social construction of gender we discussed in the last chapter: in both instances, a trivial physical difference is used to launch and justify large, consequential social differences—especially, inequalities.

But what do sociologists mean by race and ethnicity? Our understanding of the terms often differs from popular notions, especially of what it means to be of a different race. By race, sociologists mean differences based on physical or genetic characteristics that produce differences in appearance. People often equate the term race with ethnicity, but the two are significantly different. For sociologists, the term ethnicity refers to social and cultural characteristics people are believed to share.

An ethnic group, then, is a set of people who consider themselves, or are considered by others, to share common characteristics that distinguish them from other groups in a society. Typically, these characteristics are historical and unite group members by distinguishing them from others. From their set of cultural similarities, groups develop a distinctive cultural behaviour and form an ethnic group or community. Most important of these are a presumed common origin and distinctive cultural behaviours. People from the same ethnicity may appear similar, or they could look completely different and even be part of a different race.

For sociologists, both race and ethnicity are socially constructed. But it may be easier for the general public to see ethnicity rather than race as social. After all, we live in a society where racial differences are so often linked to biological differences. Some people have difficulty accepting that race has little biological basis. Instead, they see each race as possessing unique physiological characteristics, based in genetic differences that are absent in other races. Often, they also believe that cultural or personality dispositions—even intelligence—are genetically based.

Increasingly, however, scientists reject this view of race, in light of growing genetic evidence showing that the so-called human races are significantly more alike than they are different. The Human Genome Project, an international scientific project dedicated to determining the sequence of chemical base pairs that make up DNA, has identified and mapped the roughly 20,000–25,000 genes of the human genome. In doing so, it has shown that only a tiny fraction of our genetic makeup as human beings varies by characteristics historically associated with race. In fact, 85 percent of the genetic variability that exists within the entire human species can be found within a single local population.[3]

This means there could be more genetic difference between two randomly selected Cambodians than between, say, a Cambodian and a Norwegian—supposedly members of two different races. As well, the physical attributes commonly associated with race are not genetically associated with each other. For example, the pieces of DNA that determine a person's skin colour are inherited separately from the pieces that control if that person's hair is curly or straight. So, the chances of getting the entire racial package in one individual are far from 100 percent. Instead, the physical features that distinguish members of one race are a result of genetic adaptation to specific environmental influences, for example, to prolonged sunlight. Skin colour darkens where strong sunlight shines most of the time, as it does near the equator.

Race and ethnicity are not necessarily connected. People who look different—for example, French-Canadians and Chinese-Canadians—may share the same cultural values, and people who look the same—for example, Texans and Swedes—may think in strikingly different ways. So, racial and ethnic groups are quite different. Yet, racial and ethnic inequalities are linked fundamentally, since both racial and ethnic minorities suffer from prejudice and discrimination. As well, both racial and ethnic differences ignite bitter conflict. Around the world, racial and ethnic conflicts still erupt, sometimes resulting in genocidal bloodbaths that kill hundreds of thousands. Today, in a global, post-industrial world, we should be witnessing fewer genocidal wars, not more. Classical sociological theory predicted the decline of racial and ethnic divisions. Why, then, do they persist?

First and most important, it is difficult—perhaps impossible—to completely change people's perceptions, prejudices, and stereotypes.

Perhaps that's because there's a grain of truth to them. But there's a lot that is untrue—often, too conveniently untrue. As a result, there is a tendency for ethnic and racial stereotypes to persist. Some conclude that you have to give into them—get bleached if you are a dark-skinned minority, for example. Others conclude that there is no true melting pot, since differences will never disappear. Yet, there are signs it may be disappearing.

Throughout the twentieth century, Marxists expected class identities to replace ethnic identities, especially in the minds of class-conscious workers. Marx and other progressive thinkers viewed racial and ethnic distinctions as distractions from class warfare. However, ethnic sentiment has proved more binding than class sentiment in the twentieth century—something that would have surprised Marx. Racial and ethnic identities have proved more resistant to change than nineteenth-century thinkers had ever imagined.

This fact would have also surprised Emile Durkheim and Max Weber—the other two founders of sociology. They imagined that occupational and professional identities would replace ethnic identities, through the development of what Durkheim called organic solidarity. Instead, however, people in modern societies developed compartmentalized ethnic and occupational identities, keeping them separate but intact. How can we explain this persistence of ethnic and racial inequalities, ethnic and racial communities and identities, and ethnic and racial conflict?

The short answer is that ethnic communities and identities persist because they are dynamic, adapting creatively and changing with the times. In this way, they are like organisms that adapt to new and changing habitats, constantly evolving and reinventing themselves to survive. In fact, new ethnic groups are always being formed as populations move between countries. Of course, some ethnic communities—ethnic groups in particular cities or countries—disappear. It would be fair to say there is no Australian, Tibetan, Ghanaian, Monacan, Bolivian, or Moldovan ethnic community in Canada. These groups are too small or poorly organized to survive in the Canadian context. They soon blend into other similar language or racial groupings.

Other ethnic communities survive for many generations. They do so, in Canada and elsewhere, by purposely maintaining their ethnic distinctiveness—for example, their proudly distinctive ethnic identities and customs. In Canada, these ethnic communities are helped along by Canada's official policy of multiculturalism.

This policy was originally intended to ensure that Canadian institutions would reflect the values of cultural pluralism. So-called traditional multiculturalism was concerned especially with protecting the rights of people against prejudice and discrimination. Present-day modern multiculturalism is more concerned with protecting the survival of ethnic communities. Some critics argue that multiculturalism today accentuates the differences between Canadians and segregates them from one another, rather than contributing to a unified nationhood.

Besides multiculturalism, high rates of immigration also support the survival of ethnic groups. Chain migration—a process in which one family member successfully migrates to an area, and then other family members and even acquaintances slowly immigrate to join them—tends to reproduce original communities in a new land, in effect, to transport and replant a section of Calabria or Hong Kong in Vancouver. This transplant has the effect of slowing immigrant assimilation and explains why it may take several generations before an immigrant group is fully assimilated. The more committed a group remains to its home community, the harder it is to assimilate, and the more slowly it gains full acceptance by other Canadians.

Ethnic groups and ethnic communities are related but different. An ethnic group is just a set of people who share the same ethnic origins; an ethnic community is an ethnic group with boundaries, often living together in a defined geographic location. In a sense, this distinction is like the one Marx made between a class in itself and a class for itself. Like the class for itself, the ethnic community is self-aware and self-conscious about its difference from outsiders. Residential proximity may be important, but the survival of an ethnic community depends on more than mere proximity. It depends on imagination.

Imagined Communities

What is remarkable about ethnicity is its sheer staying power in the face of wars, migrations, and out-marriages. No wonder people have been studying ethnicity and race for a long time—even, in fact, for millennia. The Greek historian Herodotus, in the fifth century BCE, was the first to study ethnic groups. Witnessing the continued conflict between major Mediterranean empires, Herodotus looked into the roots of cultural difference—especially, cultural differences between the Greeks, Egyptians, and Persians, the leading contenders for dominance in the Mediterranean region in his day. To explain why they were so often at war with one another, Herodotus studied their languages, gods, and customs. Why, he wondered, couldn't they live in peace? And why did they have so much trouble understanding one another? It had something to do with competing political and economic interests; it also had something to do with beliefs and lifestyles.

Emile Durkheim, a nineteenth-century French sociologist, looked at the same problem another way. He recognized the importance of social cohesion for groups, and wondered what made small tribal societies so cohesive, compared to modern, industrial societies. His research led him to conclude that shared group sentiments—what he called a collective consciousness—were the primary source of cohesion and personal identity in these societies. People needed the survival of their community for their own survival, and both survived through the cultivation of similarity. In these early communities, everyone had a similar identity, similar values, beliefs, and desires. Similarity led to group cohesion, and group cohesion led to personal well-being. So, for those groups around the Mediterranean, forming groups based on similarity was a way of ensuring protection.

In his final work, *The Elementary Forms of Religious Life*, Durkheim proposed that collective consciousness is mobilized by rituals and ritual objects called totems.[4] Totems could be animals, plants, or even imaginary beings. Yet regardless of their concrete qualities, these totems were all objects of veneration for members of the group. By constructing a meaning for the totem and celebrating it, the tribe celebrated its social cohesion. In religious rites, anything could serve as the basis for group solidarity: a bird, an animal, a rock. It was people's ability to share an imagined meaning for the totemic object—a story, a myth, or a fable about the totem—that gave them stability and strength.

Translate this finding to Canada today. For example, Ukrainian songs, foods, and heroes all play this cohesive, totemic role in a present-day Ukrainian-Canadian community. These activities and objects are boundary markers and sources of collective ritual. What's more, they mark the boundaries that separate insiders from outsiders. Any ritual object can play that role, even a portrait of a long-gone hero.

Historian Benedict Anderson coined the term *imagined communities* to describe people who group together around a common history and culture.[5] Doing so forces them to ignore obvious differences—for example, class or religious differences—and search for sometimes hidden or trivial similarities. The common origins of an ethnic group need not be real, but they must be believed to be real. Remember the quotation we mentioned in the introductory chapter. Sociologists W.I. Thomas and D.S. Thomas once said: "If men define situations as real, they will be real in their consequences." In other words, what people believe to be real will have real outcomes.

Like Durkheim, Max Weber, another founder of sociology, paid attention to the ways ethnic communities control their members. He noted that, as status groups, ethnic groups practice closure (exclusion) and usurpation (capture) to maintain themselves. That is, they create and police their boundaries, reward insiders and punish outsiders, and capture (or monopolize) valued resources for their members' use, especially in India, which is the setting Weber primarily studied in relation to this finding. This is also what members of the capitalist class do, according to Marx and Erik Olin Wright, as we mentioned in the first chapter.

Thus, ethnic groups are more effective status groups than social classes, since they have managed to achieve the level of group awareness and consciousness that Marx hoped classes would do. Like social classes, ethnic groups practice control and exercise power in the interests of their members. The creation of ethnic communities means highlighting, or even inventing, cultural markers that unite subgroups and separate them from people in neighbouring groups deemed culturally different. This means distinguishing Greeks from Turks, or Poles from Ukrainians. Typically, this requires the use of symbolic markers such as language, rituals, and ceremonies.

However, merely imagining an ethnic community is not the same as maintaining it. To survive, ethnic communities rely on what Canadian sociologist Raymond Breton has called *institutional completeness*—a set of institutions (stores, schools, churches, newspapers, and so on) that help people maintain their culture and social connections.[6] These community institutions preserve ethnic sentiments, and they also promote them. Often they do so to the advantage of their members. Initiatives undertaken to promote the community's merchants and businesses, for example, are certain to provide small-scale, short-term benefits—especially for newcomers who have trouble speaking English. It may even improve the fortunes of the community, and of community members, in the larger society.

There are downsides to ethnic enclaves, however. Enclaves mean segregation, and segregation sometimes means a concentration of poverty and other social issues. The level of segregation in Canadian cities is lower than in the more unequal American cities, but it seems as though visible minorities are excluded from the British or French majorities to a greater extent than immigrants from other European backgrounds. This is sometimes due to racism in the real estate market, as many minority groups experience difficulties in buying a house. Research has found that some racial groups have lower rates of home ownership than what would be expected considering their income, education, and careers.[7]

Ethnic segregation in neighbourhood contexts may also make it difficult for community members to compete in the larger world, where there are more varied and bigger prizes to be won. In a multicultural society, minorities have to decide whether to stay within their community or cross boundaries and even assimilate economically, socially, and culturally. Doing this, individuals risk becoming marginal, in the sense of having one foot inside the group and one foot outside. They may belong to two worlds and sometimes feel like they belong to neither. Worse, they may find themselves rejected by both worlds.

Sociologists used to think of ethnic minorities in Canada and the US as isolated, even stranded, in a foreign sea—that is, until they assimilated. But this is no longer a useful way to understand ethnic communities since today communication and travel are easier than in the past, making the idea of global ethnic communities increasingly possible. How different this is from a century ago, when immigrants to Canada often had to cut their ties to the homeland and risk everything on success in the New World. And yet, once they arrive they still often face discrimination and difficulties integrating into the host society.

The Vertical Mosaic

In his classic work, *The Vertical Mosaic*, Canadian sociologist John Porter explored the reasons certain groups are not as integrated into the host society as others.[8] In doing so, he put to rest common misconceptions of Canada as a classless society.

Like the United States, and contrary to popular mythology, Canadian society is vertical—a social hierarchy of wealth and power. However, unlike the United States to which people often compare it, Canada is a mosaic of unassimilated ethnic groups who hold different positions in this hierarchy of wealth and power. Canada is not a melting pot like the US, nor is it socially equal. Porter found that Canada is socially stratified, with economic power in the hands of a small group of elites who act to promote and protect one another's interests. Of greatest interest is that this small group of Canadian elites is mainly comprised of people with a WASP (White Anglo-Saxon Protestant) background, though a few elites have a French background. Porter calls these two ethnic groups the charter groups.

Porter proposes that many historical and social factors forced Canada's ethnic mosaic into a vertical position with the two charter groups—the British and the French—on top. Supporters of the vertical mosaic argument contend the charter groups, especially the British, have maintained their favourable positions. Meanwhile, Eastern and Southern Europeans and, in particular, visible minorities and people of Aboriginal ancestry continue to occupy the lower positions in Canada's socio-economic ladder.[9]

Because of limited educational opportunities, lower-status, non-WASP groups are locked into inferior economic positions, generation after generation. At the same time, descendants of the charter groups preserve and extend their historic advantage, largely by monopolizing higher educational opportunities. Without a higher education, non-charter group Canadians have little chance to get ahead—little chance to escape the entrance statuses their forebears achieved on arriving in Canada and even less chance to enter the elite.

To improve this situation, Porter called for a transformation of Canada's educational system to make it equally open to everyone, so the most able have the opportunity to advance occupationally and economically, regardless of ethnic background. Porter also encouraged cultural assimilation, to break down social and cultural barriers that have protected the WASP elite and kept down the newcomers.

Porter said all this in 1965, fifty years ago, and some would say that Porter's study is dated. Today, people's ethnic origins do little to hinder their educational or occupational advancement. Others might say that, today, opportunities for upward social mobility are beside the point: what matters for Canada is the persistence of a small, ruling elite, whatever its ethnic composition. However, the book remains significant today. By challenging previously held misconceptions, Porter led sociologists and policy-makers to develop new ideas about Canadian society. The book set off twenty years of sociological research on power, mobility, ethnicity, and immigration in Canada.

Most important, Porter's call for a transformed educational system was hugely influential. The expansion of Canada's post-secondary education in the 1960s and 1970s was fueled in part by Porter's arguments (among others), and many Canadians have since benefited. So, if ethnicity is no longer an important determinant of education, occupation, or income (as it once was) that is largely thanks to Porter's sociological research.

Has more recent research shown that the vertical mosaic does, in fact, exist? Rebuttals to the Porter thesis highlight that Porter had nothing to say about women or racial minorities in the Canadian mosaic.[10] Looking at the 1991 data, Jason Lian and David Matthews examined the earnings of different ethnic groups at ten levels of education ranging from no degree, certificate, or diploma, to an earned doctorate.[11] They found that while people of European ethnicity have achieved equality with the British, visible minorities have significantly lower earnings than the British reference group at most educational levels. The authors conclude that while the traditional vertical mosaic of ethnic differences may be disappearing, it has been replaced by a strong coloured mosaic of racial differences.

Why the continued inequalities among some ethnic, but especially racial, groups? Ethnic affiliation may be one factor. Strong ethnic attachments may cause social bordering that often isolates people from information about mainstream job opportunities.[12] The result of this is limited educational and occupational attainment. Another explanation for persisting inequality may be the structural barriers faced by members of various communities. From this perspective, racial prejudice and discrimination are systemically woven into the fabric of Canada's socio-economic structure, denying members of certain groups the full range of job opportunities and similar resources despite whatever human capital they possess.[13]

Racial inequality seems to be tied to income inequality in many countries, including developed societies. This is especially noticeable when comparing black and white income disparities. When comparing Canada and the United States, for example, it's obvious there is a greater racial income gap in the US than in Canada, but black people are under-represented in the highest household income categories in both countries.[14]

However, black Canadians seem to fare considerably better than their American counterparts, with a higher ratio of affluent blacks to affluent whites in Canada. Black Canadians are 82 percent as likely as whites to be found in the top income category, while this is true for only 39 percent of black Americans, even after controlling for population size.[15] As well, the Canadian middle class, with incomes over $120,000, is more racially balanced than that of America.[16] Furthermore, Canada does not seem to have the over-representation of black people in low-income categories as dramatically as the United States.

Many believe the racial income gap is smaller in Canada than the US, but once the relative sizes of each generation of immigrants in the country have been taken into account, these gaps become similar in both countries. All in all, racism affects where and how people live, and can also induce long-term effects on income and wage differences. Race, it seems, still matters.

Ladder of Separation

We know that immigrants—especially visible minorities—are economically unequal to native borns in our society. But how do we measure how far apart they are socially? And are Canadians coming together, moving farther apart, or merely isolated in distinct ethnic or racial communities?

In the early twentieth century, psychologist Emory S. Bogardus invented a handy way to measure the social distance between pairs of ethnic and racial groups.[17] He designed it to measure intergroup segregation and, conversely, the willingness of group members to mix with other groups.[18] Specifically, the Social Distance Scale measures the extent to which survey respondents say they would accept members of a certain racial or ethnic group into closer social relationships, as follows (listed from the closest to the most distant):

1. Close relative by marriage
2. Close personal friend
3. Neighbour on same street
4. Co-worker in same occupation
5. Citizen in own country
6. Temporary visitor in own country
7. Someone excluded from own country

For example, the researcher might ask a French-Canadian to show his willingness to have a Pakistani person as a close relative—say, to marry his daughter. If not, would he be willing to have a Pakistani person as a close friend? As a neighbour on the same street or co-worker at the same workplace? And so on. If the French-Canadian shows a desire to exclude the Pakistani person from Canada, he would receive a score of seven for this question. The respondent would then be asked the same question about, say, Brazilians or Nigerians. For each question, the respondent would get a score ranging from one to seven.

This yields an average social distance measure for each respondent, each respondent group (for example, French-Canadians), and each target group (for example, Pakistanis, Brazilians, Nigerians, and so on). By analyzing these averages, we can determine what types of people are most open to minorities and which types of minorities are most accepted or rejected by a majority of respondents. Equally valuable, we can use this method to chart change of attitudes over time.

In the Bogardus scale, the closest measure of social distance is a close relative by marriage. So, while the Bogardus scale itself is a useful measure of social distance, we can also look at rates of intergroup marriage as an indication of groups either getting closer over time or not, implying lesser social distance. In fact, intergroup marriage is often seen as the "last barrier to social integration."[19] Typically, where there is little intermarriage across group lines, it means the groups are sharply divided socially, and likely are unequal. On the other hand, a high degree of marriage across racial or ethnic lines means people think these differences are unimportant or inconsequential.

People marry across group lines under two conditions. First, they must have many opportunities to meet members of the other group, whether in their neighbourhood, at school, or at work. Second, there must be a relative abundance of eligible mates in the other group and a shortage of them in one's own group. For our purposes, cross-comparative data on intermarriage is an indicator of the level of inequality between ethnic and racial groups in different societies. In other words, we expect societies with higher levels of inequality to also have lower levels of intergroup marriage, given the differences in status among groups.

In a cross-comparative study conducted by Tim Heaton and Cardell Jacobson,[20] the prevalence and pattern of intermarriage gives us a good assessment of any remaining barriers to inter-group connections. However, we must be careful when comparing racial relationships across countries since, for example, black–white relationships have different meanings in South Africa than in the United States. Results can also be biased by many factors, such as segregation, geographic isolation, and culture on top of many other third party factors such as religious affiliation and history of conflict between groups. Nevertheless, Heaton and Jacobson's study considered six regions: Canada, the US, the US state of Hawaii, New Zealand, South Africa, and Xinjiang province in China. Through various techniques, they determined that Hawaii and New Zealand are the most tolerant, South Africa and Xinjiang exhibit the highest strain, and Canada and the US as a whole are in the middle on this continuum.

Heaton and Jacobson's findings imply that intermarriage has been increasing over time in Canada. This is supported by the 2006 Census, which found an increasing number of mixed unions, with a growth rate five times larger than other couples.[21] As for the US, interracial or interethnic marriage rates have doubled since 1980 (even though they are slowing among certain racial groups).[22] Further, more than six in ten Americans said they "would be fine" with one of their family members marrying someone of a different race or ethnicity.[23] New Zealand's rates are increasing, as well as South Africa's, concluding the race barriers between black people and whites in those countries are also wearing away.

Yet, despite rates of higher intermarriage, native populations of these countries still have high endogamy (same-group marriage) ratios among groups that live in remote areas, including reserves.[24] Individual group parameters of this experiment showed even greater variation, with whites (the vast majority in the US, Canada, and New Zealand) having low rates of homogamy. Heaton and Jacobson explain that when minority groups marry exogenously, they marry into the majority, supporting the theory that intermarriage is at least in part a function of group size, and of minorities having more contact with the dominant group.

But the group size theory only accounts for some of the intermarriage rates. Heaton and Jacobson's study concludes the highest homogamy rates are in societies where opportunities of interracial mingling are abundant and least in countries where parties have strong interests against interracial marriage, such as in Xinjiang, China. Race and ethnicity still continue to be a critical part of a marriage decision, and third party influences have an effect on the decision, especially the bride and groom's families.

What about other nations? If developed countries are becoming more racially tolerant, we should see the rates of intermarriage increasing over the last decades. Consider Australia, where out of all registered marriages in 2007, over 60 percent of the couples were both born in Australia, 9.5 percent were both born in the same overseas country, and about 30 percent were born in different countries.[25] The number of marriages registered yearly has been fluctuating greatly, rising then falling; the number of couples both born in the same country as well as those born in different countries has been steadily increasing since 1998. Meanwhile, those with both partners born in Australia have been the same, fluctuating each year since 1988. This could be the result of the overseas-born population in Australia increasing by around 13 percent from 1996 to 2006, with the top three groups either born in England, New Zealand, or China.[26]

Japan, on the other hand, tends to show more endogamous marriages. Out of all marriages in Japan in 2006, 93 percent were between people of Japanese ethnicity.[27] Japanese men marry interracially more often than women, with a higher percentage of brides originating from Korea, China, the Philippines, and Thailand. Lower percentages occur in the US, the UK, Brazil, and Peru. To show a better comparison, around 36,000 men married another ethnicity while only 8,700 women did the same. The rest of the marriages unaccounted for were between various foreign ethnicities, neither of Japanese descent.

As for intermarriage in France, one study found that 36 percent of immigrants are intermarried, and this included large variations in the individual's country of origin.[28] Following normal patterns, immigrants exogenously married tend to be younger than their endogamous counterparts.[29] Interestingly, the longer a person remains in the country after migration the more likely they were to be in an interracial relationship. European immigrants are more inclined to have mixed marriages with a rate very close to 50 percent while Turkish people, on the other hand, have had the lowest rates in France.[30]

In fact, in Europe Turks are highly pressured to marry strictly within their ethnic and religious group. Being mainly of the Muslim faith, Turks endure strong parental pressures and are limited by the rules set by their religion. For example, in Germany, Turkish men marry proportionally more German than Turkish women; Islam permits them to do so, while it forbids women from marrying non-Muslims.[31] Nevertheless, their rates of intermarriage are extremely low, and many women will even go as far as importing Turkish husbands from other areas.

Now consider one of the Scandinavian countries, Sweden. This country is supposed to be less unequal than most of the world, so how do their rates of interracial marriage compare to the rest? Interestingly, we do not have a very clear answer to this question. There has not been a lot of research conducted on intermarriage in Sweden, so we lack the kind of precise statistics we have been looking at for other countries. In fact, people in Sweden do not even officially register their ethnicity or race.[32] According to their 2010 Statistics, 173,000 couples started a family during 2004 to 2008, and only 9 percent consisted of one partner born in Sweden and one born abroad.[33]

In the city of Malmö, an anonymous survey was conducted among white Europeans to explore their outlook on marriage between people of different races or ethnicities.[34] Their answers to this questionnaire show that they were open to dating or marrying people of a different race, but that they preferred certain groups over others. Those from other Scandinavian countries were most preferred, followed by other types of Europeans and Latin Americans, while Africans and Middle Easterners received the least positive response. Not surprisingly, these findings held true when respondents were asked to consider having children with someone of a different race.[35]

Another survey was carried out in Sweden in 2004. Among other statements, participants were asked if they agreed with the following: "I would not like having an immigrant from another part of the world married into my family."[36] While 15 percent of respondents agreed "completely or largely," this was still a decrease from the 25 percent who agreed in 1993. Another statement was: "Persons from a different culture and race should not build a family and have children," and in this respect, about 10 percent of the respondents agreed. However, only about 4 percent chose total agreement on the scale.[37]

People with interracial friendships are more likely to have a positive attitude toward interracial dating or marriage, and are correspondingly more likely to marry someone of a different race.[38]

The survey conducted in Malmö revealed that respondents who were friends with people of different races were three to eight times more likely to have positive attitudes toward intermarriage, depending on how close they were to these friends.[39] Another study showed that people who had been in previous interracial relationships were more likely to be married to someone of another race later on than those who had never experienced such relationships. This all seems to support the increased contact hypothesis: "the more contact you have with people of a different race, ethnicity [or] culture, the more tolerant you become to these groups."[40]

Yet, despite progressive trends in other areas of inequality, Sweden still has a strong tendency toward racial homogamy. Even their intermarriages are not very diverse, as they are mainly between Swedes and people of other Scandinavian or European descent. What does this tell us? It may suggest that part of the reason Scandinavian countries are more equal economically is because they do not have racial or religious differences, and that may account for their tendency to be more accepting of less privileged members of their own group—that is, those who are one of them.

The Race Myth

In the beginning of the chapter, we said that, according to sociologists, race is a social construct, just like ethnicity. And yet, we've just presented research that shows that racial differences still matter in people's lives. Sociologists would say that this is because certain groups are racialized. Sociologist Steve Martinot[41] describes this process as follows:

> [Racialization is] the way race is produced and bestowed on people by institutional social actions, and not as a condition found in people as their racial category. Racialization means that race is something people do rather than what they are.

Race is sociologically important because large numbers of people continue to think that race makes a difference in how we think and act. A constant concern with race in social interactions, the result of racializing social relations, may end up causing more racial conflict by focusing people's attention on racial differences. So we want to avoid over-racializing society. However, we also need to be aware of racial myths and their harmful effects.

Racial distinctions are not static: they have varied noticeably over space and time. For example, Irish immigrants to North America were once considered black whereas Arab immigrants were once considered white. The position of sociology today is that race is a social construct—an imagined community, just like ethnicity. However, it is a community that only outsiders have imagined. Ukrainian people have freely chosen to celebrate their Ukrainianness without any prodding from non-Ukrainians. Racialization is partly a result of European imperialism, a foreign imposition on Africans and Asians. Humanity might never have invented racial differences—the stereotypical colours of black, white, red, and yellow—or invested them with importance, without wars of imperial conquest and colonization.

Racial differences, like ethnic differences, are socially constructed. Out of these social constructions come social institutions—such as the Jim Crow racial segregation laws in post–Civil War America—in which these distinctions are codified and become ingrained in society. Even racial classifications, for the most harmless reasons can cause harm. In his 1992 book, *The Racialization of America*, Yehudi Webster argues against the racial classifications commonly used by governments and academics.[42] He calls for an end to the practice of describing Americans as either black or white, since this classification defies logic, ignores history, and creates a self-defeating system of race relations. In effect, through racial classification (and therefore, racialization), government and academics worsen race relations.

As well, it is extraordinarily difficult—actually many argue it is impossible—to exclude considerations of class and gender when discussing the social inequalities linked to race. We mentioned this in the introduction, when we talked about the process sociologists call intersectionality. For example, a working-class black woman faces the inequalities of class, gender, and race simultaneously. In the case of a particular woman it is impossible to say which factor is most influential. Further, racialization affects men and women differently.

For example, according to one study, African-American men are racialized more rigorously than African-American women, and rightly feel more threatened by this process, since the consequences can be severe.[43] African-American women, for their part, are often viewed as exotic or sexy because of racialization. Myths about the sexual energies and skills of African-American women make them more attractive to white men, while the same sexual energies and skills make African-American men appear dangerous.

As well, racialization reportedly affects people's sense of identity. For example, sociologist Anthony Chen studied Asian-American men in San Francisco, finding that racialization by others undermined his subjects' sense of masculinity.[44] Treatment as racial minorities distressed them and caused them to feel resentment. Some compensated by striving even harder to achieve career success, extreme fitness, and displays of wealth. In the long run, however, these efforts led to frustration, stress, and poor personal health.

In short, the notion of racialization underlines the socially constructed basis of race. The stance of sociology is clear on this point: categorizing people by race is not based on biologically important differences in the genetic make-up of differently identified races. But, if racial groups are merely imagined communities, why are racial designations (like white, black, Asian, Inuit, and so on) able to predict outcomes like school success or occupational achievement?

While forms of racial discrimination used to be obvious, and even blunt, today they tend to be more subtle and less likely to be detected by the general public. Many social psychologists believe that, despite the fact that people consciously support racial equality, deeply ingrained stereotypes remain about certain ethnicities concerning their work ethic, criminality, intelligence, and overall temperament that affect our evaluations and decision-making in many social situations. This is the case especially with hiring practices.

For example, in one well-known study, researchers Marianne Bertrand and Sendhil Mullainathan mailed five thousand fake resumés to thirteen hundred employers in response to want ads from two newspapers in Chicago and Boston.[45] The study's title was "Are Emily and Greg More Employable than Lakisha and Jamal?" and targeted positions for sales and administrative support as well as clerical and customer service positions. The resumés they sent had either black-sounding or white-sounding applicants' names. Even though names do not always show race, that association seemed strong enough for the white-sounding applicants to be favoured.

Bertrand and Mullainathan found that resumés with white names were 50 percent more likely to result in a job interview than resumés with black names. As expected, higher-quality resumés generated more call-backs than average, and even here, resumés with white names were 30 percent more likely to result in a job interview than the same resumes with a black name. White names also received more payoffs to additional qualifications, showing the racial gap among applicants was larger the more highly skilled the applicants were than among those with fewer qualifications, which is perhaps an even more depressing finding.

Similar types of experiments have been conducted globally, all with the same conclusion: race matters in hiring decisions. Bertrand and Mullainathan's study was replicated in Greece, with Albanian minorities facing a 43 percent reduction in opportunities for jobs than their Greek counterparts.[46] And it was replicated in Germany, where a correspondence survey was conducted with two student internship applications, one with a German-sounding name and the other with a Turkish one.[47]

Sociologist Devah Pager reviewed the results of various such studies conducted in the United States. After considering a range of findings from New York, Chicago, Boston, Milwaukee, and Washington between 1991 and 2005, she determined that the magnitude of discrimination can vary anywhere between 1.5 to 5 times more success for white job applicants than equally skilled black applicants (or for favoured versus unfavoured groups, whoever they may be).[48] Employment opportunities for black applicants can be anywhere from 50 to 500 percent less likely to be considered by employers as an equal candidate to white job seekers. However, variation across cities may account for some of the differences, with Washington DC showing the highest levels of discrimination (the *capital* of the United States!).

In Canada, a similar experiment was done in 2009 by Phil Oreopoulos. Four different types of resumés were sent to potential employees over two to three days, with their order randomized.[49] These resumés consisted of either:

1. Canadian name, education, and experience
2. Foreign name, Canadian education and experience
3. Foreign name and education, Canadian experience
4. Foreign name, education, and experience

The first finding was that Canadian-born applicants with English names were the most likely to receive callbacks compared to those who were foreign born, but this did not apply to people supposedly born in Great Britain. It was also determined that employers value experience in Canada. Education seems to play a minor role in explaining the gaps, since a degree from a highly esteemed foreign school did not help, and neither did a Canadian master's degree. The name-based discrimination was extremely significant, even for resumés that seemed to show no other foreign details, leading to substantial callback differences. There seemed to be extreme discrimination against Chinese, Indian, and Pakistani names in particular, but this discrimination was reduced if the resumés listed job experience in Canada.

Cross-comparison studies seeking the cause of racism show that racialization is strongly influenced by the unique history and institutions of each nation. Canada and the United States provide useful comparisons because they have equivalent standards and styles of living, but very different political and institutional histories. Sociologist Seymour Martin Lipset once suggested that Canadians and Americans are "probably as alike as any other two peoples on earth," and would be useful for comparison because "the more similar the units being compared, the more possible it should be to isolate the factors responsible for differences between them."[50] Both Canada and the United States are multi-racial, multi-ethnic societies, with complex social hierarchies, and yet they have quite different approaches when it comes to racial inequality.

In their book *Regions Apart*, James Curtis and Edward Grabb agree with Lipset's classic work that, while the original North American colonies were very similar some time ago, they changed during the American Revolution.[51] Over time, internal divisions in the two countries compounded these differences. Canada is unlike the American south, while the US is unlike Quebec, speaking from a cultural and political standpoint. Over the course of the past century, the two countries have become more similar, through the spread of American culture northward and the arrival of global immigrants in both countries. Yet differences remain.

Consider recent work on Canada's multiculturalism policy, which attempts to ensure that a variety of cultural heritages are valued. As a result, Canadian immigrants are more likely to acquire citizenship, participate politically, and be represented in elected bodies by fellow-ethnics than is the case for US immigrants.[52] On the other hand, while in both countries legislative efforts have been made to guarantee equity in hiring, affirmative action policies to promote opportunities for blacks in both employment and education have a far more extensive history in the US.

One US study contrasted two groups of native-born black Americans: one group who were descendants of recent black immigrants from the Caribbean, and another indigenous group whose ancestry suggested their families had lived in the US since the era of slavery.[53] They found that black descendants of immigrants earned more than longer-standing black Americans. But in Canada, a comparable study found that immigrants earned less than native-born people.[54] They also found that immigrants to Canada were less economically disadvantaged than immigrants to the US, and proposed that this difference was mainly due to the fact that Canadian immigrants on average had more education than native-born Canadians. That educational advantage was not the case for immigrants to the US. As Porter originally proposed, education is an institution that can provide access to valuable social resources, and can be a mechanism used to reduce social inequality.

Yet how can we explain the persistent disparity in test scores among black and white students, as well as other compared disadvantaged and advantaged groups? In the US, the famous and influential Coleman Report during the 1960s found that family background was a stronger predictor of educational achievement than were school characteristics, including school funding.[55] This rightly focused attention on the condition of American families. The Moynihan Report called attention to the deterioration of the structure of the black family.[56] Moynihan proposed that there was a crisis in the black family, with the prevalence of female-headed households. His research shows that children from poor, single-parent black families had a higher-than-average probability of dropping out of school and of engaging in deviant behaviour. Moynihan's critique of the black family made the public aware of the pressing need for better economic opportunities for black people, such as better jobs.

Many explanations have been offered for the educational and earnings gap between immigrant black people and native-born black people in the US. Some older studies pointed to cultural differences between West Indian and US black people dating back to differences in the slave systems.[57] Others pointed to the structural position of black immigrants, who, as a minority within a minority, have often filled roles as service providers and political brokers for a larger and less well-educated native-born black community.[58] Still others have pointed to the psychological advantages that come from growing up in predominantly black societies abroad, as opposed to growing up part of a stigmatized minority group in America.[59] And yet what these studies ignore is the role of economic differences between people, with race or ethnicity often being a cover for more fundamental economic disparities.[60]

Canada is typically thought of as a country that is inclusive of all races, but even here, research has shown evidence of democratic racism.[61] That is, Canada maintains the illusion of equality while at the same time marginalizing particular racialized minorities. Instead of practicing overt or institutionalized racism, racism in Canada is typically practiced so subtly that either the targets are not aware of it or only the targets are aware of it.

Yet unlike in the US, in Canada, blame is placed especially on Aboriginal peoples.[62] Blaming victims for their troubles helps Canadians ignore issues that conflict with their belief that Canada is fundamentally a country that treats everyone equally. Such issues include the government's failure to provide a public school in Attawapiskat, an Aboriginal community in Northern Ontario.[63] It may be impractical and costly to provide what is needed, but Canadians recognize that practicality cannot trump equality under all circumstances.

Thus, in some situations, Canadians victimize people based on their race. But what about Scandinavian countries? Does their better stance on equality, partly a product of political history, show less discriminatory hiring practices? Unfortunately, despite doing better on many other instances of inequality, research seems to suggest that institutional discrimination is just as prevalent in Scandinavia as in many other societies. One famous study by Magnus Carlsson and Dan-Olof Rooth used a two-stage field experiment, the first part measuring the typical call-back differences for interviews with Arab or Muslim names in comparison to applicants with Swedish-sounding names.[64] This ethnic group was used in this experiment since previous studies seem to show that Arabs and Muslims suffer the worst discrimination among all immigrants in Sweden.[65] The researchers sent out two identical job applications to 1,552 employers with either a Swedish or Arabic/Muslin name, and determined that those with a Swedish name received 50 percent more callbacks.

In the second stage of the experiment, the researchers measured the implicit and explicit attitudes of the recruiters regarding performance stereotypes using the Implicit Associations Test (IAT), as well as explicit questions. Out of the 193 recruiters who participated, the results showed a significant negative correlation between the implicit performance stereotypes and the callback rate for applicants with foreign names, but not Swedish names. This shows that implicit discrimination may be just as important as explicit discrimination in explaining unequal hiring practices.[66] In other words, some employers may not even know they are being discriminatory, and yet their actions discriminate against this group in the population.

In addition, half of the employers stated explicitly that they would prefer to hire, or had more positive reactions to, a majority Swedish employee over an Arabic/Muslim employee; however, the majority stated there was no difference in productivity between the two groups. This hints that there is a strong negative attitude toward Arabic immigrants, but that it is not necessarily the result of a shared explicit productivity stereotype. The evidence suggests that sometimes the attitudes and the stereotypes people foster exist in an unconscious mode. This, on top of existing explicit attitudes, explains the racism present in the hiring processes of the labour market.

So, undoubtedly, discrimination on the basis of race and ethnicity does occur in Sweden and other parts of Scandinavia. But in terms of observable dimensions of inequality economically and socially speaking, ethnic and racial minorities are at an advantage in countries like Sweden and Norway, with more generous social safety nets. The policies of income equality in Scandinavian countries allow non-working families to maintain a standard of living close to that of working families. And they also benefit many immigrants of visible minority status, allowing them to enjoy a good standard of living.

Especially compared to other European countries, there is relative economic equality among different racial and ethnic groups, though the minorities often experience real and painful discrimination. The point is that discrimination is not as extensive when we examine data on economic and social well-being. For example, the United Kingdom restricts immigrants from receiving non-contributory benefits such as social assistance, while Sweden does not.[67] This highlights the point that inequality is a complex topic with many dimensions and considerations, so we need to think about all the ways in which inequality may be expressed differently around the world.

An Unanswered Question

The research we have presented in this chapter mostly proposes that racial and ethnic inequality is an issue in Scandinavian countries as well as other developed countries. In terms of discrimination, it appears that visible minorities are often targets of prejudices, even in the more equal Scandinavian nations. But in terms of economic conditions, there is greater parity. This proposes, in effect, that not all types of inequality are perfectly correlated: despite a high degree of income and gender equality, you can still have a moderate degree of racial or ethnic inequality.

Comparisons are difficult, however, given that in most cases the proportions of visible minority groups in those countries are nowhere near those in more diverse countries such as Canada. In fact, some have even suggested that countries like Sweden or Denmark have been able to achieve their better levels of income equality because of their more ethnically and especially racially homogenous populations. By this token, they do not experience a lot of group divisiveness precisely because of their more integrated population.

Does this mean that more ethnic and racial homogeneity is a necessary trade-off if Canada wants to become a more economically equal society? This question remains unanswered. Perhaps time will tell, given that an increasing number of immigrants are interested in coming to the prosperous northern European countries. Perhaps if Scandinavian countries begin to accept more immigrants than in the past, they will face increasing challenges to maintain the current level of income equality.

One thing is certain: in terms of their societal values, Scandinavian countries like Sweden put more emphasis on solidarity and equality, rather than diversity. Meanwhile Canada holds fast to multiculturalism, one of only a few tenets of Canadian identity. Given this commitment to multiculturalism and high immigration rates, the question of whether economic equality is a trade-off for racial equality is an important one. And it is also one that will have to take into account considerations of how other types of inequalities are also relevant to the discussion.

As we saw in this chapter, some ethnic and racial groupings are stronger in 2012 than they were in 1912, while other groupings, like classes, have largely been defeated and are left without resources. This says something about the power of social construction, and more broadly, about the power of human imagination. In the next chapter, we will discuss age groups and draw parallels to this theme as we look at this other type of social inequality which is discussed less readily than others.

CHAPTER 4

Exclusion

———————— ◆ ————————

"Age is whatever you think it is. You are as old as you think you are."
Muhammad Ali, worldchampion heavyweight boxer

A New Life Stage

Time is a strange thing: sometimes a minute seems to last an hour, and other times an hour seems to go by in a minute. Many factors influence our experience of time. It drags when we are locked in a state of inactivity we did not choose, when we cannot even foresee the next time we will be able to make our own decisions. This is the experience of people who are bedridden with a debilitating chronic illness, according to Kathy Charmaz, the author of *Good Days, Bad Days*.[1] Physical disability (and extreme aging) undermines our ability to make plans and carry them out, which undermines our sense of a personal future; this, in turn, undermines our sense of self as a unique, independent entity.

Ultimately then, our planning abilities contribute a lot to the social roles we play and, as a result, to who we are. Because aging has a huge effect on our ability to make and execute plans independently, it also has a huge effect on our ability to play chosen social roles and, therefore, to be who we want to be. This is true for old and infirm people, but it is equally true for infants, toddlers, children, adolescents, young adults, and twenty-somethings.

Perhaps because of this intense impact on our sense of self, research on age and aging is often surprisingly popular, even with non-academic audiences. In 2000, for example, an academic study on this topic went viral. Scientific studies and the discussions about them are hardly ever as popular. This article became as well-known and widely referenced as an online home video of a piano-playing dog. No doubt about it: psychologist Jeffrey Jensen Arnett's "Emerging Adulthood: A Theory of Development from the Late Teens through the Twenties" struck a chord.[2] In addition to the hype generated around this article, Arnett went on to publish an extremely successful book on the same topic, called *Emerging Adulthood: The Winding Road from the Late Teens through the Twenties*.[3] To add to his widespread popularity, Arnett's book was featured in the *New York Times* in 2010.[4] Perhaps unsurprisingly, due to all of this publicity, Arnett's work on age stimulated widespread discussion. Keeping with the trend, many other studies have also attempted to conceptualize new age groupings, addressing the cluttered nest syndrome and the sandwich generation.

All of these age-related formulations help us make sense of our current realities, whatever they may be. On the one hand, they hit home with the twenty-somethings of the early twenty-first century—especially with those who live in their parents' basement while having a PhD award on the wall. On the other, they also resonate with the parents of these young adults who cannot make sense of their children's lives. In their eyes, though they might not say the words, their children seem on the verge of failure: they hover uncertainly between the identity confusion of adolescence and the mature responsibility of adulthood. Arnett, for one, seemed to capture this in-between status effectively, even coming up with a catchy concept to describe it.

His analysis probably seems so accurate because he had the opportunity to observe and interact with his subjects in their natural environment. Like many academics, Arnett spent his adult life surrounded by young adults, so he knows what he's talking about. As a professor at Clark University (in Worcester, Massachusetts) in the 1990s, he noticed a disconnect between what classical theories said about aging and what he saw in his students. Even though he was in his early thirties himself, making his students only a few years younger, he remembers thinking, "They're not a thing like me."[5]

Arnett then began to wonder why, and found that past theories about human development did not give him satisfactory answers.

At the time, the reigning idea was Erik Erikson's fifty-year-old eight-stage theory, which divides adulthood into three stages— young (20 to 45), middle (45 to 65), and late (65 and up).[6] Maybe those distinctions had worked fifty years earlier, but for Arnett, the young period seemed too broad: it contained too many different life experiences, from still living with your parents at twenty, to owning a home and having a family by forty-five. These different experiences, according to Arnett, meant the younger of young adults were going through a complex developmental sequence of their own. At twenty or even thirty, they were grown-ups, but not quite. By forty-five, however, they were middle-aged, and therefore not the same people they had been two decades earlier. Arnett called these twenty-somethings *emerging adults.*

The sociological take on development was always different than the psychological one, focusing as it did on important social transitions, rather than personality transitions (as Erikson's theory highlighted). In classic sociological theory, the transition to adulthood is characterized by five milestones: completing formal education, moving out of the parental home, becoming financially independent, getting married, and having a child. The sociological approach is useful because it sets clear, concrete criteria to be fulfilled at each stage, making comparisons with the past quite easy. For example, the *New York Times* article that featured Arnett noted another Canadian study that had found: "a typical 30-year-old in 2001 had completed the same number of milestones as a 25-year-old in the early '70s."[7] Judging by these kinds of statements, more and more people have been taking varied and non-traditional routes to adulthood, including delaying marriage until their thirties, childbearing even later, returning to school after a period of full-time paid work, and so on.

And yet, there was something special about the twenties that made them different from the thirties and early forties. To clarify this difference, Arnett began interviewing twenty-somethings to find out how they differentiated themselves from thirty-somethings.

He heard a few things over and over again: for one, his participants kept saying they were taking their time, finding themselves, and enjoying life. But at the same time, the big 3-0 weighed heavily on most of their shoulders. They saw it as a threshold full of symbolic significance. In their minds, real life seemed to start at thirty. After that, a final acceptance of adult responsibilities—having a stable career, getting married, and having children—was inescapable. In this developmental sense, thirty was the new twenty. Arnett found that women were especially likely to hold this view, since they were even more concerned than men about the biological clock and their declining fertility.

The emerging adulthood that twenty-somethings experience is therefore a period of instability, exploration, and self-analysis. During this time, according to Arnett, young adults try out different kinds of relationships before settling down and commiting themselves to one stable relationship.[8] This exploration may, at times, be overwhelming and stressful. However, it is also characterized by a sense of possibility and a desire to try out many things that these young adults realize they will not (otherwise) be able to do until their own children are grown up. By then, they may not have the energy or enthusiasm to try these new things any more. Emerging adults thus tend to embrace change and new opportunities, while rejecting commitment, so they can be sure that the path they take through life will be a satisfying one.

Unsurprisingly, however, many parents are ambivalent about such open-ended, flexible alternatives and opportunities, as many see this approach as getting something without giving anything back. Emerging adults get to explore and find themselves while being financially supported fully, or at least partially, by their parents, who themselves may not be able to afford it. Cue the misunderstanding, negative feelings, stereotypes, disagreements, and ultimately intergenerational conflict between these parents and their children.

In the end, Arnett thinks that taking this time to be self-focused is a wise decision. People used to look forward to adulthood because it was associated with independence in decision-making, financial gain, and a socially accepted love life. But many people weren't ready for all of this in their twenties. Today however, emerging adults have access to all of these benefits before they become independent adults in the traditional sense. And as a result, they are able to try out some of their options before making a commitment, ensuring that the choices they make will be satisfying. They are looking for self-fulfillment, sure enough, but eventually that may mean a more self-fulfilled and content population, instead of one that feels stuck with the choices that were actually thrust on them.

In support of the unstable, exploratory experiences of emerging adulthood, Arnett writes:

> Parents as well as emerging adults themselves find it really reassuring to hear that this is what's normal now, is to be very unsettled for most of your twenties. And it's reassuring to know too that for everybody, by about the age of thirty, emerging adulthood is over, they're ready to move on to the commitments of adult life. They don't remain emerging adults forever.[9]

What We Can Learn from Car Rental Companies

Arnett is a psychologist, so he talks about emerging adulthood in psychological terms, calling it a developmental stage. Consistent with his scientific approach, neurological research has shown that the brain keeps developing until about age twenty-five. This prolonged development is especially true for the pre-frontal cortex, the part of the brain responsible for rational planning. That's why car rental companies charge enormous rates for those under the age of twenty-six, because, according to the stats, these young people are most likely to get into accidents.[10]

Arnett realizes that people had the same brains fifty years ago as they do today, so he doubts that today's new adults are incapable of taking on responsibility. Instead, they are facing a new period of uncertainty and exploration that suits what is going on in the brain at this point in time.

In this sense, Arnett's argument is quite sociological if we look beneath the surface. He says, for example, that emerging adulthood is a universal phase, and he describes it in terms of perceptions, thoughts, and world views. Arnett realizes that it is the social context that creates this developmental phase for young adults. Mainly, this context is found in developed countries, where current social, cultural, and economic conditions allow for this newly emerging period of life. These conditions are rooted in trends that started decades ago, including the need for more education, the globalization of manufacturing jobs, the replacement of those jobs with positions that deal with information technology, and the destigmatization of premarital sex and cohabitation. All of these factors mean that today's twenty-somethings are delaying the developmental steps traditionally associated with adulthood.

For young people and their parents, emerging adulthood represents another period in the continually lengthening life course—an extension and refinement of an age category that used to be called young adulthood. In many ways, a similar lengthening has occurred on the other end of the life span, with the emergence of centenarians (people over one hundred years old), and even supercentenarians (people over 110 years of age). These changes in life phases occurred for sociological reasons, even though psychological explanations might help us understand why these stages are more fitting than those we had before.

Though we have been focusing on Arnett's analysis, he is not the first researcher to have explored youth development, or to have found signs of ambivalence, confusion, and even alienation among young people. Another famous example of this kind of work was done by psychologist Kenneth Keniston, who, in 1965, published a book on adolescence and young adulthood.[11] As you may have noticed from the date, his work came out when today's baby boomers (the parents of today's twenty-somethings), were twenty-somethings themselves.

Keniston based his study on interviews with male undergraduates at Harvard University, who were studying in the 1960s. As each of his participants was alienated, that is, uncommitted, Keniston described these young people as ambivalent, unsure, and even aimless, unable to settle down into life. Like many others writing at that time, he saw some evidence of young people's alienation from consumer capitalism and the military-industrial complex; mainly, however, he related this to childhood experiences.

Despite some of the assumptions and stereotypes embedded in Keniston's assessment (like gender inequality), this excerpt reminds us of a famous 1960s movie about one uncommitted youth: *The Graduate*, played by Dustin Hoffman.[12] Perhaps every generation develops its own theories about discontented or uncommitted young people as a way of criticizing contemporary society. What we can say for certain, however, is that the period of youthful dependency is growing all the time, and this is bound to extend the length and depth of youthful anxiety.

In this chapter, we will see that age categories are socially constructed, just as are those surrounding gender, race, and ethnicity. Therefore, inequalities based on age are also socially constructed. These age inequalities often translate into exclusion from full membership in society. For example, the economic system encourages such age inequalities by requiring younger people to complete a lengthy education before they are considered economically viable. The same system also offers few opportunities for older people to continue to work if they want to; but, simultaneously, it has made retirement difficult to sustain, given the present economy.

We began this chapter with a discussion on the lower portion of the age continuum. But we will spend most of this chapter talking about the upper portion of this age continuum, since sociologists are conducting most of their age-related research on this group today. This focus is partially due to the fact that older Canadians already make up a substantial and costly proportion of our population. Aging is also academically interesting because it takes every one, both male and female, by surprise. Old age is never what they expected, and it brings fewer benefits than it brings disadvantages. Women are especially likely to feel the high price of aging since they benefit more from their good looks in youth than men usually do. As Agatha Christie remarks, only archaeologists, such as her husband, are likely to value their wives more as they get older.

On the other hand, however, childhood is no picnic either. While it's often imagined to be an idyllic period of innocence and ease, childhood has come to be ever more weighted down by parental expectations and demands.

The Invention of Childhood

From a sociological point of view, we can easily think of age groups (like childhood) as social constructions. The boundaries defining each age group are imprecise and flexible, and are often renegotiated in response to scientific or medical discoveries. Even more importantly, these groupings reflect the demands of important social institutions, like schools and workplaces. In fact, schools have defined childhood, just as workplaces have defined retirement age. And as the requirements for schooling and work change, our notions about the ages of childhood and retirement change accordingly. For example, as more schooling is required to prepare young people for paid work, they spend more years being economically dependent (on parents, loans, or a spouse). In turn, as economic dependents, young people are infantilized—freed of adult responsibilities, adult norms, and adult respect. In effect, this means extending the period of childhood beyond its original pre-adolescent meaning.

Age, then, is a social marker: a way of designating the number of years since a person was born. But age is also a kind of performance: we all perform our age, just as we perform our gender. Sociologists refer to this as "doing age" in the way that researchers West and Zimmerman argue that people "do gender" on a continual basis.[13] When people perform an age that is very different from their apparent chronological age, they are criticized or ridiculed. Some examples would include older people dressing too young, or being too interested in sex. But without the performance of age, chronological age has no intrinsic social meaning: people can't tell whether the person in question wants to be taken for thirty-five, fifty, or sixty-five.

If age groups are nothing but social constructions—nothing but imagined communities of people with economic dependence (or independence) in common—it's easy to see how age-related myths and stereotypes arise. For example, people often construct myths around infantilized young people, myths of innocence, or of irresponsibility. In line with this mentality, what have people been thinking about childhood and children over the last few centuries? That is, how have adults imagined childhood, and thus, molded their children?

This is the question that motivated the work of French historian Philippe Aries, author of a classic book on childhood, *L'Enfant et la vie familiale sous l'Ancien Régime*, translated as *Centuries of Childhood*.[14] Though some have criticized the book as Eurocentric, it is interesting and provocative nonetheless. In this work, Aries proposes that the notion of childhood was invented at a particular time in European history, for particular reasons. Before that time, children—people of say, ten years old or younger—were thought of differently than they are today. Accordingly, ideas about childhood changed as ideas of children changed. This means that what we think of today when we say childhood is something new in human history. Notions of exploration, play, discovery, dependence, and imagination have not always been linked to this life stage. Therefore, conceptions of childhood as a protected, idealized, and even revered time of life were invented at a particular time and place.

As we mentioned earlier, institutions like schools play a large role in shaping our ideas about age, and these ideas change as these institutions evolve. Aries confirms this theory, noting that before the sixteenth century few European children went to formal schools like the ones we have today. Some were educated in the military, where they learned to mature early, taking on adult roles as fighters. For those who did receive a formal education, the schools they went to were not like our own: for example, students were taught all together, rather than being divided into different classes according to age. In this respect, age was unimportant before industrial times, so the notion of childhood did not exist for most young people. Aries thus concludes that it was only with the invention of formal schooling and age-based segregation of students that adults started to view children as significantly different from themselves.

As education became more common, schoolchildren—and especially those who were privileged—became objects of conspicuous consumption, to be treasured, protected, and enriched. With the rise of compulsory public education in the nineteenth century, all families were forced to give up their children to education for at least some part of their youth, since learning was seen as children's developmental duty. Even children whose families wanted them to work became subject to newly legislated child protection laws, and could no longer do so until they reached a certain age.

As this example suggests, the industrialization of work had a deep, unexpected effect on schooling. As a result, the industrialization of schooling changed people's conception of childhood. Universal mandatory education shaped the idea of universal childhood because it created a distinct life stage that segregated children from adults. No longer were young people to be viewed as proto-adults with adult-like tasks to perform in the home and workplace. Now, people came to view them as different kinds of beings altogether, with pre-adult developmental needs to satisfy before they could enter adult life.

Increasingly, according to Aries, children were segregated from adult society by ever-lengthening periods of formal education. As we know, this process continues today, with people staying in school for as long as fifteen to twenty-five years. And when they do end this prolonged economic childhood, many are already parents themselves. The point here is so simple it is easy to miss: it was the economic need to educate and isolate children that led to new, imagined images of childhood, not the reverse. That is, it was not the discovery of childhood—nor the discovery of childhood's unique requirements—that brought about prolonged schooling, but instead, the social and economic circumstances of the times during which childhood as a distinct period of life emerged.

Thus, Aries's argument meshes well with Arnett's, which we discussed at the beginning of this chapter. Arnett's notion of emerging adulthood merely reflects a continued extension of cultural childhood into the period traditionally considered adulthood. Yet this new phase of emerging adulthood is not full adulthood in the traditional sense: it has its own unique, socially constructed characteristics. These include social marginality, behavioural irresponsibility, and economic dependence—three conditions that are necessarily correlated. And although these factors are newly important, they are not new in themselves. In some European countries, for example, marriage used to be a requirement for adulthood, and since it was economically out of reach for some poorer citizens until later in life (if ever), some people could be considered children even into their later thirties.

Unsurprisingly, the same process that Aries describes in the invention of childhood also invented adolescence around the beginning of the twentieth century, decades earlier. In 1904, a psychologist named G. Stanley Hall published a study called *Adolescence,* which considered how changes in the social, cultural, and economic contexts had created a new period of life between childhood and adulthood.[15] He noted that with the expansion of education and child labour laws, children became more financially dependent on their parents for longer periods of time. This preface to adulthood gave them time and opportunity to attend to developmental tasks that would have been otherwise ignored, including finding themselves, identifying their life goals, and gaining psychological independence from their parents.

Of course, the chronological period of adolescence—roughly the ages twelve to eighteen—is also a time of important, visible changes that typically distinguish older children from younger ones. These include hormonal changes that bring on menstruation for girls, increased sexual attraction for both sexes, and the emergence of secondary sexual characteristics, such as breasts on girls, and deeper voices and facial hair on boys. But what of the belief that adolescence also means a greater emotional volatility than that of younger children? Was this a real result of hormonal change, a real result of extended economic dependency, or merely imagined—another socially constructed idea about age?

Some have questioned this strictly social constructionist analysis of aging, with its focus on the social invention or creation of childhood and adolescence. After all, even before the seventeenth century, some people believed that children made up a separate age group. This belief was largely based on the fact that infants and young children are more fragile than older children, and therefore have higher mortality risks; consequently, they have likely always had special needs for food, shelter, affection, and protection. So, this argument holds that children's physical vulnerability has always made them distinct from older, self-sufficient adults. Of course, all of this is true, just as it is true that men and women have different chemistries and therefore, different needs. But for sociologists, the issue is not that these age differences exist, but rather, how they are magnified, dramatized and performed—and we have no doubt that industrialization caused changes in each of these respects.

While this perspective is closely linked to Aries's work, his theory has been criticized for being based on unrepresentative data and relying too heavily on the writings of moralists and educationalists. However, his analysis of the ways in which age groups become more distinct over time, in response to emerging social concerns, is crucial to understanding age group relations today. We cannot understand Arnett's discovery of prolonged childhood among twenty-somethings unless we understand Aries's path-breaking theory of the development of childhood in human history.

With such an understanding, then, we can make some sociological predictions about how age groups will develop in the future. For example, as we live increasingly longer and the population becomes increasingly older, there will be even more social differentiations between age groups. History suggests that we will have to keep inventing age groups as people lead ever longer lives, under conditions of ever longer, or recurring, dependency.

Langer's Time Machine

In 2009, a woman named Olga Kotelko received Sport BC's "Master Athlete of the Year" honour.[16] Kotelko was ninety years old at the time. The holder of numerous world records in track and field, Kotelko did not become an athlete at a young age. For most of her ninety years, she led the life of her generation and circumstance; she did not get involved with sports until much later.

Born into a large Ukrainian immigrant family with eleven children, Kotelko grew up on a farm, tending the farm animals.[17] At the school she attended, sport meant playing with an old and broken softball. She led a humble but checkered life, eventually becoming a teacher in a one-room schoolhouse. She married a man from whom she later had to run away, taking her two daughters with her. Shortly after that, she decided to complete a bachelor's degree at night school, despite the pressures of being a single mother. With all of these immediate demands, sport and exercise were never on the horizon.

Then, in 1984 at the age of sixty-five, Kotelko joined a softball team and found that she loved it—especially the competitiveness.[18] At seventy-seven, one of her teammates suggested she might like to try track and field.[19] Kotelko, always keen to learn, sought the help of a local coach and trainer who was obviously far younger than her. She brought to this task the energy of a fifty-year-old.[20] As her eventual world records show, Kotelko turned out to be exceptional in track and field.

How was she able to do this? Biology played some role, as her genes appear to have influenced her incredible longevity and resistance to degeneration. Beyond that though, Kotelko refuses to be excluded or lead the rest of her life in roles that society has ascribed to her. She is far from infirm, and continues to think about the future, not the past. Kotelko is likely the exception, but she represents the reality that older people today are unlikely to renounce life and wait for death by the sidelines.

And yet, that is exactly the kind of picture of older people drawn by an early, influential sociological theory of aging, Disengagement Theory, as put forth by Elaine Cumming and William Henry in 1961. They proposed that the exclusion of older adults from the labour market is functional for society as a whole.[21] They note that as people age, they decline both physically and mentally: muscles weaken, bones become fragile, perceptual abilities decline, and cognitive faculties dwindle. Elderly people are also more prone to illness and disability. Perhaps due to these declining abilities, elderly people are often less efficient at work than their younger, stronger, and more energetic counterparts. For the good of society and for themselves, then, elderly people must give up their positions and withdraw to the borders of society, where they can prepare for their certain death. According to Cumming and Henry, they must—and do—disengage from the normal activities of adulthood that they have spent forty or fifty years practicing.

This theory suggests that older people's retirement from paid work serves several functions for society as a whole. First, it empties important social positions, allowing people from the next generation to move up the social hierarchy. Second, it allows retiring individuals a moment of recognition—like a retirement party—for their contribution. Third, retirement ensures that society regularly replaces outdated skills and ideas with more useful ones. Though the theory may sound cold and cynical, it reminds us that change is both natural and crucial to society's effectiveness. Without such personnel turnover, the economy might be less efficient and less equipped to compete globally.

However, many people disagree with this theory, especially with the assumption that excluding older people from financially rewarding and socially important roles is good for society. Some sociologists, for example, argue that forced retirement or so-called disengagement is merely age-based discrimination. This kind of ageism does not serve society as a whole, but rather is merely a form of inequality exercised by the younger majority to further their own interests. If society needed to displace people who were no longer useful, we would test and evaluate people's usefulness directly; we wouldn't assume it was predicted by age.

As well, not all old people have gone along with this disengagement agenda. Some continue to learn new skills and compete for a place in society, Kotelko among them. Contrary to what disengagement theory predicts, many elderly people remain active and fight obsolescence. As for those older people who do seem to fit with disengagement theory, they have rarely withdrawn from society of their own will. Instead, employers and retirement rules push them out of the workforce. Without these pushes, many elderly people would remain active for as long as possible because the health benefits of being active have made us value such a lifestyle. We can see this in the majority of retired people who stay active as long as opportunities in the family and the wider community allow. When elderly people do finally disengage, it is often because of other people's wishes and perceptions, not their own.

Even the common decline in physical and mental abilities over the aging process—senescence—is partly rooted in social causes. Although these changes are biological, our society also tends to view old people as frail, weak, and dependent, regardless of their actual condition. So are these characteristics inevitable for everyone? How might we act and treat others if we made different assumptions about aging? This was the line of reasoning followed by social psychologist Ellen Langer at Harvard University in 1979.[22] She recruited male volunteers over the age of seventy-five and put them through a special test they would never forget.[23]

Langer's idea was to turn back the clock to 1959, twenty years earlier, when all of her participants had been in their fifties. She arranged for her subjects to watch old television shows and eat meals like the ones they ate in those days. Additionally, they were to become responsible again, and do everything for themselves, without the care and support of others they had come to need and expect. They would experience all of this for one week, as Langer explains in her description of this experiment:

> We created this environment they were going to be totally immersed in. It was a timeless retreat that we had transformed. So for a full week they would be living there as though it was that earlier time. They were talking about things from the past, watching movies from the past, seeing props from the past. And all of their discussions were going to be in the present tense.[24]

Langer was determined to have her participants act independently during this week. They didn't even get help carrying their heavy suitcases when they got to the house the researchers had set up. Though some had to carry every single item from their suitcase up to their room one at a time, Langer remained determined not to intervene. Unsurprisingly, her subjects initially protested against these rules and conditions. But by the second day, everybody had begun helping in the kitchen as they grew accustomed to their new situation.

As thoughts about their own capabilities began to change, Langer's participants lost many of their inhibitions and started to express themselves autonomously and individually. As she reports,

> When the men were in discussion groups they would decide for themselves whether or not they were going to speak, without any anybody signalling subtly, as the culture often does, that they're incompetent. When old people start to act in ways that young people think is uninhibited and think they've regressed, they've progressed. And they're disinhibited. They say, "Why am I paying attention to some of these rules that just don't make sense?"[25]

Remarkable things began to happen as the week went on—not just cognitive changes, but physical ones as well. Langer found improvements in the men's dexterity, walk, posture, IQ, vision, hearing, cognitive abilities, joint flexibility, blood pressure, and arthritis—all in a just one week, and simply by asking them to go back in time. By forcing her participants to assume that they could and should do things for themselves, Langer changed their outlook, and then their actual health.

Langer's research showed that our abilities decline with aging not only because of biological changes, but also because these changes are socially expected. The way other people treat us as we age—whether they are relatives, friends, or strangers— makes a huge difference to our actual competence and abilities. Negative expectations and beliefs are exclusionary, and they are also disabling—they make people less competent than they could otherwise be. Equally, exclusion promotes ageism and the mistreatment of older adults, since we start to devalue people once we put them out to pasture. In the end then, exclusion is a form of dehumanization.

With experiments like Langer's, we are realizing more than ever that old age is a social invention, just like childhood or adolescence (or middle age, for that matter). And, if we study history, we can see that old age was only recently invented. People did not used to think about old age since most died young, leaving only a select few to cope with life beyond the age of sixty. In an average preindustrial town or village, populated by several hundred people, only a few would have been old people. The handful of these who were in good health may have continued to participate fully in social life. However, those who were infirm quietly watched the younger people from the sidelines until they died.

This pattern changed in part with the German invention of paid retirement in the 1880s. At this time, the Iron Chancellor, Otto von Bismarck, defined people as being of old age if they were over sixty-five. As a result of this legislative step, a new difference between middle-aged and elderly people became widely recognized. The new concept of paid retirement, although designed to aid aging people, also signalled the invention of old age, which only truly came into effect with industrialization. Paradoxically then, the invention of retirement led to the idea of old age, not the other way around. In this sense, old age was created by the spread of paid retirement, just like childhood and adolescence were created by the spread of education.

For more than a century after Bismarck made this defining move, most aged people in the West were viewed as unproductive, and, as such, they were expected to retire from work with a pension. Today, however, many people continue working past the traditional age of retirement, earning an income and feeling socially useful. Self-employed professionals like doctors and lawyers, for example, usually retire later than sixty-five: they are often deeply engaged in their work and feel free to continue with it as long as they wish.

In fact, elderly people are no more willing to take a backseat, and watch social life from the sidelines, than are poor people, women, or racial and ethnic minorities. This has been made evident through the abolishment of mandatory retirement in Canada, which allows people to stay employed regardless of their age. As of December 16, 2012, the Canadian Human Rights Act and the Canada Labour Code were amended to prohibit federally regulated employers from setting a mandatory retirement age, unless there is a genuine occupational requirement to do so. No one knows yet how long people will continue working now that they are no longer obliged to retire. Likely, those who enjoy their work will continue working, at least for a while. Likewise, people who need the extra money will probably remain employed. And, given the widespread increase in poverty following the 2008 economic recession, many will likely continue working well beyond Bismarck's mandated (and arbitrary) age of sixty-five.

So, to return to the idea with which we opened this section, disengagement theory is at best a partial truth, as it fails to account for the experiences of many elderly people in our society today. At worst, it is a fanciful misrepresentation of age-based interests as a social good. In other words, disengagement theory suggests that what is good for young people is good for society as a whole, which, as studies like Langer's have proved, is simply untrue.

A Shared Fate

Perhaps the most significant twenty-first century phenomenon related to the human population is that the average age is rising all over the world. Estimates have been made that roughly one in four Canadians will be sixty-five years of age or older by 2051.[26] It is paradoxical, then, that as old people have become more and more numerous in our society, they have lost the power to control and exclude younger people, as they have been able to do in the past. In present-day societies, old people are more numerous but simultaneously less powerful and more excluded than they were in some (but not all) premodern societies. As we have just discussed, they are forced or urged to retire from paid work, as though doing so is good for them and necessary for the benefit of society. Like all types of inequality, this forced exclusion is justified by differentiation and justification.

Of course, older people were not always excluded in these ways. In some parts of the world, and throughout human history, elderly individuals held positions of authority and power in communities made up of mostly younger members. In these gerontocracies, old people ruled the roost: they dominated the young and were at the centre of community life, not at its sidelines. Even today, many Aboriginal communities remain gerontocracies, where the wisdom and advice of elders is held in high regard.

There are still many societies around the world where older people are treated with this kind of respect. Consider the Chinese ethic of filial piety, based on Confucian teaching. This belief holds that in return for their upbringing, children must support, honour, and care for their aging parents. Such duties are even owed to deceased parents, grandparents, and other relatives, with respect for preceding generations being required of all living people. Within this framework, both the cultural and legal system is biased in favour of parents over children. However, this system has started to break down with the industrialization and urbanization of East Asia. Children increasingly avoid their duties of filial piety, or look for easier ways to fulfill them. The Confucian ethic made sense in an agricultural society with little geographic or social mobility, but it does not work in a society like our own.

These kinds of beliefs highlight the different expectations that people of different age groups have of one another, and they can also help us see how differently younger and older people are expected to behave. One result of this kind of social differentiation of age groups is that social distance forms between them, just like the social distance we saw between various ethnic or racial groups. Each age group occupies its own social and cultural sphere, so no group has a clear sense of what the other groups are about, and sometimes they feel contempt or fear toward each other. Occasionally, people of different ages ally themselves against a common generational enemy, based on mutual opposition. However, such alliances are the exception. Largely, people of different ages, like people of different genders, live in different worlds.

Because of this social distance, people harbour prejudices that can lead to discrimination. Whether people are considered young, middle-aged, or old, the stereotypes attached to each age group are often applied to its members. The young, for example, are typically seen as disobedient, unmotivated, and lazy, whereas the elderly are considered infantile and unable to care for themselves. Both sets of stereotypes are usually untrue, with many young people working hard to establish a satisfying future for themselves, and elderly people staying active and fully functioning well into their eighties and nineties, and even beyond. Despite evidence to the contrary, these stereotypes continue to be invoked, often resulting in different forms of exclusion.

Sociologists typically use the term exclusion in discussions of social problems like unemployment, low income, poor housing, deficient health, or social isolation. However, the term is also applicable to age grading and its effects. In fact, sociologists have developed three distinct ideas of exclusion that are useful here. The first defines social exclusion as a barrier to exercising social rights. When used in this way, exclusion is related to notions of citizenship: it suggests that people are being deprived of their rights to participate fully in society.

A second approach defines social exclusion as a state of social (and therefore normative) isolation from the wider society. This idea of exclusion is related to notions of anomie and social integration. It helps us understand why, for example, young people riot and do other antisocial and otherwise inexplicable things. It also helps to explain why younger and older people are more likely than middle-aged people to commit suicide.

Finally, a third approach that is particularly applicable to multicultural societies defines social exclusion as extreme marginalization. By marginalization, we mean denying a group or individual access to important positions and symbols of economic, religious, or political power. A marginal group may constitute a numerical majority, as in the case of black people in South Africa during Apartheid. Regardless of size, this marginal group often has little or no access to political and economic power. As a result, we sometimes call these marginalized groups minority groups, even if they are in the numerical majority. Examining these marginalized groups can help us understand how a society defines itself, and what it bases its key cultural values upon.

Another concept related to marginalization and exclusion is closure. As we explained in the third chapter on racialization, Max Weber was the first to use this term. The idea emerged as an alternative to Marxist theories of class-consciousness, with the aim of providing a more general, panoramic notion of group mobilization. This means that Weber's term is not limited to social class. Later scholars saw closure as the basis of all inequality, whether it results from material reward, authority, or status honour. So, all unequal groups—including classes, genders, ethnic groups, castes, and age groups—can practice closure to secure their advantage, or to resist domination.

Closure works through both exclusion (and marginalization) and inclusion. It relies on the power of one group to deny another group access to rewards or positive life-chances. The group with more power controls the selection of criteria for exclusion and inclusion, and the practices of imposing these criteria. So, for example, powerful groups dictate whether educational credentials, party membership, skin colour, religious identity, property, social origins, manners and lifestyle, or region are socially important. They then work to justify or legitimate these criteria, explaining why such conditions are required of included people. Of importance in this chapter, the group with more power can define whether people must meet a particular age requirement to gain or keep a job, office, rights, or other privileges. Typically, the dominant group invents legitimizing ideologies to justify this domination and exclusion.

Sometimes, then, closure is based on a single attribute. A good example related to age is the ineligibility of younger people to vote. Often, however, there are competing modes of closure that conflict with each other. These are sometimes rooted in different opinions about who should be excluded, and on what grounds. As well, elites defined by one criterion may not always use the obvious means to achieve closure. So, even if age dictates elite status, this privileged group may not exclude people based on their age, but on other grounds, like gender, ethnicity, or education.

At this point you might be feeling a kind of déjà vu, the sense that certain things that we are saying now have already been thought about and said before in this book. If you're thinking this, you're right. Throughout this chapter, we have been arguing that both young and old people—like all disadvantaged individuals— are singled out for special (but not necessarily good) treatment on the grounds of supposedly innate differences. Like ethnic group- ings, youth and elder groupings are largely imaginary. Like women, young and old people are subjected to domination on the assump- tion that they require (or deserve) it. So the causes and effects of age-related inequality are similar in a lot of ways to those of other forms of inequality, such as those based on ethnicity and gender.

However, there are also some differences between these var- ied types of inequality. For example, adolescents and elders are less likely to be exploited economically than workers, women, and racial minorities. This is not true in all cases, of course: many teenagers and post-retirement seniors earn a small income doing poorly paid service work, making them like women and recent immigrants in this respect. But for the most part, young people are kept out of the economy until they reach a certain age, and old people are pushed out around age sixty-five—supposedly for their own good. This kind of age discrimination is still widespread and it occurs on both sides of the age spectrum; though unfair, it saves the young and old from economic exploitation.

Employment discrimination among the elderly also occurs for different reasons than it does for women or racial minorities. Employers do not usually hire older people because they tend to have more health related problems, require more-than-average training, and are often seen as incapable of adapting to new technology. As research by American Vincent Roscigno and his colleagues showed, employers tend to perceive older adults as slow, difficult, inflexible, and expensive.[27] The same can be said for Canadian employers. According to economist Morley Gunderson, our human rights laws protect people against employment discrimination *unless the worker is sixty-five years of age or older*.[28] In this way, discrimination is built into our employment system.

But age-related employment discrimination exists elsewhere too—even in progressive Scandinavian countries. A study of fictitious job applicants in Sweden found that a hypothetical thirty-one-year-old was three to four times more likely to be offered a job than a fictional forty-six-year old.[29] Likewise, public polls from Norway from 2003 to 2007 showed that 20 percent of the population reported experiences of work-related age discrimination.[30] These findings are all the more interesting (and puzzling) because, in 2006, the European Union obliged member countries to implement legislation barring employment discrimination on the basis of age.[31]

Younger adults also face age discrimination, but for different reasons, such as being perceived as immature or poorly prepared for the demands of employment. These views are reflected in the case of Michael Sisler, a twenty-five-year-old New Jersey man who was fired from his job as vice-president of credit card operations at a major bank after letting his colleagues know his age.[32] After only five months of work, during which he demonstrated satisfactory job performance, Sisler was fired, and an older employee replaced him.[33] Sisler took his case to court, where he was informed that New Jersey law against age discrimination applied only to persons over forty years of age.[34] The judge explained that employers are not restricted from basing their hiring decisions on age-related factors, but that they were discouraged from making decisions based solely on age. Sisler's particular case had enough evidence to demonstrate his employer's inclination to discriminate against younger workers, but the judge was clear that it is very rare for a young adult to win a court battle over age discrimination.

These realities reflect a process called ageism: prejudice and discrimination based on age. Ageism is different in its effects than the other isms discussed in this book so far, such as sexism and racism. However, it is no different in its goals: that is, to ensure status advantages for the powerful group (in this case, the middle-aged) on the basis of supposed differences that justify domination.

There are at least two sociological theories that explain ageism. The first is functional theory, which posits that ageism helps younger people deny self-threatening aspects of old age.[35] By antagonizing people who are older, young people can pretend that aging will not have the same (negative) outcomes for them.[36] The second is the terror management theory that argues that young people distance themselves from older people to deny the mortality that is inevitable for everyone.[37] So, it appears that ageism, like all of the other forms of discrimination we have been discussing, is a protective cover for the fears that people hold about the aging process. Both older and younger people experience ageism, but older adults (and especially the elderly) are usually the main target.

The Life Course: Ages and Stages

It is an undeniable fact that all people are dependent on their caregivers (typically, their parents) at birth. They start out small, weak, and dependent and gradually become big, strong, and independent.

Therefore, one of the first developmental tasks associated with becoming an adult is declaring maturity and independence. As a result of this universal process, young people are united by a feeling that they have to prove themselves, become free of parental interference, and show that they can lead their own lives. This common stage of development—and, as Marx might say, common relation to the means of production—is what gives young people a sense of solidarity.

Building on these foundational insights, another sociologist, Glen Elder, created what has become one of the most useful concepts in the sociological study of age relations today: the life course.[38] The life course is a patterned sequence of individual experiences over time, which is subject to varied social, historical, and cultural influences. This life course approach involves studying one generation over its lifespan, while taking into account all of the relevant cultural, economic, social, and psychological influences that would have been exerted upon it. This concept is based on the idea of aging as a process by which we pass through historical events as members of a particular age group or cohort, in comparison with (and sometimes opposed to) other age groups.

Thinking about age within this kind of long-term context helps us to understand the inequalities between age groups, as well as the social and cultural dimensions of biological aging. Elder starts by stating that, in each society—and even within each social group—people have expected life courses.[39] By this, he means that everyone has certain expectations for what their lives will be like when they are at specific ages. So there are periods of life, or different life stages, that follow in sequence and that most of us expect to experience at a certain age.

Alongside this ideal life course or sequence, Elder suggests that there is also an actual life course, and the two—ideal and actual—are not always the same.[40] The gap between the expected life course and the experienced life course often causes people a lot of distress. This is because people want to feel normal by leading the idealized life course: completing school before starting to work, starting to work before marrying, and marrying before producing children. Most people become concerned and upset if their lives do not turn out like this, since they feel abnormal, or as if they aren't doing things the right way. However, an increasing number of people today have deviated from these ideal life course patterns, meaning that most of us are not leading the lives we expected we would.

Elder's life course approach makes the following five assumptions:[41]

1. Human development and aging are lifelong processes.
2. The consequences of life transitions, events, and behaviour patterns vary according to their timing in a person's life.
3. Lives are lived interdependently, and socio-historical influences are expressed through this network of shared relationships.
4. People's life courses are embedded in and shaped by the historical times and places they experience over their lifetime.
5. People construct their own life courses through the choices and actions they take based on the opportunities they are offered, and within the social circumstances in which they find themselves.

Elder's first assumption is that human development begins at birth and stops only with death; that is to say, we develop and change continuously throughout our lives. As people get older, their lives inevitably change, and at each stage certain concerns become supreme, while others become trivial. Specific life events typically concentrate in certain periods of a lifetime, such as education in youth, and parenting in adulthood. Social institutions are gatekeepers in this respect: they divide and regulate life course transitions, pushing people in and out of school, in and out of marriage, in and out of jobs, and so on. The same institutions—families, schools, workplaces, churches, and so on—also teach and reward the fulfillment of social expectations connected with the life course.

So, in order to understand why people act in certain ways or believe in certain things at a given age, we must understand how they got to that age—that is, the developmental pathway they followed. For example, among American young people who grew up during the Vietnam War, it makes a great deal of difference whether they were drafted and went to war, were drafted and fled the country, escaped the draft, or were never eligible for military service. This means that longitudinal studies are the best ways through which we can develop our understanding of people's lives. It also means that we need to be able to understand how a single turning point can be of crucial life importance, influencing all further developments.

Elder's second assumption is that the age at which you make a key life transition has an impact on the way you experience this transition. For example, it makes a difference if you divorce at twenty-five or at fifty-five, or if you graduate from college at twenty or at forty. The age at which people make such transitions affects the way they view themselves because people often base their self-image on comparisons they make with others. People who are far later or far earlier than others in their transition to a new status— whether as a graduate, grandmother, or retiree, as a few examples— may feel abnormal or ridiculous.

Further, the sequence in which these major changes unfold affects the experiences we have and the people we meet. Consider the important differences between students who have been working full time, versus students who have not. Many young undergraduates (say, under twenty-two) will say that older undergraduates (say, over thirty) hang out with one another, ignore younger students, and behave abnormally in the classroom. They ask too many questions, for example, demand a lot of the professor's time, and interject endlessly boring information about their own lives and views. They seem to think that they have more insight than anyone else, just because they've been working for the last ten or twenty years— at least, this is how it appears to the younger undergraduates. For their part, the older (mature) students are likely to think that their younger counterparts are goofing off all the time, don't take their education seriously, and don't know about the real world.

Third, Elder assumes that everyone has some kind of social relationships, which means that we cannot study individual lives separately, as though lived in a vacuum. One of the reasons for this is that we often find ourselves entering new statuses because of the actions of others, not through our own choosing. For example, the pregnancy of a teenage daughter may turn a woman into a grandmother before she is ready for this transition, just as the early death of her spouse may make her a widow before her time. Our degree of preparation for new roles and statuses affects how we experience and perform these roles and statuses. Equally as important, those life transitions that occur because of the actions of others remind us just how much of life is outside of our own control.

His fourth assumption is that historical circumstances shape each of our life experiences. Coming of college age means something different in wartime (as it did, for example, in the 1940s) than it did in peacetime (as in the 1970s); in prosperity (the 1950s) than in financial slump (the 1980s); or in a period of gender equality (the 1990s) than in one of male dominance (the 1890s). The historical period in which we live affects our opportunities and the choices we are likely to make, given these opportunities; in turn, these choices affect other opportunities we will have and choices we will need to make later in life. And these opportunities and choices are all situated in a particular historical context.

This observation creates the need for Elder's final assumption, which is that social forces create the context within which we exercise choice. Within this social context, we exercise our own agency or free will, allowing each of us to lead different lives. People living in any different social category or historical period will follow different life paths because they are free to choose their own course through life. This is the reason why all twenty-year-olds are not the same, nor are all fifty- or eighty-year-olds. Often, these differences among twenty-year-olds (or fifty-year-olds or eighty-year-olds) are a result of different, earlier choices.

To illustrate his ideas about the life course, Elder carried out a classic longitudinal study, *Children of the Great Depression*.[42] In gathering his data, he followed a cohort of 167 children who were eleven years old and living in Oakland, California, during the 1930s. The children were separated into two groups: deprived and non-deprived. The deprived children were from families that had lost at least 35 percent of their income between 1929 and 1933. Their sudden financial loss altered, among many things, the dynamics of the relationships between their family members. One notable consequence was a shift in power from the father to the mother, who often assumed the role of wage-earner and decision-maker, as well as providing emotional support.

Elder therefore found that the Depression changed parents' roles, but he also saw how it changed the roles of their children. To compensate for their fathers' lost income, many teenage sons had to leave school and start working. Doing so gave them more independence, as well as a sense of importance. It also gave them the opportunity to mingle with adults and form extended social networks. As a result, these deprived children were more likely to seek advice from their strong social networks of friends and acquaintances than they were to look to their family members.

Their early exposure to the adult world also led the deprived children to mature sooner than their non-deprived counterparts. Having assumed adult roles in the home at a younger age, these kids started to date earlier, and went out more often on school nights. In particular, the daughters of deprived parents often took over some of the household chores that traditionally belonged to the homemaker. Likely because they had experienced more distant relationships with their fathers and strong socialization into the homemaker role, these deprived girls married and had children earlier than other (non-deprived) girls, starting their families during or just after World War II. So, the scrambling of roles and the generational redistribution of power created a more egalitarian family structure.

While we have been discussing them as a homologous group, these children each had individual experiences of deprivation, influenced in part by their own personal qualities. On one hand, positive personal traits—like intelligence for boys, physical attractiveness for girls, and an easy temperament for both—lessened the negative effects of financial hardship. In addition, those children who had strong relationships with their mothers tended to be less affected by their fathers' negative behaviour.

The individual relationships they had with their parents also had an impact on deprived children's conception of the family unit. As we might expect, the experience of a deprived childhood led people to place a greater value on family, as opposed to work or leisure. Maybe the absence of a secure, loving relationship with their fathers made these young people yearn for the kind of caring family life they had lacked growing up. Or perhaps they learned to see family as a valuable resource and children as a worthwhile investment, capable of making the same kind of contribution they had made during their own difficult childhood.

As we can see from their valuing of family life, the shortened childhood and earlier entry into adulthood that these deprived children often experienced did not always produce negative effects. In addition to developing this appreciation for the family, many deprived children grew up to become useful, successful members of society. They even reported more life satisfaction than their non-deprived counterparts. So, financial hardship, though undesirable, can still produce positive outcomes.

Elder's study, while uncovering the positive and negative effects of deprivation, also shows that longitudinal research can reveal a lot about the aging process. Some have disputed his results, saying that the children he studied "passed through the Depression at an 'optimum age' for minimizing its detrimental effects."[43] However, most have praised Elder's work for showing that people experience the various phases of life—childhood, adolescence, middle age, and

so on—in different ways, depending on their socio-historic contexts. In addition, his study highlights how economic changes shift
social roles and family relations. For example, many of the teenage
sons he studied had to work for pay during the Depression. As a
result, they had the opportunity to mingle freely with adults and
form extended social networks—and these effects were strength-
ened by military service in the 1940s. The daughters in his sample,
for their part, took over some of their mothers' household chores
and, in this way, quickly entered a phase that was something like
adulthood. Paradoxically then, deprived children matured sooner
than their non-deprived counterparts, and these differences were
largely due to the economic context in which they were raised.

Even more importantly, Elder's study provides insights into age
group relations today. Based on his research, we can assume that
Group A might grow up with one set of assumptions, while Group
B might grow up with a quite different set of assumptions, because
of their different circumstances and the inequalities between them.
Further, his findings suggest that there are misunderstandings and
conflict between people in every generation, and accusations are
always made against members of other age groups. Like people
of different gender and racial and ethnic groups, people who are
different ages have different experiences, and therefore different
outlooks. The important question this raises is whether varied
outlooks lead to social differentiation and if this differentiation, in
turn, leads to inequalities.

Another important implication of Elder's work is that aging
well has a lot to do with social context, including the social policies
that either help to support elderly people or that take this support
away from them. As communication researcher Elizabeth Fussell
pointed out, supportive policies are more likely to be adopted if
the tension and competition between different age groups is
reduced.[44] Of course, part of this process involves rejecting the
stereotypes associated with different age groups. Just like the oth-
ering of women and racial and ethnic minorities, stereotypes of
youth and the elderly lead to justifications about their dependent

and vulnerable status. For example, the belief that all older people are infirm and in need of support makes it challenging for the elderly to live independent lifestyles. It is therefore difficult to age well while living in a society that assumes this kind of aging to be almost impossible. Aging well is also difficult in societies that do not recognize the social reasons for why people are in the positions and situations that they are, be it highly educated youth who cannot find a niche in the labour market, or elderly people without the support of retirement funds.

What can we say, then, about the social inequalities between different age groups, at the end of this chapter? If our fellow Canadian Olga Kotelko can teach us anything, it is that age is both biologically determined and socially constructed. At the age of ninety, Kotelko and others like her continue to reject obsolescence and embrace the opportunities that come their way. We can say the same about the emerging adults whom Arnett studied. Like Kotelko, they struggle to survive in a society that expects everything of them, but yet offers them few opportunities in harsh economic times. All of this suggests that many Canadians, both younger and older, are simply doing their best with the cards they have been dealt.

So, some people actively reject the stereotypes associated with their age, behaving in ways that overturn people's expectations of them; others merely accept age-based mistreatment as inevitable. In the next chapter, we will see how the homosexual community has taken the former approach, rejecting victimhood and fighting back against exclusion and oppression. In doing so, we will recall the social benefits of institutional completeness that we discussed in connection with ethnic minorities—something that people of different age groups have not always been able to achieve.

CHAPTER 5

Victimization

———•◆•———

*"What is straight? A line can be straight, or a
street, but the human heart, oh no, it's curved
like a road through mountains."*
Tennessee Williams

More than a Headline

On October 17, 2011, the flag at A.Y. Jackson Secondary School flew
at half-mast. Students and teachers at the school in Kanata (near
Ottawa, Ontario) huddled below it, some crying, some offering
hugs, and all thinking about Jamie Hubley. Hubley, a high school
student, committed suicide due to the bullying he experienced at
school and the depression he suffered as a result. He had declared
his unhappiness on his blog, where he wrote, "I wish I could be
happy, I try, I try, I try. . . . I just want to feel special to someone"—
so we can be fairly certain that his decision to take his own life was
related to this discontentment.[1]

Hubley's struggles to fit in and be accepted are familiar to
most teenagers, all of whom are trying to forge a sense of identity
within the often tumultuous high school setting. Yet for Hubley,
this process was even more difficult as he was openly gay. He had
reportedly seemed like a happy person on the outside, always smil-
ing and offering hugs in the hallways.[2] But inside, Hubley despaired
about being called a "fag" and having no one to love and be loved
by in return. He also didn't think that his situation could get better, and one fateful Saturday, this led him to end his own life with
a handful of pills.

Jamie Hubley's tragedy fits within the unfortunate context of our fairly high youth suicide rate. In 2009, 202 Canadian teens between the ages of fifteen and nineteen took their own lives.[3] Suicide therefore accounts for almost one quarter of the deaths among this age group.[4] But that's not the whole story. Youths who identify as gay, lesbian, bisexual, or transgender are more susceptible, even though they make up a smaller percentage of the population. What's more, unlike Hubley, many of these young people will remain in the shadows of anonymity. Hubley's case only became so widely known because his father was a public figure (a councillor for Kanata South)[5] and because Jamie was being bullied, which in 2013 is a hot topic in the media. And, as Hubley's own father pointed out, different groups used his story to promote their own agendas.

Even though his story is only one of many, it points to several themes surrounding suicide. For one, mental health and homosexuality come to the fore in discussions of cases like Hubley's. But we can also see how his story highlights the victimization that certain members of society face. Hubley was bullied for several reasons, but the fact that he was gay is a prominent one. Of course, this particular kind of bullying happens in all high schools, with people throwing around the words "fag" and "gay" to describe things they consider stupid or silly, or to label their fellow students as such. To address this issue, C.J. Pascoe conducted an ethnographic study that she eventually called *Dude, You're a Fag.*[6] In her work, Pascoe proposes that boys in particular use this epithet in order to police the boundaries of what is considered masculine. But in doing so, they lock in the negative connotation of the word and its original implication of minority sexual practices.

All this is to say that gay, lesbian, bisexual, and transgender people still struggle with issues surrounding their orientation, though these issues may be different from the ones they would have faced several decades ago. Despite the gay rights movement and the progress that has been made toward tolerance, Hubley's suicide and that of many others shows that it is still tough to be gay in our society.

Social Construction

When talking about gender and sexuality, sociologists often use the term socially constructed. By this, we mean that sexuality or sexual orientation is not embedded within our biology, but rather, that it is a product of our social context, just like the other types of inequalities we have talked about so far.

Undoubtedly, biology does influence how we experience and express our sexuality. Men and women are obviously differentiated by biological markers that limit their respective sexualities in some form. But as with any other example, biology exists and is expressed within a social environment. In our society and many others, people put forward arguments about sexuality that are commonsensical. You've heard phrases like, "Heterosexuality is natural because the male and female reproductive organs just fit naturally together." Unfortunately, these commonsensical arguments don't make sense sometimes. But despite their ineffectiveness, these arguments tend to overshadow the significant role of social context in shaping human sexuality.

To show why social context matters, let's assume that sexual orientation—whether we are attracted to people of the same or the other biological sex—is a genetic given. If sexual orientation is not chosen by the individual, nor mandated by society, culture, religion, or any other institution, a great deal is still left to social construction. For example, we still would not be able to confirm whether a homosexual is someone who is regularly having sex with someone of the same sex, occasionally having sex with someone of the same sex, has only done so in the past, has only imagined doing so, has identified him- or herself as a homosexual but practices heterosexuality, practices both homosexuality and heterosexuality, and so on. So we can see that it matters a great deal how we define and measure whether someone is homosexual because we get quite different numbers when we take one approach rather than another.

Even more obviously, social construction is implicated in a culture's decision to highlight sexual orientation as a topic of interest.

We don't single out men who are attracted to women with red hair, or gaps between their front teeth, or small breasts as requiring a special name or identity, nor do we make them the topic of public discussion or special legislation. What, then, can we say about a society that singles out men who are attracted to other men, or women who are attracted to other women? For one, it appears that our fascination with homosexuality in particular has something to do with our fascination and confusion about sex in general.

People who deviate from what has been labelled normal sexual behaviour are largely the cause of this intrigue and confusion. Think about how differently we would behave in a society that assumed that the main purpose of sexual activity is pleasure, where different people take pleasure from different kinds of sexual activities and sexual partners. Or in a society that sees our definition of sex as a social construction, and recognizes that other people in different societies and times thought about sex very differently. In either of these hypothetical societies, sexual preferences would be just like sandwich preferences; deviance would be impossible because normal preferences would not even exist.

Many societies label heterosexuality as the norm and homosexuality the deviation; married monogamy the norm and multiple partners the deviation; procreative sexual intercourse the norm and other types of sexual behaviour the deviations; and so on. There are many varieties of sexual expression but, at one time or another, someone has condemned or labelled all of them as deviant. Perhaps because of the strong feelings sex produces, people want to regulate sexual behaviour more than most other actions.

However, homosexuality has proven to be difficult to regulate since we cannot even seem to come up with a satisfying definition. While it has formally been defined as a physical and emotional attraction to people of the same sex, it is hard to say whether homosexuality is an act (or set of acts), a preference, or an identity. We also haven't been able to come to a consensus on whether it is something occasional, regular, or permanent. Views vary on these topics because sexuality is multi-layered: people experience their sexuality in thoughts, fantasies, desires, beliefs, attitudes, values, roles, and relationships, as well as in behaviour. Further, sexuality manifests itself at the intersection of many factors—biological, psychological, economic, political, cultural, ethical, legal, historical, religious, spiritual, and social. With all of these variables to consider, it's no wonder we have had a hard time developing a universally applicable definition of homosexuality. But this plethora of factors has also led to the invention of the "sociology of sex." We study sex, gender, and sexuality because they are important parts of social reality and not only biological reality.

To repeat, these social factors that contribute to the construction of sexuality mean that our conception of sexuality changes over time. Thirty years ago, for example, many people viewed homosexuality as both a medical condition and a legal condition punishable by law. A great deal has obviously changed since then. On July 20, 2005, Canada became the fourth country in the world to legalize same-sex marriage nationwide with the enactment of the Civil Marriage Act, which provided a gender-neutral marriage definition. That said, the national legislation followed court decisions, beginning in 2003, that had already legalized same-sex marriage in eight provinces and one territory, which cumulatively made up about 90 percent of Canada's population. This recent development shows that Canadian public opinion on sexual topics has changed dramatically over the last thirty years, with attitudes about same-sex intimacy and marriage becoming more liberal.

In fact, most Canadians today consider outwardly anti-homosexual behaviour—not homosexuality—to be a social problem and a potential violation of hate laws—the Canadian Human Rights Act or one of the provincial human rights codes. Many of us think that other people's sexual activity is only of public concern if it is harmful to us or to others. Yet in some places—even within Canada—homosexual people are still victimized, and they continue to experience a disproportionate amount of discrimination, exclusion, and even violence. In severe cases, as we saw with Hubley, some become so desperate that suicide seems like a better option than enduring this kind of mistreatment.

Canadians have also come a long way in that most of us appear to feel that governments (and churches, schools, and workplaces) have no business judging people's sexual preferences. Where two consenting adults are concerned, sex is private business, not public business. Despite this widespread view, homosexuality remains stigmatized in many quarters, making secrecy necessary and coming out a painful process for gay and lesbian people. So, while we have made big improvements in a relatively short period of time, there is still a lot of work to be done.

Define Normal

The common wisdom in early twentieth-century Canada and the US was that sexuality is fixed and binary. Normal people were supposed to be entirely heterosexual and those who were homosexual, while not "normal," were considered entirely homosexual. However, American sexologist Alfred Kinsey—who conducted research at the end of what some people called Victorian prudery during the 1950s—showed that human sexual orientation lies on a continuum, with heterosexuality at one end and homosexuality at the other.

Kinsey was working in response to biologists and psychologists who assumed that heterosexuality was part of an animal's innate or instinctive equipment. He was especially critical of the view that varied non-reproductive sexual activity is perverse or abnormal. So in 1947, Kinsey founded a research lab, now known as the Kinsey Institute, where he surveyed roughly eighteen thousand Americans on their sexual practices.[7] The survey showed that men of different social classes were very different in terms of their sexual behaviour, including factors like masturbation, homosexuality, oral sex, sex with a prostitute, and premarital and extramarital sex. On the other hand, women's class was less significant than their age and gender ideologies for explaining sexual variations. These findings, although disputed today as not being entirely accurate, shocked the nation. As a result, Kinsey's study played a part in opening up the conversation about sex.

But Kinsey's most important contribution is his Heterosexual-Homosexual Rating Scale, a seven-point continuum showing a complex and sophisticated understanding of sexual tastes. Using this approach, Kinsey avoided labelling people themselves as heterosexual or homosexual, but rather, he was able to label their life histories or cumulative sexual experiences as such. This nuance gave him more flexibility, allowing him to rate people differently at different times in their lives. This approach also implied that no position on the continuum is intrinsically normal or abnormal, any more than it is fixed or fundamental.

In other words, Kinsey proposed that most people are not entirely heterosexual or homosexual in their sexual desires; rather, they exist somewhere between the ends of the continuum at different points in time. Further, he noted that not all people act on their sexual wishes: some people who think of themselves as heterosexual may be attracted to people of the same sex, yet may not act on their desires for fear of attracting censure or stigma. Some are not even entirely aware of their preferences, owing to the stigma attached to exploring one's options.

So, by Kinsey's reckoning, it is difficult, and maybe even impossible, to label someone as strictly homosexual or heterosexual throughout his or her entire life. Perhaps it was this very blurring of the boundaries between homosexuality and heterosexuality that drove some people to try to re-enforce these divisions more rigorously. As well, we think about sexuality in a certain way because we think about sex and gender in a certain way—namely, in oppositional, mutually exclusive terms. For all of these reasons, people have a tendency to place themselves and others into binary categorizations.

Since Kinsey conducted his research, many sociologists have proposed that heterosexuality has been socially defined as normal, in opposition to the belief that it is inherently so. In the 1980s, Mariana Valverde suggested that arguments normalizing heterosexuality are rooted in a biological determinist perspective that sees heterosexuality as natural and innate.[8] This view is based on the simplistic reasoning that heterosexuality was invented by Mother Nature to ensure that, after procreation, men would not abandon the mother and child, but would continue to provide them with protection in exchange for sexual favours from the woman.[9] This kind of heterosexist perspective is everywhere in our society—just watch some television or open a magazine to see it being acted out.

Yet, despite its conventionality, the biological reductionist view is both stereotypical and illogical. It is stereotypical in that it sees Mother Nature as a "manipulative mother-in-law," men as predators concerned only with sex, and women as weak and sexually passive.[10] It is also illogical, since it does not clarify why women would turn to predatory men for protection when by pairing off or banding together, they could protect themselves just as effectively.

Even though researchers like Valverde have shown that heterosexuality is merely constructed as the norm, most people continue to see it as such. Sociologist Karin Martin defines this view as *heteronormativity*—the sense that heterosexuality is to be taken for granted as normal and natural.[11] The spread of heteronormativity relies on a variety of "social institutions, practices, and norms that support heterosexuality," and shows itself when people automatically assume that another person is heterosexual, even when there is no reason for them to think so.[12] Martin proposes that heteronormativity is so subtle, that we often practice it without even realizing. No wonder, then, that we are sometimes surprised to find out someone is homosexual: we have learned to assume that everyone is heterosexual, unless evidence shows otherwise.

Martin used these theories to explore how parents contribute to shaping their children's sexuality. In her ethnographic study, she describes the ways in which mothers privilege and take for granted heterosexuality, thus constructing their children's sexual views and experiences on a daily basis. These processes, according to Martin, occur through two sets of practices. First, many mothers imagine and create a world for their children in which only heterosexuals exist.[13] By assuming universal heterosexuality, these mothers interpret their children's behaviour as showing heterosexual interest, thus projecting their own expectations about appropriate sexual interaction onto the usually gender-neutral interactions between young children. One example is when mothers label their children's friends as girlfriends or boyfriends if they are of the opposite sex and only as friends if they are of the same sex.

Second, mothers manage heteronormativity when they allow themselves to consider the possibility that their children may one day show homosexual preferences. A few mothers consciously prepare for this possibility, but more hope their children will turn out heterosexual, despite signs to the contrary. The largest group of parents tries to discourage or even prevent homosexuality in their children.[14]

Within this heteronormative context, children are free to interpret, resist, or alter the messages they receive from their mothers. However, their parents' heteronormative perspectives structure the social circumstances that shape "older children's and adults' sense that heterosexuality is natural."[15] Martin stresses that mothers are not to be blamed for this behaviour; after all, many are unaware of the assumptions they promote. Others are understandably reluctant to parent in unconventional ways, since mothers are themselves constrained by the social expectations that surround mothering. They want to be able to consider themselves successful mothers, not failures in a conventional sense. Further, many are concerned that their children will be the targets of bullying if they aren't considered normal, so, by discouraging sexual deviation, they feel as though they are protecting their children from social rejection.

In the heteronormative process, heterosexuality is put forward as the only valid form of sexual expression. Certain social situations reinforce this social definition, like when we automatically assume that others are heterosexual. While this happens innocently enough at times, as we saw with the mothers whom Martin studied, the privileging of heterosexuality can also be intentional and even spiteful. Some people believe in heteronormativity to such an extent that they enact heterosexism, a belief in the moral superiority of heterosexual institutions and practices. It's not difficult to see how such heterosexist views can lead to victimization.

Bull's Eye

As a group suffering from social inequality, homosexuals are unique. Unlike women, who form half the population, and unlike ethnic, racial, class, or age groups, which are often very large, the homosexual population is very small. Only 1 percent of Canadians who are eighteen years of age or older identify themselves as "homosexual."[16] This is consistent with figures from local communities in the United States, indirect measurements, and statistics from the UK, France, Norway, and Denmark. While gay and lesbian leaders have occasionally estimated that as many as 10 percent of the general population is homosexual, those estimates are far off the mark. At best, they only apply to geographical areas where homosexuals are concentrated, such as the gay neighbourhoods in big cities like Montreal and Toronto.

Because homosexuals typically represent a small fraction of the population, they are especially vulnerable to victimization. But victimization is not inevitable: sociological research shows that the risk of victimization varies depending on the context in which people live their lives. This area of sociological study, focusing on the victims of crime, is called victimology. Victimology has been stimulated in recent years by the increased use of surveys to collect data on the hidden incidence of crime, an advance in our knowledge that takes us beyond the crime rates reported by the police. Researchers have long recognized there are many more victims out there than those whose cases are reported to and by the police and other social services; victimization surveys are designed to target these uncharted cases.

The findings of such surveys show that typically, victimization is most common among disadvantaged people. As a general rule, victimization is rooted in social inequality, with hate-motivated forms of victimization being especially insidious. We will use the homosexual population as our example in this chapter, though we could make similar points about the bisexual, transsexual, transgendered, and polyamorous populations. We chose to focus on homosexuality because it is both a poignant example and one that has received increasing research attention from sociologists in the last few decades.

Because so many studies have been conducted on the topic, we have lots of data on victimization prevalence rates. A 2009 study by Statistics Canada shows that people with higher-than-average risks of violent victimization fall into a few main categories: they self-identify as an Aboriginal person, have some form of activity limitation or physical handicap, or self-identify as homosexual.[17] Another survey shows that, in 2004, about 12 percent of hate-motivated incidents were focused on the victim's sexual orientation.[18] Among people who identified themselves as gay or lesbian, the rate of violent victimization was about two and a half times higher than the rate for self-identified heterosexuals.[19]

Active homosexuals who are victimized are an example of what we might call victims of conscience. They cannot, in good conscience, deny who they are and must risk danger and rejection by others in order to be true to themselves. Throughout history, victims of conscience appear in various social forms: as heretics, whistle-blowers, conscientious objectors, war resistors, or merely bohemians and members of counter-culture. Eventually, people may come to remember many of them as the heroes and heralds of a new society. Yet, in their own time, an ignorant populace—sometimes even a fearful power structure—may victimize them. So, victimization is partly a result of people's characteristics and partly a result of what a society labels as deviant or worthy of condemnation. In some societies, this labelling is taken to the extreme, and homosexuality is seen as so completely unacceptable that it demands capital punishment.

Such fear or hatred of homosexuals is called homophobia. George Weinberg introduced the term in 1972, challenging traditional thinking about homosexuality and helping to focus society's attention on the problem of anti-gay prejudice and stigma.[20] However, the term does have its limitations. The most important is its implication that anti-gay prejudice is a phobia—that is, an irrational feeling based mainly on fear and, consequently, a defence mechanism against that fear.

Today, this understanding of anti-gay sentiment seems inappropriate. Instead, we argue that the hatred of gay and lesbian people is not a phobia, but a socially learned anti-homosexual attitude. Without this perspective, we cannot account for historical changes in the way societies regard homosexuality. For example, we mentioned earlier that Canadians have become more tolerant of homosexuality in recent decades, as have people in other Western societies. However, things used to be a lot worse for many homosexual people. If we are to gain a sociological (versus psychiatric) understanding of anti-homosexuality, and of the historical changes in anti-homosexual sentiments, we need a new vocabulary for discussing so-called homophobic behaviour.

The tendency that has been labelled homophobia comes in various forms. They range from mild social distance, as when people are unwilling to form close friendships with homosexuals, to stereotyping, including the view that all gays and lesbians are the same. Homophobia has also been considered to involve religious injunctions, bullying and harassment at school or work, and hate crimes that have even amounted to murder.

However, we feel that it would be more accurate to characterize these homophobic thoughts and behaviours as belonging to a type of anti-homosexual subculture—to some degree, a response to the increasingly organized homosexual subculture. One principle behind this anti-homosexual subculture is essentialism, or the belief that all homosexuals essentially have the same characteristics. In 1954, psychologist Gordon Allport proposed that any belief in this kind of group essence constitutes part of a prejudiced personality.[21] This means that essentialism is often accompanied by a rigid way of thinking that cannot accept ambiguity or changeability—the same problem we mentioned in our earlier chapter on racism.

Recent research confirms that essentialist beliefs about homosexuals are strongly associated with anti-gay or anti-lesbian attitudes. People who demonstrate essentialist thinking are usually hostile toward homosexuals, even when they are not hostile to other minorities like women or immigrants, for example. Research also suggests that essentialist beliefs about sexual orientation vary along two dimensions: the immutability of sexual orientation and the fundamentality of a classification of people as heterosexuals and homosexuals. First, immutability refers to the belief that under no circumstances can one change a personal feature—in this case, homosexuality. In other words, homosexuality is like skin colour: people are born with it and cannot do anything to change it. Second, fundamentality refers to the belief that a certain feature—homosexuality, for our purposes—is central to a person's entire character.

People who believe in immutability and fundamentality have been found to hold hostile attitudes toward lesbians and gay men. In other words, people are more likely to hold anti-gay attitudes if they think homosexuals have a choice in their sexual orientation. They are also more likely to hold anti-gay attitudes if they think of homosexuality as an essential or key feature of a person. The worst combination of these two tendencies can often be found in societies fraught with extreme forms of victimization based on sexual orientation.

However, ideas like immutability and fundamentality are not rooted in any concrete evidence. People who believe in these concepts are likely to believe in other, equally unsupported ones as well. For example, people who think that homosexuality is a choice tend to think that it is also a result of developmental experiences, or those that a person has while growing up. These could include negative heterosexual encounters at a young age, which would (supposedly) lead to homosexuality later in life. Anti-homosexuals may also believe the reverse to be true: if a person has a positive homosexual experience when young, he or she will eventually become a homosexual. Or, people may think that someone with a dominant, domineering, or smothering mother, and a weak or absent father is more likely than average to develop a homosexual orientation.

But again, there is no evidence to support any of these firmly held, anti-homosexual beliefs. Most gay rights activists today argue that a person is born gay and that sexual orientation is not a choice, but rather that homosexuality is permanent and uncontrollable. The idea that people are homosexual from birth is widely accepted within the gay community, and it is also gaining acceptance and support from the heterosexual public. Just as heterosexuals think of themselves as naturally heterosexual, they are increasingly coming to think of homosexuals as naturally homosexual.

Clearly, those whom we have labelled anti-homosexual do not share these views. Rather, anti-homosexual beliefs are grounded in three concepts that Gregory Herek identified in 2004.[22] The first of these is sexual stigma, or the tendency to hold non-heterosexual behaviour, identity, or the community as a whole in low regard. Second, heterosexism, as we briefly mentioned earlier, is the belief that only heterosexuality is natural and normal. Third and finally, sexual prejudice is the tendency to hold negative attitudes about people based solely on their sexual orientation. When we talk about anti-homosexuality in the following paragraphs, we are referring to all three of these ideas: stigmatization, prejudice, and heterosexism.

There is no shortage of speculation about the causes of anti-homosexuality. True, it appears to be founded on faulty beliefs about homosexual people and about the essentialism and controllability of their sexual orientation. But where do these beliefs come from, how do they arise, and why do some people continue to hold them? To try to answer these questions, we looked at related social science research, where we found four groups of factors that appear to influence anti-homosexuality. These were: openness to human diversity, openness to sexual diversity, familiarity with homosexuals, and membership in an anti-homosexual culture.

Openness to human diversity. A classic study by Theodor Adorno and his collaborators, which was originally about the psychological bases of authoritarian thinking, found unexpectedly that those with this thinking style also tend to be anti-homosexual. Authoritarian people, according to these researchers, are more likely than other people to hate homosexuals, as well as black people; Jews; and other ethnic, racial, and social minorities. This anti-homosexual, racist orientation is rooted in a complex of superstitious beliefs and conservative political and economic views. Other studies have come to similar conclusions, confirming the correlation between anti-homosexuality and political conservatism.

In fact, conservatism appears to be the single best predictor of anti-homosexuality. This is particularly true for conservative people who are religious, uneducated, and older, but it is also true for highly educated people as well. For example, politically conservative freshmen at an Ivy League university were found to hold more negative attitudes toward homosexuals—and more traditional ideas about female sexuality and male dominance—than liberals.[24] Similarly, heterosexual college students with traditional social views, and a reliance on conventional rules about human behaviour, were more likely to hold anti-homosexual attitudes.[25] Because they are so often supporters of convention, people with anti-homosexual attitudes also usually reject a wide variety of other deviant groups.

Familiarity with sexual diversity. In a survey conducted by the Kinsey Institute in 1989, Americans responded to statements designed to gauge their attitudes and beliefs about homosexuality, among many other sexual topics.[26] Robert Fay and his colleagues found sexual experience to be a determining factor in people's acceptance of homosexuality. This means that people who have had a wide variety of sexual experiences, or are personally acquainted with others who have had such experiences—whether with premarital sex, extramarital sex, or homosexuality—are less anti-homosexual than people with a more limited lifetime sexual environment.

Familiarity with homosexuals. People who live in large cities or communities where they are likely to meet many homosexuals tend to be more accepting of homosexuality. Fay's study also found that people who are more familiar with homosexuality and homosexuals, usually because they know more homosexuals at work, school, or in the neighbourhood, tend to score lower on anti-homosexuality measures.[27] This finding is supported by other research that shows the great importance of acquaintanceship or contact with known homosexuals in reducing anti-homosexuality. In 1993, for example, Gregory Herek and Erik Glunt reported that personal contact with gay friends and relatives has more influence on attitudes toward gay people than any other social or demographic variable.[28]

Membership in an anti-homosexual culture. Certain cultural characteristics also contribute to the prevalence of anti-homosexual attitudes. A study conducted by Anissa Hélie in 2004 reports that in the eighty-three countries where homosexuality is a punishable crime, people often follow fundamentalist religions that support these laws.[29] The heterosexist ideas we've been describing, including a belief in the moral superiority of heterosexual institutions and practices, are also related to anti-homosexuality.

However, some research suggests that the best single predictor of anti-gay sentiment is sex-role rigidity: a belief in the essential difference between men and women, and the need to keep women in their place. Sex-role confusion and anxiety around sexual matters may also explain why heterosexual men are more prejudiced against gays than women are, why gay men elicit more negative reactions than lesbians, and why effeminate gay men are less threatening to heterosexual men than are their macho counterparts.

Overall, the research that revealed these four factors shows that anti-homosexuality is a result of social variables, or even idiosyncratic psychopathologies. Yet, as Thomas and Thomas said in their famous Thomas Dictum, what is defined as real is real in its consequences.

We have also seen that anti-homosexuals appear to be fixated on whether lesbian and gay people choose their sexual orientation. So far, it has been impossible to locate a gene that accounts for homo- or heterosexuality. Some researchers, like Aaron Greenberg and J. Michael Bailey, believe that there would be positive aspects to being able to select the sexuality of your child.[30] In opposition, the belief that homosexuality is based in genetics has also been linked with negative eugenic agendas.[31] This is clearly a sensitive topic and one that seems to have a big influence on people's perception of homosexuality as normal or abnormal.

Today, societies that marginalize homosexuality and promote heteronormativity are less numerous than they once were. These changes reflect both an increased tolerance for homosexuality and reduced victim-blaming. The Scandinavian societies we have been mentioning so often—Sweden, Norway, Denmark, and Iceland— typically have weak just-world beliefs and place blame on social practices that foster discrimination and disadvantage. As a result of these views, such societies have collectively had the most success in decreasing anti-homosexual attitudes.[32] For example, homosexual HIV/AIDS victims in Scandinavian countries are typically treated more generously than those in Canada and the United States. So we can see that blaming the homosexual's suffering on social institutions and practices that foster discrimination, and not on the individual him- or herself, is the best way to decrease negative attitudes toward homosexuals. This approach still allows people to express just-world beliefs by placing blame, but it deflects this blame away from the victims.

The question for sociologists, then, is not, "Is homosexuality something inborn and unchangeable?" Instead, we wonder, "Why is there so much concern about whether homosexuality is something inborn and unchangeable?" The second question does not take sides in the debate, but asks what social factors make this issue so important. Gay and lesbian rights groups are understandably concerned that the claims they have used to found and legitimate their movement are being questioned. And if they are overturned, that says something about the narrow way in which our society has agreed to grant legitimacy to sexual diversity. In short, this debate highlights the social construction of inequality issues and the consequences that these mere constructions have for people's lives.

Anti-homosexuality as a Development Problem

Though not all countries are as opened-minded about sexual diversity as Canada, not all countries have victimized homosexuals to the same degree. Today, homosexual rights are, in many ways, at the forefront of the human rights agenda in the developed world.[33]

Within the last decade and a half, ten countries have legalized gay marriage, and many others are strongly considering the possibility. Recently, the prime minister of the United Kingdom threatened to withdraw foreign aid from receiving countries that do not respect gay rights.[34] This is a dubious threat, however, considering that the United Kingdom has yet to allow same-sex partners to get married.

This shows that the whole world has not embraced or condemned homosexuality to the same degree. Some societies, such as the Netherlands, have been very welcoming in both their laws and attitudes, while other countries have not. African countries are particularly discriminatory in their treatment of gay people—in fact, thirty-eight African countries currently have laws prohibiting homosexuality, whereas homosexuality is only legal in thirteen.[35] In those countries that have outlawed homosexuality, many have also ruled that it is an offence punishable by death.

Is it merely by chance that one continent is so anti-homosexual? We believe there are likely social factors at work in sub-Saharan Africa that account for its strong anti-gay laws and attitudes. For example, heavy impoverishment, instability, corruption, and authoritarianism are hugely problematic. It is the poorest and most underdeveloped continent, and has been characterized by governments guilty of many human rights violations. It is a place where the average life expectancy is fifty-three and the average annual income is only a little over one thousand dollars.[36]

North African and Middle Eastern countries also have similarly harsh laws condemning homosexuality, with some like Sudan and Saudi Arabia ruling that it is punishable by death.[37] In North Africa and the Middle East, people live longer, with an average life expectancy of seventy-one years, and they are better off economically. Still, people in these areas only have an average income of about thirty-five hundred dollars, less than a tenth of what the average Canadian makes.[38]

These statistics on income are important because comparative cross-national research on homonegativity and modernization has confirmed a link between economic development and homosexual approval.[39] In fact, Singapore is the only one listed among the IMF's thirty-five advanced economies that still outlaws homosexual behaviour.[40]

This suggests that anti-homosexuality flourishes in countries that are the most impoverished and the least developed. Perhaps if aid-providing nations make gay rights a precondition for their services, we might see some progress in the LGBT movement in sub-Saharan Africa and other anti-homosexual areas. However, this could also result in cutting the aid that is provided to anti-homosexual countries, which could, in turn, promote anti-homosexual sentiments in those countries pushed further into poverty by the withdrawal of this aid. If modernization theory is right, and economic development helps produce homosexual tolerance, withdrawing aid from anti-homosexual governments might do more harm than good.

Homosexual tolerance, however, is not only dependent on development. For instance, one of the nine countries in the world with no legal homosexual discrimination happens to be a fairly impoverished country in sub-Saharan Africa—South Africa. If gay rights were just a development issue, we would see a lot of countries allowing same-sex marriage a long time before South Africa (such as Japan, France, the UK, and the United States). Likewise, the entire developed world has not been equally accepting of homosexual populations. Societies at the same stage of economic development vary significantly in their tolerance of homosexuals; so, there is more to the story than mere modernization.

That said, the less developed world is still the most dangerous for homosexuals. In 2002, Robin Mathy from the University of Minnesota conducted a cross-continental study on the link between suicidality and homosexuality.[41] In the end, she had to exclude Africa from the study because only five Africans had dared to out themselves on the survey. Even without statistics from Africa, Mathy discovered that male homosexuals in every continent, except Europe, were significantly more likely than heterosexuals to have attempted suicide.

Other research has confirmed this link between suicide and homosexuality.[42] On this relationship, Mathy notes that the lower risk of suicide in Europe may have something to do with European culture. She remarks that Europeans have "a much more laissez-faire attitude toward sexual matters," but is also quick to point out that this attitude is not uniformly spread across the continent.[43] North American trends also diverged from Mathy's main findings, but in a different way: it was the only continent in which suicide and homosexuality were also linked for females. This reality, in many ways, seems puzzling. There are many similarities between Canada and the US, and Europe, including that they are mainly highly developed with liberal democratic governments. Also, these countries have been strong protectors of human rights.

Yet Europe appears alone at the tolerance end of the spectrum, being the only continent with no link between homosexuality and suicidality. Canada and the US are at the other end, with both men and women equally at risk of suicide related to homosexuality. What is Europe doing so well that prevents their gay men from wanting to kill themselves? And more importantly, what is North America doing so badly, making it the only continent where gay women want to kill themselves too?

The "Not-So-United" States of America

Throughout the United States, homosexuals have actively campaigned for civil liberties and social acceptance. They have done so, however, in the face of anti-homosexual militants who have actively challenged their agenda. Here are some examples that highlight the hostility of American society toward homosexuals.

The Ding-Dong Defense. On May 21, 1979, anger lingered in the air as five thousand gay protestors gathered outside of San Francisco City Hall. Many of them had been marching all day through the streets, but they were not satisfied with their efforts. The time for peaceful protest had ended and the time for rioting had begun.[44] The San Francisco protestors were not trashing city hall for the right to have sex, get married, or adopt kids. Sodomy laws in California had been struck down three years earlier, and the right to marry or adopt children was not at the top of the gay agenda. Instead, they were protesting because the first openly gay politician to be elected to office in California, Harvey Milk, had been murdered, and the killer had gotten off with only a seven-year sentence for voluntary manslaughter.[45]

When Milk decided to run for the city board of supervisors in San Francisco, he had an invigorating idea that set him apart from many others in his position. Rather than reach out to powerful members of society for support, he reached downward to some of society's most vulnerable members: disenfranchised homosexuals. Milk successfully rallied the gay community to vote for him, finally winning a seat on the board on his fourth electoral try. His success is perhaps surprising, given that this was still a time when many psychiatrists referred to homosexuality as a mental illness.

Several months later, a conservative supervisor on the board named Dan White decided to resign, for a variety of reasons. He later had second thoughts and asked the mayor to reinstate him. The mayor was originally willing to do so, but changed his mind after being lobbied by other supervisors on the board, including Milk. White, disgruntled about this outcome, expressed his anger by shooting both the mayor and Milk in cold blood in city hall. At the time of his death, Milk had only served in office for eleven months.

During the ensuing murder trial, his defence team proposed that White was bipolar and that the shooting was the result of a severe mood swing. Normally an advocate for nutrition and fitness, White had eaten a lot of junk food on the day before the murders. His lawyers proposed that high sugar intake had likely worsened his mood swing and further diminished his decision-making capacity. Junk food—Ding Dongs and Ho Hos, to be specific—had sent him over the edge. The jury bought what came to be known as the Twinkie Defense, and White, pleading guilty to manslaughter, received only a seven-year sentence.[46] He would end up serving only five years for the murder of two men; he committed suicide less than two years after getting out of prison.

The case received widespread public acclaim and lived on under the moniker of the Twinkie Defense.[47] While it's possible that the jury did believe that Ding Dongs and Ho Hos were the real killers in this case, we cannot help but consider that Milk's homosexuality also played a role in influencing their decision. The jury was composed entirely of white, middle-class San Franciscans, most of whom were Roman Catholic. As we noted earlier, research has shown a link between religiosity and negative attitudes toward homosexuals.[48] Regardless of what role anti-homosexual attitudes played in the jury's decision, San Francisco's gay community did not agree with White's sentencing. They felt angry, leaderless, and disempowered. It was this anger and frustration that fueled their siege of city hall, which eventually came to be called the White Night Riots.

San Francisco was not the only city where homosexuality was being challenged. In fact, it had been decisively challenged in a famous riot ten years earlier, in the so-called Stonewall Riots in New York City, which some see as the beginning of the gay rights movement in the US. After World War I, gay neighbourhoods began to form in Greenwich Village and Harlem. Many men and women recently demobilized from the military had settled here to seek a more satisfactory, independent, and somewhat bohemian lifestyle. Not surprisingly, in the next two decades, they developed a distinctive community and subculture. New York City had passed laws against homosexuality in public and private businesses but, thanks to the proliferation of underground drinking establishments following the enactment of Prohibition, the police were unable to prevent homosexual gatherings in these less well-known places.

But the laws still stood, and by the early 1960s, Mayor Robert Wagner, in his concern about the city's image during the coming 1964 World's Fair, attempted to rid New York City of gay bars. Many liquor licences were revoked and undercover police officers set out to entrap homosexual men in bars, gyms, bath houses, parks, and other public places. If a conversation initiated by a police officer looked as though it was headed for sexual consummation, the homosexual was arrested for solicitation. Eventually, the militant Mattachine Society persuaded Mayor John Lindsay, newly elected in 1965, to end the practice of police entrapment in New York, but they were unable to influence the liquor licencing authority, which enjoyed considerable discretion; gay bars therefore continued to face closure. This posed a significant problem, since homosexuals had few places other than bars where they could meet openly without being harassed or arrested.

Interestingly, almost all of these bars were owned and controlled by organized crime rings, whose owners and operators held their homosexual clientele in low regard, but paid off the police to prevent frequent raids. The Stonewall Inn in Greenwich Village was one such establishment, owned by the notorious Genovese crime family. It was in dilapidated condition, provided poor service, and had no liquor licence; it also lacked fire exits and reliably useable toilets. But it was the only bar in New York City where gay men could dance with one another.

While the police raids eventually became somewhat less common, they were far from over, and on the night of June 27, 1969, the Stonewall Inn was raided. What makes this particular raid notable is that, unlike those in the past, the crowds in the bar fought back. And for several nights afterward protest continued. These few days of vocal outrage constitute what we now know as the Stonewall Riots, which marked the beginning of the gay liberation movement. A little over four decades later, this movement had managed to legalize same-sex marriage in several US states and countries across the world, including Canada.

What Do You Do When the Supreme Court Tells You You're Wrong? Christian fundamentalist groups across the US were faced with this dilemma after the landmark ruling that officially banned anti-sodomy laws throughout the country. On June 26, 2003, the US Supreme Court decided in *Lawrence v. Texas* to strike down the Texas same-sex sodomy law; in this 6-3 ruling, it declared that private, consenting sexual conduct is protected by liberty rights implied by the due process clause of the United States Constitution.

Nonetheless, the Westboro Baptist Church has continued its anti-gay campaign with regular protest activities that include the picketing of homosexual funerals and even flag-burning.[49] The church is based in Kansas, one of the fourteen states that had been forced by the federal government to legalize gay sex.

One group took their cause a step further. After the Supreme Court had granted homosexuals the constitutional right to practice their sexuality, this group managed to infiltrate another country altogether; due to their efforts, the anti-homosexuality movement in Uganda remains alive and kicking today. In 2009, a group of American evangelical preachers travelled to Kampala for a conference designed to educate thousands of Ugandans about the the gay agenda. For three days, these people presented themselves as experts on homosexuality, making unfounded claims about gay men sodomizing teenagers and the gay movement's aim to "defeat marriage-based society and replace it with a culture of sexual promiscuity."[50]

While these two examples show how the US has mistreated its homosexual population in the past, American society to date has not granted equality to gay and lesbian people. In 1996, President Clinton passed a bill that explicitly defined marriage as only occurring between a man and a woman. In 2013, a few states have allowed same-sex couples to marry, but there is still no federal recognition of same-sex marriage. Despite increased support for recognition of the civil liberties of homosexuals, rights legislation has lagged behind in America compared to most other developed liberal democratic countries.[51] Under Prime Minister Pierre Trudeau, Canada repealed its sodomy laws in 1969, thirty-five years before Texas did so—and this was the result of an act of political leadership, not constitutional compulsion. Even the Chinese government, world-famous for its human rights violations, has been more progressive than fourteen US states in repealing their sodomy laws in 1997.

Since Milk harnessed the gay community in San Francisco in order to get elected, gay politics have flourished in the US. Yet influential segments of American society have remained hostile to gay rights. For example, a 2008 ruling of the Supreme Court of California based on an equal protection argument was successful in legalizing gay marriage, until a ballot initiative several months later overturned the decision. On November 5, 2008, the passage of Proposition 8 amended the California Constitution that limited marriages to those between one man and one woman. The political victories of gay America have never swept the whole country; gay sex remains illegal in Texas and thirteen other states, and the political will to change this fact has never existed.

In this context, it is especially good to know that Canada is one of the few countries in the world today that doesn't have any form of legal discrimination against homosexuals. Legal and constitutional institutions were important in bringing about this change. In 2005, Miriam Smith traced the growth of homosexual rights in Canada to Supreme Court decisions based on the Canadian Charter of Rights and Freedoms.[52] Government legislation came after this, but it was prompted by court decisions that protected gay rights.

One of these was the 1995 Canadian Supreme Court ruling that sexual orientation was analogous to other grounds of discrimination covered in the equality clause of the Charter of Rights and Freedoms. This analogy led to many cases that successfully struck down Canadian laws that were deemed anti-homosexual. For example, *M v. H* in 1999 prompted federal recognition of same-sex couples; *Halpern v. Canada*, which legalized same-sex marriage in Ontario, eventually prompted federal legislation in 2005.[53]

Thus, Canada's laws protecting homosexuals from discrimination have not come from Canadian legislation so much as they have come from the Canadian courts. Of course, not all Canadian courts and governments have been equally progressive. For example, Alberta's provincial government actively contested the legal rights of homosexual citizens throughout the 1990s.[54] Nonetheless, Canadian governments and Canadian society have been more favourable to homosexuals than those of the United States.

At the same time, it is important to remember that courts— even Supreme Courts—do not represent popular opinion. They are an elite who are expected to use abstract notions like equality and right to privacy to stop governments from unfairly locking up people like Lawrence and Garner, two Texan men arrested at home in 1998 for having consenting oral sex.

What's interesting about the homosexual movement in Canada and the US is how much gay and lesbian people have had to rely on the judiciary to protect their rights. And because the judiciary has played such a large role in legalizing gay sex in the US and marriage in Canada, it seems as though it is our courts that have become progressive toward homosexuals. Our elected politicians, on the other hand, are lagging behind in protecting gay rights, because they are ever-sensitive—and perhaps overly sensitive—to the wishes of the most traditional segments of the electorate. Modernization theory seems unequipped to explain why this is so. Canada and the US are highly developed, so why are our politics still so anti-homosexual? And why is Canada still faring better than the United States, despite a lower level of economic development?[55]

The Laissez-Faire Europeans

Europe, in many ways, has been at the forefront of homosexual rights. In 2001, the Netherlands, where sodomy laws were abolished in the early 1800s, was the first country to legalize same-sex marriage. Of the ten countries that have nationally legalized same-sex marriage, seven are in Europe. An additional fifteen permit registered civil unions for homosexuals. So, European countries have always treated homosexuals far better than the United States, especially in the case of Scandinavian countries like Sweden and Denmark. For example, Denmark was the first country in the world to recognize a civil union between homosexuals—essentially marriage, but called something else.

But why are these European countries—particularly the Netherlands, Sweden, and Denmark—so much more accepting of homosexuals?[56] What do these societies have in common that could lead them to adopt these pro-homosexual attitudes? For one, Sweden and Denmark have the lowest levels of income inequality of all European countries.[57] In addition, socialist parties in Northwestern Europe tend to have a better record of homosexual emancipation than conservative, Christian, and liberal parties.[58] This seems to suggest that socialism, income equality, and the equal treatment of homosexuals are all related. We will give you more details on this relationship in Chapter 9 , but for the moment, consider some additional evidence that this link really does exist.

First, it seems likely that American and European attitudes toward homosexuality are so different in part because there is a higher level of income equality in Europe, compared to the US. The United States ranks fourth in the world in economic development, yet it ranks sixtieth on measures of income equality.[59] Only two countries that have legalized gay marriage have higher levels of income inequality than the United States: Argentina and South Africa. In general then, we can see a pattern linking income equality and pro-homosexuality (or income inequality and anti-homosexuality).

In this respect, the Netherlands is an anomaly. As the first to legalize gay marriage, it stands out as arguably the most pro-gay European country.[60] And yet the Netherlands has less income equality than other pro-homosexual European countries such as Sweden, Denmark, Norway, and Iceland. Nevertheless, the Netherlands is still a highly developed country with a high level of income equality, compared to most other countries across the world (including Canada).[61]

So, the Netherlands appears to possess the key characteristics needed for homosexual rights to flourish: a high level of development, a high level of income equality, and a tradition of secularism, literacy, and education. But, because other less tolerant countries are also well endowed with these features, these variables alone do not seem to account for why the Netherlands is so far ahead in their gay rights.

Another factor we may need to consider is religion. A study at the University of Oxford found that, throughout the seventies and early eighties, Dutch people became increasingly tolerant of homosexuality. During this time, Dutch religiosity was also on the decline, leading the researchers to conclude that extreme devotion is the most important factor in causing anti-homosexual attitudes.[62] These findings have been found to hold true across Europe.[63] All of the Scandinavian countries that are accepting of homosexuality have low levels of religiosity, compared to the rest of the world. So, if Dutch tolerance comes from a low level of religiosity, likely American anti-homosexuality comes from a high level of religiosity.

A recent survey seems to confirm this theory.[64] The question, "Is religion an important part of your daily life?" was used to measure religiosity in the US. According to the findings, the three most religious states are Mississippi, where 85 percent of the population answered positively; Alabama, at 82 percent; and South Carolina, at 80 percent.[65] All three of these states were among the fourteen that were forced by the Supreme Court to legalize sodomy; seven of the top ten religious states identified by the survey had also been forced to abolish their anti-sodomy laws. On the other hand, four of the top ten *least* religious states currently grant marriage licences to same-sex couples.

So, we have a good deal of research showing that religiosity is often associated with negative attitudes toward homosexuals in the US.[66] This seems to make sense, as many religious texts condemn homosexuality outright. So while some religious denominations have accepted homosexuality, many others have refused to do so, and continue to adhere to religious edicts. It is under religious (for example, Muslim sharia) law that Middle Eastern countries like Saudi Arabia put homosexuals to death.

But if religion is mainly responsible for anti-homosexuality, why does economic inequality appear to be related as well? A study from the University of Illinois shows that a society's level of economic inequality is positively related to the level of religiosity of all of their members, both rich and poor.[67] In other words, countries with higher levels of economic inequality are also more religious. Further, economic inequality may be the precursor to religiosity. Longitudinal research that has been conducted in the US over fifty years found that economic inequality drives religiosity, not the other way around.[68]

One reason for this is that economic deprivation, which can result from economic inequality, increases religiosity. Consider how poorer members of society become needier, and how religious organizations often provide material resources and hope to these people; in turn, poorer people channel their thanks toward religious institutions. If we think about it this way, it makes sense that research has shown that economic inequality produces more religiosity among the poor. However, the same research also shows that the same effect occurs among the richer members as well. Seemingly, this is because religion appeals to the rich as a mechanism of social control, since it explains and justifies the social order: why some people are rich and others poor. Religion is also useful for the rich since it tranquilizes the poor by giving them the hope of heaven, for example. In short, religion promotes the status quo.

Still, religion is not the only problem when it comes to anti-homosexuality. As we noted earlier, people in the Netherlands have a higher level of religiosity than people in Scandinavian countries such as Sweden and Denmark—and yet they are still the least anti-homosexual country in Europe. Even though this seems like a contradiction, it actually points to the more general cause of pro-homosexuality (rather than singling religion out as the cause of anti-homosexuality). Namely, the Dutch are a secular, tolerant, and liberal people: in addition to their acceptance of gay and lesbian people, they have also decriminalized the sale of cannabis, provided prescription heroin to long-term addicts, and legalized prostitution. Dutch laws thus reflect a more liberal notion of what people should be allowed to do, making them laissez-faire not just toward sex, but toward personal choices more generally. The low level of religiosity in Holland is related to this tolerance of alternative lifestyles, allowing gay rights to flourish throughout the country.

Not surprisingly, the United States seems to be on the opposite end of the spectrum, with the world's highest imprisonment rate for drug offenders and harsh laws against people in the sex trade.

The United States—and especially the most traditional, religious states—has repeatedly criminalized these alternative lifestyles by attaching harsh punishments to them. Their intolerant attitude has created a political culture in which anti-homosexuality thrives. And this culture of intolerance is not unrelated to income inequality: as we have seen, vastly unequal societies maintain religiosity, conformity, and the status quo.

Homosexual tolerance, ultimately, rests on an assumption that people with different tastes and desires can be equal nonetheless. Scandinavian and other Western European societies accepted this notion sooner and more thoroughly than did Canadian and US societies—especially the United States. European politicians succeeded in extending rights to homosexuals, but, for a long time, American and Canadian politicians were unable or unwilling to do so. Instead, both the Canadian and American Supreme Courts have had to grant these rights in the face of vocal anti-homosexual minorities. Economic development, though important in spreading secularism and permissiveness, is surely related to homosexual rights. But economic development alone does not ensure the culture of tolerance that we have seen in the Netherlands and Scandinavia.

Stadtluft Macht Frei

(City Air Makes You Free)[69]

Faced with stigma, rejection, and even violence by the people around them, sexual minorities like homosexuals are victims of inequality, just like poor people and racial minorities. The struggle they have faced to gain a measure of acceptance has been especially difficult given their small numbers. As we mentioned earlier, the estimates on sexual orientation vary, depending on how it is defined—if it is based on practices, experiences, self-identification, and so on. But the numbers are undoubtedly small, at around 1 to 2 percent of the total population.[70] So how have homosexuals managed to gain the resources and protection they need to survive as a group?

In the 1970s, an American sociology student named Stephen Murray approached his master's graduate supervisor at the University of Arizona and said that he was interested in researching how gay communities form. He was told, "No one is interested in your lifestyle." But Murray persevered, and what became the book *American Gay* was one of the first studies on how gay and lesbian people mobilize and support one another through the formation of communities powerful enough to influence public opinion.[71]

Murray, like others, noted that cities provide special safe havens for homosexuals, since they allow them to build their own special communities and subcultures. This trend goes back to World War II; according to John D'Emilio, the war itself tended to bring together large numbers of sexually active young men in isolation from family and community constraints.[72] This provided an opportunity for homosexuals to find other homosexuals, just as factories in the Industrial Revolution provided an opportunity for working people to meet large numbers of other working people.

After the war, the gay rights movement was encouraged by a period of general sexual liberation, characterized by the women's movement and the birth control revolution. The availability of safe and certain birth control after 1960 allowed both males and females to concentrate on the pleasures of sex, while avoiding procreation. It was this de facto separation of sexuality from procreation that justified unmarried sex between people of the same gender, as it did between people of different genders. Also, the decreasing double standard around sexuality both increased gender equality and lowered moral anxieties about recreational sex.

Within this context, homosexuals in large cities like San Francisco and New York flocked to the gay life. They created a subculture world with its own institutions, customs, and even language that served to distinguish members from the out-group. These gay/lesbian communities established public places where homosexuals could gather, meet, and socialize, whether at cafés, clubs, or elsewhere. Such communities also provided a training ground for gay norms and values, a milieu in which people could live safely and comfortably, and a chance to receive social support from other members. Today, homosexual communities are increasingly visible in urban centres, with Toronto's gay community among the best known in North America.

These gay communities, like ethnic communities, are institutionally complete, a term the sociologist Raymond Breton created to describe communities that are self-sufficient and self-aware. Institutionally complete communities include all the products and services a person is likely to need, like clubs, newspapers, schools, churches, clinics, and advocacy groups. These communities, by providing for all the practical needs of their members, do a great deal to promote and protect them. We know that ethnic communities do the same by publicizing community issues, promoting local activities, and using schools and churches to maintain group traditions. This is equally true and equally important for other minority groups, which helps to explain the development and existence of communities designed to protect and facilitate homosexuality.

Homosexual communities in more dangerous places—though small and powerless in such an anti-homosexual environment— also help their members to overcome loneliness and isolation, and to deal with the stigmatization they face. In fact, group mobilization and institutional completeness is precisely how most disadvantaged minority groups survive. And through community survival, minority identities are also preserved.

Of course, community formation is often difficult. Like the gay and lesbian communities of New York City and San Francisco, Toronto's gay community used to be routinely harassed and raided by the police. The year 1981, for example, marked a turning point in the history of the Canadian gay rights movement with what has come to be known as the Bathhouse Riots. In response to police victimization, the LGBT community launched a protest in which two thousand people gathered at Queen's Park (the home of Ontario's provincial legislature) to express their outrage. At the time, this was the largest gay demonstration seen in Canada. But in its wake, many new gay organizations sprang up in Toronto and existing ones grew rapidly, all the while with growing access to resources. The City of Toronto also commissioned a report to examine and improve the relationship between police and the LGBT community; progress was eventually made.

The communities that have managed to form are increasingly celebrated. City planner and policy researcher Richard Florida[73] has noted that cities with large homosexual populations typically have high levels of the artistic and intellectual creativity that are central to the prosperity of knowledge-based economies. The result is a high level of innovation and economic growth in the service sector and a higher quality of life for all city residents. So, in this case as in many others, we discover that human diversity pays off economically, as well as socially and culturally.

PART 2

The Power of
Life and Death

CHAPTER 6

Sickness and Stigmatization

———— • ◆ • ————

"Of all the things I've lost, I miss my mind the most."
Mark Twain

In this chapter and the next two, we will show that inequality carries heavy costs for society. This chapter will focus on health problems that are a consequence of the inequalities we have discussed so far. In the two chapters that follow, we will consider crime and large-scale societal conflict, including war, as other consequences of inequality. In the end, the costly consequences of inequality—widespread sickness, crime, and death—are what make inequality an important topic not only for sociologists but for the public as a whole.

We start by acknowledging that a great many factors influence people's health. Some causes of ill health are genetic or present at birth, although genetic predispositions are probably activated by environmental factors we will discuss. Some causes of ill health are related to biological aging; we all decline physically and sicken before we die—some for longer periods than others. And of course, there are many social factors that affect poor health—factors like workplace dangers and poverty, for example. However, in this chapter we will focus on the role played by social inequality, especially economic inequality, but also inequalities stemming from other differences that have been defined socially as important in societies.

There is probably nothing that Canadians care about more than good health, as shown by the fact that the largest and most rapidly growing portion of Canada's gross national product is devoted to health care. Also, most Canadians consider any threat to good universal health care—for example, evidence that waiting times are too long—is a serious issue. At the same time, more and more Canadians are concluding that bad health is easier to prevent than it is to cure. In Canada, and even more in the US, people lose more person-years of healthy life through preventable causes than they do through infectious or even degenerative diseases. Thus, there is a general growing understanding that public health measures are the best way to guarantee Canadians remain healthy. Such measures aim to reduce smoking, improve eating patterns (thus reducing obesity), and promote exercise, for example—three main ways to increase the likelihood of a long, healthy life.

But good health requires both a sound mind and a sound body. The mind and body are connected; they work together, and an illness in one is likely to harm the other. Therefore, "good health" means both good mental health and good physical health. As we will see, both mental health and physical health are undermined by social inequality. And good health is easily lost: we must all take preventive measures to ensure we remain healthy against the endless ravages of time and an (often) unforgiving environment.

Current views on the topic reflect, first, the present-day public health conception of health—best enunciated by the World Health Organization (WHO). In WHO documents, we see stated clearly the view of health as a state of general well-being—not merely the bodily response to a targeted medical intervention.

So, Canadians are in favour of preventing premature death and suffering, and they know this can be done by stressing good diet, exercise, and the cessation of smoking. What fewer Canadians know is that we can also prevent premature death and suffering through the reduction of social inequality and the stigma surrounding health problems. That is, we can increase the health and longevity of Canadians by breaking our habits of inequality. This chapter argues that we need to look at our habits of social inequality as a public health problem, and we need to be as dedicated in the battle against inequality as we have been in the battle against smoking and obesity. Our goal, then, will not merely be justice and fairness, it will also be better health and increased longevity.

Social Inequality and Health

Increasingly in the last few decades, health has gained interest in the social research community for several reasons. First, with the aging of national populations in the West, health and health care have become increasing sources of concern—and expense—in all Western societies. Second, Canadians, like most other people, place a great deal of value on good health as a type of well-being and life quality, as we have already said.

Beyond these factors, health is particularly interesting to social scientists as a way of measuring whether society is working well or not. The overall health or sickness of a population tells us how well government, the economy, the family, and other social institutions are playing their expected role. In this respect, health is a more sensitive and secure indicator of well-being than happiness or life satisfaction. Naturally, happiness and life satisfaction are important, since we all strive to maximize our happiness and satisfaction, though we may define these things in different ways. The problem is that people tend to readjust their expectations of happiness downward when they encounter adversity.

Said simply, people who experience disappointment over an extended period tend to lower their goals, so that they can be happy (or satisfied) with relatively little. Thus, we find reasonably high levels of satisfaction in all populations above the most deprived 20 percent or so of humanity. Once the minimum needs for food, shelter, and safety are met, people find similar degrees of happiness in family life, social life, religion, and even work—despite widely divergent material conditions.

So, the human mind is almost infinitely capable of persuading itself to settle for what is available. However, the human body is less able to continually adjust downward. Under conditions of adversity—especially, continued adversity—both minds and bodies show signs of stress, decline, and diminished functioning. These signs include mental illnesses like anxiety and depression and physical illnesses like chronic pain, psychosomatic disorders, and poor cardiovascular functioning, among others. The mind may often let us lie to ourselves about happiness, but the body is less compromising in this respect: our bodies don't lie, even when our minds want to do so. That is why physical and mental illnesses are better indicators of societal malfunctioning than are measures of happiness and life satisfaction.

Health is also an easy measure to use, because medical doctors have become so good at measuring health precisely. What's more, researchers have even found that people's self-reports of their health are usually quite accurate. That said, using health to measure social functioning is not without its difficulties. The main problem is that so many factors influence health. Age, sex, genetic makeup, living conditions, work stress, environmental pollution, and transient germ populations all influence a person's health on any given day. Then there are the chronic and transient stresses in people's lives that also influence their health: events such as divorce, job loss, family crisis, and so on. Amid this welter of competing factors, we have trouble separating out the contribution of social inequality—our variable of key interest in this book.

However, it is not merely the volume of influences that causes us analytical problems. It is also the interconnection of influences. Consider the many connections between inequality, poverty, work stress, and environmental pollution: comfortably well-off, middle-class people are typically freer of all these influences than homeless, unemployed, underemployed, and low-income working people (for example). So, it is difficult to isolate the unique contribution of inequality if our goal is to determine how a reduction of inequality might reduce adverse health outcomes.

Another problem is called the "ecological fallacy," and it appears in one of the earliest sociological works—the classic study *Suicide* by French sociologist Emile Durkheim.[1] In that work, Durkheim proposes that suicide rates are highly correlated with social integration and social stability—as society becomes less integrated and less stable, the suicide rates go up. Further, Durkheim suggests, at any given moment, people whose lives are less socially integrated and less socially stable are more likely than average to commit suicide, because people cannot stand to be isolated or unregulated. This he demonstrates by showing, for example, that highly isolated, unregulated people—for example, men who are divorced or single—are at greater risk of suicide than people (especially women) who are married with children.

The problem here, as critics have pointed out for over a century, is that Durkheim's method—what he deems the uniquely sociological method of correlating rates of occurrence—is subject to the ecological fallacy. Simply put, this fallacy consists in attributing to individuals the characteristics of groups. Imagine two groups: A and B. People in Group A have a low average level of social integration and high rate of suicide. People in Group B have a high average level of social integration and low rate of suicide. It is tempting but unjustified to conclude from these facts that a low level of integration increases the risk of suicide—unjustified because we do not know, from these facts, whether the individuals committing suicide in either group are poorly integrated. Other variables may account for the suicides. Only a direct study of individuals can make the link between suicide and integration, and such a direct study is hard to carry out, especially where the outcome is relatively uncommon, as suicide is.

Consider now the problem of social inequality and its effects on health. What will it take to prove that a 10 percent increase in inequality causes a 10 percent (or 5 percent or even 1 percent) increase in premature mortality, heart disease, or depression? First, we will need statistics from at least two different moments or periods, to measure change in the variables of interest. Second, we will need to show how an increase in societal inequality may have translated into higher numbers of dead, sick, or depressed people. Third, we will (ideally) want to show that the people most directly affected by inequality are the same people whose health goes into the deepest decline.

So, for example, consider the period 1980 to 2008, when a widespread increase in social inequality began with Reaganite policies in the US and Thatcherite policies in the UK, with similar effects in parts of Canada (for example, in Ontario under Premier Mike Harris's severely anti-welfare and anti-union Conservative government). Such increases in inequality were associated with widespread deregulation of markets and businesses, and cuts in social spending and taxes on the wealthy. Combined with the export of manufacturing jobs to low-wage foreign countries, these increases of inequality threw many people out of work and, in 2008, also took away many people's homes and life savings.

What was the effect of this increased inequality on people's health? As mentioned, the answer is hard to calculate precisely. To answer this, we would need to know whether and to what extent the losses in health were mainly suffered by people who endured the main consequences of inequality: that is, by the people who lost their jobs, homes, and savings, for example.

Now, suppose that we could show that the people who lost their jobs, homes, and savings, among other things, were indeed the people whose health declined the most. How would we then prove that inequality was to blame for this health decline and not poverty—the absolute deprivation that results from inequality—and the stresses associated with poverty? In principle, it would be possible to separate these factors, but we would need a lot of precise data to do so.

Solving this problem is important, because different research results would point to different social policies. If poverty were to blame for worsened health, then the appropriate social intervention (arguably) would be to grow the economy and improve welfare payments, employment insurance, and job creation programs. If inequality were to blame, then the appropriate social intervention would be to raise taxes at the upper end of the income scale and increase regulation of the means by which the rich get richer (for example, through more regulation of stock and land speculation, and more restrictions on the export of jobs and capital).

This simplified account of the methodological problem helps us understand the conclusion drawn in a thoughtful review of the literature by Adam Wagstaff and Eddy van Doorslaer,[2] which ends in the following way:

> We have concluded that data from aggregate-level studies of the effect of income inequality on health . . . are largely insufficient to discriminate between competing hypotheses. Only individual-level studies have the potential to discriminate between most of the advanced hypotheses. The relevant individual-level studies to date, all on U.S. population data, provide strong support for the "absolute-income hypothesis," no support for the "relative-income hypothesis," and little or no support for the "income-inequality hypothesis." . . . Overall, the absolute-income hypothesis, though >20 years old, is still the most likely to explain the frequently observed strong association between population health and income inequality levels.[3]

By absolute-income hypothesis, the authors mean the hypothesis that poverty—a shortage of actual dollars—causes a person's health problems. The relative-income hypothesis is the one about inequality. So it is absolute poverty, rather than relative deprivation, which causes ill health, according to these authors. The problem is not inequality, such as a shortage compared to the nextdoor neighbour, nor the extent of inequality in the community, state, or country as a whole. The problem is just a deficiency of dollar bills.

Why, in the face of such an unambiguous conclusion, does a debate continue to rage about the link between inequality and health? There are several important reasons. First, as Wagstaff and van Doorslaer note, their conclusions are based entirely on US data. As we have seen repeatedly, the US is an unusual country—indeed, the most unequal and unregulated of all developed Western societies. So, it would be foolhardy to draw strong, universal conclusions from US data. Second, aggregate-level studies have predominated—and continue to predominate—because they are easier and less costly to do, in this and every other area of social science inquiry. However, for many reasons, they are largely inconclusive for policy purposes. There is no telling what we will find out when more individual-level, longitudinal studies have been completed on large populations.

Consider an example of such a study. Swedish research by Ulf-G. Gerdtham and Magnus Johanneson[4] used "a random sample from the adult Swedish population of more than 40,000 individuals who were followed up for 10–17 years." The researchers found "that mortality decreases significantly as individual income increases. For mean community income and community income inequality we cannot, however, reject the null hypothesis of no effect on mortality."[5] This supports Wagstaff and van Doorslaer's conclusion, but leaves open at least one other possibility: that poverty is the immediate cause of health problems, but it is also a common outcome of inequality. Thus, inequality is the final cause of health problems, even if poverty is the efficient (or immediate) cause.

One might reasonably argue that inequality causes poor health by means of increasing poverty (or a shortage of absolute income), and there are many reasons to make such a claim. But Wagstaff and van Doorslaer may also be right to argue that researchers haven't yet connected all the dots in this argument. As yet, much of the "social inequality causes poor health" argument remains compellingly and coherently suggestive—but only suggestive—especially when we look at keystone works like the Whitehall Studies we will discuss shortly.

Today, the dominant viewpoint among population health researchers is that "social inequality causes poor health" and is indeed the strongest, most comprehensive understanding of how social factors affect health. Indeed, when one speaks to other researchers about population health or the social determinants of health, one is almost axiomatically assumed to be speaking about social inequality.

Thus, in the current population health literature, we find repeated validation of the "social inequality causes poor health" conclusion. Consider here only a few of the many recent studies that have made this claim. John Asafu-Adjaye concludes from panel data for forty-four countries covering six time periods that

> income inequality (measured by the Gini index) has a significant effect on health status when we control for levels of income, savings, and education. The relationship is consistent regardless of the specification of health status and income.[6]

Backlund, Rowe, Lynch, Wolfson, Kaplan, and Sorlie conclude from the US National Longitudinal Mortality Study that

> income inequality is not a major driver of mortality trends in the United States because most deaths occur at ages 65 and over. This [current] analysis does suggest, however, the certain causes of death that occur primarily in the population under 65 may be associated with income inequality . . . but further research is needed to provide a definitive answer.[7]

Karlsson, Nilsson, Lyttkens and Leeson use a

> dataset containing information collected in 2006 on individuals aged 40–79 in 21 countries. . . . The dependent variable is self-assessed health, and as a robustness check, activities of daily living (ADL) are considered. . . . Correcting for national differences in health reporting behaviour, . . . in the high-income sample, there is strong evidence that average income within a peer group is negatively related to health, thus supporting the relative income hypothesis. . . . Finally, there is evidence of a negative relationship between income inequality and individual health in high-income countries.[8]

In the pages that follow, we will unpack this debate and consider the best-known, most visible evidence that social inequality has important health consequences.

Where the Halls Are White

The classic and most famous proof that inequality causes bad health is found in the so-called Whitehall Studies.[9] These two studies, carried out over the period 1967–88 examined detailed health information on British civil servants. Their findings were shocking for the time. They found that death rates from chronic heart disease were three times higher among workers in the lower civil service jobs than among workers in the higher civil service jobs. Even after controlling for lifestyle risks like smoking and obesity, a worker in the lowest job grade was still twice as likely to die of cardiovascular disease as a worker in the highest grade. The conclusion is that being on the bottom rung of the inequality ladder is dangerous for your health.

This gradient in health and health-related behaviours was observed across the entire job spectrum and every decrease in job grade corresponded with an increase in health risk. For example, not only were the civil servants in the highest grade more likely to be healthier than the civil servants in the lowest grade but they were also more likely to be healthier than the civil servants in the grade immediately below. This fine grain gradient in health gives support to the phrase, "the poor are always with us." In this way, economic inequality is not only relevant at the lower end of the class hierarchy, though it is at this end where inequality takes its greatest toll on well-being. That equality has the potential to benefit the entire society makes economic inequality everybody's problem.

Another way to make sense of this finding is there is not just one class divide between the haves and have-nots along which good health is distributed. There are gradations of health, just as there are gradations of income and class, and the two are related. The question is, how are they related? How does lower (relative) income, status, or rank, translate into lower (relative) health? We are not talking about poverty now—indeed, in the Whitehall Studies, we are talking about people with secure, adequate incomes.

Start with the observation that social inequality tends to correlate with social fragmentation, poorer social relations, and a lack of autonomy for people in the lower ranks. Poorer communities, for example, tend to be less safe, less beautiful, and less relaxing than richer communities. These and other social factors increase the stress level of people who live in these communities. Such social stressors can cause mood disorders that compromise health, such as depression and anxiety.

These social experiences, in turn, are linked to the release of cortisol, a hormone produced by the body as a response to stress. When cortisol is released into the body, the immune system loses some of its effectiveness. The more times that stress causes this to happen, the more the immune system is compromised and the more vulnerable a person becomes to infectious disease. One theory is that infectious pathogens are at least partly responsible for coronary diseases. Therefore, a person with a severely suppressed immune system will be less able to prevent cardiovascular disease.

Cortisol levels fluctuate over the day, and they respond to dangers (or stresses) in the environment. For example, in one study, workers showed no significant difference in cortisol levels upon awakening, regardless of their socio-economic position.[10] However, within thirty minutes after waking, the lower employment grades showed significantly higher levels, especially on workdays, presumably because they were anticipating chronic stress at work.

Work naturally occupies a substantial portion of adult life, such that the work environment can play a crucial role in influencing health. Differences in job control appear to produce differences in stress: lower status means more stress, since the worker is less able to control the work setting. People in low-status jobs have less control over their work than people in higher-status jobs. When combined with more or harsher demands, this absence of control produces more stress. This uncontrolled stress may lead to higher blood pressure and higher risk of chronic heart disease, or to infection that is connected with heart disease, as mentioned earlier.

In the second Whitehall Study, researchers tried to capture stress at work in three different dimensions: effort-reward imbalance, job strain, and organisational justice.[11] Organisational justice refers to the fairness of decision-making processes and interpersonal relationships in the workplace. All three indicators of stress at work have been linked to coronary heart disease, with risk of heart disease escalating with increasing unfairness. Additionally, coronary heart disease has been linked to poor social support and low autonomy in the workplace, as well as to depression, anxiety, and hostility. Even though the Whitehall cohorts constitute employed, well-adjusted adults, the results are likely applicable to a vast number of people.

The Whitehall Studies have been replicated many times and continue to be replicated today; similar findings are reported for many occupations. The Whitehall Studies are classic because they changed the way social scientists thought about problems such as health issues. In the past, researchers believed that the relationship between income and health was driven by the poor health of those groups of people within society that lived in poverty.[12] These groups had low absolute levels of income, and the associated deprivations that come with not being able to purchase even the most basic of needs was seen as the channel by which income and health were related.

As the average income of citizens increased over time in developed countries like the United States and Canada, the conditions of life changed, and only a small number of people can now be classified as living in a state of absolute poverty.[13] However, the income-health gradient has not diminished over time, suggesting some other income-related effect is creating health inequalities. Contrary to what busy executives might like you to believe, it is far more stressful to be a waitress than to be a bank president. This is because, while a bank president can get rid of irritating people, a waitress has to serve them.[14]

So, both relative deprivation (that is, inequality) and absolute deprivation (that is, poverty) affect people's health and longevity.

Absolute income speaks to the direct impact of the material environment on health as well as the indirect, psychosocially mediated, impact of material wealth. Meanwhile relative deprivation speaks to the issue of income inequality—the fact that income is not distributed equally to all members of a society. A small number of people receive a disproportionately large share, a larger number get amounts close to the country's average income, and many groups receive significantly less than the national average.[15]

While income inequality has an influence on both high- and low-income groups, it has a much greater negative effect on low-income groups.[16] Although an average increase in income leads to increases in average health, low-income earners do not benefit from this, because of relative deprivation.[17] For example, looking at American research (because that is where most of the studies are found), people who live in American states that have high levels of income inequality are more likely to report poor or fair health than people who live in states with low levels of income inequality.[18] Similarly, people who live in areas with high income inequality report fewer healthy days on average.[19] People living in regions of high income inequality also have a higher risk of premature mortality.[20] Researchers estimate that lowering the Gini Index of inequality below the threshold of 0.3 would help prevent 1.5 million adult deaths in the United States per year.[21]

What links income inequality to health inequality continues to be the subject of considerable debate. One hypothesis is that income inequality causes health inequality due to a disinvestment in human capital. According to this hypothesis, states that are less egalitarian in their income distributions spend less on social programs.[22] They do so because people with high incomes want lower taxes and consequently less government investment in public services for the poor. People with more wealth and power are able to do this, without harm to themselves. They can cut taxes to protect their personal wealth, have the means to privately fund education and health care for themselves and their families, and do not depend on the public safety infrastructure that the taxes fund.[23]

Less money being spent on health education and preventive care means social environments that cannot develop and maintain healthy behaviours.[24] Ironically, poorer but more equal countries have better health outcomes for the mass of the population because they distribute social resources—health care, education and welfare, among others—more fairly.[25] They achieve this by taxing the wealthier members of society and redistributing resources to the poorer members of society.[26]

Another hypothesis focuses on inequalities in access to resources. Not everyone has the same access to important and beneficial goods, services, and information.[27] Several important resources—income, education, power, and social prestige—can all be related to health.[28] A person with more of these resources is better able to maintain a healthy lifestyle, for example. The same person is also better able to get the best medical treatment available, in the event of an illness. The resources that are associated with a high SES (socio-economic status) are flexible: they can be used in many different ways under different scenarios. And, as we know, they are unequally distributed in a society.

Thus, understanding socio-economic inequality is key to understanding health inequality. These "flexible resources" are central to understanding the causes that operate at both individual and contextual levels.[29] They do so by influencing whether people know about, have access to, can afford, and receive social support for their efforts to engage in health-enhancing or health-protective behaviours.

At the individual level, flexible resources shape individual health behaviours. Income inequality causes health inequality through its influence on behaviours that can be damaging to or protective of health.[30] For example, people might smoke to compensate for unpleasant living conditions that result from low income.[31] The unequal distribution of protective behavioural factors across people of different socio-economic statuses can also be explained in part by the unequal access to material factors. People occupying the lower stratum of an unequal society may not be able to afford dental care and other services not covered by Canadian Medicare and many provincial health plans, and as a result, certain important aspects of their health are neglected.

At the community level, a high-SES person is more likely to live in a high-SES neighbourhood, where there is a significant emphasis on ensuring that crime, noise, pollution, violence, and traffic are minimized, or eliminated entirely. Such neighbourhoods are often near top-notch health care facilities, excellent schools, clean and safe playgrounds, and well-stocked, high-quality grocery stores.[32] On this last matter, consider access to healthy food. Healthy and nutritious foods are more expensive than junk foods, and poorer people are less able to readily access healthy foods than wealthier people.[33] And even if poorer people wanted to eat healthier, they are more likely to live in areas with little or no access to grocery stores selling good-quality food and better-quality restaurants they can afford. Therefore, income inequality can potentially lead to poorer eating patterns among the poor, which in turn can lead to poorer health.

Another hypothesis about how inequality leads to health problems focuses on the role of social capital and trust as primary determinants of health disparities.[34] Social capital refers to the strength of the connections people feel to one another. The hypothesis says income or class inequality increases the risks to health by breaking down social cohesion. Greater income inequality leads to communities that are low in social capital and are thus less able to achieve cooperation for mutual benefit.[35]

Another problem is that inequality impedes the formation of new social capital.[36] For one thing, reduced cohesion increases the risk of social conflict. People who live in non-cohesive neighbourhoods are more likely to suffer from isolation, loneliness, and criminal victimization. Studies have also found that high social capital in communities advocates individual and community health by increasing and promoting access to local processes, healthy norms of behaviour, psychosocial support toward leading a healthy lifestyle, and following health-related norms set by community leaders or experts.[37]

Less social cohesion also means less social support in the event of a problem: less financial and social aid, less emotional and spiritual support, less health care information and access, and more high-risk behaviours. A socially non-cohesive society reduces the level of trust among people in the society, and leads to feelings of vulnerability and isolation. This in turn harms health by causing stress and depression. Stress and depression are often gateways to drinking, smoking, and other health-compromising behaviours.[38] More social inequality, combined with high levels of distrust, also decreases people's confidence that public money will be spent to improve health.[39]

In a recent study, researchers even calculated how many people social inequality kills.[40] They asked, "If we can say that behaviours like smoking cigarettes kill people, why can't we make the same argument for social factors, such as inequality and poverty?" The researchers reviewed earlier studies on the effects of six social factors, all based on large national surveys. They then pooled the data and calculated what proportion of deaths each social factor accounts for. It turns out that 291,000 US deaths a year are due to poverty and income inequality. For the sake of comparison, consider the numbers for accidents (119,000) and lung cancer (156,000). So, more people die from being absolutely or relatively poor than those from accidents and lung cancer combined. Even in societies that are highly developed, the health impact of income inequality is not offset by other positive societal factors (for example, overall prosperity and the general availability of health care).

The Cuckoo's Nest: Mental Health and Addiction

Perched on an island a short boat ride from St. Mark's Square in Venice stands the grand San Clemente Palace. Today it is a luxurious, five-star hotel and resort, complete with high Venetian ceilings, gourmet restaurants, Old World bars, a shimmering pool, tennis courts, and a luxury spa. But the palace also has a darker history, which it does not readily acknowledge.

During the Crusades nine hundred years ago, the island was the site of a hospital for pilgrims returning from the Middle East. It was later converted to a convent and then used as a quarantine station during the Black Death to separate the plagued bodies from the healthy. It then became Europe's first mental institution for women and offered psychiatric procedures until 1992.[41]

The present-day hotel does not boast about its long and (some might say illustrious) past as a mental hospital. Today, the only shock therapy you'll receive is when the bill arrives. Otherwise, there is no allusion to the hotel's association with mental illness, which is potentially stigmatizing. But what exactly is a mental illness or disorder, and why is it stigmatizing? According to Health Canada, a mental disorder is any condition "characterized by alterations in thinking, mood, or behaviour (or some combination thereof) associated with significant distress and impaired functioning over an extended period of time."[42] Mental disorder and mental illness are often used interchangeably, but it is important to distinguish the two.

Formally, the term mental illness should only be used for clinical diagnoses that require medical or psychiatric treatment. Mental disorders, on the other hand, are more numerous and wide ranging, but they are far from trivial. Nor are mental illnesses and disorders to be confused with the momentary feelings of loneliness, sadness, or emotional agitation that we all experience. Mental disorders and illnesses pose serious limits to people's ability to carry out their daily lives and interrupt the normal functioning of families, schools, workplaces, and other social institutions.

At the same time, their causes are poorly understood, and public ignorance—or at least, unawareness of the facts—contributes to a general sense of unease and stigmatization by the public. The professionally accepted classification for mental illnesses is the American Psychiatric Association (APA) *Diagnostic and Statistical Manual of Mental Disorders (DSM-IV)*.[43] It describes the most common categories of mental illnesses, including anxiety disorders, mood disorders (including depression and bipolar disorder), schizophrenia and other forms of psychosis, dementias (including Alzheimer's disease), eating disorders (including anorexia nervosa and bulimia), and personality disorders, such as obsessive compulsive disorder (OCD).

Experts now agree that most mental illnesses arise from an interaction of genetic (or biological), psychological, and social (or environmental) factors. Let's focus on the social elements of mental illness, since they are the least often discussed. Major social disruptions, such as wars or natural disasters, for example, can trigger the development of mental illness through stress and the breakdown of social order; they also trigger or release antisocial tendencies that, in stable times, might remain dormant. In general, the individualistic nature and fast pace of life in present-day industrial societies erode traditional sources of social stability like family and religion, also increasing the risks of mental illness. And, most relevant to our current interest, social inequality—through its creation of stress and blame—contributes importantly to the development of mental illness.

In industrial nations, major depression, bipolar disorder, schizophrenia, and OCD are four of the ten leading kinds of mental illness. Mental illness is the leading cause of disability in Canada.[44] In Canada, mental disorders have a combined lifetime prevalence rate of 20 percent, meaning one person in five—or six million Canadians—will suffer from a mental disorder at some point during their lifetime.[45] And often, the presence of one mental disorder—for example, depression—predisposes an individual to another one—for example, addiction. This condition is known as co-morbidity. According to a major study of mental illness involving ten thousand adults in the United States, 45 percent of people who experienced any mental illness within the past twelve months suffered from more than one disorder during that time.[46] So, paradoxically, mental illnesses—though widely feared, ridiculed, and stigmatized—are all around us, affecting all our lives, and sapping the productivity of our society.

No social class or social group is free of mental illness. Mental illness affects all types of people. However, not everyone is equally at risk for mental illness, and that's the point to keep in mind. There are in fact social patterns and social causes to mental illness—to its onset, trajectory, and control. For example, research continues to show that depression is more common among poor people, who typically suffer more stress due to poverty, inequality, and work-place control. And mental health is poorer among marginalized ethnic and cultural groups, especially Aboriginal populations, prob-ably for reasons associated with stress, deprivation, and experien-ces of violence.

It remains unclear whether the mental illnesses found among poor people are mainly because of poverty or because mentally ill people are more likely than healthy people to drift down into pov-erty. Both processes—what sociologists call social causation and social selection—are likely at work. One thing is certain: mental illness arises out of adverse social conditions, thrives in adverse conditions, and further worsens those conditions for the mentally ill individual.

Mental illness rates vary for all of the dimensions of inequality discussed in this book. For example, overall rates of most mental illnesses are higher among women than among men, though sub-stance abuse and addiction are higher among men. Mental health is also poorer among marginalized groups, especially Aboriginal populations, as we mentioned. As a result, Aboriginal communities have much higher suicide rates than those for the general popula-tion. In short, groups disadvantaged by other forms of inequality—by exploitation, prejudice, discrimination, and victimization, for example—are also at the greatest risk of mental illness and the stig-matization that results from it.

Today, the stigma of mental illness is weaker than in the past, as we have come to better understand its causes. Over the past two centuries, views and norms bearing on mental illness have come under the domination of (especially medical) experts, through medicalization. They have been taken out of a religious and moral context and viewed in terms of the disease model of illness, to be cured through medical, pharmaceutical, or psychiatric treatment.

Early explanations of mental illness involved evil spirits and demons. Some pre-industrial societies were gently tolerant of mentally ill people, whom they viewed as simpletons or holy fools. Others, however, believed that the strange behaviours associated with mental illness were a result of spells or a punishment for wrongdoing, or were due to the acts of malevolent witches or devils. As a result, some communities tortured people who suffered from mental illnesses (especially, people suffering from delusions) in an attempt to drive out the demons.

Andrew Scull, a medical sociologist, gives an example of the kinds of procedures performed during the eighteenth century in an attempt to cure madness:

> Benjamin Rush was probably the most famous American physician of the revolutionary era. Rush was known as "The Bleeder." He bled his patients for madness. He also invented something called "The Tranquilizer." It's a chair that looks a little bit like an electric chair. The patient was confined in this apparatus, sometimes with cold water applied to his or her head for some hours at a time.[47]

Not surprisingly, torture failed to return people to sanity, and there is a long human history of efforts, some more successful than others, to look for alternative (that is, scientific) cures. One long-lived treatment was hospitalization in places like Bedlam—the early and notorious mental hospital in London, whose proper name is the Bethlem Royal Hospital. There, in Europe's first and oldest institution to specialize in mental illnesses, mentally ill people were sometimes chained to walls, so the rest of the world could forget they existed. Or, the public could visit to watch (and perhaps be entertained by) the suffering of imprisoned maniacs.

In time, the name Bedlam came to be synonymous with the uproarious behaviour of mentally ill inmates. Bedlam was the earliest, but far from the last, attempt that people made to isolate and warehouse mentally ill people, supposedly for their own safety and that of others. However, as time passed, hospitals and asylums began trying to cure the mentally ill, using the medical knowledge at their disposal. They also began to treat mentally ill patients in the same way as other patients, providing cleaner surroundings, better care and nutrition, fresh air, and light. Nineteenth-century advocates fought successfully to see mental institutions adopt more humane treatments toward the mentally ill.

War contributed significantly to an improved treatment of the mentally ill. A growth of compassion was especially marked with the rise of professional nursing during the Crimean War, and surge in casualties associated with warfare. During World War I, medical caregivers discovered that emotional problems and shell shock had disabled many soldiers returning home from the front. Many previously normal people had fallen into mental illness because of their combat experiences. We see similar problems among soldiers returning from warfare today (from Iraq and Afghanistan, for example) and call the illness post-traumatic stress disorder (PTSD).

A century ago, doctors began to reason that if a trauma such as warfare could cause mental disorder, then lesser traumas, occurring more often, might produce the same effect. This was a crucial insight about the effects of stress and trauma on mental functioning, and in due course, this insight would transform our understanding of mental illness.

However, popular opinion about mental illness was slow to change. Most people continued to view shell shock as a disgrace rather than an illness—as a demonstration of cowardice and moral weakness. Many imagined that soldiers suffering from shell shock lacked the moral strength (the guts) needed for combat. There was a tendency to view mental illness as a moral flaw, rather than as a medical problem or the result of a traumatic experience. Such moralistic, stigmatizing interpretations likely contributed to the continued concealment (and worsening) of mental illness.

Our modern understanding of mental illness began around the time of World War II and the development of modern chemical treatments. In the 1940s and 1950s, researchers found medications that helped the severely mentally ill to cope with their illness. And with these discoveries, people began to realize that if the cures of mental illness were chemical then the causes might be chemical as well—not moral.

Social research also helped to increase popular understanding of mental illness. With the rise of modern quantitative social science in the latter half of the twentieth century, researchers developed a better sense of the way social factors influence mental illness. Modern surveys of mental health, like modern surveys of crime and physical illness, have helped to spread public health conceptions of mental illness—an understanding that social factors contribute to the problem. In principle, anyone at all could become mentally ill if they lived in pathogenic conditions or endured a pathogenic experience (for example, traumatization at war or life in a violent household).

Thanks to this research, we know that some mental illnesses are more prevalent in some communities and some population groups than others. Neighbourhood disadvantages—poverty and danger, for example—are associated with higher-than-average rates of major depression and substance abuse. In low-income neighbourhoods, high rates of residential mobility—that is, high rates of people moving in and out of the neighbourhood—are also associated with higher rates of schizophrenia, major depression, and substance abuse. This means that normal, healthy people run an increased risk of becoming mentally ill if they move into a neighbourhood characterized by poverty, danger, and weak social ties.

Definitions of mental illness have also broadened in the last fifty years, and the rejection and stigmatization of mentally ill people has decreased. Today, we are all more familiar with a wide variety of less dramatic, less visible forms of mental illness—chiefly, neuroses. We all know people with anxiety issues, occasional depressive issues, impulse control issues, compulsions, obsessions, and addictions, for example. However, the view that mentally ill people are typically violent or frightening continues to persist, thanks in large part to the terrifying treatment of the topic by the mass media. As a result, fearful and exclusionary attitudes toward people with mental illnesses remain common in some communities.

This is partially because those who are mentally ill, even more than those who are physically ill, are stigmatized. The term stigma has a long history. In ancient Greece, it referred to a brand or mark of shame placed on outcast groups, so others could readily identify and shun them. The term entered sociology mainly through the work of Erving Goffman, who wrote a classic book on the topic titled *Stigma*.[48] This useful concept turns our attention to a process of devaluation that creates and maintains inequality. Stigma, then, is not a fixed characteristic of people, but a social attribution made by some people against other people, under particular conditions.

In his book, Goffman reports studies of people who are not seen as normal and who are stigmatized by other members of society for their appearance or other discreditable features. Goffman opens the book with a letter to an advice column written by an unusual young girl. She claims to have been born without a nose; her letter describes how her classmates mock her and her mother cries whenever she looks at her. This is only one poignant example among many that Goffman uses to illustrate his point. The reasons for stigmatization are many and varied. They include anything that distinguishes a person socially from the ideal or the statistical average. But because mental illness is often something that is unseen, in the past and even in the present it tends to be more severely stigmatized than physical conditions.

Stigmatization in general arises out of social interaction. In any interaction, both parties try to present themselves and others involved as normal, avoiding any reference to taboo or stigmatized characteristics. Typically, everyone wants the interaction to succeed, and Goffman is interested in the processes by which people make this happen. So, much of his book explores the ways in which stigmatized people try to manage their interactions to appear more normal. Usually, they do so by using the strategies of passing and covering.

Passing is the effort to disguise discreditable facts (for example, past imprisonment or treatment in a mental hospital) through a process of impression management. Some people take more active steps to disguise the facts: for example, they hide their histories by inventing new ones, and hide their ethnic origins by changing their surnames or resorting to plastic surgery. In every case, the potentially stigmatized person tries to appear as typical or mainstream as possible. However, some potentially discrediting features, such as dark skin colour, are harder to disguise than others, so passing is not always possible.

Covering is the strategy used by people whose stigmatizing feature is visible or well-known. Their strategy is not to manage that information—that is impossible—but to manage the tension arising from their discreditable features. The discredited person tries to deflect attention from the stigmatizing feature so the interaction can continue in a normal, relaxed way. So, for example, a blind person might learn how to copy the behaviours of people who can see. They don't pretend they can see—they only strive to make their blindness less noticeable or intrusive. Joking is another way to reduce tension about the stigmatizing feature: for example, a blind person might make jokes about bumping into things, or a black person jokes about black people. A third tactic is to associate mainly with other people who are similarly stigmatized. This leads, eventually, to the formation of subcultures and communities of stigmatized people.

Goffman's book is important because everyone deviates from some norm in one way or another, so this book is about everyone. The concerns and techniques he discusses in his book are merely extreme versions of the concerns and techniques that affect everyone in everyday interaction. Everyone has some discreditable feature to hide. The strategies of passing and covering are more visible among the most stigmatized members of society. In truth, we are all discreditable, all trying to appear more normal and meritorious than we really are.

Stigmatization is one form of a more general process sociologists call labelling. Labelling means attaching interpretations to others: this person is fat, that person is a drunk, another person is a slut, and so on. When we define others as deviant—stigmatizing them and treating them as devalued—we are labelling them, and often the labels stick. Doctors, as we have seen, have the power and the right to label people as sick (rather than deviant or immoral). This is one of the things that gives doctors so much power in our society. At the same time, such labelling is also a factor in people's sickness and recovery. Whether applied by people in authority (like doctors) or others (like family and friends), such labels can hurt people by attacking their self-esteem and increasing their stress levels. By contributing to stress, labelling can worsen people's health and delay their recovery from illness.

Doctors play a central role in our society in labelling sick people—in effect, by laying blame on them or relieving them of blame. In the twentieth century, with the rise of the medical profession, a great many social problems became medicalized. The power of doctors to medicalize people's behaviours and pronounce on issues of blame—to label people as sick, rather than lazy or wicked, for example—results from the high social and professional status of physicians in our society. (In turn, this reflects the high value of science in our culture). Medical and pharmaceutical industries have been complicit in the process of medicalization—they have had an interest in viewing behavioural issues as medical issues. After all, the more people labelled as sick, the more drugs get prescribed to treat them. The more the drugs that are prescribed, the greater is the profitability of the pharmaceutical industry.

And more than ever today, just as mental health has been medicalized, so has addiction. Today we are all used to hearing, and even using, the word *addiction* to refer to any behaviour, not just alcohol and drugs, that is repeated or frequent, disapproved socially, and possibly harmful. Recently, we have started to hear about addictions to gambling, sex, shopping, the Internet, food, gaming, and even work. By calling these behaviours addictions, we give them a medical label and imply that they are as important as other behaviours labelled addictions and that we should deal with them medically, perhaps using public funds.

So addictions are interesting sociologically because they have been medicalized as a health problem, and yet they remain socially stigmatizing—like obesity and anorexia. Their stigmatization and medicalization, in turn, leads to the expectation that people will accept professional treatment and patient status. At least by medicalizing addictions, we do not blame the victims, and recognize that, like mental illnesses, addictions are extremely common, widely misunderstood, and often hidden or ignored.

The medical definition of addiction, based on criteria used by the American Psychiatric Association (*DSM-IV*) and the World Health Organization (*ICD-10*), has seven criteria. To summarize, the questions to ask are about tolerance, the person's desire to cut down, withdrawal symptoms, control, and adverse effects the source of the addiction has had on the person's life. However, there is nothing in the question about how often a person uses the drug or alcohol—whether once a month or once an hour. That's because the issue is whether you have trouble controlling your use and whether there are negative effects when you do, rather than the frequency.

Professionals consider the use of substances problematic—as addictions—when they begin to affect health, family life, relationships and friendships, and work life, and because of the cost of treating and fixing the addicts. In addition, there are crime and safety issues at stake as well. Where the medical approach focuses attention on the addicted individual and his or her personal pathology, the sociological and public health approaches focus on the social forces that increase the risks that certain people, or groups, will develop addictions. This, in turn, proposes that we need to understand what it is about our society, and our social policies, that promotes harmful, addictive behaviour, and how we can change society to reduce these risks, rather than what it is about the individual that leads them to become addicted.

Consider one of the more recently defined addictions: gambling. Research shows there are factors in our society, our communities, and our families that predispose people to a gambling problem or gambling addiction. Gambling, like drinking, is on a continuum. It ranges from non-gamblers at one end to recreational gamblers to problem gamblers. In any population, a fraction will graduate from non-gamblers to recreational gamblers to problem gamblers. Ontario population surveys using the Canadian Problem Gambling Index (CPGI) have reported a prevalence of 2.6 percent for moderate and 0.8 percent for severe gambling problems.[49] This means that one Canadian adult in twenty has a serious gambling problem.[50]

Problem gambling has probably come the farthest among all others to truly being considered an addiction, on par with alcoholism and drug abuse. The chief difference about gambling is that we can detect physiological effects on drug or alcohol users that we can't detect on gamblers. So, the gambling addiction measure is not about how often a person gambles or how much he or she loses, but rather about the frequency of adverse effects, especially on other people. However, as with alcohol, there is a huge ambivalence about gambling and its effects in the general population. All over Canada, and even all over the world, governments are helping to promote gambling to raise their own revenues. Governments appear to reason that people are going to gamble anyway, so they should take a percentage in taxes. Like alcohol and drugs, gambling has historically also been a major source of revenue for organized crime.

Profit, then, is at the front and centre of the gambling industry, despite the casualties it leaves behind in the thousands of gambling addicts and those in their lives. And worst of all, governments are contradictory about their efforts to recognize gambling as a public issue with serious impacts on population health. While making incredible profits off problem gamblers, they simultaneously claim that they are funding programs to help those trying to recover. And where do those funds come from? From problem gamblers themselves, who pour their savings into these institutions.

There is a gradual movement to accept that gambling is an activity that, like any other, someone has learned socially in the usual ways—through observation, experimentation, reward, and emulation—in social surroundings, or through the example of social role models. Often, people learn to gamble in families during childhood. So, to understand a person's gambling, and even his or her problem gambling, we have to understand the family and socio-cultural ideas that person brings to the gambling event, however unconsciously. A failure to consider these ideas will make therapy and behaviour change slow or even impossible.

Therefore, cultural life is also a risk factor for problem gambling. Mass media advertising plays a significant role in promoting positive images of gambling. Media advertisements for casinos, for example, normalize and promote gambling—making it seem cool, fun, and desirable. As well, gambling addictions have increased because gambling opportunities have increased.

Those who stand to gain from the losses of problem gamblers endorse a psychological approach to gambling addiction. This perspective views addictive gambling as the result of cognitive distortion (bad thinking) about the odds of winning and the value of chasing losses. The goal of psychological counselling is to get gamblers to think differently about what they are doing and act differently, whatever their personal inclinations. In this model, the ability to play responsibly is put squarely on the shoulders of the individual gambler. Policy-makers, industry representatives, and the public share this individualistic viewpoint. It is reflected in everything from government gaming policies to gambling treatment and intervention programs.

Meanwhile, the problem gamblers lose their home, job, family, children's educational savings, car, prize collection of coins, or whatever else they value. And in the end, these problem gamblers are pitied and perhaps ridiculed. In turn, society blames and stigmatizes problem gamblers for their failure to act responsibly. Yet the same society provided the conditions for this social problem to occur. In the end, the society that induced and encouraged this irresponsible behaviour will get off scot-free.

International Differences in Health Inequalities

Of course, we cannot consider the effect of inequality on large-scale health problems—whether physical, mental, or addictions—without showing differences in this effect around the world. If health differences exist, as we argue, across levels of inequality, we can then look at the relationship between the two variables of interest. Of course, international differences in health are large and a result of multiple factors. Poor population health is seen as an obvious result of the deprivations that exist within developing countries; many sociology and health researchers are interested in the less obvious differences that exist between developed countries. These countries all have a relatively low percentage of citizens who cannot satisfy their basic needs, yet huge differences exist between their levels of population health.

For example, Japan has one of the healthiest populations in the world.[51] Its citizens have an average life expectancy of eighty-three years, higher than any other country in the world.[52] Japan also has low rates of premature mortality (mortality due to circulatory disease, mental illness, diabetes), and mortality due to cancer.[53] Sweden too is very healthy in comparison to other developed countries. Its citizens have a life expectancy at birth of 81.5 years, and 79 percent rate their health as good or very good.[54] Canada also ranks near the top, with an average life expectancy of 80.8 years.[55] However, Canada has the third highest rate of death due to diabetes of economically developed countries. Among the developed countries, the US too has one of the unhealthiest populations. The average US life expectancy is around 78.7 years—three years less than the average Swede.[56]

These statistical differences are mere surface representations of the deep-rooted social inequalities that exist within these countries. International studies have revealed multiple factors that explain why some populations are healthier than others. One factor is the social interconnectedness of people in the population. As we discussed earlier, research has shown that the frequency of contact with others and the quality of support networks are crucial determinants of health and well-being. Sweden, Canada, and the United States are all highly interconnected, with 92 percent of their populations saying they have at least one person to rely on in times of need.[57] Yet, social interconnectedness varies in all cases with socio-economic inequality. In Canada, 94 percent of the wealthiest Canadians say they have someone to rely on, while only 89 percent of the poorest Canadians do.[58] Six percent of the poorest Canadians are in a state of social isolation, with no one they can rely on.[59]

Other factors that influence population health have to do with the daily work experience—also related to inequality: for example, the length of the average working week and the ratio of positive to negative experiences a person has throughout the day. These factors influence the level of stress and anxiety people experience on a day-to-day basis. It is well-known that higher stress impairs personal health as the Whitehall Studies showed us. The percentage of the population that works very long hours (over fifty hours per week) is 10.86 percent in the United States, 3.91 percent in Canada, and only 1.28 percent in Sweden—another reason for the observed variations in health from one country to another.[60]

We also see international variations in time spent on leisure and personal care (including sleep). Canadians get an average of 14.25 hours for leisure and personal care, compared with 15.11 hours in Sweden.[61] And because Sweden is more egalitarian than Canada, more people cluster around this daily average. In Canada and the US, people differ more in the numbers of hours they have to work each day and, conversely, the number of hours they have free for leisure and sleep.

More generally, research reveals that people of different socio-economic status rate their health very differently. In the United States, 96 percent of the wealthiest quintile rates their health as good/very good, while only 76 percent of those in the poorest quintile do so.[62] The numbers are similar in Canada, where 94 percent in the top quintile rate their health as good or very good, while only 78 percent of the bottom quintile says the same.[63] Compare this with more egalitarian Sweden, where 89 percent of the top quintile and 82 percent of the bottom quintile rate their health as good or very good.[64] As we can see, the more the income inequality in a given country, the more unequal are people's self-reports of their health.

Publications by leading public health researchers have repeatedly shown these links between social inequality and health inequality—none more so than Richard Wilkinson and Kate Pickett.[65] Using cross-national data, they have repeatedly shown a clear connection between social inequality and health inequality on a variety of dimensions.

First, the connection is evident in relation to infant mortality, which many researchers consider the single most sensitive indicator of the overall health condition of a society. In brief, as Wilkinson and Pickett have shown, as income inequality rises, infant mortality rises apace.[66] Note, additionally, that some nations display higher- or lower-than-expected infant mortality, given their level of income inequality. This suggests that other factors—for example, race discrimination (in the case of the US), social connectedness (in the case of Japan), or corrective social programs (in the case of Scandinavia)—may intensify or mitigate the effects of social inequality on health.

Measures of child well-being are also affected by social inequality. Part of the story of child well-being has to do with maternal health, including the age of the mother at the time of childbirth. Generally, children do worse when their mothers are teenagers, especially, a single teenager with limited income or social support. This points to the importance of a link between social inequality and the risks of teenage pregnancy: the more unequal a society, the more likely teenage girls are to become pregnant. On this dimension, the US is off the charts. In the US, not only is there a high rate of teenage pregnancy attributable to social inequality, there is also a high rate due to faulty sex education, unavailability of birth control, and the over-sexualization of the mass media.

Differences in teen birth rates between countries are striking. Wilkinson and Pickett found that, "In the US, the teenage birth rate is 52.1 per 1000 women aged 15–19, more than ten times higher than Japan, which has a rate of only 4.6."[67] The rate for Canada is 14.2—half that of the US.[68] As well, Wilkinson and Pickett note that "babies born to teenage mothers are more likely to have low birth weight, to be born prematurely, to be at higher than average risk of dying in infancy and, as they grow up, to be at a higher than average risk of educational failure, juvenile crime and becoming teenage parents themselves. Girls who give birth as teenagers are more likely to be poor and uneducated."[69] This process of teenage pregnancy and childbearing maintains an "intergenerational cycle of deprivation and social exclusion."[70]

Not only is social inequality related to infant mortality, adult mortality, teenage pregnancy, and diminished child well-being, but it is also related to a variety of lifestyle-related health risks. For example, Wilkinson and Pickett show that social inequality increases the risk of obesity.[71] Here too, the US is off the charts, meaning other social and cultural factors besides inequality are pushing this health danger upward in the US. By contrast, other social and cultural factors—besides inequality—are pushing the risk of obesity downward in countries like Japan and Switzerland, where people are less obese than social inequality would have predicted. Obesity is increasing rapidly throughout the developed world. Research has shown that "in the USA, three-quarters of the population are overweight, and close to a third are obese."[72] The trends in children's obesity are most worrisome and are likely to lead to shorter life expectancies.

Not only risks of physical illness are influenced by social inequality. Research shows that risks of mental illness are too. Data from world mental health surveys organized by the World Health Organization show that rates of mental illness vary between societies.[73] Yet again, Wilkinson and Pickett demonstrate that "in some countries, only 5 or 10 percent of the adult population has suffered from any mental illness in the past year, but in the US, more than 25 percent have."[74] In general, the data show that mental illness is more common in economically unequal societies than it is in more equal societies.

The same applies to addictions of various kinds. Since addictions are related to mental illness, we should not be surprised to find that rates of alcohol and drug abuse are also related to social inequality. Wilkinson and Pickett use *The World Drug Report 2007*, compiled by the United Nations Office on Drugs and Crime, which contains the results of sample surveys on the prevalence of the use of opiates, cocaine, cannabis, ecstasy, and amphetamines.[75] They "found a strong tendency for drug abuse to be more common in more unequal countries."[76] Likewise, among the fifty states of the US, rates of drug addiction and death from drug overdoses are also predicted by levels of inequality: that is, the more social inequality, the more common are drug addiction and death from drug overdoses.[77]

Finally, social inequality also influences access to, and use of, health care services. A study by Cathy Schoen and colleagues examined the differences in the manner by which countries approach health care.[78] Sweden has universal health coverage, which covers the majority of services and necessities involved in health care. On top of this, government grants focus on specific problem areas in health care that may create inequalities (that is, geographical inequalities). Out-of-pocket expenses account for 16 percent of the total national health expenditures in 2007. However, the government has installed a safety net, in that they set a maximum amount to be paid out-of-pocket in a twelve-month period. Thus, underprivileged members of society are protected and supported if they need extensive medical care. This egalitarian form of providing health care helps undermine many of the health inequalities that result from other forms of inequality in society (that is, income inequalities).

In the United States, by contrast, health care coverage has not been available to everyone: 55 percent of Americans get health insurance from their employers and 24 percent are variously covered by federal programs. However, federal insurance programs have not covered many aspects of health care. As a result, 12 percent of total national health expenditures in 2007 were paid out-of-pocket by US care recipients. On top of this, another 16 percent of the US population was left without any assistance in paying for health care at all. The manner in which the United States has arranged its health care has exacerbated health inequalities and social inequalities more generally.

Since health insurance is expensive, and in most cases has been given to people through employment, it has left the unemployed and other poor Americans without any access to health care. It is this population that is most unhealthy and needs health care the most. Thus, America's health care system has reinforced existing inequalities within society. With the 2012 passage of a comprehensive health care plan under President Obama, these inequalities are likely to diminish in coming years, but we have yet to see how much they will diminish under the less-than-ideal health care package that Congress agreed to pass.

Canada has been a lot better in its health care provision, with physician and hospital expenses completely covered by publicly funded insurance. A significant proportion of health services are thus available to people, no matter their status in society. Canada's public health care system (Medicare) is an umbrella term for thirteen separate but linked health insurance plans that are administered separately in each province and territory. This arrangement gives Canadians something close to equal, universal health care coverage—a service unavailable in many other countries, including the US.

However, even in Canada, the coverage is not perfect. Medicare does not cover costs of prescription medicines, most dental care, most vision care, non-physician health services (for example, psychologists, physiotherapists), or long-term home care services. In part because of the rapid aging of the population, the percentage of Canadians who reported having unmet health needs more than doubled between 1998 and 2001, rising from 6 percent to over 12 percent.[79] The reported shortage of professional care is especially acute in rural communities.

As well, the costs of commonly used pharmaceutical drugs are growing rapidly; currently, only drugs taken during in-hospital treatment are covered by Medicare. In some jurisdictions, non-essential services have been removed from Medicare coverage (for example, adult eye exams and chiropractic care). These problems come at a time of greater strain on Medicare, due to the aging of the population, and with that, the greater longevity of chronically ill people. Worse still, insufficient attention is being given to preventive care strategies. So, while Canada is doing moderately well, when we consider what has been achieved by other counties, we could be doing better.

That's why inequality is important—a matter of sickness and health, life and death. In the next chapter we will add another layer to our analysis by talking about crime and punishment and their relation to social inequality.

CHAPTER 7

Crime and Punishment

———·◆·———

"Poverty is the mother of all crime."
Marcus Aurelius, Roman emperor and philosopher

Does inequality cause crime, in the same way that it causes sickness and death? We will argue in this chapter that it does: that disadvantaged people are more likely to commit common crimes, and they are also more likely to be punished for these crimes. So, crime is another of the costs of social inequality: the more unequal a society, the more often people will commit crimes, be victimized by crimes, and be punished for crimes.

Criminal behaviour is not only a result of criminal values or personalities, it is also a result of social injustice. So, to understand crime we need to understand the society that gives rise to it. On the other hand, some thinkers have proposed that crime is far too complex to be reduced to a simple, social-determinist formula. Some have noted that crime is to be found in all segments of society and, therefore, it cannot all be explained by social or economic factors like inequality.

Punishment poses other problems, both practical and theoretical. Punishment is dangerous because it is open to error and excess, and important because it is a signal of society's commitment to a certain code of rules. In principle, there can be no group, organization, or society without rules; nor any social unit that does not punish people for violating its rules. The problem is, how much punishment is too much, and what type of punishment best fits the crime? Here there are no hard and fast rules.

In this chapter, we will argue that inequality is one of the determinants of crime. However, it is only one of many causes. For example, consider the role of substance abuse in crime. There is a long recognized association between alcohol consumption and aggressive or violent behaviour. By disrupting normal brain function, alcohol encourages the commonly witnessed outward signs of heavy drinking such as slurred speech, difficulty controlling body movements, and impaired memory, but it also weakens the brain mechanisms responsible for controlling one's conductivity in society. Alcohol encourages impulsive behaviours (including inappropriate aggression), causes people to misjudge or overreact to social cues, or gives them confidence about evading any future repercussions of actions.[1] All of these alterations help to explain a tendency toward criminal activity when under the influence of alcohol.

Drug abuse may lead to similar effects. For example, it is well-known that drug users sometimes commit criminal acts in order to buy drugs. As well, those already involved in criminal activity commit far more offences after becoming drug dependent. These crimes are directed toward funding the person's addiction, and they mainly include theft, burglary, fraud, assault, and the like. Others commit criminal acts to maintain control over drug distribution.[2]

Substance abuse has an especially powerful effect on the mentally ill, who are already at risk of rule-breaking and substance abuse. In fact, while 15 percent of the general population abuses illegal substances, the numbers for the mentally ill are up at 50 percent.[3] This number is startling, especially knowing the effects of these substances on criminality. Some mental disorders are more closely linked to criminal behaviour at their core than others because their symptoms violate the rights of others. Such illnesses include antisocial personality disorder, and impulse control disorders.[4] So, mental illness may also explain people's tendencies toward criminality.

Other social factors that increase the propensity for crime include childhood maltreatment. Whether it is neglect, abuse (physical, sexual, or emotional), or the witnessing of violence in the household, negative childhood experiences are associated with increased risk of subsequent delinquent and criminal behaviour.[5]

The abused, often emotionally scarred by their experiences, often reproduce the antisocial behaviour they learned as children. Their trauma may show itself in persistent mental health problems; substance abuse as a way to self-medicate; and aggressive, violent, or criminal behaviour.[6]

Just as socialization in the home influences a person's propensity to crime, so does socialization by peers. Consider Edwin H. Sutherland's *Theory of Differential Association*, which describes this process of learning the attitudes, techniques, and motives of criminal behaviour through intimate interaction with others. It proposes that a person becomes criminal because of an "excess of definitions" favorable to violation of law over definitions unfavorable to violation of law. In other words, people break the criminal law when they are exposed to more messages favouring criminal behaviour than opposing it.[7] This argues that specific motivations to act in a criminal or deviant manner can be learned—indeed, the self can be shaped to see criminal activity as socially acceptable behaviour.

Often, group pressures contribute to the commission of a crime.[8] People innately need to feel part of a social group and are thus prone to social influence. A group can be commanding and intimidating, and when it comes to crime, probably no group is more intimidating than a gang. For instance, in the two most gang-populated cities in the United States (Los Angeles and Chicago) over half of approximately one thousand homicides in 2004 were gang-related.[9] These groups are built for crime.

Education, or more precisely the absence of an education, also plays a part in the shaping of crime. Where a quality education leads to employment opportunities and a propensity to obey the laws, a poor education leads to fewer legitimate opportunities and a greater propensity to commit crimes. This is evident in Canadian statistics on crime and imprisonment. For example, 41 percent of all Canadian prisoners have not completed high school, compared to 18 percent of the general population.[10] These numbers can be alarming when we consider that prisoners tend to be young, and that in the 2009/2010 school year, only 8.5 percent of Canadians aged twenty to twenty-four had not graduated from high school and were not trying to get their diploma.[11] So, crime and punishment select disproportionately from the ranks of the under-educated.

They also select from among the ranks of people with below-average intelligence. Like people with less education, people with a learning disability or lower-than-average IQ also have an increased disposition to criminal behaviour.[12] Having a low IQ or learning disability not only limits a person's educational attainment, itself a factor predicting a propensity to crime. It may also increase social exclusion and lower a person's self-esteem, triggering the rejection of societal norms and rules.

Policing and law enforcement also have an effect on criminal behaviour. Needless to say, people will be more inclined to commit crimes when they feel more confident of escaping capture and punishment. Some crimes (like domestic violence or drunk driving) and white-collar crimes (such as fraud or tax evasion) are particularly common because they receive a relatively tolerant response from the general public, as well as a low risk of capture and punishment.[13]

In some societies, permissive gun control also causes more crime—especially, more gun violence—because crimes become easier and more dangerous as soon as a firearm is introduced. As an example, consider the doubling of youth homicide rates between 1985 and 1991 in the United States. According to some researchers, this growth in homicides was "entirely associated with growth of handgun use in homicides (with no growth in non-handgun homicides)."[14] A more recent and disturbing example is the tragedy in Newtown, Connecticut, where twenty school children and six aduts were killed in a shooting rampage in December 2012.

Some believe that the the mass media play an important role in criminality. For example, research shows that over-exposure to criminal behaviour and violence in the media can desensitize audiences to the genuine impact of crime and make crime seem normal, or even acceptable.[15] Crime, through its sensationalized portrayal in the media, can even seem alluring or glamorous.[16] On the other hand, there may also be a selection factor here: people who are in clined to break the laws are also inclined to watch more TV programs and movies in which law-breaking is portrayed and glamorized.

So, there are many factors that affect criminality. That said, social inequality is among the most pervasive and most important of them all. And, social inequality interacts with many of the factors mentioned above to produce a variety of criminal outcomes.

The Role of Inequality in Crime

Sociologists, criminologists, and policy experts have discussed the connection between inequality and crime for a number of decades now. It would be nice to be able to say the debate has been resolved, but it hasn't. As will become obvious, there are unanswered questions.

Specifically, sociologists are likely to ask some of the following questions: What kind of crime are we examining—for example, crimes against property versus (violent) crimes against other people? What kind of person are we concerned with—for example, socially disadvantaged people versus non-disadvantaged (even, elite) people? What social, economic, and cultural factors influence the connection between inequality and crime?[17] None of these questions has been fully answered, though merely asking them takes us a long way toward answering them. As we will see, the majority of academic studies find evidence that inequality increases the likelihood of crime. For this reason, we will start with research that, on the contrary, has found no relationship between inequality and crime.

So, for example, a Malaysian study examined the connection between inequality and crime over the period 1973 to 2003, and found "no meaningful relationship with any of the various categories of crime selected, such as total crime, violent crime, property crime, theft, and burglary. Crime exhibits neither long-run nor short-run relationships with income inequality and they are not co-integrated."[18]

Likewise, a Swedish study[19] refined the problem by distinguishing between permanent and transitory changes in people's income. Disentangling these two types of income, the researchers found that "an increase in the inequality in permanent income yields a positive and significant effect on total crimes and three different property crimes [while] an in increase in the inequality in transitory income has no significant effect. Using a traditional, aggregate, measure of income yields insignificant effects on crime," perhaps accounting for the Malaysian (non-) finding mentioned above.

In the US too, some researchers failed to find a positive link between inequality and crime.[20] In fact, they argued that a far more important influence on crime is the proportion of young males in the population—as they are the type of people most likely to commit crimes.

Other researchers propose that a failure to find the connection between inequality and crime is that the connection is hard to measure.[21] One important problem is the interwoven connectedness of variables that influence both inequality and crime: factors that affect inequality also tend to affect crime. As a result, studying the link between inequality and crime can lead to confusing results.[22]

Sometimes, problems arise in defining the kinds of crimes we expect to result from inequality. So, for example, in US data from ninety-one cities, researchers found that "while total inequality and intra-racial inequality had no significant association with offending rates, interracial inequality was a strong predictor of the overall violent crime rate."[23] This finding suggests that, if we are to understand the link between inequality and crime, we need to refine our measures and specify the types of crimes, perpetrators, and victims of interest.

Another debate surrounds the relative importance of, and connection between, macro-level (or societal) variables such as social inequality and micro-level (or personal) variables (such as age, sex, marital status, education, or income). Using data from forty-two nations, a recent study of crime victimization[24] found that compared to macro-level variables, micro-level variables were much better predictors of both the likelihood that crime would occur and its intensity. In other words, social inequality proved to be less important than specific individual experiences of inequality, such as education and income.

The meaning of this finding is clarified by a Mexican study[25] that compares 1,963 municipalities from the years 2000 to 2005. Using data on both property crime and violent crime, and using two measures of inequality, income and education, the study finds a connection between crime and inequality. But at particularly high rates of crime, the results change. This suggests a nonlinear (rather than linear) relationship between crime and inequality, with one or more important turning points.

Some people are also more likely than others to turn to crime in the face of inequality. One study[26] finds that, for people already near to the crime industry—for example, who know participants in it and are morally indifferent to it—an increase in inequality provides an incentive to join. However, another study finds that inequality affects everyone equally in terms of crime, by creating a decline in legal opportunities.[27] Clearly, we have much more to learn about this issue.

That said, a large number of analyzed report the link between inequality and crime. In a study of this relationship conducted in the 1970s, cross-national data on inequality, unemployment, and various crime rates (including both property crime and violent crime) showed a strong, unmistakeable link between inequality and crime, via unemployment.[28] As unemployment rates go up, so does crime. More recent studies continue to find this connection between unemployment and crime in many different societies.[29]

For example, one study[30] examined the relationship between income inequality and homicide rates, as previous research on this topic had proved inconclusive. Comparing areas within both Canada and the United States, local levels of income inequality were found to account significantly for differing homicide rates. Further, as rates of inequality changed, so did homicide rates.

Another study using data from seven Colombian cities found that inequality has a profound effect on the criminality of a particular segment of the population, especially in connection with property crimes.[31] The connections between inequality and property crime are easiest to explain, because they are the most rational and practical responses to increased economic inequality.[32] Not surprisingly, low-income earners have a greater incentive to commit burglary than high-income earners. A regressive income tax that causes the rich to get richer and the poor to get poorer also contributes to this criminal incentive, in two ways. First, legitimate means of earning money are less appealing to low-income earners, who feel exploited by the regressive income tax program. Second, as high-income earners become richer, the expected gains of burglary become greater.[33] In this sense, burglary provides a spillover of wealth from wealthy neighbourhoods into poor ones—also, a spillover of crime from poor neighbourhoods into wealthier ones.[34]

These findings do not necessarily mean the connection exists for all types of crime.[35] In fact, many researchers find that inequality affects property crime but not violent crime.[36] Nevertheless, researchers seem to agree that increases in general income inequality increase the overall level of crime. It is not absolute poverty that causes crime, for the most part; it is the anger and resentment caused by unequal access to desired goods.[37]

Although property crime has the clearest connection with inequality, a great deal of research also finds a link between inequality and violent crime. This is especially the case in large urban centres, where people live close together and so have a greater opportunity to compare themselves with those around them, and find disparities.[38] Researchers in Chicago, for example, argue that "in addition to poverty, income inequality adds stress to individuals when they compare their situation to those around them."[39] This sometimes leads to violent crime as well as other types of crime. One study, which examined data on both homicides and burglaries from about forty countries between 1965 to 1995 found that "crime rates and [income] inequality are positively correlated within countries and, particularly, between countries, even after controlling for other crime determinants,"[40] a finding confirmed by other studies as well.[41]

To a large degree, the crime rates that result from income inequality are a result of government policies that influence inequality. For example, some argue that what separates the United

States from other rich nations is its unwillingness to reduce wage inequality.[42] Compared to other rich democracies, the United States transfers less money to the unemployed, has a lower minimum wage, and through its laws makes unionization difficult. Policies that increase and maintain income inequality therefore contribute to America's high crime rates.

China provides another example: after income inequality increased during China's so-called reform period,[43] urban workers and peasants lost much of their access to education, employment, housing, and health care, giving them fewer opportunities to achieve economic prosperity. Income disparities across regions also gave rise to a huge migrant population that is socially disorganized and has no roots in any particular community. These factors of poverty and rootlessness, along with diminished control and feelings of strain, led to high crime rates among the floating population. As in the US, in China political and economic policy has played a significant role in creating income inequality that leads to crime.

The same has happened in post-communist countries in Europe: consider their cultures of inequality, a term coined by sociologist Susanne Karstedt.[44] Karstedt noticed the recent rise of both elite crime (that is, corruption) and violent (non-elite) crime in Central and Eastern Europe and asked why some countries fared better than others after the collapse of the Soviet Union. She found that in all of these communist societies, subcultures of inequality had developed during and after World War II, despite the homogenizing forces of ethnic cleansing and communist ideology.

These subcultures included "close-knit networks at the top and bottom of society, clientelism as a pattern of linking them, and non-egalitarian and collectivist value patterns"[45]—all of which contributed to high-level corruption and violence. Some Eastern European societies—for example, Hungary, Poland, and the Czech Republic—were more immune to these outcomes, thanks to strong traditions of civil rights and the rule of law. But others like Russia and Ukraine were less immune, and there violence and corruption flourish. Of course, inequality is not the whole story; but to the extent that inequality undermines confidence and participation in public institutions, inequality promotes the flowering of crime throughout society.

Another part of the story has to do with what David Halpern[46] calls self-interested values. To find out whether self-interested attitudes and values explain crime, Halpern used cross-national data from the World Values Surveys, which were conducted in the early 1980s and 1990s. From this, he concluded that self-interested values, along with economic inequality and social trust, "explained two-thirds of variance in [criminal] victimization at the national level."[47] Said another way, societies with high levels of inequality, low levels of social trust, and high levels of self-interested attitudes and values produce the most crime—hence, the most victimization. Said yet another way, selfish, unequal societies—societies that display the habits of inequality we discuss throughout this book— have the most crime and victimization.

Inequality, Crime, and Race

In the US, compared with Canada and Europe, much of the criminological research on inequality focuses on the link between income inequality and racial inequality. That is because, in the US, the most intense, concentrated disadvantage is found in the black population. But the research is nevertheless relevant to us in Canada as well. Some of the most interesting, complex research on inequality and crime has centered on racial inequality, not income inequality per se. A prime source of information is the recent collection of research reports titled *The Many Colors of Crime: Inequalities of Race, Ethnicity, and Crime in America*, edited by Ruth Peterson, Lauren Krivo, and John Hagan (2006).

As a reviewer of the book notes, "race and ethnicity are fundamental structuring influences in society and, as such, cannot remain on the periphery in the study of crime."[48] The most revealing finding to come out of this book, according to the reviewer, is that "existing theories and the research they have generated may not be applicable to other race/ethnic groups at all, they may apply in dramatically different ways, or there may be subtle variations across and within race and ethnic groups." In short, we are cautioned to look for the link between inequality and crime in careful, subtle ways, and warned that one general theory may not fit all cases.

A similar conclusion about the complexity of connections is stated in a review of *Unequal Crime Decline: Theorizing Race, Urban Inequality, and Criminal Violence*, by Karen Parker.[49] Some reviewers noted that the improved economic conditions of the 1990s—including reduced social inequality—had more positive effects for African Americans than for white Americans.[50] The reason for this racial difference is that many social variables affect white people and black people in different ways: consider, for example, residential segregation, racial competition/threat, and industrial restructuring. In short, poor black Americans suffer more from segregation, racism, and industrial decline than poor white Americans, and the reduction of these differences in circumstances also reduces crime rates, in this case homicides.

An even stronger argument along these lines focuses on the role of imprisonment in the lives of people who are incarcerated.[51] As we note later in this chapter, social inequality not only increases crime rates for particular segments of the population, it also increases imprisonment rates for particular segments—usually, the same segments—of the population. In Canada, Aboriginal people are the most likely of all Canadians to end up in jail, while in the US, blacks are the most likely.

According to researchers Bruce Western and Becky Pettit,[52] in the US the mass incarceration of young black men—largely in connection with the so-called "War on Drugs"—has three main links with inequality. First, the organization of criminal justice in the US comes down hardest on poor black men. Racial and income inequality leads to higher rates of crime in this subpopulation and also higher rates of imprisonment.

Second, the over-imprisonment of poor black men has a variety of social effects, which include the concealment of actual rates of black disadvantage (for example, under-education, under-employment, and unemployment) in US society, since convicts and ex-convicts are left out of official statistics. Third, on release from prison, poor black men face a variety of disadvantages—including social stigma—that hinder their ability to find jobs, keep jobs, and maintain stable family lives. These circumstances increase their likelihood of returning to crime and to prison. This passes social disadvantage on to their children—that is, from one generation of poor black men to the next.

Many of these observations are developed in a masterful review by an influential sociologist in the study of deviance named John Hagan, titled "Beyond the Classics: Reform and Renewal in the Study of Crime and Inequality."[53] As Hagan points out, the link between inequality and crime is one of the abiding, trans-disciplinary themes in the study of crime. And, as an evergreen topic, the discussion has become more complex and subtle with the passage of time.

Hagan notes that

> the focus on crime and inequality joins many if not most crimin-ologists in opposition to a largely unspoken but still influential economic and political perspective on crime . . . that emphasize[s] presumed links between inequality, individualism, and efficiency. The latter perspective holds that social inequality enhances indi-vidual initiative and is necessary for economic efficiency, or in other words, economic progress and success.[54]

Hagan dismisses the evidence that equality is socially ineffi-cient (and inequality efficient) and makes several points that bear repeating.

First, Hagan asserts that research finds "economic processes that alter life outcomes more generally also have an impact on crime."[55] They do this in some of the ways we discussed above, in connection with imprisonment. They also do so by creating social disorganization, anger, and despair. In short, inequality is socially inefficient because it increases crime and punishment. Inequality creates animosities that can easily turn to feelings of frustration, hopelessness, and alienation, and can lead to crime.[56]

Further, Hagan says that "sanctions cause more crime among social out-groups and less crime among social in-groups, or said the other way round . . . sanctions are more likely to succeed in deterring crime among social in-groups but to fail in deterring crime among social out-groups."[57] So, for example, people with jobs try harder to avoid trouble with the police than do people without jobs, since the former have more to lose. However, some disadvantaged groups have more trouble getting and keeping jobs—hence, they are more likely to get into repeated trouble with the police. Hagan notes "social equality is assumed to dampen individual initiative and to produce inefficient, unsuccessful economic results . . . [thus diverting] strategic investment from declining communities and disadvantaged individuals."[58] So, for Hagan, as for many criminologists and sociologists, the problem facing unequal societies like the US is capital disinvestment in the poor.

What Hagan is saying is that in poorer communities people are so preoccupied dealing with everyday issues that just help them survive, they have little chance to develop the resources and skills—the social and cultural capital, not to mention formal education—that will help them to do well in society. This is especially pronounced during periods of economic decline and economic inequality when people have to put survival ahead of personal cultivation. As well, inequality and group frustrations lead people to band together and to organize their efforts in gangs, which represent an effort to reach attainable goals.

So, the problems caused by this link between crime, inequality, and social disinvestment are compounded when "individuals become so embedded in crime networks that they have few opportunities to leave. The combination of little schooling, poor job experience, and arrest records provide little or no social capital for affected youth to pursue legitimate career paths."[59]

Conformists, Innovators, and the American Dream

The most famous sociological explanation of crime is Robert Merton's anomie (or strain) theory. It proposes that crime is a personal adaptation to social inequality. The argument runs as follows: in modern industrial societies like our own, there is a gap between cultural goals and the means available to pursue these goals. As children, we are taught to seek material success. We are taught to strive for wealth, respect, a good job, a family, a nice car, and a big house in the suburbs. Equally, we are taught in school and elsewhere that anyone is capable of attaining these goals if only they work hard enough. By implication, if you fail to achieve these goals, you did not work hard enough and weren't patient enough. (Again, we encounter the just-world belief). And the only legitimate way to succeed, according to this cultural rhetoric, is through formal education and hard work. These are legitimate means because they obey the rules and laws of society.

But in reality, society does not work fairly. In reality, some people have less access than others to education and employment, the culturally accepted ways of attaining the good life. Some people's pathways to success are blocked—they have less opportunity for success than other people, because of their class, gender, race, age, or sexual orientation, for example—all types of inequalities discussed in earlier chapters. They may also be blocked by their lack of economic, social, or cultural capital, poor health, poor location, poor transportation, and so on. In short, life's opportunities are distributed unequally for a large number of reasons, and that means that different people will have different chances of achieving the good life by following society's rules.

According to Merton, this gap between cultural goals and the legitimate means available creates what he calls anomie or strain. Faced with this gap, people respond in any one of five ways, which Merton terms adaptations to anomie. The most common response, according to Merton, is continued conformity. By conforming, people do their best under the circumstances, using the legitimate means available to them. They maintain the belief that if they just keep doing what society tells them to do, they will eventually reach its goals. And the fact that most people are conformists means that society can keep functioning and keep its cultural goals and means intact. This steady faith in eventual success helps social inequality—and modern capitalism—to persist.

A second way people adapt to anomie is by accepting the cultural goals—the nice house, car, and mate—while rejecting the accepted means of attaining them. Merton calls this response innovation, since these adapters find innovative ways to get what others try to get through conformity. Most of the time, innovation involves breaking the law, especially stealing. Professional criminals—for example, gangsters—are the ultimate innovators, devising complex systems of activity to attain wealth while avoiding imprisonment. Innovators believe that if you cannot win by the rules, rewrite them.

Of course, not all innovators are convicted or convictable criminals. Take the example of gamblers: a person who gambles legally and happens to win the lottery attains society's cultural goal of material success, but bypasses the longer, more difficult path of education and employment. In a sense, gamblers take the easy way out by innovating. No wonder so many people gamble. And this insight can be extended to people—many of them wealthy, powerful, and respected—who speculate (that is, gamble) in stocks, land, currency, futures, and other commodities. When innovators are "too big to fail," they manage to stay out of court and out of prison, despite socially dangerous and injurious behaviour.

Or for that matter, consider tax evaders—another kind of innovator. Most tax evaders manage to cheat the government with impunity. A sizeable fraction of Canadian taxpayers innovate (that is, break the tax laws) by paying less than they should. Many respectable Canadians break the law every day, while others avoid doing so mainly because they fear being punished. According to a 2011 survey of Canadian adults, commissioned by the Canada Revenue Agency (CRA), a sizeable minority of Canadians—about 13 percent—resist warnings from the CRA and regularly cheat on their taxes. For example, they pay cash under the table to get a cheaper price on services and under-report their income. These rule-breakers think tax evasion is not a big deal, use excuses for cheating, and think a lot of other people cheat on taxes too.

In terms of social background, this outlaw group tends to have low education and income. As well, they are more likely than average to be self-employed men under thirty years of age. Compared to other Canadians, they are the least likely to see consequences attached to tax cheating, and among the least likely to fear getting caught. On the other hand, nearly half—an estimated 49 percent of Canadian adults—pay exactly what they are expected (and required) to pay. These are Merton's conformists.

That leaves the 51 percent of Canadians who are potential cheaters—people who avoid taxes by making cash payments under the table, for example. These potential cheaters fall into several categories, according to the CRA. Rationalizers (12 percent of Canadians) believe that taxation in Canada is unfair and try to rationalize or explain away tax cheating. Underground economists (12 percent) figure they can get away with it and think tax cheating is without much risk. Over-taxed opportunists (15 percent) feel they are over-taxed, and believe that many others pay cash to avoid taxes too. They say that, in future, they may break the tax laws and pay less than they owe. However, at present, these potential offenders are law-abiding and fear having to pay penalties if found cheating.

Tax evaders are, broadly speaking, an example of what sociologist Edwin Sutherland called "white-collar criminals."[60] Today, sociologists use this term to denote property crimes by white-collar workers. As the *Oxford Dictionary of Sociology* notes,

> the great value of the idea was to redress the imbalance in criminology's obsession with crimes of the working class. The concept tends to be used very broadly, to include both activities carried out by employees against their employer . . . and activities undertaken by corporate executives on behalf of the corporation itself.

In his classic study *White Collar Crime*, first published in 1949, Sutherland carried out an original study of the largely neglected illegal activities of US corporations. By white-collar crime,

Sutherland meant corporate crime committed by people of high socio-economic standing, often the holders of dominant positions in large corporations.

To carry out his research, Sutherland examined the court records of seventy US corporations prosecuted over the previous forty-five years. In this sample he found that corporate crime was widespread: in total, the corporations studied had been convicted of 779 offenses, 158 of which were criminal convictions. Most of the offending corporations (60 percent) had at least four convictions each. Sutherland notes that, if these corporations had been ordinary people, they would have been considered habitual criminals in most states. Their crimes were deliberate and consistent, like the crimes of Mafia gangs. What's more, the executives of these law-breaking corporations often expressed contempt for the law, for government, and for government personnel, including prosecutors and judges.

From this finding, Sutherland concluded that white-collar crimes are deliberate and they are organized. Sutherland explains, "We are in transition from free competition and free enterprise toward some other system, and the violations of the anti-trust laws by large corporations are an important factor in producing this transition."[61] He proposes that persistent and widespread white-collar crime has undermined the ideological justification for capitalism, a lesson not yet learned on Wall Street.

Sutherland notes that traditional theories about crime that focus solely on poverty, lack of opportunity, personality defects, or bad family experiences are unable to explain white collar and corporate crime. He urges us, therefore, to understand that all crime—including corporate crime—has an important cultural (or subcultural) aspect. That is, criminals are taught to hold criminal values and learn to perfect their criminal skills—whether they are safecrackers or Wall Street financiers. For both white-collar and blue-collar criminals (or, as they are sometimes called, "suite" and "street" criminals), "criminal behaviour is learned in association with those who define such behaviour favourably and in isolation from those who define it unfavourably."[62] Merton's theory of anomie applies as well to corporate or white-collar criminals as it does to poor street criminals. For both, the motivation is to have more: to achieve an unlimited supply of society's success symbols we are taught to want.

Youth Violence as a Response to Inequality

Violence is apparently more common in more unequal societies, because it is often triggered by people feeling looked down upon and disrespected, and by a loss of face on a smaller scale. We can see similar processes occurring in smaller social units as well, for example high school hierarchies, which are familiar to most of us. Even among high school students, issues of inequality and honour are sources of violence and danger. In 2006, Jessica Klein proposed that high school social hierarchies play a role in causing school shootings. In this sense, adolescent violence can be seen as a result of a teenage version of social inequality. Unpopular boys feel driven to literally fight for higher status, or to violently express their dissatisfaction with the social rankings that cause them so much grief. Social inequality and negotiations for popular status can culminate in extreme violence.[63]

Stereotypical markers of masculinity such as athleticism, defiance, dominance, and aggression are linked to popularity—boys who display these qualities are of higher social status within their schools. Popularity is thus defined in opposition to the feminine passivity that unpopular boys supposedly embody. In order to maintain their higher rank, popular boys must continuously prove their masculinity by behaving in ways that reflect their masculine qualities. However, the unpopular boys who don't possess these characteristics do not have alternative means by which to attain cultural capital—only masculine boys can be popular, because they need to define themselves against supposedly feminine boys. School shooters therefore show the most extreme form of masculine aggression in their efforts to build cultural capital and escape from their social marginalization.[64]

In addition to this inequality between individual students, groups of adolescents also jostle for a sort of collective popularity.

According to the classic sociologist Max Weber, a group is able to maintain its status and power by differentiating itself from other groups.[65] By defining these other groups as inferior to their own, members of the popular group establish their dominance.[66] In high schools today, for example, circles of popular boys publicly distinguish themselves from groups of unpopular boys, most commonly through name-calling and physical abuse. "Fag," "homo," and "pussy" are typical insults used to degrade unpopular boys, situating them at the bottom of the social hierarchy and the name-callers at the top.[67] Beating up non-members also allows the popular group to show their physical superiority through an assertion of stereotypical masculine strength.

Similarly, popular boys dominate and objectify girls in order to assert their supremacy. Playing sports and valuing athleticism over academic success also characterizes the popular boys in most high schools. Finally, popularity is usually linked to social class, with wealthy boys composing the popular group and working-class or less wealthy boys becoming social rejects. Clothing and self-presentation make these socio-economic status differences more apparent, as popular boys wear trendy, expensive clothing that differentiates them from the unpopular boys who wear old, torn, or "Goth" clothing.[68] Popular boys are thus expected to wear certain clothing, interact with their peers in a certain way, and participate in certain activities. Those who don't fulfill these expectations are pushed down the social hierarchy to lower status groups.[69]

The schoolhouse murderers Klein examined all had low cultural capital, in that they didn't fulfill these qualifications for popularity. As non-athletic, physically unattractive boys who weren't involved in cool activities, they were bullied by the popular boys and rejected by the girls. Having been harassed and excluded in these ways, the shooters believed that violence would allow them to build the cultural capital they lacked, and to improve their social status.[70] Other researchers also note that boys (and probably girls) who are subjected to name-calling feel inferior to their tormentors.[71]

In another article, Klein expands on her discussion of the way in which popular boys assert their power over less-popular boys by calling them "homos" and "fags," regardless of their actual sexual orientation.[72] This suggests that sexual orientation is also a factor that determines students' positioning on school social hierarchies. Popular boys assume that being gay is shameful and that their targets will recognize this kind of name-calling as insulting given the stigma attached to homosexuality.[73]

On the other hand, heterosexual people enjoy a privileged status over homosexual people, and many would prefer to claim these privileges, especially if they are, in fact, straight. In their attempts to demand the equal, respectful treatment they believe they deserve as straight men, unpopular boys who experience this name-calling may act violently in order to show that they too are "real men."[74] That these boys will go to such extreme lengths to prove their heterosexuality shows that being gay warrants an unbearably low position on school social hierarchies.

Some boys choose to commit their violent acts at school, demonstrating that they felt this institution as a whole caused their repression. The communities in which they lived also tended to be intolerant of difference and politically conservative. Many researchers (like Klein) have therefore concluded that school shooters are often reacting to a "culture of cruelty" implemented by jocks and popular kids. Accordingly, they tend to target the popular boys who had bullied them, or those who had worked to establish and reinforce their lower social status.

Overall then, the shooters targeted the people who support the values and standards that (they believe) led to their social rejection.[76] Because these people enforced a hierarchy that valued attributes the shooters didn't have, they felt as though their fellow students, as well as the school institution as a whole, were responsible for their exclusion and unhappiness. Killing these people and trying to burn down or blow up their schools was, to these unpopular boys, the only way to get rid of the forces causing the inequality that was making them so unhappy.[77]

In contrast, others have proposed that school shooters aim to harm or kill as many people as possible, rather than seeking revenge against specific people.[78] At Columbine High School in Littleton, Colorado, for example, where a school shooting occurred on April 20, 1999, two high school boys killed and injured several people whom they had never even met. A now infamous series of "basement tapes" recorded by the boys were created in their efforts to explain their motives, and their journals also give us some insight into their intentions. In both sources, the boys describe the bullying and harassment they suffered at the hands of higher-status kids and the anger this mistreatment caused them. Accordingly, they explicitly state that they intend to exact revenge. In direct contrast, however, they also reveal that they wanted to harm as many people as possible, implying that they weren't targeting their abusers in the hope of retribution.[79]

While some researchers have suggested that this seeming lack of specific targets shows the boys were deranged killers, others argue that they were trying to destroy the entire institution that enforced their lesser status.[80] By this reasoning, even those students and staff members who had never interacted with these boys played a role in maintaining their social ostracism by accepting it and doing nothing about it.[81] Shool shooters attack the school institution as a whole in order to attain the power they had been denied and to exact a sense of justice.[82]

In their efforts to destroy the people whom they felt were responsible for their low social status, these shooters attempted to rearrange the social hierarchies of their schools in order to attain some sense of power and status. As firearms are recognized as symbols of power, the school shooters who possessed them were able to exercise the control and dominance they had never experienced due to their marginalization.[83] However, this approach merely reaffirms the inequality that had led to their social rejection, as they aimed to destroy the boys who were established as powerful and popular, and to reinstate themselves as the new, high status, popular boys.

Klein proposes that abolishing school social hierarchies altogether would significantly reduce school shootings. However, she also acknowledges that these school hierarchies develop within the context of the inequality that characterizes "adult" life. Ultimately, struggles for popularity at school are similar to the negotiations of adults striving for financial and professional success. Social hierarchies at school can, therefore, not be framed as fickle, childish problems that kids will outgrow. Instead, they are the adolescent version of the inequality people face as adults. Teenage social inequality is merely a manifestation of the inequality that characterizes their broader communities.

Another scholar, Ronald Kramer, also discusses youth violence as a product of inequality, but advances his argument differently than Klein. He suggests that inequality—and the relative poverty and social exclusion it engenders—reduces the ability of families, schools, and communities to exercise the informal social control and to provide the social support necessary to keep teen violence in check. Without the support and control of functional families and communities, adolescents can harm each other both physically and verbally. That is, if youth are not being provided with the support they need, they can develop negative feelings and perspectives that might drive them toward violence.

One reason for the absence of social support and control in American society, Kramer proposes, is a strong, widespread belief in the American Dream, just as Merton argued in his classic book.[84] This outlook encourages personal financial success by any means necessary, and thereby privileges individual drive over a sense of solidarity. American society can be seen as unsupportive: the benefit of the community as a whole isn't seen as being as important as individual advancement, so community members fail to mutually support one another. A strong belief in the American Dream can therefore reduce the quality of social support networks, which, as we will see, contributes to youth violence.

In opposition, supportive parent–child relationships help prevent violence amongst teens.[85] Children who feel that they can communicate with their parents will likely share their emotions, intentions, and activities with them. These parents are thus more easily able to monitor their children's behaviour and exercise some control over their activities. Inequality contributes to preventing deprived parents from supporting and controlling their children. These parents experience anxieties related to their social and economic status that can detract from their ability to perform these parenting duties.

As well, income inequality means the number of single-parent households increase. A single parent, with his/her many commitments, is more stressed than a pair of partners who can divide household, work, and child care duties more equally. A single parent household also has a more limited income than a two-parent household. Further, these parents may have to work longer hours to compensate for lost income that a second parent would have brought in.[86] They are, therefore, largely absent from the home, unable to form supportive bonds with their children or carefully supervise them.

All of these factors mean that single, racially marginalized, impoverished parents are preoccupied with financial and class-based concerns, making them less capable of monitoring their children's activities effectively. These lower-class parents cannot devote as much time and attention to shaping their children's behaviour by punishing inappropriate actions and rewarding proper actions. As a result, their children might come to see violence as a legitimate behaviour. Inequality thus prevents parents from exercising the social control that could prevent children from acting violently.

Like Klein, Kramer also examines the ways in which cultural capital relates to youth violence. Disadvantaged communities lack social and cultural capital, meaning that residentially segregated, impoverished, and racially divided regions have less cultural capital. Parents living within these communities cannot provide their children with opportunities, resources, and support in the same way that more affluent, upper-class parents can.[87] The children within these more deprived regions thus become motivated to attain the cultural capital they have been denied. However, without the power and status associated with the upper classes, these children lack socially accepted means through which to do so, and thus they innovate, as Merton would have argued.

The American Dream also promotes financial success and personal achievement, but fails to emphasize the means of attaining these goals as being of particular importance. Rather, people who needed to take extreme measures to attain wealth and high status, fulfilling the American Dream, are often admired for their commitment.[88] Within this context, youth might come to believe that violent behaviour is acceptable if it allows them to attain their desired end of affluence. Muggings, robberies, and participation in the drug trade are a few examples of money-related violent crimes that youth may commit in their efforts to attain financial success. Because impoverished parents cannot supervise and control their children especially well, as we just discussed, lower-class children may turn to violence as an illegitimate means to attain cultural capital, without any inhibitions or restrictions imposed upon them by their parents.

Teachers, coaches, extended family members, friends, and parents can exercise informal social control. The more intimately enmeshed within these networks teens are, the less likely they are to become violent. This is because they will recognize and appreciate the values imposed by these groups, and will aim to fulfill their expectations. However, inequality can prevent social networks and institutions from exercising social control effectively. The emphasis on financial success means the economy dominates all other values and institutions. Schools and families lose power and become less important.

Kramer concludes that inequality and the relative poverty it engenders are causally linked to adolescent violence in the United States. He reminds us that inequality negatively impacts social institutions like schools, the family, and communities that might have been able to provide the support and exercise the informal social control that often prevent violent crime. But Kramer also implies that inequality can play a more direct role in youth violence by inspiring feelings of shame, humiliation, frustration, and anger within the lower classes or status groups. These emotions can drive teens to try to overcome their impoverished status through violence, trying to attain a sense of control after having been rendered powerless by inequality. Because deprived adolescents (and perhaps adults) believe that they are merely asserting the right to power and equal treatment that they have been denied, they may feel as though their violent actions are justified.

Growing Inequality and Greater Punishment

Crime, of course, is closely related to its punishment. Punishment strategies share the goal of discouraging criminal behaviour, but they vary in the degree that they satisfy one or more of the five main goals of punishment: to take retribution for criminal behaviour, deter the criminal and others from committing crimes in the future, rehabilitate criminals so that they do not commit further crimes, restore the victim and the community, and incapacitate the criminal so that he or she cannot commit further crimes.

One of the oldest goals of punishment is retribution or vengeance—literally payback for harm done, or "an eye for an eye, a tooth for a tooth." The idea of retribution continues to hold a significant appeal for some Canadians, especially in respect to serious crimes such as rape, kidnapping, and murder. However, retributive justice receives less support when applied to more common, less serious offences like theft or public nuisance.

The second, more commonly accepted, purpose of punishment is deterrence: dissuading people from committing crimes by showing that if they do, they will be caught and (painfully) punished. Cesare Beccaria, an Italian who lived in the eighteenth century and was arguably the world's first criminologist, believed the goal of criminal punishment should be to prevent or deter crime. He considered this more socially useful than exacting retribution. He believed that people would act rationally to avoid punishments. To be effective, however, punishments would have to be unpleasant, certain, publicly observable, and swift—a goal harder to achieve than to enunciate.

A third commonly accepted purpose of punishment today is rehabilitation: obliging convicted criminals to become law-abiding members of society. Today, many Canadians support this idea of punishment because they believe in our ability to change ourselves and to change others, through systematic effort. Early rehabilitation efforts were aimed at changing the character or disciplining the soul of convicts by exposing them to religion and a severe lifestyle. Rehabilitation efforts today focus on providing support and supervision to ensure that prisoners refrain from crime when they reintegrate into law-abiding society. Sometimes, parole and probation staff also supply advice, education, or vocational training, assistance finding housing, and programs of treatment for mental illness and substance abuse.

A fourth commonly accepted purpose of punishment is to repair the harm done by the commission of a crime, and to restore the victim, the offender, and the community to a healthy state. Restorative justice focuses on ensuring that offenders take responsibility for the harm they have caused. As well, the victims of the crime have an effective voice in determining the punishment given and in explaining the effect of the crime on their lives. Where possible, restorative justice also tries to ensure the offender makes restitution to the victim and repairs any harm done to the community.

The fifth and final commonly accepted purpose of punishment is to incapacitate people who have inflicted harm and are considered still dangerous to society. Even if we do not believe in retribution, deterrence, rehabilitation, or restorative justice, we can still support incapacitation, on the grounds that removing dangerous people from society will improve public safety. Banishment and execution accomplished this goal in the past; today, most modern societies rely on imprisonment.

In the past hundred years we have come increasingly to depend on prisons to achieve most, if not all, of these goals. In general, prisons are intended to separate wrongdoers from law-abiding citizens and, by doing so, to protect good people from bad ones. Prisons are also intended to punish wrongdoers, inspire rehabilitation, and assist in the reintegration of convicts into society. In this sense, prisons are supposed to be not only sites of punishment but also of resocialization or re-education.

Prisons and other methods of rigorous rehabilitation have a long and checkered history. In his classic work *Discipline and Punish*, French sociologist Michel Foucault reminds us that in earlier times, punishment was a public spectacle, often involving torture and execution.[89] However, this mode of punishment often provoked pity for the victim. It came under criticism because it was inhumane, it did not significantly lessen crime, and it seemed excessive—even unjust.

Gradually, people began to accept a deterrence point of view, wanting punishment to ensure the criminal did not repeat the crime. In the late eighteenth century, deterrence and rehabilitation became the stated goals of imprisonment, and imprisonment quickly became the standard punishment for most crimes. Prison administrators came to think of their work as correctional, not punitive. However, to maintain public order, the punishment meted out was no longer publicly visible. Few could see or watch the reformative process, to be achieved through systematic discipline and punishment.

An important part of this reformative process was discipline of the body. Bodily discipline was first employed in the military, where recruits were taught how to stand, walk, hold and fire a weapon, and so on. But discipline did not stop at the body. The goal was to discipline the mind as well. Controlling both the mind and body meant using knowledge more efficiently. Accordingly, people in power set about to record as much information about people as possible, to better regulate them.

Discipline through the use of information meant increased information collection, including increased surveillance. Surveillance also meant the appearance of continued information collection. Here Foucault recalls Jeremy Bentham's idea of the panopticon: a prison where guards can always see the prisoners, but prisoners cannot always see the guards, so they do not know if they are being watched. This uncertainty leads prisoners to regulate themselves, since they could be watched at any moment. This continued external control was considered a step toward the learning of internal control—a movement to self-regulation.

Erving Goffman called the most extreme of these disciplining organizations total institutions. Goffman's classic book *Asylums: Essays on the Social Situation of Mental Patients and Other Inmates* was the first work to examine mental institutions from the perspective of the patient.[90] In doing so, Goffman developed an understanding of the organization of total institutions: their stated goals, how they function, and their significance for society.

Goffman defines a total institution as any place where people work, live, and for a time, are cut off from the wider community in a formally managed existence. They are total in that they all engage in rehabilitation that sometimes feels like punishment. The term total institutions usefully includes hospitals, prisons, monasteries, convents, boarding schools, residential schools, orphanages, military establishments, and slave quarters. Goffman focuses on mental institutions, but he proposes that all total institutions aim to change their inmates, to make them better people. That's why every institution needs around-the-clock organization of the needs of large numbers of inmates. However, all of these institutions create as much pathology as they correct. Additionally, within all total institutions, subcultures develop to oppose the administration.

All total institutions, to preserve order and resocialize their inmates, deprive them of autonomy, dignity, and symbols of their prior status. The process begins with entry events that Goffman calls *ceremonies of degradation*, which are intended to undermine the inmates' original identity. They are stripped of their rights and liberties, often without their realizing this is happening. For example, they may be forced to wear a uniform, receive significant changes to appearance (for example, a short haircut, no makeup), and answer to a number rather than a name.

This resocialization process gradually creates a new self-concept, one that complies with the institution's needs. Inmates then go through a process of secondary adjustments by those already in the institution, gaining entry into an underlife that teaches them how to use unauthorized means to circumvent the institution's rules. Many show what Goffman refers to as *inmate syndrome*, an adaptation that makes them more able to survive inside the institution but less able to survive outside it. No wonder so many inmates, after confinement within these institutions, become recidivists, often returning for repeated stays.

Sociologist Donald Clemmer[91] agrees that, by their nature, prisons degrade people, pressure them, and take away their rights. In this way, they make people less competent to deal with life outside prison, rather than more so. Degrading treatment is almost unavoidable—in fact, it is a strategy used by prison officials to control a large community of (usually) young, unruly men. One consequence of this harsh, degrading control is that prisoners learn the prison subculture, especially its anti-administration values and codes of conduct. As well, through contact with more experienced inmates, prisoners gain new criminal skills, often learning to behave in even more undesirable and violent ways. They end with an identity that is more deviant than the one they brought into the prison.

Prisonization, as Clemmer calls this process, produces prisoners who have been well-socialized to prison life—people who fit perfectly into the inmate society but poorly outside of it. As their release from prison approaches, inmates often feel great stress. After release, they often commit even more crimes—sometimes, even more violent crimes—and many end back in prison. This process is called *recidivism* or, more popularly, the "revolving door" of prison life. The extent of recidivism is hard to measure, but Canadian studies have consistently found large numbers of offenders returning to the criminal justice system—some are even resentenced many times over.

Not only is imprisonment often ineffective given its stated goals, it also tends to target those who are least able to resist it. In Canada and elsewhere, the criminal law—and penal punishment—is unduly harsh on the people who are most likely to get into trouble with the law: the poor, minorities, and the disadvantaged. In particular, the

Commission on Systemic Racism in the Ontario Criminal Justice System has found that black people are overrepresented in Ontario jails. According to the National Parole Board (2007/2008), black people make up only 2.5 percent of the Canadian population, but they account for 7.3 percent of prisoners in federal prisons.

Likewise, Aboriginal peoples made up 3 percent of the Canadian population in 2007/2008, and yet they accounted for an astonishing 22 percent of all admissions to sentenced custody.[92] This overrepresentation is especially acute in some western provinces. In Saskatchewan, for example, Aboriginal people comprise 81 percent of the prison population, but only 11 percent of the province's general adult population.[93] Aboriginal women, in particular, are overrepresented, with many more Aboriginal than non-Aboriginal inmates making up the female correctional population.[94]

These Aboriginal offenders are also younger, less educated, less likely to be employed at the time of their admission to prison, and more likely to reoffend than non-Aboriginal offenders. In addition, 81 percent of Aboriginal offenders in Saskatchewan were found to have a substance abuse problem.[95]

Canada is a moderately punitive country, if we consider the imprisonment rate, compared to that of other countries. Over the last few years, Canada's imprisonment rate has varied between 105 and 110 prisoners per 100,000 of the population. Imprisonment rates are far lower than this in Japan, Switzerland, and the Scandinavian countries (Finland, Sweden, Denmark, and Norway)—countries that are just as developed as Canada and therefore make good comparisons. Note in passing that these other countries have lower rates of income inequality than Canada. This leads us to wonder whether societies that are more unequal are also more punitive.

Supporting this idea, we find that imprisonment rates are far higher in the United States, Russia (and members of the former Soviet Union), China, Singapore, and some rapidly developing nations such as South Africa and Brazil. These countries all have higher rates of income inequality than Canada. This variation— in punishments and in inequality—tells us we need to look for sociological and historical reasons why some nations punish their citizens more commonly and more harshly than others.

Canada and the United States are undeniably similar in many respects, but they are very different in the ways they punish rule-breakers, and the difference has a lot to do with different degrees of inequality. What's more, as the level of inequality has grown in the US, so has the rate of US imprisonment. The American imprisonment rate has exploded over the last thirty-five years and is now more than five times as high as it was in 1970. By contrast, there has been virtually no growth in the Canadian prison system, and our crime rate has continued to decline over the past two decades, currently resting at its lowest since 1972. Although inequality in Canada has grown over the same period, the continually lower crime rate can be explained by factors such as an aging population (the Baby Boomers becoming seniors). If not for the aging population, among other factors, Canada's crime rate may also have risen over this period.[96]

The expansion of the US prison system, a result of inequality, has also had a dramatic general effect on social inequality, given the extreme disparities in imprisonment for African American men born since the 1960s. Through its effect on employment and other areas, imprisonment disrupts the life course, produces enduring disadvantages, and fosters a class of social outsiders. Just as economic opportunities for unskilled young men collapsed in American inner cities, the state and federal governments adopted more punitive policies, undermining the earlier goal of rehabilitation. So, in recent years, high rates of imprisonment have weakened the integration of cohorts of young African American men into American society. This imprisonment surge has hit the most disadvantaged and poorly educated men the hardest.

High incarceration rates among low-status and minority men are unmistakable. The experience of incarceration is so widespread among disadvantaged social groups as to be a defining feature of their collective experience. Incarceration used to signal dangerousness or persistent deviance, but by 2000, it had become a common event for poor, minority males, especially those who are black.

The racially concentrated rate of incarceration has two profound effects on American social and economic inequality. First, mass imprisonment generates invisible inequality. Official statistics and data sources that measure the economic well-being of the population do not count those institutionalized. The large labour force surveys that measure the unemployment rate, for example, are drawn from samples of households and thereby conceal the stalled economic progress of black youths in prison.

The second effect of incarceration is the reduction of life chances of inmates after they are released. Through the stigma of a criminal conviction, the diminished human capital from time out of the labour force, and the weakened social connections to legitimate employment opportunities, incarceration reduces the wages and employment of those serving time in prison. In addition, it limits the types of jobs that are available to formerly incarcerated workers. Career jobs requiring a high level of trust, skill, credentials, or social connections are largely out of reach to those with prison records. As a result, incarceration channels former inmates into the secondary labour market in which employment is precarious and there are few prospects for mobility. In this way, the American penal system acts to reinforce the lines of social disadvantage. Likewise, inequality has had an impact on policing and sentencing policy, as authorities use law enforcement to respond to fears of social disorder or threat from poor and marginalized men.[97] Such a relationship would explain the rise in economic inequality and incarceration rates.

An important result of this incarceration is the negative social reaction that follows prison sentences and releases. Applying what in sociology is known as *labelling theory*, interactionists maintain that when people are labelled criminals and assumed to possess the negative traits that accompany the criminal stigma, their deviant careers expand because they accept society's negative view of them. The label conferred upon them by the criminal justice system can be irreversible, for it follows felony processing that permanently marks one's record and exacts social consequences. As a result, large cohorts of former prisoners, about 650,000 each year, return to their poor, minority neighbourhoods and face reduced economic opportunities.[98] They often live at the margins of the labour market and are precariously employed in unsteady, low-wage jobs that offer little prospect of mobility. With added barriers to overcome, former inmates are more likely to become repeat offenders. The punitive trend in criminal justice policy may, then, be even tougher on the poor than it is on crime.

The harmful results of imprisonment go well beyond their effects on work, income, and social class. Imprisonment affects social and family life as well. Being sentenced to prison often results in job loss and family breakup. Most prisoners, with little or no income before entering prison, are often unable to pay child and family support while in prison. This leaves their families dependent on welfare, leading to a new generation of children raised by single parents on welfare and in prison. And imprisonment affects the quality and survival of marriages—also, the likelihood of marriage, especially for minority populations with high rates of imprisonment.

Canadians have largely been able to escape several of the wider forces or risk factors at the root of high imprisonment rates in other countries. These include—but are not restricted to—a history of racial segregation as in the United States and an attack on social redistribution by conservative governments in both the US and the UK. The fragmenting of Canadian politics owing to regionalism and multiculturalism, and a weak central government, have so far kept Canada from adopting the same punitive policies—especially, mandatory minimum sentencing—as in the United States and the UK.[99] But, since we are becoming more unequal over time, perhaps we will see analogous increases in incarceration and their negative effects on people in the future.

In our next chapter, we will discuss the ultimate, supreme effect of inequality: war and destruction. War is a natural, inevitable outgrowth of the processes we have discussed so far: punishment, stigmatization, victimization, racialization, exclusion, domination, and exploitation inflicted on disadvantaged peoples.

CHAPTER 8

War and Destruction

———•◆•———

"War does not determine who is right—only who is left."
Albert Einstein

Robert Owen believed that equality could be achieved gradually, carefully, and sympathetically, through social and industrial experiments. Perhaps he underestimated the effects of past inequality on people's ability to take charge of their own lives. He did not think violence would play a part in this story of social improvement. However, it does play a part. In this chapter, we will examine the role of inequality in the rise and prolongation of wars. Of course, there are other factors contributing to war as well. And, given the complexity of wars and the multitude of factors influencing why they happen, it's no surprise that people's opinions vary as to their causes.

Probably the most popular view is the one based on evolutionary psychology (and biology). This view defines war as a human extension of animal behaviour, related to instinctive territoriality and competition. In this view, people fight to protect their territory and to obtain needed resources. An early advocate of this view was Konrad Lorenz, who proposed that animals are naturally aggressive, and that this aggression also shows up in humans in the form of war.[1] In the course of human development, increasingly advanced technology simply heightens the human capacity for destructiveness and self-destruction.

Critics have noted, however, that human warfare differs more than just technologically from territorial fights between animals. After all, not all human populations are equally warlike and, historically, wars come and go. Social factors and childhood socialization are also important in the creation and persistence of warfare. So while human aggression may be a universal occurrence, warfare is not.

An alternate theory, put forward by Sigmund Freud and his followers, proposes that war is inevitable because people have a destructive instinct, just as they have an instinct for love. Freud understood that, to live together in societies, people need to curtail their "death instinct"—a natural desire for outward aggression. But curtailing the outward expression of aggression creates neurosis, the inward expression of aggression. This conflict between war and neurosis represented, for Freud, one of the central, inescapable difficulties in human life.[2]

To handle this destructive instinct, nation states channel people's pent-up aggression outwards, into warfare. In a famous exchange of letters on the topic, Freud and Einstein agreed that warfare could be reduced if nations were willing to give up some of their sovereignty to an international body like the League of Nations, with adequate power to compel obedience by the member nations. However, neither Freud nor Einstein was hopeful that this would happen. In any event, since destructive urges are deemed to be universal, Freudian theories do not explain when or how wars occur. Nor do they explain the fact that some societies engage in war less often than other societies. Thus, while Freudian theories are good at explaining why humans are warlike in general, they are not good at explaining why some societies are more warlike than others.

Many theorists have observed that aggressive rulers play a part in warfare. In history, very few wars have started due to popular demand. Far more often, the rulers have drawn a reluctant populace into war. Hitler, for example, used clever propaganda techniques to goad the German citizenry into war, blaming the Communists, the Jews, and other enemies for Germany's troubles, and using this as an excuse to invade Poland.[3] The combination of national propaganda and personal charisma were instrumental in pushing Germany toward war.

Others have proposed demographic theories about war, following the lead of the eighteenth-century demographer Thomas Malthus. These theories focus on the role of expanding populations and diminishing resources as the key causes of armed conflict. Malthus famously wrote that without preventive checks (human actions that lower the birthrate, like abstinence and the postponement of marriage), populations will always increase until they are limited by positive checks (war, disease, and famine).[4] Positive checks, by this theory, would be most likely to occur in high-fertility parts of the world, because these populations grow the most rapidly.

Still other demographic theorists have highlighted the role of young people in war-making (just as researchers have highlighted the role of young people in criminal behaviour). The so-called youth bulge theory proposes that war tends to break out when large youth cohorts (especially male) experience a lack of regular, peaceful job opportunities. This youth bulge becomes problematic when 30 to 40 percent of the males of a nation belong to the fighting age cohorts (fifteen to twenty-nine years old), as would commonly be the case in high-fertility countries.

Some have used this theory to explain Islamic terrorism.[5] According to this theory, however, religions and ideologies are secondary factors that merely legitimate violence; they do not result in violence unless a youth bulge is present to do the fighting. So, for example, violence in the high-fertility Gaza Strip may have been driven by this kind of youth bulge. An absence of violence in nearby Lebanon, on the other hand, is explainable by the much lower level of fertility. Both Lebanon and Gaza have similar religious and ideological profiles, but very different demographic profiles, suggesting that demography—not ideology—drives Islamic violence. The same theory is often applied to revolutions. Some have suggested that recent political events in Libya, Syria, and Egypt—in Africa and the Middle East more generally—are the result of a *youthquake* and a corresponding lack of job opportunities for young people. The combination of too many young men and too few jobs is a recipe for political explosion.

But this theory, as attractive as it may be, fails to explain the wars begun by more developed, lower-fertility countries, without an excess of unemployed young men. Some wars involving developed countries begin with the pursuit of territory for natural resources and wealth. Indeed, Marxist theory proposes that all modern wars are caused by a competition for resources and markets between capitalist powers. These wars are a natural result of the free market system, which must always expand or else implode. By this reckoning, war will disappear only after a world revolution has overthrown the global capitalist class.

For similar reasons, some say that bankers cause wars. War is particularly lucrative for banks, which are often called on to lend governments the money to make war. As well, banks lend money to war industries, so they can produce the material needed for war-making. Some theorists even propose that international bankers secretly control central banking systems like the US Federal Reserve. Allegedly, they manipulate the public to believe in an imaginary enemy in order to initiate the war-making process.

However, this theory also has its limitations, since not all wars are economically profitable, even for capitalists. Moreover, many wars appear to have purely strategic, rather than economic motives. The so-called rationalist theory views war as a betting game—a game of strategic moves, aimed at achieving strategic political (or geopolitical) goals under conditions of uncertainty. Sometimes, despite the great risks involved, some countries cannot avoid war. However, this theory too has its limitations. First, it is hard to apply cost-benefit calculations to explain the most extreme genocidal cases of war—for example, those in Rwanda and Kosovo—where no bargain is ever offered. Second, rationalist theories seem to assume the state acts as a unitary individual. This may make sense when analyzing dictatorships or monarchies, but makes less sense when the country's leader is controlled by a congress or parliament. Third, rationalist theories assume the actors involved can accurately assess their likelihood of success or failure. But usually this is not the case, and it ignores the role of irrational prejudices, fears, hopes, and fantasies.

War and Inequality

On the surface, the connection between inequality and violence is simple: more inequality, by creating more frustration, creates more aggression, hence more violence. In support of this, one interesting study by Robert Macculloch surveyed a quarter-million randomly sampled individuals and asked about their desires for revolution.[6] The findings show that more people express a preference for revolt when their nation is highly unequal. Indeed, Macculloch argues that "a 1-standard deviation increase in the Gini coefficient explains up to 38 percent of the standard deviation in revolutionary support."[7]

Intuitively, this makes sense. It argues that reductions in inequality will reduce people's support for revolution. However, one wonders how willingly people with a stated taste for revolt would actually translate their feelings into risky actions, even under the worst possible conditions. The connection between inequality and violence—whether we are discussing domestic violence, civil warfare, rebellion, revolution, or foreign war—is not a simple one at all. We know this, for example, from the numerous studies of frustration and aggression carried out by social scientists nearly eighty years ago.

Consider research on the so-called frustration–aggression hypothesis, a theory of aggression proposed by John Dollard, Neal E. Miller, and colleagues in 1939 and further developed by associates and students of these researchers in later years. The theory proposes that aggression results when a person's efforts to attain a goal are blocked or frustrated. Simply stated, frustration causes aggression. However, when the source of the frustration cannot be challenged, the victim directs (or displaces) the aggression onto an innocent target, or even channels it into dreams. So, for example, anthropologists J.W.M. Whiting and I.L. Child argued in their book *Child Training and Personality* (1953) that such displacement can be seen in dreams and fears of witchcraft in highly repressive societies.

As already noted, in many social and cultural contexts aggression—at least, direct aggression against one's oppressors—is not an option. The frustration caused by social inequality may, among men, express itself as aggression against wives and children, and, among women and children, express itself in suicide and psychosomatic illnesses. So, in short, frustration does not guarantee aggression, nor does the expression of aggression guarantee warfare.

On a societal level, the linkages are even more complex, as a great many elements go into the translation of frustration into political violence. This is evident in a clear statement of the problem by Walter Goldfrank, who studied inequality and revolution in rural Mexico.[8] Reducing his findings to a few overarching principles, Goldfrank writes:

> First, inequality and oppression do not in themselves produce revolt (or dissensus). . . . Second, it is false to argue that the greater the inequality, the greater the rebelliousness. . . . Third, the activities of the dominant rural class are crucial to the analysis of inequality and revolution. . . . Fourth, the government's ability to suppress rebellion was most limited in the areas where rebellion was most likely. . . . In sum, rural revolt in Mexico suggests no easy or linear correlations between inequality and discontent, or between discontent and revolt. . . . Varied aspects of class relations and political structure intervene between inequality and revolt. Hence it is also true that revolution, while a conclusive indicator of "dissensus," cannot be the only one.[9]

Similar findings are present in the research of others who have studied revolution and social movements. The expression of violence in response to unfair and oppressive conditions depends, to a great extent, on opportunities, resources, and expectations. Where people expect little or have few opportunities or resources by which to express their discontent, rebellions are unlikely, no matter how great the inequality. Where people's expectations are higher, and people have more opportunities and resources to express their discontent, rebellions are much more likely, even if the injustices (objectively viewed) are much less severe than in the previous instance.

This tells us that an important factor in rebellious behaviour is the direction of movement—in society and in people's heads. If things are getting better, or people think they are getting better, then people are less likely to rebel. In part, this is why globalization has reduced political protest throughout the world. Mills notes that, by exporting manufacturing jobs to low-wage parts of the world, globalization has reduced inequality in developing economies, while increasing inequality in industrialized nations.[10] This suggests that globalization is likely to quell rebellious behaviour in the less-developed countries that were at highest risk of it in the past and stimulate rebellious behaviour in industrial countries. But again, the revolutionary potential of developed societies depends on what people expect, what they think is happening, and how they explain their declining conditions. In the most developed industrial societies, people tend to hope for the best.

By contrast, in states without a strong tradition of good government—sometimes called failed states—worsening economic conditions and increased inequality produce violence and rebellion. The precipitating conditions are economic decline and growing income inequality, but other factors play a part. Perhaps most important of all, "economic regress and political decay bring about relative deprivation or perception by influential social groups of injustice arising from a growing discrepancy between what they expect and get."[11]

That said, some societies are able to develop effective ways of channeling conflict peacefully, despite inequality. The Whitehall Papers note that:

> Despite high and rising levels of inequality in key regions of the world over the last two decades, the number of armed conflicts has declined. An important part of the explanation for this decline appears to lie in the increasing ability of some societies to develop mechanisms for the peaceful resolution of distributional conflicts, most notably through the spread of democratic political system.[12]

A case in point is Latin America, which remains highly unequal in economic terms yet much more peaceful and stable in recent decades than in the past. By contrast, problems remain in so-called weak or failed states like Somalia, or where (as in Northern Ireland), economic deprivation combines with strong ethno-nationalist traditions.

Summing up our current state of knowledge, Cramer asserts that while economic inequality is important for explaining civil conflict, the link between inequality and conflict is not direct.[13] Different kinds of inequalities have different effects, as do the mechanisms and processes that turn inequality into violent conflict.[14] With all this in mind, Cramer urges us to be cautious about the claims of studies that attribute more predictive power to inequality measures than they deserve.

So, we will have a hard time tracing a simple link between inequality and violence under all circumstances. On the other hand, we have clear evidence that inequality affects people's propensity to violence—their "taste for revolt" as we discussed above. As for translating this propensity into action, low levels of trust can play an important role.[15] So can provocative shows of force by the police and military. More unequal societies tend to use guard labour to monitor and control the symptoms of inequality. A society with a large part of its workforce committed to guarding, policing, soldiering, supervising, prosecuting, and judging is a society with a high potential for rebellion.[16]

Often, the link between inequality and violence is easiest to see in rural, pre-industrial settings. Consider, for example, the finding by researchers who studied the connection between land inequality and conflict intensity in a variety of societies.[17] They note that the most severe violence between landlords and landless people occurs at intermediate levels of land inequality—not under conditions of the most extreme inequality.

This finding permits several possible (and mutually compatible) interpretations. First, it suggests that rebellion is most likely when the peasantry has risen above abject poverty but is still far from equitable land-sharing. It is at this stage that the peasantry has the resources it needs for a prolonged struggle, yet still has good reason to enter into such a struggle. Second, it suggests that rebellion, as social scientists used to argue fifty years ago, is driven by expectations that are rising more quickly than the rate of social improvement. Third, and finally, it suggests that the transition from old to new ways unleashes aggression that stays in check so long as the old ways appear to be permanent.

This reminds us of Rosemary Gartner's finding that femicide—homicidal violence by men against women—is most common in societies in the midst of a changeover from traditional to modern ways. It may be true, as other research shows, that violence against women (including sexual violence) is prevalent where women's status is lower than men's.[18] But it is apparently even more prevalent where the status of women is starting to rise, threatening men's traditional standing in the society.

A second key factor in the expression of "taste for revolt" is the strength of forces arrayed against rebellion—for example, the ability of government to respond flexibly to demands for change. Governments that want to control people's rebelliousness should avoid unduly violent responses and make clear that people who stay away from rebellion—the politically innocent—will be spared punishment.[19] Punishment that is disproportionately and carelessly dispensed, on the other hand, may encourage rebellion and serve to recruit more rebels. Most important for our current discussion, the outbreak of rebellion depends on "the level of preexisting inequality between the poor and the ruling elite, the relative military capabilities of the two groups, and the "destructiveness of conflict." Thus, if a society tries to repress the suffering caused by inequality through threats of military backlash, widespread fear makes rebellion more likely.[20]

The same social conditions that are conducive to rebellion—or at least, a taste for revolt—are conducive to urban violence. As Richard Wilkinson, whom we mentioned in Chapter 6, points out, "the tendency for rates of violent crime and homicide to be higher where there is more inequality is part of a more general tendency for the quality of social relations to be poorer in more hierarchical societies."[21] Compared with more affiliative and egalitarian societies, unequal societies are more likely to inspire tastes for violence as well as rebellion.

So far, we have focused on the conflict-producing effects of economic inequality. However, recent research has also focused attention on horizontal (ethnic-, regional-, or religious-based) inequalities—that is, on inequalities between culturally defined groups. As James Robinson notes, "class conflict is not necessarily worse than ethnic conflict. In fact, ethnic conflict is generally worse when the distribution of income is more equal,"[23] since ethnicity is immutable while class position is not. As individuals, people can do nothing (or very little) about the social disadvantages of belonging to a particular ethnic (or racial, religious, or caste) group. They cannot solve the problem through educational attainment and social mobility, for example. For this reason, horizontal inequalities have become a far more explosive source of civil violence than any other source.

Marie Besançon, agreeing with Robinson, notes that "traditionally deprived identity groups are more likely to engage in conflict under more economically equal conditions, while class or revolutionary wars fall under the conditions of greater economic inequality and war."[24] This means that we must consider genocides—aimed at particular ethnic, tribal, or religious groups—differently from other, equally violent types of civil war and political upheaval. Besancon asserts that political and social equalities are important in mitigating ethnic violence. She concludes that peace and stability in ethnically divided states will require the equalization of incomes and also the inclusion of all groups, especially minorities, within the political agenda and the equal distribution of public goods.[25]

Just as with finding a link between economic (or class-based) inequality and violence, we also encounter problems finding a link between horizontal (or culture-based) inequality and violence. While identity politics and horizontal inequalities mobilize groups for conflict,[26] the patterns in the relationship are far from simple.[27] For ethnic conflict over "horizontal inequalities," we will need to find not only perceived injustice in one or more ethnic communities, but also a strong communal identity and strong institutional resources for seeking justice.[28]

Disentangling these effects requires a subtle, powerful methodology. Through the use of geocoding, researchers have concluded that "in highly unequal societies, both rich and poor groups fight more often than those groups whose wealth lies closer to the country average."[29] Perhaps poorer groups fight because they have little to lose and a strong motivation to improve their standing. Richer groups fight because they have a great deal to lose and a strong resource base with which to wage the battle.

Indonesia is one country that has had to deal with the problems of horizontal inequality, using a strategy researcher Rachael Diprose has described as political decentralization.[30] This decentralization has reportedly relieved tensions between rich and poor groups and has also addressed long-standing inter-group tensions and horizontal inequalities at the local level, "particularly where geographically concentrated ethno-religious groups have previously been marginalized from government."[31] However, while solving old problems, decentralization has created new ones. For example, it has promoted ethnoreligious segregation and a great deal of migration, as groups relocate themselves for self-protection and self-advancement.

These outcomes have not led to violent conflict in Indonesia, Diprose notes, and they may not do so. It may be that conflict cannot be reduced below a certain level, given persistent horizontal inequalities and identities, and the best that can be hoped for is the channeling of hostility into peaceful electoral processes. We see such processes at work in multi-group, multi-party, multi-identity polities like Israel, for example.

An alternate strategy—or hope—is that the conflict between horizontally unequal groups can be moderated by cross-cutting cleavages. One study that looked at the risk of civil war in one hundred multi-ethnic societies finds that civil war is more likely in countries where "ethnicity is crosscut by socioeconomic class, geographic region, and religion."[32] These are countries like Canada circa 1950, when francophone ethnicity was centered in a particular region (the province of Quebec), characterized by a particular religion (Roman Catholicism), and disproportionately absent from the dominant financial, commercial, industrial, and professional classes. Though Canada weathered a brief so-called October Revolution in Quebec, there was no mass uprising, and Canada escaped the 1960s and 1970s without a civil war, leading us to conclude that conditions between Quebec and the rest of Canada were never as dire as the separatists were painting them.[33]

A theory linking horizontal inequalities to political violence may work best for less developed societies. For example, an analysis of civil conflict across thirty-six developing countries in the period 1986–2004 investigated ethnic, social, and economic polarization, as well as social and economic inequalities.[34] Focusing on the inequalities between groups, the study found that horizontal social inequality indeed predicted the outbreak of conflict, under specific conditions: notably, it is the interaction between group identity, segregation, institutionalization, and disadvantage that creates conflict. Taken on their own, these variables—ethnic polarization, inter-individual inequality, and ethnic or socio-economic polarization—have no significant effect. It is only when they come together that violence is likely to break out.

Issues of population pressure and resource scarcity also play an important part in the struggles between competing ethno-cultural or regional groups, and in fact research shows the effect of demographic pressure on violence risk.[35] Taking Indonesia as an example again, in the period 1990–2003 "demographic pressure and inequality seem to have little effect in isolation. However, in provinces where population growth is high, greater levels of inequality between religious groups appear to increase the violence risk."[36]

Given the importance of ethnic polarization and inequality, we need to consider the processes (such as exclusion, social division, and class formation) that lead to these outcomes. Here, Pauline Peters notes the role of processes "including commodification, structural adjustment, market liberalization and globalization . . . that limit or end negotiation and flexibility for certain social groups or categories."[37] This insight reminds us that processes of inter-group inequality and violence take place in a highly globalized, capitalized world.

Nowhere is the importance of this global context stated more forcefully than in a review by Gjermund Saether of several books published by the OECD on violence and inequality in Africa.[38] Saether concludes:

> There has been a tendency to focus only on internal political causes and, in particular, "ethnic" factors in explaining violent conflict in the region. However, ethnicity cannot be seen as the root cause of conflicts, although ethnic identities may con-tribute crucially to the spiral of violence. An economic analysis also places heavy responsibility on the major power centres out-side the continent for violent conflict in sub-Saharan Africa. . . . International economic strains increase both the potential and intensity of violent conflicts.[39]

Saether urges us to pay more attention to issues of debt and access to markets in any discussion of violence in developing societies.

Horizontal Inequality and War

It is difficult to speculate about all the causes of war and, among all of these causes, the relative importance of inequality.

There are, however, theorists who are attempting to take on this difficult task. Among the most prominent is a social scientist at the University of Oxford, Frances Stewart. In her work *War and Underdevelopment*, Stewart argues convincingly for the link between inequality and war.[40] While involved in another project on human development, Stewart noticed that all the countries on the bottom rungs of human and economic development were currently involved in wars, or had been very recently. It was obvious there was something lurking beneath simple explanations focusing exclusively on poverty or on conflict. That something turned out to be inequality.[41]

Stewart acknowledges, as we have, that wars are extremely complex social events, with a wide range of factors at play. Root causes of war may include poverty; economic stagnation; crime; lack of government services; high rates of unemployment; and shortages of land, food, and water, among other things. Reducing the likelihood of war, then, requires investing in development so that unemployment can be reduced, illicit trade can be controlled, and more services can be provided by the state. As well, social and cultural factors need to be considered, including ideology, public opinion, confidence in the government, and people's "taste for revolution."

Charismatic leaders in particular are often central in the cause and maintenance of warfare. Yet, while these people can help initiate war, leadership does not determine the extent and significance of warfare. Instead, it is the long-simmering historical grievances related to certain social factors—whether economic anxieties or political disagreements—that are the real fuel for protracted warfare. In her book, Stewart considers four hypotheses to explain why war happens. Some are similar to ideas we discussed earlier. As well, these theories are not mutually exclusive, so we do not have to choose between them. Stewart's four hypotheses are as follows:

> *Private motivation hypothesis*: War confers benefits on people . . . that can motivate people to fight. Young uneducated men, in particular, may gain employment as soldiers. War also generates opportunities to loot, profiteer from shortages and from aid, trade arms, and carry out illicit production and trade in drugs, diamonds, timber, and other commodities.

> *Failure of the social contract*: People accept state authority so long as the state delivers services and provides reasonable economic conditions (employment and incomes). With economic

stagnation or decline, and worsening state services, the social contract breaks down, and violence results.

Green war hypothesis: This [hypothesis] points to environmental degradation as a source of poverty and cause of conflict. For example, rising population pressure and falling agricultural productivity may lead to land disputes. Growing scarcity of water may provoke conflict.

Group motivation hypothesis: If there are important differences between groups, especially in the distribution and exercise of political and economic power . . . deprived groups are likely to seek (or be persuaded by their leaders to seek) redress . . . privileged groups may also be motivated to fight to protect their privileges against attack from deprived groups.[42]

Stewart most strongly supports the last hypothesis, a choice that is in line with our own ideas. While the other three are important, it is this last one that highlights the often overlooked role of inequality. Stewart's contribution lies in recognizing that inequalities related to group membership, not inequalities between individuals, pose the greatest risks of conflict. *Horizontal inequalities*—those based on economic, social, or political differences—cause the conflicts that are most likely to explode into war.

According to Stewart, conflict ensues either when deprived groups try to gain some of the privileges of the upper classes, or when "privileged groups [are] motivated to fight to protect their privileges against attack from deprived groups."[43] Horizontal inequalities are those that, aside from class and income inequality, we have been discussing throughout this book: inequalities between genders, racial and especially ethnic groups, age groups, neighbourhoods, sexualities, regions, nations, and empires.

Wars, then, despite their variations over time, place, and circumstance, usually build on conflicts about inequality. As such, the key to reducing war, according to Stewart, is getting to the root of inequality. By focusing on horizontal inequalities, Stewart highlights a newer theme in the scholarly research on inequality and conflict. She shows that, where inter-group inequalities are severe, intra-group inequalities (for example, between the wealthy and poor members) will not be a primary cause of organized political conflict.[44]

This insight is important for the study of all collective protests, even including civil wars, which are driven by conflict between groups.[45] More recent studies that take this new approach have found that horizontal inequalities that divide people along ethnic lines increase the risk that disadvantaged people will express themselves in violence.[46]

It is important to note that non-economic or symbolic goals can also motivate people to revolt. Modern studies of civil war have defined two types of rebellion: those that are greed-driven and those that are grievance-driven. Greed-driven rebellions aim to increase people's access to financial and natural resources. Grievance-driven rebellions, on the other hand, tend to be seeking equality or political rights for their own sake, or for symbolic reasons.[47]

However, just because people feel that they are being treated unfairly does not mean they will react violently. Group identification is critically important in mobilizing people to fight.[48] Groups that differ in wealth and power are not likely to identify with each other. So a society divided between two well-defined groups that are very different from one another is likely to experience political instability and even rebellion.[49] In effect, the combination of high levels of identification *within* groups, and high levels of alienation (or distance) *between* groups, is conducive to civil wars.

Evidently, then, group dynamics and horizontal inequalities play a significant role in causing civil war. One study by Ted Gurr used the Minorities at Risk (MAR) database—the only worldwide dataset that includes information on inequality at a group level.[50] Gurr found that civil protest is more likely to occur in societies where groups with strong identities also have strongly shared grievances. Presumably, these grievances motivate people to act violently in order to bring about change. In line with Stewart's thinking, it appears that group identities and the horizontal inequalities that divide these groups play an important role in civil conflict.

This is not to ignore the role of economic differences. Gudrun Ostby is one of the many scholars who have found that civil unrest is more likely to occur in areas in which both economic and social polarization are extreme.[51] Strong socio-economic divisions between groups make people within the same group feel closer to one another, while at the same time alienating them from people in different groups. That said, social polarization has an even stronger impact on civil unrest than economic polarization. So educational inequality (one example of a horizontal inequality) is more important in making an entire group resentful than unequal wealth (a vertical example).[52] The link between horizontal social inequality and conflict was especially strong in Ostby's study. This suggests that other studies on the topic may not have been sensitive to the influence that horizontal inequalities have in generating civil conflicts.[53]

When Stewart identified those nations at the bottom of the development ladder that were seemingly always at war, she was unwittingly identifying what others have called "failed states." Since 2005, the US government has posted an annual list of failed states, in part to explain American military and foreign policy initiatives throughout the world. These failed states, as Stewart notes, are often the locus of civil war and promoters of wars in other nearby countries. At the top of the US government's failed states list, we find Somalia, Zimbabwe, Sudan, Chad, Democratic Republic of the Congo, Iraq, Afghanistan, Central African Republic, Guinea, and Pakistan. By contrast, at the top of the sustainable (that is, non-failed) states list, we find Norway, Finland, Sweden, Switzerland, Ireland, Denmark, New Zealand, Australia, Netherlands, and Austria. Canada is one of the next three states, alongside Luxemburg and Iceland. In contrast to failed states, sustainable states tend to stay out of wars.

The Failed State Index measures the weakness, ineffectiveness, and illegitimacy of a national government, and its inability to control the economy and the borders and maintain rule of law. Notably for our purposes, these are not trivial or unimportant contributors to war. Items important in identifying a failed state include uncontrollable demographic pressures, refugees, group grievances, human flight, economic decline, corruption, public lack of confidence in the state, poor public services, violations of human rights, factionalized elites, and external intervention. In calculating a country's rating on this scale, each of twelve dimensions is scored from 0–10, with a top possible score of 120 and a bottom possible score of 10. The most failed state on the list, Somalia, has a score of 114.7 out of 120, showing failure on virtually every dimension. The most successful or sustainable state, Norway, has a score of 18.3, showing success on virtually every dimension of rule.

To say that a nation has "failed" is seemingly to stigmatize it. However, given the criteria used to classify these states, we see some justification for this label. Moreover, consider that each of these failed states has a history of internal or external war. That leaves us to ask, is war a cause or effect of state failure? Or, are both war-making and state failure a result of social inequalities?

We also know from the news media that societies with high scores on the Failed State Index have high degrees of racial (or tribal) strife and troubling issues around gender. This leads us to wonder whether failed states, which are so enmeshed in gender and ethnic inequality, also manifest other forms of inequality like income inequality, for example. Let's find out by determining if the Gini Index of income inequality is highly correlated with the Failed States Index.

To do so, we will consider published data for both of these measures for the top and bottom twenty countries on the Failed States list. If inequality is a generalized cultural tendency or "habit," as we have suggested, societies that score highest on the Failed States Index will also score highest on the Gini Index. To further simplify our analysis, we will split the Gini indices around the median (that is showing countries that are above and below average in their income inequality), in order to view the data in a simple two-by-two table.

The data (Table 1) from this experiment show that income inequality (as measured by the Gini Index) is indeed highly correlated with gender inequality and racial inequality (as measured by the Failed States Index). Said more simply, with a few exceptions, societies that have a high degree of income inequality (i.e., score high on the Gini Index) also have a high degree of gender and racial inequality (i.e., score high on the Failed States Index).

The correlation between income inequality and state failure also suggests that states engaged in a lot of warfare are also states with failing governments and high levels of income, gender, and ethnic inequality. Thus, as we have been arguing, inequality tends to predict—and possibly cause—violence, rebellion, and war.

In Table 1, only eight out of forty societies do not conform to this pattern. First, Afghanistan, Iraq, Pakistan, and Ethiopia have lower levels of income inequality than we would expect from their Failed State score. Perhaps Western intervention in these four societies has reduced the level of income inequality below its expected level—the level that is common in neighbouring nations, like Syria and Saudi Arabia. Second, the US, the UK, Portugal, and New Zealand have higher levels of income inequality than we would

Table 1 Cross-Tabulation of Indices of Inequality, Gini Index[a] and Failed State Index			
Failed State Index	Gini Index <35 (24–34)	Gini Index >35 (35–60)	No Gini information
>98 (98–113) 20 Most-Failed States	4 (Afghanistan, Iraq, Pakistan, Ethiopia)	13	3
<35 (20–35) 20 Most-Sustainable States	16	4 (US, UK, Portugal, New Zealand)	0

[a]Before taxes and transfer payments

Sources: "Gini Index." World Bank, Development Research Group. http://data.worldbank.org/indicator/SI.POV.GINI; "Failed States Index 2012." The Fund for Peace. http://www.fundforpeace.org/global/library/cfsir1210-failedstatesindex2012-06p.pdf.

expect from their Failed State score. The US result is not surprising, since it is well known for racial strife. However, the UK, Portugal, and New Zealand do come as surprises. More research is needed to understand these eight anomalies.

Gender Inequality and Warfare

As noted, failed states are also largely characterized by the horizontal inequalities Stewart and others have identified—for example, horizontal inequalities by gender and horizontal inequalities by race and ethnicity.

One kind of gender inequality is violence perpetrated by men against women, including rape and physical abuse.[54] Violence is one of the ways by which men maintain their power and control. Further, the dominant ideology in patriarchal societies affirms the weakness of women while rewarding the aggressiveness of men.[55] Therefore, the subordination of women goes hand in hand with male violence, broadly defined by Johan Galtung to include the exploitation and marginalization of women, as well as their fragmentation as a group.[56] The result is a patriarchal culture in which violence against women is alternately accepted or ignored, and assertions of male dominance like rape and abuse come to be viewed as an unavoidable (though of course horrible) part of life.

This norm of violence plays out in national and international politics, and numerous studies link higher rates of domestic violence to higher rates of violent conflict resolution.[57] As Mary Caprioli says, an acceptance of individual, societal, and structural violence strengthens the validity of using violence to resolve global conflicts.[58] Caprioli finds that states characterized by low levels of gender equality are more likely than other states to initiate international violence in response to a dispute. In other words, a culture marked by gendered violence on the individual level has been primed for other forms of violence on a larger scale, resulting in higher levels of both inter- and intrastate violence.

Not only does violence against women point to gender inequality and predict inter-state violence: other indicators of gender inequality—such as high fertility rates and low female employment rates—do the same. In societies with high fertility rates, women tend to have less access to education and jobs than men.[59] Moreover, high fertility rates are associated with a perception of women as mainly baby-producers and homemakers. Accordingly, women in societies with high fertility rates tend to have modest occupational aspirations and are more financially dependent on men.[60] As a result, decision-making authority for women both inside and outside the home is reduced in societies with high fertility rates.[61]

Caprioli found that high fertility nations (in which women bear three or more children each) are twice as likely as low fertility nations to experience internal conflicts (i.e., rebellions and civil wars). Other studies have confirmed these findings, noting that with increases in gender equality, the likelihood of intrastate armed conflict (i.e., civil war) decreases.[62]

A state's gender equality can also be measured by female employment rates. Women tend to gain a sense of empowerment in the work force, as they are better able to support themselves financially and reduce their reliance on men. By increasing women's self-esteem, social and financial status, and power, employment can level the playing field between men and women. Again, Caprioli found that states with only 10 percent of women in the paid labour force are thirty times more likely to experience intrastate conflict than states with 40 percent (or more) of women in the labour force.[63]

Studies on international conflict yield similar results. As Caprioli found, higher levels of international violence are related to both high fertility rates and low female participation in the labour force.[64] Notably, even a slight increase in female employment rates results in a drastic drop in the use of military force to resolve international conflicts.

Gender inequality relies on a construction of women as lesser, weaker people who lack agency. Stereotyping and socialization have helped to maintain this perception of women as inherently inferior to men.[65] In turn, discrimination against women determines their social roles, access to power and resources, responsibilities, and the behaviour expected of them.[66]

These socially constructed gender relations produce violence against women, as we have noted, but they also cause violence on behalf of women. The latter form of violence works through a form of benevolent sexism, marked by chivalry and often considered benign. Hegemonic masculinity, on the other hand, describes a dominant culture of manhood characterized by courage, competitiveness, and aggression. Both benevolent sexism and hegemonic masculinity contribute to a culture of militarism: an ideology that calls men to protect their country, women, and children. Nation-states often appeal to male citizens on these grounds, as a call to arms.

Gender inequality thus leads to violent conflict by promoting the idea that strong men must defend their weak women—an inequality that mobilizes men through the use of stereotypes and gendered language (for example, "the motherland"). War efforts have traditionally relied on the notion of masculine heroes fighting to protect the gendered motherland and the defenceless women who live within it.[67] As such, researchers have proposed the stereotyped roles of female caretakers and male defenders lay the foundation for patriarchal militarism.[68] Thus gendered hierarchies are used as an explanation of violence against women, and as a justification of men's use of violence against other men.

However, this is not the only way in which allegedly powerless women have been used to justify violent conflict. When the United States faced dwindling support for the current war in Afghanistan, they turned to the familiar trope of the helpless Eastern female. This conflict, which has lasted over ten years and killed thousands, was launched as part of the War on Terror. However, it has been increasingly portrayed under the guise of saving women from an oppressive regime. Therefore the relationship between masculine superiority and peace is two-sided, encouraging men to act as protectors of women at home and saviours of women abroad. Joshua S. Goldstein, in his book *War and Gender*, suggests that this cultural construction of tough men who need to care for tender women also supports male aggression by framing conflict as a test of manhood.[69]

The stereotypes of male aggressiveness and female peaceful-ness also play out in leadership styles. Societies with a high propor-tion of female politicians are one-fifth as likely to use violence to solve international disputes as societies with a low proportion of female politicians.[70]

That said, female politicians do not reduce violence by reduc-ing gender inequality. Both male and female leaders encourage women to support the collective goals of their nation, whether these goals reduce gender equality or not.[71] Further, female leaders tend to avoid gender-related issues altogether in their efforts gain elected office or maintain communal solidarity.[72] Women leaders may fear that an attempt to address issues of gender inequality drive a wedge between men and women, thereby weakening a sense of unity across the nation. Accordingly, gender inequality is rarely addressed on a national scale—not even by female political leaders.

Many studies show that women are more opposed to war and violence than men, but that may not translate into policy decisions, since no nation-state has achieved complete gender equality in pol-itics. However, one study found that a mere 16.6 percent of female-led countries had ever been in an international conflict; also, the women leaders of these countries were not responsible for initiat-ing the conflicts in which their countries had become involved.[73] These findings suggest that increasing gender equality in politics would very likely also reduce international conflict. Along simi-lar lines, data confirmed that higher levels of gender equality in political participation, including female leadership and suffrage, resulted in lower levels of violence.[74]

What about conflict between communities of men and women? Inherent differences between men and women div-ide them into distinct cultural groups in every society, meaning that male-female distinctions exist within each nation, as well as globally.[75] Dichotomizing the sexes in this way enhances a sense of belonging in one way, but increases alienation in another. As

Caprioli argued earlier, intrastate violence is most likely to occur when groups have a strong common identity.[76]

Such an identity naturally follows from in-group/out-group distinctions,[77] frustrations based on relative deprivation,[78] and a history of discrimination.[79] In principle, women are thus united worldwide through a shared identity, which develops out of their shared grievances against the men who have discriminated against and repressed them. In turn, these grievances can serve as a motive for violent action.[80] So, groups who feel they have been treated unfairly or unequally often feel driven to assert their rights, sometimes through violence.[81]

By this argument, we would expect women to violently revolt against their male oppressors in an effort to gain equal treatment, in the same way that other groups that have been oppressed and discriminated against have done in the past. However, it seems that gender roles and stereotypes prevent women from rebelling and advocating for greater gender equality.

For one thing, gendered divisions of labour mean that men and women have unequal opportunities to develop on a personal level.[82] For example, women are not usually provided with the job opportunities outside of the home that are needed to create a sense of efficacy.[83] Their status as homemakers also means that women are typically burdened with greater family responsibilities than their male counterparts. So while women may resent the men and the gendered hierarchies that allow for their repression, they lack the unity needed for a rebellion against these oppressive forces.

In the absence of such rebellion, deeply rooted gender inequality allows men to exercise social control over women, as social norms and expectations encourage women to conform to the role of subservient housewife, while they allow men to dominate women both socially and physically.[84] However, as Galtung proposes, violence on a personal level does not allow for the same kind of extreme dominance as structural violence.[85] And, more likely than not, with continued declines in childbearing, gender differentiation and gender inequality will continue to decline throughout the world. In the end, increased gender equality will reduce both intra- and interstate violence and war.

Ethnic Inequality and Warfare

Ethnicity has long been recognized as a major contributor to violence within regions—that is, to civil wars. Indeed, civil wars often seem to have an ethnic dimension, with well-defined identity groups fighting each other.[86]

Ethnically-based civil wars make up the vast majority of all recorded civil wars that have occurred since 1945,[87] and these internal conflicts have resulted in over five times the number of deaths occurring in interstate wars.[88] In order to understand the role ethnicity plays in these devastating wars, we must understand how divisions along ethnic lines can affect group identities and grievances.

With ethnic diversity comes increased fractionalization and polarization between groups.[89] Fractionalization is the process that occurs as the number of ethnic groups in a society increases. Ethnic polarization, on the other hand, increases when there are a few equally large groups. Because fractionalization and (especially) polarization can both unite group members while alienating them from other groups, rebel leaders often use ethnic identities to further their own political and financial agendas. One of the ways by which they can do so is through the creation of narratives of goals shared amongst the group, and grievances against other groups. Thus, it is easier for leaders to mobilize people living in societies that are made up of only a few rival groups (that is, polarized societies), where the ethnic divisions are obvious.

By this reasoning, higher levels of ethnic polarization should lead to a higher risk of civil conflict. And yet there are many examples of ethnically diverse countries that have avoided such violence. For example, Tanzania and Ghana have avoided the internal conflicts that have plagued many of their neighbouring regions. The greater socio-economic equality found in Tanzania and Ghana may explain the limited conflict in these countries.[90]

In contrast, other regions experience ethnic divisions and horizontal socio-economic inequalities. These factors may enhance
both collective grievances and group cohesion among disadvantaged people, creating the motivation and opportunity for group
mobilization. In this way, a common cultural identity can become
a powerful mobilizing agent that can increase the likelihood of
civil unrest.[91]

Ethnicity is important because it can affect a rebel leader's
ability to mobilize a group in a variety of ways. First, ethnicity can
promote group identification with certain goals. It also helps rebel
leaders exercise social control, since people of the same ethnicity
will tend to uphold the same values and have the same expectations
of each other. Finally, communication within a more homogenous
group is relatively easy.

First, ethnicity can be used as a means of getting people to identify with a nationalist cause, leading to the subsequent formation
of a national group.[92] This is one reason why ethnic civil wars often
involve disputes over national issues. Because ethnicity is an aspect
of identity over which people have little control, it is easier for leaders to motivate an ethnically homologous group to identify with
nationalist goals, and to mobilize them to fight for these goals.

Rebel leaders also use social control to minimize threats to
their mobilization goals—especially the loss of recruits. Social control is the process through which a person's decision to take part in
a group effort is influenced by the values, expectations, and actions
of the people around them.[93] Accordingly, social control has been
directly linked to the onset of civil wars, as people can encourage or discourage each other from participating.[94] This concept is
especially relevant for ethnic groups because membership in such
groups is typically based on language, religion, or cultural heritage,
and sometimes even skin colour—characteristics that are not easily changed. Acquiring membership in, or being excluded from, an
ethnic group is therefore more difficult than movement along other
differences that aren't as readily apparent. Consequently, rebel
leaders exercise social control by using ethnicity as a justification

for co-ethnics to stay within the group, even when these people may oppose the leader and want to leave the group. Social control allows rebel leaders to maintain a large following of people, united by a shared ethnic identity.

The final mechanism by which ethnicity enhances mobilization is through its facilitation of group communication. Members of an ethnic group often share a common language, which naturally makes communication easier. In addition, ethnicity is strongly related to culture, which can enhance understanding among members and thereby make communication flow more easily.

Ethnic differentiation can play a role in group mobilization for conflict, yet there are many ethnically diverse countries that do not experience civil wars. In order to understand why, we must first explore two theories: *social cleavage theory* and the notion of *cross-cuttingness*.

Developed by Seymour Martin Lipset and Stein Rokkan in the 1960s, a society marked by social cleavage meets three conditions.[95] First, groups within the society are divided along demographic or socio-economic lines such as class, ethnicity, and religious affiliation that distinguish group members from non-members. Second, individuals on one side of a social divide (or cleavage) must be aware of the characteristics that unite them, and must be willing to take action in support of their social group. Finally, institutions exist to provide organizational support to those on a particular side of the social divide. Thus, social cleavages produce patterns of political behavior that reflect these deeply entrenched social divides.[96]

The concept of cross-cuttingness, on the other hand, describes how two cleavages relate to each other. Imagine a society in which all people of ethnicity A belong to religion X, while all people of ethnicity B belong to religion Y. A society in which each ethnic group belongs to its own unique religion does not have any cross-cuttingness. Each social cleavage—for example, ethnicity—is completely and perfectly reinforced by another cleavage—for example, religion. On the other hand, imagine a scenario in which half of all the people in ethnicity group A belong to religion X and the other half to religion Y; and the same is true of the people in ethnicity group B. This is a case of perfect cross-cuttingess, where there are no links between an individual's memberships in various groups. Knowing a person's ethnicity tells us nothing about his or her religious affiliation.

Societies with deep and overlapping cleavages are, by their nature, very divided and unstable, but people in societies with cross-cutting cleavages are not.[97] People in cross-cutting societies have relatively weak affiliations and loyalties to any one particular group, since a high degree of cross-cutting leads to more associations. Cross-cutting links diversify people's interests, giving them larger, more diverse social networks and reducing their commitment to any one group or ideology.

These dynamics have a direct influence on the risk of civil war, since overlapping cleavages tend to justify the ideological and nationalistic goals put forward by rebel leaders.[98] However, when ethno-linguistic identity is crosscut by other social cleavages such as religion, socio-economic class, and region, the likelihood of a rebellion drops.[99]

Cross-cutting cleavages, to repeat, reduce the mobilization of ethnic populations, as they reduce the ability of rebel leaders to mobilize ethnic sentiments and identities. Rebel leaders are more successful in mobilizing an ethnic group that is not divided along other social differences. For example, an ethnic group that practices a different religion than most others, is significantly poorer, and is geographically isolated will be easier to mobilize toward nationalist goals, since rebel leaders can use all of these differences to advance their claims of political repression and exclusion.

Cross-cutting cleavages also decrease a rebel leader's ability to exercise social control. People who can align themselves along non-ethnic cleavages, such as social class or religion, can identify with others on grounds other than ethnicity. Such a group would be more difficult to control and mobilize. Finally, cross-cutting cleavages reduce in-group communication and enhance communication with members of other groups. This kind of external communication tends to weaken the influence that rebel leaders have in appealing solely to ethnic ties and expose people to alternate views.

The reverse of these concepts also holds true: states with few cross-cutting cleavages are more likely than other states to experience civil war. Joshua Gubler and Joel Selway[100] examined data from over one hundred countries that included cross-cuttingness measures for three pairs of cleavages: ethnogeographic (EGC), ethnoincome (EIC), and ethnoreligious (ERC). They found the majority of countries that experienced civil war (twenty-two out of thirty-five) had low EIC—or a high degree of overlap between ethnicity and income.

They found that EIC had a mean risk ratio of 6.48, meaning that the risk of civil war was six and a half times greater in countries with low EIC than in countries with high EIC. (The effects of EGC and ERC were also significant, but much smaller: EGC had a mean risk ratio of 2.33, while ERC had a risk ratio of 1.71.) These results provide strong evidence that ethnic differentiation is an important predictor of onset civil war, especially when it overlaps with income inequality.

The researchers concluded that cross-cuttingness significantly reduces the likelihood of civil war, while overlapping cleavages significantly increase the likelihood of civil war. In fact, the highest risk occurred when all three cleavages were combined (yielding a risk ratio of 11.64). Stated in words, the onset of civil war is twelve times more likely in countries with the low combined levels of cross-cuttingness (or a high degree of overlap) than in countries with high combined levels of cross-cuttingness. Simplified even further, countries in which differences of ethnicity, region, income, and religion overlap closely are very likely to explode in civil war.

Having established that inequality increases our risk of sickness and death, crime and punishment, violence and war, it is now time to draw some final conclusions about inequality: its causes and consequences, and what we can do to minimize the harm.

PART 3
Making Society Better

CHAPTER 9

Imperfect Equality

———— • ◆ • ————

"We must be the change we want to see."
Mahatma Gandhi

We opened this book with a vision of Robert Owen's perfect world—a utopia where everyone would live in peace and prosperity. Throughout history, people have been searching for this sort of perfect world. Plato's *Republic*, Atlantis, El Dorado, Marx's communist state, as well as Owen's New Harmony, are only a few examples of the visions people have had of a better world, whether lost in the past or waiting for us in the future. This continuous search for a better world suggests that, fundamentally, we humans care about inequality.

Of course, people's ideas about what makes a perfect future have differed widely over the course of time. There is little similarity, for example, between Plato's ideal society in the fifth century BCE and Karl Marx's ideal society 2,300 years later. Plato's ideal society, based on reason, would be deeply unequal, ruled by philosopher kings. Marx's ideal society, on the other hand, would be (mainly) equal and ruled only temporarily by the vanguard of the proletariat. Both of these images of the ideal future have had a great influence on actual political and legal systems, though each is imperfect and impracticable in its own way. Neither is likely to come to fruition in our lifetimes, so we need to ask ourselves what is possible—what goals can we realistically hope to achieve? But, within these realistic boundaries, we also need to consider what is fair and just. We need to keep searching for equality because failing to do so is not only unfair, but also harmful to human life.

As we saw in the second part of the book, research clearly links social inequality to heightened risks of illness and mortality, crime and punishment, and war and destruction. We may choose to dismiss these as merely heightened risks rather than certainties, but doing so would be like dismissing the problems connected to climate change. We can try to deny the evidence of climate change, but the ice caps keeps melting, the waters keep flooding, the average temperature keeps rising, and tropical storms become more destructive. At some point, even the most uninformed and skeptical people will begin to see a pattern. Likewise, with sickness, crime, and war, the pattern is clear: we see more of these unwanted intrusions into human life wherever inequality is most extreme.

These three outcomes are important because, if you ask people what they care about, they say the same things: health, safety, and justice for themselves and their loved ones. No one prefers illness over good health, or death over life. Similarly, no one prefers a high crime rate compared to a low one, and no one wants high rates of imprisonment. Likewise, most people prefer peace over war—especially if they have had any firsthand exposure to war and its human costs.

So, inequality is measurably important to human society, and it has consequences that matter in ways we all care about. The question we need to ask, and one that has inspired a good deal of speculation, is: Why does inequality persist? First and most likely, many people have been led to believe that inequality is natural and inevitable. According to this view, we are stuck with the inequality that exists in our society. However, this belief is untenable, since different societies have different levels of inequality. So there must be another reason why people so persistently cling to this notion or habit of inequality.

One obvious reason is that some people benefit from the existing system of inequality. It would be against their immediate economic interest to oppose inequality. That said, we have shown in this book that greater equality would actually improve most people's economic benefit in the long run. And we have shown that greater equality would be beneficial in non-economic ways as well, promoting health, peace, and order. So, most people would likely subscribe to more equality, if only they knew about the significant advantages.

This means that we need to consider how people change their minds, especially when it means giving up beliefs they have always held. We know, for example, that it took smokers a very long time to believe the evidence that smoking was bad for their health. In fact, a sizeable number of Canadians continue to smoke, despite their awareness of this evidence. Likewise, many obese people continue to eat too much, many alcoholics continue to drink too much, many indebted people continue to gamble too much, and so on. From time to time, they may pledge to change their behaviour because they know that they need to do so. But most of them have trouble finding a way to quit smoking, over-eating, getting drunk, or gambling.

We call these people addicts, to highlight their inability to change; yet these addicts are just like the rest of us, only a bit more extreme. We all have trouble coping with new information—whether about climate change or social inequality. The reason is really quite simple: we have all made a habit of clinging to our beliefs, and ignoring contrary evidence. To do otherwise, we would have to disengage ourselves from old patterns and invest time and effort in new ones. And we all hate to admit we were wrong in the past.

The Problem of Just-World Beliefs

This is especially true when our patterns of thinking and behaviour developed when we were children, learning our first lessons about right and wrong, good and bad. And it seems that no lesson in our society is more deeply rooted than a belief in the just world. Yet we cannot begin to understand the persistence of economic inequality in Canada unless we understand the problem of just-world beliefs.

The evidence of social inequality is staring us in the face. Thanks to the so-called Gini Index, we can measure economic inequality very precisely and chart its change over time. A score of one on the

Gini Index means total income inequality, while a score of zero means total income equality. According to recent research, Canada scores around 0.35 on this index, compared to scores of 0.25–0.30 in Scandinavia and 0.45 in the United States.[1] Recent research also shows that economic inequality measured in this way is higher in 2013 than it was two decades ago. Therefore, despite the continued growth of the Canadian economy, income inequality has gotten worse.[2] In fact, most of the benefits of economic growth have gone to the top 1 percent of the Canadian population, widening the gap between the rich and the poor.[3]

So why aren't Canadians protesting their worsened financial condition? Likely, the answer is that along with this rise in income inequality, there has been an increase in just-world beliefs, which people use to explain this increased inequality. They seek something or someone to blame. They may blame people poorer than themselves, and they may blame themselves; they rarely blame the rich. In this way, just-world beliefs colour the way we interact with economically disadvantaged populations, including the poor and the working class.

In Canada and the US, there have always been three main ways of explaining poverty. Some people blame personal failings, such as laziness, addiction, or lack of intelligence. This view is in line with the victim-blaming just mentioned. Some people blame social and economic causes, like discrimination or low wages. Finally, some people blame bad luck.[4] These latter fatalistic people view themselves and others as the helpless victims.[5] However, the first two views are more common—that is, the majority of people tend to blame the victim or blame the people in power.

Most Canadians recognize that many factors go into determining a person's economic condition. However, people differ in which factor they believe plays the most important role. In the United States, most people tend to believe that individuals are responsible for their own poverty or wealth. They think that, with enough effort, even the most disadvantaged could pull themselves up by their bootstraps.[6]

Canadians are different. Most Canadians believe that external social factors play an important role in creating poverty and wealth.[7] That is why they tend to support the creation of social safety nets, such as welfare and unemployment insurance.[8] In this respect, Canada has a more positive attitude toward equality than the US, making it more similar to northern European countries like Norway, Sweden, and Iceland.[9]

This popular American belief that poverty is caused by an individual's own personal failings—laziness, addiction, or some other preventable moral flaw—is correlated with a high level of poverty. Within the US about 15 percent of the population lives at or below the poverty line; this means that 46.2 million Americans live in poverty.[10] By contrast, only 9.2 percent of Canadians live on a low income—admittedly a large number, but very much smaller than in the US.[11] Canadians maintain a greater concern for justice in the face of economic inequality and shift the blame from people to social structures and processes.[12]

Ways of viewing poverty and inequality are distinctive cultural patterns, rooted in a nation's history and connected with what we are calling habits of inequality. An individual's particular way of reacting to the poor and the working class is embedded within his or her country's specific history. Yet, within Canada, different habits of inequality persist side by side.

For example, differing views of the cause of poverty show up along political lines, with people on the right tending to blame the victim and people on the left blaming social and economic factors.[13] Interestingly, these differences are also connected to the just-world beliefs we discussed earlier. Compared with people who hold left-wing politicals views, people with right-wing political views tend to hold stronger just-world beliefs and to believe that people control their own destiny.[14]

Research has also linked strong just-world beliefs to authoritarianism and political conservatism.[15] Such beliefs in a just world, and the related tendency to blame poor people for their poverty, pose a moral dilemma for Canadians. That is because just-world beliefs maintain the illusion of justice in the face of injustice and undermine efforts to solve our social problems. Even Canadians, who tend to place most of the blame for income disparity on social practices and policies, still make internal attributions for poverty by victim blaming. For instance, even though panhandling and squeegeeing in Toronto had significantly decreased between 2000 and 2010, the amount of fines issued to Toronto's homeless youth increased from 2,000 to nearly 16,000.[16] This kind of thinking overlooks the fact that innocent people can be impoverished and made homeless by external causes beyond their control.

The way the public sees poverty is important because it dictates how we help impoverished people—or fail to do so. For example, popular attributions of poverty influence political decisions on whether or not to create social programs that will aid the poor and the working class.[17] So we need to ask how just-world beliefs get translated into public policy.

Part of the barrier to change is that many people distrust government to solve society's problems. Americans are even more suspicious of government interference than either Canadians or Scandinavians. The American belief, that individuals are responsible for their own situation, is reflected in American values, including the idea that people need freedom not welfare, more than anything.[18] Canada and Scandinavia have not had the same historical or cultural experiences as the US and so are more likely to support government assistance in the redistribution of wealth.

These different beliefs are reflected in the proportion of taxes paid in different countries. According to 2011 OECD statistics, taxpayers in Sweden pay 45 percent of GDP and taxpayers in Finland pay 43 percent, compared to the 31 percent paid by Canadian tax payers.[19] Taxes in the US are even lower, at only 25 percent of GDP.[20] Societies that accept government intervention to equalize society do not mind paying higher taxes. However, the opposite is true for societies that reject such involvement. And that's why more unequal societies spend less on redistributive government spending.[21]

The amount a country taxes its citizens determines how much money is available for policies and programs to help the poor. This means that people in countries like the US, with a high Gini Index of inequality, have the greatest need for the programs and policies that these redistributive efforts would fund. Paradoxically though, these are also the people who receive the least amount of help, since (proportionally) the least taxes are collected and redistributed in their countries.

To repeat, both Canada and the Scandinavian countries have lower levels of inequality than the US, and understand poverty in ways that lead to greater aid for the poor. But, while Canada is doing relatively well in this respect (compared to our neighbours in the south), Scandinavia has been even more successful. One reason is the number of women holding government offices. In Canada, women hold only 25 percent of seats in the federal parliament, whereas in Sweden, women hold 45 percent of the seats. The trend holds true for other egalitarian societies as well, with 40 percent of the seats in Norway being held by women, and 39 percent in Denmark.[22] Research has shown that women—even those with strong just-world beliefs—empathize more with victims than men do. Having more women in government positions increases the likelihood of progressive social policies.[23]

Unfortunately, even though the overall rate of poverty in Canada has decreased, poor Canadians continue to become poorer, and the gap between the rich and the poor has continued to increase over recent decades, just as it has in the US.[24] Nevertheless, we have grounds for optimism: because Canadians have weaker just-world beliefs and tend to blame the victims less, we are more able to develop progressive solutions to the problem of economic inequality.

The US has not always fallen behind other developed countries in terms of poverty rates. In the 1970s, Canada, Norway, and Sweden all had higher rates of absolute poverty than the United States. But since the late 1990s, all three have had lower rates of poverty. The US experienced an economic boom in the 1990s, significantly decreasing poverty levels, but they failed to create an adequate social safety net. By 2005, the United States was experiencing high poverty rates once again, while countries that had worked to aid the poor, like Norway and Sweden, saw steadily improving conditions for the working class.[25]

People have suffered to different degrees from this setback. Just-world beliefs often target victims based on their age. They tend to homogenize people within the younger and older age brackets,[26] meaning that they see all adolescents or all elderly people as essentially the same. As a result, just-world beliefs tend to have a particularly strong impact on both the old and the young. For this reason, and because of the steadily aging world population, Americans for Generational Equality (AGE) prophesies that an age war will develop around the world, and especially in the United States. AGE fears that age-related conflict will intensify around Social Security and Medicare, as entitlement programs for the growing number of aging and elderly persons leave less funding for the young.[27] Given the rising number of elderly people in our world, and the amount of money that will be needed to care for them properly, it seems likely that the elderly will be blamed for keeping needed money from younger people.

Bearing this age-based conflict in mind, it's easier for us to see why just-world believers often hold discriminatory attitudes toward the elderly.[28] A hostile perception of the aging process is largely the result of just-world beliefs, since just-world believers are likely to think the elderly are already receiving a fair share of the pie.[29] Again, just-world believers tend to blame older people for their plight if they failed to take the necessary steps to maintain their health, remain useful to society, or accumulate wealth.

As a result of this mentality, some people use just-world beliefs to victimize the elderly. Paradoxically, just-world beliefs work in a different way when elderly people use them. Research shows that older people who hold strong just-world beliefs feel happier, healthier, and more satisfied with their lives.[30] Consider a study by Ramzi Nasser, Jacqueline Doumit, and James Carifio,[31] who focused on elderly nursing home residents—people who tend to experience a great deal of stress and anxiety. These are people who often struggle with sleeping disorders, guilt, headaches, psychosomatic symptoms, and negative feelings.[32] This study, however, found that nursing home residents with strong just-world beliefs have better than average experiences in nursing homes than other residents— also, a better than average perception of their own well-being.

Maybe this is because just-world beliefs help them cope with the disadvantages of being older in a society that tends to value youth.[33] In any case, it seems that people can use just-world beliefs to deal with the difficulties they experience in old age, much as they use these beliefs to justify other hardships.

As we mentioned, just-world beliefs also cause problems at the other end of the age continuum. For example, adolescents are often stereotyped as delinquents. Consider that, in 2007, youth crime rates in Canada were the lowest they had been for twenty years, and yet 80 percent of Canadians believed that youth crime rates were actually rising.[34] This discrepancy between popular perception and reality was probably a result of increased media coverage of violent crime.[35] Media depictions also likely contributed to the idea that younger offenders are less competent than older ones, and that youth shouldn't be held accountable for their delinquent actions. All of this points to a view of teenagers as irresponsible criminals and as people who deserve to be treated as immature and incompetent.

So, like the poor, the young and the old also suffer because of just-world beliefs, and so do sexual minorities. In Chapter 5, we noted that gay and lesbian activists maintain that their sexuality is unchosen, or determined at birth. However, according to just-world advocates, they make this claim to avoid being blamed for "choosing" homosexuality. If sexual orientation is not a matter of choice because it is inborn, no one—not even the most rabid anti-homosexual—could reasonably blame a gay or lesbian person for their sexual orientation. They could still despise and exclude homosexuals, but logically, they would not be able to blame them.

Research confirms that some people actually do think this way. Someone who believes that sexual orientation is an inborn predisposition is more likely to be tolerant toward gay and lesbian people than someone who believes that sexual orientation is a matter of choice.[36] This belief has twice the negative consequences for homosexual HIV/AIDS victims, who are blamed both for "choosing" homosexuality and for "choosing" unsafe sex.[37] Again, these examples show how just-world beliefs lead to victim blaming—a tendency to blame people for conditions and experiences they did not choose.

This is not to say that people who believe in a just world are necessarily anti-homosexual; little research has been done that would show a direct link between these views. However, research does show that people with religious beliefs and politically or socially conservative beliefs think that homosexuality is a choice; they therefore tend to have anti-homosexual attitudes due to the way of thinking we just described.[38] In addition, we showed earlier that people with strong religious and conservative beliefs often hold strong just-world beliefs too. No wonder, then, that Americans—who usually believe strongly in a just world—blame homosexuals more than either Canadians or Scandinavians, and typically give traditional moral or religious reasons for this blaming.[39]

What If this Is Not the Best of All Possible Worlds?

Today, Canada is somewhere in the middle, where income inequality is concerned; we are less unequal than many societies, but more unequal than many others. Even though ours may only be a moderate (rather than extreme) form of income inequality, each of us still pays a steep price for it in the form of health problems, crime, and conflict, as we saw in the last three chapters.

As we have also seen throughout this book, all of the forms of inequality in our society are linked in some way to just-world beliefs. People who hold these beliefs think that if they have made sacrifices—have given up, or at least postponed, their gratification—they will be rewarded, in due time. People will be compensated for their patience and virtue, because that is what happens in a just world like ours: those who are good are rewarded, and those who are not good are punished. It follows from this that people who enjoy many advantages and comforts must deserve them, and people without any advantages or comforts must not deserve them. That's because in this "just world" of ours, people get what they deserve. Indeed, as Voltaire's Dr. Pangloss was fond of saying, "Everything is as it should be," and, "This is the best of all possible worlds," no matter what happens.

When people buy into this just-world belief, they find it hard—almost impossible—to accept information that suggests that this is not the best of all possible worlds. They find it hard to believe that many people are not, in fact, getting what they deserve—indeed, that a privileged few are getting a great deal that they do not deserve. To accept these discomforting facts would mean having to change a great many beliefs about the world, perhaps, even revising one's life. So, people find it easier to deny the facts and to deny the scientific evidence that many suffer from unwarranted disadvantage and inequality causes sickness, crime, and war. And so the habitual ways of thinking and acting persist, through willful ignorance and inaction, because this persistence is easier and more psychologically comfortable than change, at least in the short term.

Now, consider this in the longer-term, global context for a moment. Cross-national research has found that in countries where a majority of people are powerless, the level of belief in a just world is generally lower than average. Likely, this is because powerless people, and others who are familiar with large numbers of powerless people, have had more firsthand experiences that proved the world is not fair, just, or even predictable.[40] By contrast, people who believe in the just world tend, more often, to endorse right wing authoritarian beliefs.[41]

Just-world believers facilitate war making because they tend to group together for mutual support and to form collective narratives that blame their opponents. As an example, think about the Jewish–Palestinian conflict that has now lasted for nearly a century. Here, each party has heightened their sense of nationalism and used symbolic kin terms such as son, sister, brotherhood, and motherland to create stronger bonds between their citizens.[42] By doing so, they have accentuated the division between the two parties, making it easier for each to blame their opponent. In this and most other conflicts, citizens do not know the details of why they are fighting; often, it takes the death of a group member before this obscure battle changes into tangible reality.[43]

These kinds of conflicts are often perpetuated by an unfamiliarity with others, which frequently accompanies just-world beliefs. Studies have shown that all people—even just-world believers—are more sympathetic to people with whom they associate; they are more likely to believe that the people they know are good people. When innocent members of their society are harmed by war, even just-world believers experience anger, agony, and despair, since this harm challenges their idea of the world as a fair place, where people get what they deserve.

As we have pointed out, Americans tend to have a secure sense that the world they live in is just, so they think that bad things will never happen to good people. However, the events of September 11 shattered their vision of a just world when thousands of innocent victims perished. One study by Cheryl Kaiser and her colleagues investigated how Americans' just-world beliefs influenced their reactions to the 9/11 attack.[44] As we might have predicted, people with an especially strong belief in the just world felt the most fearful, vulnerable, and uneasy, compared to people with weaker just-world beliefs. Also, these just-world believers had the strongest desire to seek revenge against the people responsible for this attack. With this in mind, we can see how just-world beliefs would lead to war: because everyone supposedly gets what they deserve, according to this theory, people who harm the innocent must pay the price. All conflict requires blame and, as this example shows, nothing supplies blame more readily than a belief that the world is normally fair and just.

In short, people who are deeply invested in just-world beliefs are blame-seekers, and resist changing their minds about matters of fairness and equality. Consequently, they try to ignore or deny evidence that contradicts their belief in a just world, and often they cling even more feverishly to this belief when reality should make them question it. However, people also resist changing their minds and their behaviours because they realize such change would need to be comprehensive. This is because all social inequalities are similar and, under many circumstances, they are connected. It would be difficult, or perhaps even impossible, to change only some inequalities and not others, because our entire social, cultural, and economic system is built on a network of different inequalities.

In other words, to solve the inequality problems in our society, we cannot simply reject justifications for income inequality, or gender discrimination, or homophobia. We have to reject the ideas and practices of inequality as a whole, ultimately breaking our habit of inequality.

Habits of Inequality Theory

Throughout our book, we have made repeated references to what we are calling habits of inequality, and it is now time to spell out our thoughts on this matter. The evidence shows that societies differ in their general predisposition toward inequality, and this predisposition shows itself in all the major domains of social life, in relation to class, gender, race, aging, and so on. As a result, societies that are highly unequal on one dimension tend to be highly unequal on other dimensions as well. So, societies with a high degree of income inequality also tend to have a high degree of gender inequality, racial or ethnic inequality, and regional inequality, and to support a high degree of international inequality. This is because these societies— their governments and their citizens—have bought into the idea of inequality and have built inequality into their main social institutions. But paradoxically, if you read the founding documents of these societies or speak with their citizens, you will learn that they think they are committed to equality.

Take the US as an example. Rather than being committed to establishing equal outcomes for everyone, most Americans feel strongly that everyone should have equal opportunities. Societies like this are actually less committed to equality of any kind than they are committed to freedom or liberty. Liberty is freedom from external constraint, so by setting their sights on liberty, the American and other similar societies often come up with small government, low taxes, and a relative absence of government regulation. Yet, it is only through larger government, higher taxes, and more government regulation that we can bring about something like equality, or even equality of opportunity.

Consider, for a moment, why an unregulated market economy might fulfill some people's desire for liberty, but cannot possibly bring about equality. The mythology is that uncontrolled markets are able to create the right supply of goods at the right prices. These ideal markets do not discriminate against women, poor people, black people, or homosexuals (as examples); they simply balance supply and demand, given prevailing desires. However, we know from the stock market (and property) collapse in 2008 and since that some groups have more protection than others in the marketplace. For example, some people are better able to obtain and use inside information and to create illusions about the stocks, bonds, and commodities being traded on the market.

Though seemingly fair to everyone, the market is not fair in the same sense as a roulette wheel whose odds never change. In fact, the market is more like the board game Monopoly; as people acquire more money and property, they are better able to acquire even more money and property, even though they continue to follow the same, seemingly unbiased rules. In much the same way, it is easier to acquire your second million dollars on the market than it is to acquire your first million, because the rules tend to favour people who start with an advantage.

Consider an example closer to home. Despite the widespread belief that everyone has a similar opportunity to go to college, children from more prosperous homes remain more likely to graduate from college than children from less prosperous homes. This is true even when tuition is very low or free, as it has been in some countries. In trying to figure out why this is so, some people have pointed to the importance of encouragement and role models at home: children are more likely to attend college if their parents went to college, for example. However, we cannot ignore the "opportunity costs"—the costs of foregone earning opportunities—caused by higher education, even where tuition is low or free. Children in households under heavy financial pressure will find it much harder to continue their studies, because they feel like they are missing out on potential earnings by going to school instead of getting a job.

In this sense, certain subpopulations are particularly vulnerable to low incomes and relatively low education. These include the Aboriginal people in Canada and the black population in the US (and increasingly, in Canada.) So, because they are not committed to equalizing people's opportunities, societies that are highly unequal on one dimension are likely to be highly unequal on other dimensions as well. As a result, we frequently see an overlapping of economic inequality, racial or ethnic inequality, and regional inequality.

As we have seen throughout this book, different forms of inequalities actually share many similarities. That is, all types of social inequality display similar patterns or cultural habits. We call these patterns social differentiation, narratives of blame, practices of oppression, narratives of validation, and strategies of resistance. Let's take a moment to examine each of them.

Common Features of Inequality Domains

First, in all societies we find social differentiation. This practice involves identifying different kinds of people who are assumed to be essentially and unchangeably different, and defining this difference as consequential for social and economic life.

Without social differentiation, inequality does not exist. For example, in all societies, sex and age are used to differentiate people and are thought to be socially consequential. By contrast, class, race, ethnicity, and religion are bases of social differentiation to varying degrees in different societies. This means that they are considered less important definers of identity and rights in some societies than in others. However, every society differentiates people based on what are considered important social factors. Social inequalities are, in turn, built on these social differentiations.

In all societies, these inequalities are then culturally justified. This brings us to our second cultural habit, which is the use of narratives of blame. These are socially constructed accounts that attach social or moral qualities to different groups to explain why advantaged people are advantaged and disadvantaged people are disadvantaged. People turn to these narratives because they give meaning and moral weight to their world. Often, narratives of blame are manipulated by organized interest groups. And yet, most of the time, we take these narratives of blame for granted, as though they are self-evidently valid.

These narratives of blame draw their emotional energy from just-world beliefs. To repeat, believers in a just world ignore or deny anything that threatens their belief in the stable, orderly, and fair nature of their world. When just world-believers encounter events that simply cannot be ignored, they shift the blame or re-interpret the situation in non-threatening ways. For example, in 2011, Elizabeth Krumrei and her colleagues found that 48 percent of the Americans they studied referred to demons when explaining their recent divorce.[45] They blamed the devil for their failed marriage, saying that this demon had worked through themselves or their former spouse to create marital discord. People with a powerful need to believe that the world is just and meaningful, and also that they are personally blameless, are more inclined than others to blame misfortune on devils they cannot see.

In general, however, people who believe in the just world want to ignore long-term suffering—both their own and other people's. In order to sustain their beliefs in a just world, they need to rationalize pain and suffering as deserved consequences. This need to make sense of and to justify inequality intensifies along with rising income inequality. This helps to explain what Richard Sennett and Jonathan Cobb famously called the "hidden injuries" of social class: everyone blames the victims, including the victims themselves.[46]

To repeat, what we call narratives of blame stem from these beliefs in a just world. People construct narratives of blame to explain why certain groups are poor or victimized: for example, because they are lazy and lack a work ethic, or have below-average intelligence. Sometimes, narratives of blame may also try to account for why certain groups are hated, suggesting, for instance, that they are clannish, greedy, and unattractive. They may also provide arguments for why certain groups are ridiculed or stigmatized; a good example is accusing men of effeminacy and women of masculinity, and arguing that they act "against God's will."

Typically, these narratives of blame support a third pattern common to all types of inequality: practices of oppression. These include exploitation, domination, exclusion, discrimination, and stigmatization, all of which punish certain groups and reward others. Often, many of these practices are inflicted upon disadvantaged groups at the same time. These practices of oppression tend to follow the creation of narratives of blame, with people being punished because they are shown to be blameworthy. Sometimes, however, the practices of oppression precede explanations, and the narratives serve to justify or rationalize existing oppressive practices.

Fourth, in all societies we see the disadvantaged fighting back, starting with narratives of validation. These socially constructed accounts reply to narratives of blame and may take various forms. Some of them reject the factual accuracy of the blame narratives, denying any fault, defect, or misdeed. Others deny any choice, guilt, or control over the actions for which they are blamed. Or, they may hold advantaged people responsible for creating the conditions that are blameworthy. So, for example, gays and lesbians explain that they are not to blame for their sexual desires, on the grounds that sexual orientation is inborn and unchangeable. Similarly, women and the elderly often say that they are just as capable as men or younger people, effectively denying the factual accuracy of blame narratives.

The development of narratives of validation is an important step in the formation of collective consciousness and action. As

Marx says, this is the stage at which a group moves from being a class in itself to being a class for itself—a group aware of its needs and the reasons for these needs. It is at this time that a disadvantaged group moves from being a set of oppressed people to being a community.

Fifth, after having developed these narratives of validation, disadvantaged people begin to use strategies of resistance. These include all of the collective actions that combat practices of oppression and aim to reduce the effects of inequality. They include activities designed to raise awareness, and social movements formed to achieve social and political goals. Another strategy is institutional completeness, the formation of self-sufficient communities of disadvantaged people, as described by the Canadian sociologist Raymond Breton. People also fight back by disseminating information via social media, schools, and churches aimed at changing public attitudes, and sometimes they challenge oppression legally, through the courts.

Whenever there is inequality, there is a struggle between narratives of blame and narratives of validation and between practices of oppression and strategies of resistance. Struggle and conflict are inevitable so long as inequality exists. Different kinds of inequality may produce different kinds of struggle, but often, the struggle over one form of inequality (such as race) will influence and energize the struggle over another form of inequality (such as gender). Since the struggles against different forms of inequality are often consciously connected, we cannot have separate theories for class, racial, gender, or any other form of inequality. We need unified theories—and perhaps even a single theory of inequality.

Different forms of inequality are also connected because they all follow the five patterns that we have outlined: social differentiation, narratives of blame, practices of oppression, narratives of validation, and strategies of resistance. We refer to this package of behaviors as habits of inequality because they are merely habits. By this, we mean that people have merely learned each of these behaviours—they are not innate or preordained. And because they are learned, they are cultural, that is they are quite different from the beliefs of people who live in a different culture. Like other habits, habits of inequality are so customary that we tend to take them for granted and see them as natural; yet they are not natural, merely customary. One of the goals of this book is to bring our unconscious attitudes and beliefs, and the taken-for-granted elements of everyday life, to full awareness. We cannot hope to consider and then change our habits of inequality if we are not fully aware of them.

First, we need to become more aware of our tendency to distinguish between different kinds of people based on characteristics such as age, race, ethnic ancestry, social class, and sexual orientation. We make these distinctions because we think they will reveal useful, socially important, and culturally meaningful differences that will let us understand people better. But if we take a closer look, we can see that distinguishing between people like this and looking for essential differences is often lazy and prejudiced.

Second, we need to inspect our tendency to attach moral labels—labels of blame and unworthiness—to the people we have distinguished in these ways. Such moral labels or narratives are also lazy and prejudiced, as they merely allow us to justify the status quo and, perhaps, our comfortable social advantage. Not every person or action can be classified on a moral scale; by trying to separate the world into black hats and white hats, good people and bad people, we are merely buying into the just-world ideology, labelling all circumstances as fair and deserved.

Third, we need to examine our patterns of oppression. *Oppression* is such a heavy, emotional word that we may think we cannot be guilty of any such behaviour. Yet, we have seen throughout this book that oppression takes a great many forms, some less visible than others. Exploitation and stigmatization, for example, are common in our society, and everyone who enjoys the advantages of this unequal system is part of the oppression, whether they take an active role or not. As for domination and victimization, we have more pleasant words we use to describe them when we perform them, though we are perfectly capable of recognizing them for what they are when they are done to us. Again, the point here is to bring our behaviours to consciousness and make them less habitual. To this end, we need to consider whether our patterns of oppression are unjustified, unnecessary, or excessive, and whether there are other (better) ways we might act as a society.

Fourth, we need to recognize that disadvantaged people will develop habits and practices of resistance—and they will eventually fight back. We need to get out of the habit of ignoring them on the grounds that they are disadvantaged and that they must therefore be lacking in merit. By doing this, we will be able to hear their complaints more openly and potentially act to resolve them.

How can change begin, given that we have different amounts of power over the way society works and different degrees of investment in the current social order? Obviously, people with the most wealth and power benefit the most from current patterns of inequality, so they want to keep our society as it is. They rely on the rest of us to maintain the status quo by retaining our habits of inequality. That is why change has to begin with the rest of us, and specifically with our habits of thinking.

For most of us—the 99 percent who do not rule Canadian society—culture is the master pattern, the repository of thinking about inequality. The cultural tendency we are calling habits of inequality is shaped by underlying assumptions like the just-world belief and the so-called dominant ideology, both of which promote the economic and political interests of a ruling elite.

Culture, as we know from the work of Max Weber, sets the stage for the legitimation of power: it records, justifies, and transmits habits of inequality into all of the domains of life, where they take root. People's expectations about inequality, in turn, reflect their experiences; and their aspirations reflect their expectations. To a very large degree, people who have had little expect little, are satisfied with little, and long for just a little more. As conditions worsen, they adjust to more inequality and they long for only a slight improvement. Their hopes and aspirations are humble, in line with their actual experiences.

This is because when societies establish a point of view about inequality—for example, that inequality is normal and inevitable—that view tends to permeate all domains of life. It serves to justify a wide variety of inequalities and to dampen any serious discussion of the topic. This is what sociologists typically mean by the term *dominant ideology*—a point of view on inequality that narrows the possibilities for thought, action, and discussion in every domain.

Our theory proposes that societies that are highly unequal on one social dimension—say, income—are likely to be highly unequal on the others too, for example, on race or gender. If true, this idea is important for several reasons. Theoretically, it means we need to look for a general explanation of inequality both within and between societies, rather than conducting separate investigations of class, gender, race, and so on. Practically, it means that if we want to solve the social problems associated with inequality in any particular society—problems of poverty, discrimination, exclusion, or stigma—we need to change that society's overall approach to inequality. A piecemeal method will not suffice, theoretically or practically, if our theory is correct. Consider the similarities between all of the inequalities we have discussed in this book.

All of these social inequalities are socially constructed and most are collectively imagined on the basis of supposedly important natural differences, such as sex, skin colour, age, or sexual orientation. Sometimes, these differences are totally invented, and the vast majority of people cannot even see them. In other instances, the natural differences are real enough; men and women, for example, are different physiologically, as are old people and young people. The social constructions, in these cases, are the meaning and significance of the given difference: they tell us why we should care about the difference between men and women, or old people and young people, for example.

Societies vary in the overall degree and the kinds of social inequality they display. In general, the Scandinavian countries—Sweden, Norway, Denmark, Finland, and Iceland—show the least inequality of every kind. Less-developed societies like Pakistan and Bolivia show the most inequality, while Canada and the other industrial societies (except the more unequal US) fall somewhere near the middle. Anyone who doubts that Canada and the US are this different in terms of inequality need only examine the indicators on class, racial, gender, and other inequalities to see the difference for themselves.

Because they are socially constructed, habits of inequality are closely related to other cultural patterns—especially to traditionalism, religiosity, militarism, and parochialism. Less-developed societies that are culturally traditional or parochial are typically the most unequal. That is, they are most discriminatory toward women and minorities, and provide the least-developed social welfare net. People there rely on their family members and communities to keep order and provide support. As we discussed earlier, such societies are most often underdeveloped, or are so-called failed states. But, even though it is considered a developed nation, the highly unequal United States also fits this pattern, since it is the most traditional, religious, militaristic, and parochial of all the industrial societies, and also the most unequal.

How do we explain this link between inequality and traditionalism, religiosity, militarism, and parochialism? First, militarism diverts public attention and spending away from hard-to-remedy social problems. It is far more satisfying to confront external enemies with modern technology than it is to confront internal problems with the less-developed tools of persuasion and legislation.

As for traditionalism, religiosity, and parochialism, each of these discourages people from seeking new solutions to public problems by promoting complacency. They all encourage the idea that social experimentation is unnecessary because no society is as good as or better than the present one. No society embraces this complacency more fiercely than the United States, with its belief in American exceptionalism and one nation united under God. However, no society can afford to imagine that it can do without planned social change—that it can leave everything up to God and the marketplace. These beliefs therefore perpetuate the various forms of inequality that have become a part of American society.

Canada, while less complacent, is increasingly becoming a more unequal society. In the last twenty years, the Gini Index of income inequality has risen considerably in Canada as it has in other industrial societies. The social welfare net, built with such difficulty during the middle of the twentieth century, is in danger of being dismantled. In our country, the top 20 percent of income earners already take about 40 percent of the total income, while the lowest 20 percent take only about 7 percent.[47] Canada is not as bad as the United States, where the top ten percent take roughly half of the total income, and where income inequality is even higher than it was during the Roaring Twenties, but Canada can definitely do a lot better.[48] We just need to look around, since there are plenty of more equal societies we can learn from.

The fact is, there are countries that have managed to reduce inequality while increasing the quality of life. In this regard, Scandinavia is the leader. It is important that we have this real example to work from; our standard of comparison should be other industrial nations that currently exist, not imaginary utopias like Robert Owen's New Harmony.

It is also important that we use scientific methods of evaluation and comparison to judge how well we and other nations are doing in terms of reducing inequality and increasing the quality of life. We can base these judgments on objective measurements, rather than subjective beliefs about which country is best to live in. One of these scientific tools that we have talked a lot about is the Gini Index, which sociologists use to measure income inequality. Currently, Norway, Sweden, and Denmark have the world's lowest inequality ratings, around 25.0, and Namibia has the highest, around 70.0. With an Index of roughly 45.0, the United States falls somewhere in the middle. This puts it behind all other industrialized nations, with coefficients around 25.0–35.0.

Should we model ourselves on the Scandinavian countries and, if so, can we do it? Do we know how they got to be the way they are, and can we get to be that way too? What trade-offs will be needed? Will we have to trade off political sustainability or a high standard of living? Based on a comparison with other industrial countries, we can confidently say that reducing inequality in Canada will not require such sacrifices.

We have a distance to go. As the data in Table 2 show, Canada ranks tenth in sustainability and twenty-third on the Gini Index for OECD countries, after taxes and transfer payments. On both indices of inequality, Canada falls below Finland, Norway, Sweden, Denmark, Ireland, Luxembourg, and Austria. That means we could

Table 2 Indices of Inequality and Failure/Sustainability by Country

Country	Gini Index[a]	Country	Sustainability Index[b]
Slovenia	23.6	Finland	19.7
Denmark	24.8	Norway	20.4
Norway	25.0	Sweden	22.8
Czech Republic	25.6	Switzerland	23.2
Slovak Republic	25.7	Denmark	23.8
Finland	25.9	New Zealand	24.8
Sweden	25.9	Ireland	25.3
Belgium	25.9	Luxembourg	26.1
Austria	26.1	Austria	27.3
Hungary	27.2	CANADA	27.7
Luxembourg	28.8		
France	29.3		
Ireland	29.3	Australia	28.1
Netherlands	29.4	Netherlands	28.3
Germany	29.5	Iceland	30.1
Iceland	30.1	Japan	31.0
Switzerland	30.3	Portugal	32.3
Poland	30.5	Germany	33.9
Greece	30.7		
Estonia	31.5		
Korea	31.5		
Spain	31.7		
CANADA	32.4		
Japan	32.9		
New Zealand	33.0		

[a]After taxes and transfer payments, most recent year available
[b]The Sustainability Index is the Failed State Index, viewed from the top down

Sources: "Income Distribution—Inequality." OECD StatExtracts. http://stats.oecd.org/Index.aspx?QueryId= 26068; "Failed States Index 2012." The Fund for Peace. http://www.fundforpeace.org/global/library/ cfsir1210-failedstatesindex2012-06p.pdf.

be doing a lot better in terms of economic equality and still be politically sustainable—stable, progressive, and livable.

These social differences were a long time in coming, and historical differences shape current economic and social differences.[49] In every country, domestic institutional traditions moderate global economic trends; in particular, these include habits of inequality, as embodied in the kind of welfare regime that evolves gradually in a given society. The extent of inequality in a country like Sweden today is the result of decades of state policy-making designed to encourage equality on many different levels. Sweden's high level of equality therefore reflects a strong welfare state embedded in a strong industrial economy. In egalitarian societies, the early participation of women in the labour market set early precedents for welfare state restructuring. Women's participation in politics also helped to generate more progressive ideologies, labour practices, and social regulations, while encouraging higher wages, national daycare subsidies, and other progressive programs of particular interest to women and families.

The data from these more equal European countries confirm that it is not necessary to lower the standard of living by choosing more equality. Most northern European and especially Scandinavian countries are doing fine economically and politically, while having managed to reduce their levels of inequality far below those that we see in Canada. The data in Table 3 confirm that we do not have to sacrifice our standard of living to achieve more social equality. In fact, many countries like those in Scandinavia and northern Europe have already achieved both a higher degree of equality and a higher standard of living than Canada, once we adjust the data for local purchasing power.

These results suggest that Canadians should stop comparing themselves with the United States, which is doing worse than Canada on these social equality measures. Instead, Canadians might want to compare themselves with prosperous, progressive northern European societies. These nations demonstrate that through social, economic, and political changes, we can reduce

Table 3   Measures of Per Capita Income, Adjusted for Purchasing Power Parity, Most Recent Years Available

	GDP per capita (USD)*	GNI per capita (USD)*
Luxembourg	84,829	63,950
Norway	53,376	57,100
Switzerland	43,508	48,960
Netherlands	42,330	42,610
Austria	41,805	39,660
Sweden	40,613	39,390
Canada	40,457	37,280

Sources: "GDP Per Capita, PPP (Current International $)." World Bank, Development Research Group. http://data.worldbank.org/indicator/NY.GDP.PCAP.PP.CD; "Gross National Income Per Capita 2011, Atlas Method and PPP." World Bank, Development Research Group. http://databank.worldbank.org/databank/download/GNIPC.pdf.

our habits of inequality while still remaining prosperous, content, and stable.

In closing, we note that Canada is already doing well on measures of inequality in comparison to many other societies across the world. We should also recognize that over the last twenty years, Canada has resisted pressures to significantly increase social inequality, placing us ahead of many other nations that have been unable to do so. In light of these accomplishments, we can be proud that we have largely stood our ground against the pressures for change in the wrong direction. That said, we Canadians can do even better if we can manage to recognize and dismiss our habits of inequality.

If we want to continue improving our society by reducing social inequality, we need to find out what more equal societies have that we lack. How do these counties achieve their success, when it comes to inequality? Can we, through careful planning and legislation, become more like Sweden, Denmark, Iceland, Norway, the Czech Republic, Slovakia, Austria, and Luxemburg?

Canadians need to start considering what obstacles we will need to overcome in order to accomplish these goals. Is Canada's population too large, too geographically dispersed and regionally diverse, to achieve what the northern European states have achieved? Are our immigration rates too high and would we have to become more culturally homogeneous to achieve a higher level of equality? If so, should that concern us? Are we unable to reduce our inequality because Canada is closer to the highly unequal United States, and therefore heavily influenced by its economy, culture, and politics? What trade-offs, in the form of productivity, taxation, or spending, have other countries had to make in order to achieve their levels of equality? Is there any downside to what they have so obviously accomplished?

These and many other questions need to be addressed soon so that Canada can begin to work toward the greater equality that we know, from the examples of other countries, can be achieved. The potential benefits are enormous.

As we all know from experience, bad habits are hard to break—but that doesn't mean it's not worth trying. Challenging our habits of inequality will help us reduce injustice, poor health, criminal behaviour, and the risk of war. Surely, as Robert Owen believed, this task is worthy of our attention and effort.

Notes

Preface

1. However, in ancient Athens those deemed non-citizens—including women and slaves—did not have the privilege of equality. In this sense, New Harmony was different, since women were considered equal with men and there were no slaves.

2. George B. Lockwood and W.T. Harris, *New Harmony Movement* (Montana: Kessinger Publishing, 1905 [2010]), 62.

3. Rosabeth M. Kanter, *Commitment and Community: Communes and Utopias in Sociological Perspective* (Cambridge: Havard University Press, 1972), 123.

4. Brittany Huckabee, *Heaven on Earth: The Rise and Fall of Socialism* (Washington: New River Media, 2005), DVD.

Introduction

1. Max Weber, *Economy and Society*, eds. Guenther Roth and Claus Wittich (Berkeley, California: University of California Press, 1968).

2. Kimberlé Crenshaw, "Demarginalizing the Intersection of Race and Sex: A Black Feminist Critique of Antidiscrimination Doctrine, Feminist Theory and Antiracist Politics," *University of Chicago Legal Forum* (1989): 139–67. See also, Leslie McCall, "The Complexity of Intersectionality," *Signs* 30, no. 3 (2005): 1771–1800.

3. Gerhard Lenski, "Status Crystallisation: A Non-Vertical Dimension of Social Status," *American Sociological Review* 19, no. 4 (1954): 405–13.

4. *Webster's New World College Dictionary* (Cleveland: Wiley Publishing Inc., 2010).

5. Jean-Jacques Rousseau, *Discourse on the Origin and the Foundations of Inequality Among Men*, trans. Maurice Cranston (Harmondsworth: Penguin Books, 1754 [1984]), 136.

6. E. Tricomi, A. Rangel, C.F. Camerer, J.P. O'Doherty, "Neural Evidence for Inequality-Averse Social Preferences," *Nature* 463, no. 7284 (2010), 1089–91.

7. Christopher Jencks, "Whom Must We Treat Equally for Educational Opportunity to be Equal?" *Ethics* 98, no. 3 (1988): 518–33.

8. John Rawls, *A Theory of Justice* (Cambridge: Harvard University Press, 1971).

9. Kingsley Davis and Wilbert E. Moore, "Some Principles of Stratification," *American Sociological Review* 10, no. 2 (1970 [1945]): 242–49.

10. Friedrich Hayek, *A Free-Market Monetary System* (Auburn, AL: Ludwig von Mises Institute, 2008).

11. Melvin J. Lerner and Carolyn H. Simmons, "Observer's Reaction to the 'Innocent Victim': Compassion or Rejection?" *Journal of Personality and Social Psychology* 4, no. 2 (1966): 203–10.

12. Melvin J. Lerner, Dale T. Miller, and John G. Holmes, "Deserving and the Emergence of Forms of Justice," *Advances in Experimental Social Psychology* (1976): 133–62.

13. Lerner and Simmons, "Oberserver's Reaction." .

14. Natasha W. Morgan, Karen A. Hegtvedt, and Cathryn Johnson, "Expressing Emotional Responses to the Injustice of Others: It's Not Just What You Feel," *Social Structure and Emotion* (2008): 203–26.

15. Iram Fatima and Kausar Suhail, "Belief in a Just World and Subjective Wellbeing: Mothers of Normal and Down Syndrome Children," *International Journal of Psychology* 45, no. 6 (2010): 461–68.

16. Carlos Valiente, Kathryn Lemery-Chalfant, and Jodi Swanson, "Prediction of Kindergartners' Academic Achievement from Their Effortful Control and Emotionality: Evidence for Direct and Moderated Relations," *Journal of Educational Psychology* 102, no. 3 (2010): 550–60; Felix Peter and Claudia Dalbert, "Do My Teachers Treat Me Justly? Implications of Students' Justice Experience for Class Climate Experience," *Contemporary Educational Psychology* 35 (2010): 297–305.

17. Hatem Ocel and Orhan Aydin, "Adil Dünya İnancı ve Cinsiyetin Üretim Karşıtı İş Davranışları Üzerindeki Etkisi," *Turkish Journal of Psychology* 25, no. 66 (2010): 73–86.

18. Helder Alves and Isabel Correia, "Personal and General Belief in a Just World as Judgement Norms," *International Journal of Psychology* 45, no. 3 (2010): 221–31.

19. Mattew Feinburg and Robb Willer, "Apocalypse Soon? Dire Messages Reduce Belief in Global Warming by Contradicting Just-World Beliefs," *Psychological Science* 22, no. 1 (2011): 34–38.

20. Michelle Bal and Kees van den Bos, "The Role of Perpetrator Similarity in Reactions toward Innocent Victims," *European Journal of Social Psychology* 40, no. 6 (2010): 957–69.

Chapter 1

1. Michael Apted, "Seven Plus Seven," *UP* series (Manchester, UK: Granada Television, 1970), DVD.

2. Huckabee, *Heaven on Earth*.

3. Ibid.

4. Friedrich Engels, *The Condition of the Working Class in England*, eds. W.O. Henderson and W.H. Chaloner (Oxford: Blackwell, 1958).

5. Karl Marx and Friedrich Engels, *Manifesto of the Communist Party* (Moscow: Foreign Languages Pub. House, 1955).

6. Ibid., 79.

7. Ibid.

8. Ibid.

9. Erik Olin Wright, *Interrogating Inequality: Essays on Class Analysis, Socialism, and Marxism* (London: Verso, 1994); *Class Counts: Comparative Studies in Class Analysis* (Cambridge: Cambridge University Press, 1997).

10. Harry Braverman, *Labor and Monopoly Capital: The Degradation of Work in the Twentieth Century* (New York: Monthly Review Press, 1974).

11. Melvin Seeman, "On the Meaning of Alienation," *American Sociological Review* 24, no. 6 (1959): 783–91.

12. Robert D. Putnam, *Bowling Alone: The Collapse and Revival of American Community* (New York: Simon & Schuster, 2000).

13. Max Weber, *The Protestant Ethic and the Spirit of Capitalism*, trans. Talcott Parsons (London: Unwin, 1985).

14. James Burnham, *The Managerial Revolution: What Is Happening in the World* (New York: John Day, 1941).

15. Annette Lareau, "Invisible Inequality: Social Class and Childrearing in Black Families and White Families," *American Sociological Review* 67, no. 5 (2002): 747–76.

16. Ibid., 754.

17. Annette Lareau, *Unequal Childhoods: Class, Race, and Family Life* (Berkeley: University of California Press, 2003), 2.

18. Thorstein Veblen, *The Theory of the Leisure Class: An Economic Study of Institutions* (New York: B.W. Huebsch, 1919).

19. Pierre Bourdieu, "Cultural Reproduction and Social Reproduction," in *Knowledge, Education, and Cultural Change*, ed. Richard Brown (London: Tavistock Publications, 1973).

20. Ibid.

21. Edna Bonacich, "A Theory of Ethnic Antagonism: The Split Labor Market," *American Sociological Review* 37 (1972): 547–59.

22. Richard Wilkinson and Kate Pickett, "The Problems of Relative Deprivation: Why Some Societies Do Better than Others," *Social Science and Medicine* 65, no. 9 (2007): 1965–78.

Chapter 2

1. Jayme Poisson, "Parents Keep Child's Gender Secret," *Toronto Star*, May 21, 2011, http://www.thestar.com/life/parent/2011/05/21/parents_keep_childs_gender_secret.html; Jayme Poisson, "Star Readers Rage about Couple Raising 'Genderless' Infant," *Toronto Star*, May 24, 2011, http://www.thestar.com/life/health_wellness/2011/05/24/star_readers_rage_about_couple_raising_genderless_infant.html.

2. Poisson, "Parents Keep Child's Gender Secret."

3. Ibid.

4. Ibid.

5. Ibid.

6. Ibid.

7. Lois Gould, *X: A Fabulous Child's Story* (New York: Daughters Publishing Company, 1978).

8. Poisson, "Parents Keep Child's Gender Secret."

9. Ibid.

10. Candace West and Don H. Zimmerman, "Doing Gender," *Gender & Society* 1, no. 2 (1987): 125–51.

11. Simone de Beauvoir, *The Second Sex* (New York: Vintage Books, 1973), 301.

12. Ibid.

13. Ibid., 22.

14. Meg Luxton, *More than a Labour of Love: Three Generations of Women's Work in the Home* (Toronto: Women's Educational Press, 1980).

15. Ibid., 12.

16. Ibid.

17. Ibid., 17.

18. Ibid., 48.

19. Ibid., 11.

20. Ibid., 57.

21. Ann Oakley, *The Sociology of Housework* (New York: Random House, 1974).

22. Arlie Hochschild, *The Second Shift* (New York: Avon Books, 1990).

23. Ann Oakley, *Woman's Work: The Housewife, Past and Present* (New York: Vintage Books, 1976), 222.

24. Ibid., 196.

25. Ann Oakley, *Taking It Like a Woman* (London: Jonathan Cape, 1984), 123.

26. Ann Oakley, quoted in *Observer*, October 27, 1991.

27. Judith A. Hammond, review of *The Sociology of Housework*, by Ann Oakley, *Social Forces* 55, no. 4 (1974): 1104.

28. Katherine Marshall, "The Family Work Week," *Perspectives on Labour and Income* 10, no. 4 (April 2009): 5–13. Statistics Canada Catalogue no. 75-001-X.

29. Peter Burton and Shelley Phipps, "Families, Time, and Well-Being in Canada," *Canadian Public Policy* 37, no. 3 (2011): 395–423.

30. Andrew Jackson, "Families, Time and Well-Being," *Behind the Numbers: A Blog from the CCPA*, October 31, 2011, http://behindthenumbers.ca/2011/10/31/families-time-and-well-being.

31. Bonnie Fox, *When Couples Become Parents: The Creation of Gender in the Transition to Parenthood* (Toronto: University of Toronto Press, 2009).

32. Weber, *Economy and Society*, 212.

33. Ibid.

34. See for example, Michel Foucault, *The History of Sexuality, Volume I: An Introduction*, trans. Robert Hurley (New York: Vintage, 1990).

35. Warren Farrell, *Why Men Earn More: The Startling Truth Behind the Pay Gap and What Women Can Do About It* (New York: AMACOM, 2005).

36. Manwai Ku, "When Does Gender Matter? Gender Differences in Specialty Choice Among Physicians," *Work and Occupations* 38, no. 2 (2011): 221–62.

37. Ibid. See also, Ashley Herzog, *Feminism vs. Women* (Maitland, FL: Xulon Press, 2008).

38. Nicki Gilmour, "2010 Gender Equality Is Here, and Other Media Myths that Keep Unconscious Bias Alive," *The Glass Hammer*, January 7, 2010, http://www .theglasshammer.com/news/2010/01/07/2010-gender-equality-is-here-and-other -media-myths-that-keep-unconscious-bias-alive.

39. Ingrid Peritz and Adrian Morrow, "If You Want Collective Smarts, Include Women in Your Group," *Globe and Mail*, August 23, 2012, http://m.theglobeandmail .com/news/national/if-you-want-collective-smarts-include-women-in-your -group/article1736571/?service=mobile.

40. A.W. Woolley, C. Chabris, A. Pentland, N. Hashmi, and T. Malone, "Evidence for a Collective Intelligence Factor in the Performance of Human Groups," *Science* 330, no. 6004 (2010): 686–88.

41. Elizabeth Kelan, *Performing Gender at Work* (New York: Palgrave Macmillan, 2009).

42. Elizabeth Kelan, "Gender Inequality Still at Work," *Diversity Executive*, November 16, 2009, http://diversity-executive.com/articles/view/gender-inequality-still-at -work/1.

43. Barbara Annis, "We Need Gender Intelligence, Not Myths, in the Workplace," *Globe and Mail*, October 12, 2010, http://www.theglobeandmail.com/news/national/ time-to-lead/women-in-power/we-need-gender-intelligence-not-myths-in-the -workplace/article1754094.

44. Rosabeth M. Kanter, *Men and Women of the Corporation* (New York: Basic Books, 1977).

45. Amina Yaqin, "Islamic Barbie: The Politics of Gender and Performativity," *Fashion Theory* 11, no. 2–3 (2007): 173–88.

46. Simon Duncan and Birgit Pfau-Effinger, *Gender, Economy, and Culture in the European Union* (New York: Routledge, 2000).

47. Johan Verweij, Peter Easter, and Rein Nauta, "Secularization as an Economic and Cultural Phenomenon: A Cross-National Analysis," *Journal for the Scientific Study of Religion* 36, no. 2 (1997): 309–24.

48. Sylvia Chant and Nikki Craske, *Gender in Latin America* (New Brunswick, NJ: Rutgers University Press, 2003).

49. Ibid.

50. Duncan and Pfau-Effinger, *Gender, Economy, and Culture*.

51. Ibid.

52. Ola Sjöberg, "Ambivalent Attitudes, Contradictory Institutions: Ambivalence in Gender-Role Attitudes in Comparative Perspective," *International Journal of Comparative Sociology* 51, no. 1–2 (2010): 40–41.

53. Duncan and Pfau-Effinger, *Gender, Economy, and Culture*.

54. Statistics Canada, "Women in Canada: Paid Work," *The Daily*, December 9, 2010, http://www.statcan.gc.ca/daily-quotidien/101209/dq101209a-eng.htm.

55. Suzuki, *Gender and Career in Japan*.

56. Ibid.

57. Tahany M. Gadalla, "Gender Differences in Poverty Rates after Marital Dissolution: A Longitudinal Study," *Journal of Divorce and Remarriage* 49, no. 3–4: 225–38.

58. Leah F. Vosko, Nancy Zukewich, and Cynthia Cranford, "Precarious Jobs: A New Typology of Employment," *Perspectives on Labour and Income* 4, no. 10 (2003). See also "Invest in Women and Young Women Says YWCA Canada to Federal Government," World YWCA, January 30, 2009, at http://www.worldywca.org/Member-Associations/Regions/North-America/YWCA-Canada-Broad-Investments-2009.

59. Canadian Women's Foundation, "Fact Sheet: Moving Women Out of Poverty," 2011, http://www.canadianwomen.org/sites/canadianwomen.org/files/PDF-FactSheet-EndPoverty-Jan2013.pdf.

60. Fred Rothbaum, Martha Pott, Hiroshi Azuma, Kazuo Miyake, and John Weisz, "The Development of Close Relationships in Japan and the United States: Paths of Symbiotic Harmony and Generative Tension," *Child Development* 71, no. 5 (2000): 1121–42.

61. Aisha K. Gill and Sundari Anitha, *Forced Marriage: Introducing a Social Justice and Human Rights Perspective* (London: Zed Books, 2011).

62. Khatidja Chantler, Geetanjali Gangoli, and Marianne Hester, "Forced Marriage in the UK: Religious, Cultural, Economic or State Violence?" *Critical Social Policy* 29, no. 4 (2009): 587–612.

63. Ibid.

64. Mudita Rastogi and Paul Therly, "Dowry and Its Link to Violence Against Women in India: Feminist Psychological Perspectives," *Trauma, Violence, & Abuse* 7, no. 1 (2006): 66–77.

65. Ruchira T. Naved and Lars A. Persson, "Dowry and Spousal Physical Violence against Women in Bangladesh," *Journal of Family Issues* 31, no. 6 (2010): 830–56.

66. Rastogi and Therly, "Dowry."

67. Amy R. Elman, *Sexual Equality in an Integrated Europe* (New York: Palgrave MacMillan, 2007).

68. Rothbaum et al., "Development of Close Relationships."

69. Lorraine Davies, Julie Ann McMullin, William R. Avison, and Gale L. Cassidy, *Social Policy, Gender Inequality and Poverty* (Ottawa: Status of Women Canada, 2001).

70. Huma Ahmed-Ghosh, "Chattels of Society: Domestic Violence in India," *Violence Against Women* 10, no. 1 (2004): 94–118.

71. Rastogi and Therly, "Dowry."

72. Tracey Peter, "Domestic Violence in the United States and Sweden: A Welfare State Typology Comparison within a Power Resources Framework," *Womens Studies International Forum* 29, no. 1 (2006): 96–107.

73. Ibid.

74. Immaculada Valor-Segura, Francisca Expósito, and Miguel Moya, "Victim Blaming and Exoneration of the Perpetrator in Domestic Violence: The Role of Beliefs in a Just World and Ambivalent Sexism," *Spanish Journal of Psychology* 14, no. 1 (2011): 195–206.

75. Lorraine Sheridan and Adrian J. Scott, "Perceptions of Harm: Verbal Versus Physical Abuse in Stalking Scenarios," *Criminal Justice and Behavior* 37, no. 4 (2011): 400–16; John D. Murray, Jo Ann Spadafore, and William D. McIntosh, "Belief in a Just World and Social Perception: Evidence for Automatic Activation," *Journal of Social Psychology* 145, no. 1 (2005): 35–48.

76. N.T. Feather, "Reactions to Penalties for Offenses Committed by the Police and Public Citizens: Testing a Social–Cognitive Process Model of Retributive Justice," *Journal of Personality and Social Psychology* 75, no. 2 (1998): 528–44; Anthony F. Bogaert and Carolyn L. Hafer, "Predicting the Timing of Coming Out in Gay and Bisexual Men from World Beliefs, Physical Attractiveness, and Childhood Gender Identity/Role," *Journal of Applied Social Psychology* 39, no. 8 (2009): 1991–2019.

77. Mitchell J. Callen, Nathaniel G. Powell, and John H. Ellard, "The Consequences of Victim Physical Attractiveness on Reactions to Injustice: The Role of Observers' Belief in a Just World," *Social Justice Research* 20, no. 4 (2007): 433–56.

78. Leslee R. Kassing, Denise Beesley, and Lisa L. Frey, "Gender Role Conflict, Homophobia, Age, and Education as Predictors of Male Rape Myth Acceptance," *Journal of Mental Health Counseling* 27, no. 4 (2005): 311–28.

79. Kathy Doherty and Irina Anderson, "Making Sense of Male Rape: Constructions of Gender, Sexuality and Experience of Rape Victims," *Journal of Community and Applied Social Psychology* 14, no. 2 (2004): 85–103; Emma Sleath and Ray Bull, "Male Rape Victim and Perpetrator Blaming," *Journal of Interpersonal Violence* 25, no. 6 (2010): 969–88.

80. Margaret De Judicibus and Marita P. McCabe, "Blaming the Target of Sexual Harassment: Impact of Gender Role, Sexist Attitudes, and Work Role," *Sex Roles* 44, no. 7–8 (2001): 401–17; B.J. Rye, Sarah A. Greatrix, and Corinne S. Enright, "The Case of the Guilty Victim: The Effects of Gender of Victim and Gender of Perpetrator on Attributions of Blame and Responsibility," *Sex Roles* 54, no. 9–10 (2006): 639–49; Adrian Furnham, "Belief in a Just World: Research

Progress over the Past Decade," *Personality and Individual Differences* 34, no. 5 (2003): 795–817.

81. John D. Murray, Jo Ann Spadafore, and William D. McIntosh, "Belief in a Just World and Social Perception: Evidence for Automatic Activation," *The Journal of Social Psychology* 145, no. 1 (2005): 35–48.

Chapter 3

1. Philip Zimbardo, *The Stanford Prison Experiment: A Simulation Study of the Psychology of Imprisonment* (Stanford, CA: Stanford University, 1971).

2. William Peters, *A Class Divided* (PBS, 1985), http://www.pbs.org/wgbh/pages/frontline/shows/divided.

3. Guido Barbujani, Arianna Magagni, Eric Minch, and L. Luca Cavalli-Sforza. "An Apportionment of Human DNA Diversity," *National Academy of Sciences of the USA* 94, no. 9 (1997): 4516–19.

4. Emile Durkheim, *The Elementary Forms of Religious Life*, trans. Joseph Ward Swain (London: G. Allen & Unwin, 1915).

5. Benedict Anderson, *Imagined Communities* (London: Verso, 1983).

6. Raymond Breton, "Institutional Completeness of Ethnic Communities and the Personal Relations of Immigrants," *American Journal of Sociology* 70, no. 2 (1964): 193.

7. Valerie Preston and Ann M. Murnaghan, "Immigrants and Racialization in Canada: Geographies of Exlusion?" *Canadian Issues* (2005): 67–71.

8. John Porter, *The Vertical Mosaic: An Analysis of Social Class and Power in Canada* (Toronto: University of Toronto Press, 1965).

9. Hugh Lautard and Neil Guppy, "Revisiting the Vertical Mosaic: Occupational Stratification Among Canadian Ethnic Groups," in *Race and Ethnic Relations in Canada*, ed. P.S. Li, 220–52 (Toronto: Oxford University Press, 1999).

10. Carol Agocs and Monica Boyd, "The Canadian Ethnic Mosaic Recast for the 1990s," in *Social Inequality in Canada: Patterns, Problems, Policies*, eds. J. Curtis, E. Grabb, and N. Guppy, 330–52 (Scarborough, ON: Prentice-Hall Canada, 1993).

11. Jason Z. Lian and David R. Matthews, "Does the Vertical Mosaic Exist? Ethnicity and Income in Canada, 1991," *Canadian Review of Sociology and Anthropology* 35, no. 4 (1998): 461.

12. Jeffrey G. Reitz and Sherrilyn M. Sklar, "Culture, Race, and the Economic Assimilation of Immigrants," *Sociological Forum* 12, no. 2 (1997): 233–77.

13. Feng Hou and T.R. Balakrishnan, "The Integration of Visible Minorities in Contemporary Canadian Society," *Canadian Journal of Sociology* 21, no. 3 (1996): 307.

14. Paul Attewell, Philip Kasinitz, and Kathleen Dunn, "Black Canadians and Black Americans: Racial Income Inequality in Comparative Perspective," *Ethnic & Racial Studies* 33, no. 3 (2010): 473–95.

15. Ibid., 482.

16. Ibid., 482.

17. Emory S. Bogardus, *Social Distance* (Los Angeles: University of Southern California Press, 1959).

18. Ibid.

19. Tim B. Heaton and Cardell K. Jacobson, "Comparative Patterns of Interracial Marriage: Structural Opportunities, Third-Party Factors, and Temporal Change in Immigrant Societies," *Journal of Comparative Family Studies* 39, no. 2 (2008): 130.

20. Ibid.

21. Anne Milan, Helene Maheux, and Tina Chui, "A Portrait of Couples in Mixed Unions," *Canadian Social Trends* 89 (2010). Statistics Canada Catalogue no. 11-008-X, http://www.statcan.gc.ca/pub/11-008-x/2010001/article/11143-eng.htm.

22. Jeffrey Passel, Wendy Wang, and Paul Taylor, "One-in-Seven New U.S. Marriages Is Interracial or Interethnic," *Pew Research: Social and Demographic Trends*, June 4, 2010, http://www.pewsocialtrends.org/2010/06/04/marrying-out.

23. Ibid.

24. Heaton and Jacobson, "Comparative Patterns of Interracial Marriage."

25. Australian Bureau of Statistics, "Marriages, Australia, 2007," October 14, 2008, http://www.abs.gov.au/ausstats/abs@.nsf/mf/3306.0.55.001.

26. Australian Bureau of Statistics, "2006 Census of Population and Housing: Media Releases and Fact Sheets, 2006," June 27, 2007, http://www.abs.gov.au/AUSSTATS/abs@.nsf/7d120f6763c78caca257061001cc588/ec871bf375f2035dca257306000d5422!OpenDocument.

27. Ministry of Health, Labour, and Welfare, *Specified Report of Vital Statistics* (Tokyo: Governemnt of Japan, 2007), http://www.mhlw.go.jp/english/database/db-hw/report/5.html.

28. Catherine Borrel and Chloe Tavan, "La vie familial des immigrés," *France, portrait social 2003/2004* (2003): 109–24.

29. Xin Meng and Dominique Meurs, "Intermarriage, Language, and Economic Assimilation Process: A Case Study of France," Institute for the Study of Labor, Discussion Paper Series, 2006.

30. Borrel and Tavan, "La vie familial des immigrés."

31. Diana Fong, "Low Rate of German-Turkish Marriages Impedes Integration," Deutsche Welle, February 24, 2008, http://www.dw.de/low-rate-of-german-turkish-marriages-impedes-integration/a-3134365-1.

32. Sayaka Osanami Törngren, "Attitudes towards Interracial Dating and Marriages—Examination of the Role of Interracial Contacts in Malmö, Sweden," Malmö Institute for Studies of Migration, Diversity and Welfare, Malmö University, 2011.

33. Ibid.

34. Ibid.

35. Ibid.

36. Ibid.

37. Ibid.

38. Ibid.

39. Ibid.

40. Ibid., 7.

41. Steve Martinot, *The Rule of Racialization: Class, Identity, Governance* (Philadelphia: Temple University Press, 2003), 13

42. Yehudi O. Webster, *The Racialization of America* (New York: St. Martin's Press, 1992).

43. For example, see Stever Martinet, "The Rule of Racialization: Class, Identity, Governance," *Contemporary Sociology* 33 (2004), 291–92; Becky Pettit and Bruce Western, "Mass Imprisonment and the Life Course: Race and Class Inequality in U.S. Incarceration," *American Sociological Review* 69 (2004), 151–69.

44. Anthony S. Chen, "Lives at the Center of the Periphery, Lives at the Periphery of the Center: Chinese American Masculinities and Bargaining with Hegemony," *Gender and Society* 13 (1999), 584–607.

45. Marianne Bertrand and Sendhil Mullainathan, "Are Emily and Greg More Employable than Lakisha and Jamal? A Field Experiment on Labor Market Discrimination," *American Economic Review* 94, no. 4 (2004): 991–1013.

46. Nick Drydakis and Minas Vlassis, "Ethnic Discrimination in the Greek Labour Market: Occupational Access, Insurance Coverage and Wage Offers," *Manchester School* 78, no. 3 (2010): 201–18.

47. Leo Kaas and Christian Manger, "Ethnic Discrimination in Germany's Labour Market: A Field Experiment," *German Economic Review* 13, no. 1 (2012): 1–20.

48. Devah Pager, "The Use of Field Experiments for Studies of Employment Discrimination: Contributions, Critiques, and Directions for the Future," *Annals of the American Academy of Political and Social Science* 609 (2007): 104–33.

49. Phil Oreopoulos, "Why Do Skilled Immigrants Struggle in the Labor Market? A Field Experiment with Six Thousand Resumes," National Bureau of Economic Research Workign Paper No. 15036 (June 2009).

50. Seymour M. Lipset, *Continental Divide: The Values and Institutions of the United States and Canada* (New York: Routledge, 1990), xiii.

51. Edward Grabb and James Curtis, *Regions Apart: The Four Societies of Canada and the United States* (Toronto: Oxford University Press, 2010 [2005]).

52. Paul Attewell, Philip Kasinitz, and Kathleen Dunn, "Black Canadians and Black Americans: Racial Income Inequality in Comparative Perspective," *Ethnic & Racial Studies* 33, no. 3 (2010): 473–95.

53. Ibid.

54. J.G. Reitz and R. Breton, *The Illusion of Difference: Realities of Ethnicity in Canada and the United States* (Toronto: CD Howe Institute, 1994).

55. James S. Coleman, Ernest Q. Campbell, Carol J. Hobson, James McPartland, Alexander M. Mood, Frederic D. Weinfeld, and Robert L. York, *Equality of Educational Opportunity* (Washington, DC: US Department of Health, Education and Welfare, 1966).

56. Maureen T. Hallinan, "Social Perspectives on Black-White Inequalities in American Schooling," *Sociology of Education* 74 (2001): 50–70.

57. Paul Attewell, Philip Kasinitz, and Kathleen Dunn, "Black Canadians and Black Americans: Racial Income Inequality in Comparative Perspective," *Ethnic & Racial Studies* 33, no. 3 (2010): 473–95.

58. Ibid.

59. Nancy Foner, "Race and Color: Jamaican Migrants in London and New York City," *International Migration Review* 19, no. 4 (1985): 708–27.

60. Annette Lareau, *Unequal Childhoods: Class, Race, and Family Life* (Berkeley: University of California Press, 2003)

61. Rebecca L. Malhi and Susan D. Boon, "Discourses of 'Democratic Racism' in the Talk of South Asian Canadian Women," *Canadian Ethnic Studies* 39, no. 3 (2007): 125–49; Carol Tator and Frances Henry, *Racial Profiling in Canada: Challenging the Myth of a "Few Bad Apples"* (Toronto: University of Toronto Press, 2006).

62. Malhi and Boon, "Discourses of 'Democratic Racism.'"

63. Charlie Angus, "What If They Declared an Emergency and No One Came?" *Huffington Post*, November 21, 2011, http://www.huffingtonpost.ca/charlie-angus/attawapiskat-emergency_b_1104370.html.

64. Magnus Carlsson and Dan-Olof Rooth, "Evidence of Ethnic Discrimination in the Swedish Labor Market Using Experimental Data," *Labour Economics* 14 (2007): 716–29.

65. Ibid.

66. Ibid.

67. K. Groenendijk, E. Guild, and R. Barzilay, *The Legal Status of Third Country Nationals Who are Long-Term Residents in a Member State of the European Union* (Nijmegen, Netherlands: Centre for Migration Law, University of Nijmegen, 2000).

Chapter 4

1. Kathy Charmaz, *Good Days, Bad Days: The Self in Chronic Illness and Time* (New Brunswick, NJ: Rutgers University Press, 1991).

2. Jeffrey J. Arnett, "Emerging Adulthood: A Theory of Development from the Late Teens through the Twenties," *American Psychologist* 55, no. 5 (2000): 469–80.

3. Jeffrey J. Arnett, *Emerging Adulthood: The Winding Road from the Late Teens through the Twenties* (New York: Oxford University Press, 2004).

4. Robin Marantz Henig, "What Is It About 20-Somethings?" *New York Times*, August 18, 2010, http://www.nytimes.com/2010/08/22/magazine/22Adulthood -t.html.

5. Ibid.

6. Erik H. Erikson, *Identity and the Life Cycle* (New York: Norton, 1959).

7. Marantz Henig, "What Is It About 20-Somethings?"

8. Arnett, *Emerging Adulthood*; Jeffrey J. Arnett, "Young People's Conceptions of the Transition to Adulthood," *Youth & Society*, 29 (1997), 1–23.

9. Jeffrey Jensen Arnett, interviewed by Steve Paikin, *The Agenda*, TVO, September 20, 2010, http://www.youtube.com/watch?v=Y_f8DmU-gQQandfeature=relmfu.

10. Pamela L. Ramage-Morin, "Motor Vehicle Accident Deaths, 1979 to 2004" *Health Reports* 19, no. 3 (2008). Statistics Canada Catalogue no. 82-003-X. http:// www.statcan.gc.ca/pub/82-003-x/2008003/article/10648/5202440-eng.htm.

11. Kenneth Keniston, *The Uncommitted: Alienated Youth in American Society* (New York: Harcourt, 1965).

12. Mike Nichols, *The Graduate* (California: Metro-Goldwyn-Mayer Studios Inc., 1967).

13. Candace West and Don H. Zimmerman, "Doing Gender," *Gender and Society* 1, no. 2 (1987): 125–51.

14. Philippe Aries, *L'Enfant et la vie familiale sous l'Ancien Regime* (Paris: Plon, 1960).

15. Granville Stanley Hall, *Adolescence: Its Psychology and Its Relations to Physiology, Anthropology, Sociology, Sex, Crime, Religion and Education* (London: Appleton, 1905).

16. Sport BC, *Annual Report 2009–2010*, http://sportbc.com/files/Sport-BC-2010 -Annual-Report.pdf.

17. Bruce Grierson, "The Incredibly Flying Nonagenarian," *New York Times*, December 6, 2011, http://www.brucegrierson.com/?p=29.

18. Ibid.

19. Ibid.

20. Ibid.

21. Elaine Cumming and William E. Henry, *Growing Old: The Process of Disengagement* (New York: Basic Books, 1961).

22. Nicola Stockley, *Don't Grow Old* (London: BBC, 2009–10), http://www.bbc.co.uk/ programmes/b00qm7zr.

23. Ibid.

24. Ibid.

25. Ibid.

26. Human Resources and Skills Development Canada, *Canadians In Context – Aging Population* (Ottawa: Government of Canada, 2013), http://www4.hrsdc .gc.ca/.3ndic.1t.4r@-eng.jsp?iid=33.

27. Vincent J. Roscigno, Sherry Mong, Reginald Byron, and Griff Tester, "Age Discrimination, Social Closure and Employment," *Social Forces* 86, no. 1 (2007): 313–34.

28. Morley Gunderson, "Banning Mandatory Retirement: Throwing Out the Baby with the Bathwater," *C.D.Howe Institute Backgrounder* 79 (2004): 1–8.

29. Ali M. Ahmed, Lina Andersson, and Mats Hammarstedt, "Does Age Matter for Employability? A Field Experiment on Ageism in the Swedish Labour Market," *Applied Economics Letters* 19 (2012): 403–6.

30. Trude Furunes and Reidar J. Mykletun, "Age Discrimination in the Workplace: Validation of the Nordic Age Discrimination Scale (NADS)," *Scandinavian Journal of Psychology* 51 (2010): 23–30.

31. Colm O'Cinneide, *Age Discrimination of European Law* (Luxembourg: Office for Official Publications of the European Communities, 2005).

32. Joy L. Lindo, "Employment Discrimination: Youth-Based Termination," *Seton Hall Law Review* 30, no. 2 (2000): 682–89.

33. Ibid.

34. Ibid.

35. Todd D. Nelson, "Ageism: Prejudice against Our Feared Future Self," *Journal of Social Issues* 61, no. 2 (2005): 207–21.

36. Ibid.

37. Ibid.

38. Glen H. Elder, *Children of the Great Depression: Social Change in Life Experience* (Chicago: University of Chicago Press, 1974).

39. Ibid.

40. Ibid.

41. Glen H. Elder, Monica Kirkpatrick Johnson, and Robert Crosnoe, "The Emergence and Development of Life Course Theory," in *Handbook of the Life Course*, eds. Jeylan T. Mortimer and Michael J. Shanahan, 3–19 (New York: Springer, 2003); see also, Glen H. Elder, "The Life Course and Aging: Some Accomplishments, Unfinished Tasks, and New," presented at the annual meeting of the Gerontological Society of America, Boston, MA, November 11, 2002.

42. Edler, *Children of the Great Depression*.

43. Jay Mechling, review of *Children of the Great Depression: Social Change in Life Experience*, by Glen H. Elder, *Journal of Social History* 9, no. 3 (1976): 419.

44. E. Fussell, "The Transition to Adulthood in Aging Societies," *Annals of the American Academy of Political and Social Science* 580, no. 1 (2002): 16–39.

Chapter 5

1. Blair Edwards and Jessica Cunha, "'I Wish I Could Be Happy.' Glen Cairn Teen Takes His Own Life," *Your Ottawa Region*, October 17, 2011, http://www.yourottawaregion.com/article/1227169--i-wish-i-could-be-happy.

2. Louise Boyle, "'I Just Want to Feel Special to Someone': Gay 15-Year-Old Kills Himself after Chronicling His Unhappiness Online," *Mail Online*, October 18, 2011.

3. Tanya Navaneelan, "Suicide Rates: An Overview," *Health at a Glance* (2012). Statistics Canada Catalogue no. 82-624-X, http://www.statcan.gc.ca/pub/82-624-x/2012001/article/11696-eng.htm.

4. Ibid.

5. Jon Willing, "Jamie Hubley's Dad Defends Anti-bullying Legislation," *Ottawa Sun*, April 6, 2012, http://www.ottawasun.com/2012/04/06/jamie-hubleys-dad-defends-anti-bullying-legislation.

6. C.J. Pascoe, *Dude, You're a Fag: Masculinity and Sexuality in High School* (Berkley: University of California Press, 2007).

7. Alfred D. Kinsey, Wardell B. Pomeroy, and Clyde E. Martin, *Sexual Behavior in the Human Male* (Philadelphia: W.B. Saunders Co., 1948); Institute for Sex Research, *Sexual Behavior in the Human Female* (Philadelphia: W.B. Saunders Co., 1953).

8. Mariana Valverde, "Heterosexuality: Contested Ground," in *Family Patterns, Gender Relations*, ed. B.J. Fox, 212–18 (Don Mills, ON: Oxford University Press, 2009), 212.

9. Ibid., 213.

10. Mariana Valverde, *Sex, Power, and Pleasure* (Toronto: Women's Press, 1985), 49.

11. Karin A. Martin, "Normalizing Heterosexuality: Mother's Assumptions, Talk, and Strategies with Young Children," *American Sociological Review* 74, no. 2 (2009): 190–207.

12. Ibid., 191.

13. Ibid., 203.

14. Ibid., 204.

15. Ibid., 205.

16. Statistics Canada, "Gay Pride . . . by the Numbers," July 8, 2011, http://www42.statcan.gc.ca/smr08/2011/smr08_158_2011-eng.htm.

17. Samuel Perreault and Shannon Brennan, "Criminal Victimization in Canada, 2009," *Juristat* (Sumemr 2010), http://www.statcan.gc.ca/pub/85-002-x/2010002/article/11340-eng.htm.

18. Susan McDonald and Andrea Hogue, *An Exploration of the Needs of Victims of Hate Crimes* (Ottawa: Department of Justice, 2012), http://www.justice.gc.ca/eng/pi/rs/rep-rap/jr/jr14/p7.html.

19. Ibid.

20. George Weinberg, *Society and the Healthy Homosexual* (Garden City, NY: Anchor Press, 1972).

21. Gordon W. Allport, *The Nature of Prejudice* (Cambridge, MA: Addison-Wesley Pub. Co., 1954).

22. Gregory M. Herek, "Beyond 'Homophobia': Thinking about Sexual Prejudice and Stigma in the Twenty-First Century," *Sexuality Research and Social Policy* 1, no. 2 (2004): 6–24.

23. Theodore W. Adorno, Else Frenkel-Brunswik, Daniel J. Levinson, and R. Nevitt Sanford, *The Authoritarian Personality* (New York: Harper, 1950).

24. I.L. Lottes and P.J. Kuriloff, "The Effects of Gender, Race, Religion, and Political Orientation on the Sex Role Attitudes of College Freshmen," *Adolescence* 27, no. 3 (1992): 675–88; see also K.S. Larsen, M. Reed, and S. Hoffman, "Attitudes of Heterosexuals toward Homosexuality: A Likert-Type Scale and Construct Validity," *Journal of Sex Research* 16, no. 3 (1980): 245–57.

25. L.A. Kurdek, "Correlates of Negative Attitudes toward Homosexuals in Heterosexual College Students," *Sex Roles* 18, no. 2 (1988): 727–38.

26. Robert E. Fay, Charles F. Turner, Albert D. Klassen, and John H. Gagnon, "Prevalence and Patterns of Same-Gender Sexual Contact among Men," *Science* 243 (1989): 338–48.

27. Ibid.

28. Gregory M. Herek and Eric K. Glunt, "Interpersonal Contact and Heterosexuals' Attitudes toward Gay Men: Results from a National Survey," *Journal of Sex Research* 30, no. 3 (1993): 239–44.

29. Anissa Hélie, "Holy Hatred," *Reproductive Health Matters* 12, no. 23 (2004): 120–24.

30. Aaron S. Greenberg and J. Michael Bailey, "Parental Selection of Children's Sexual Orientation," *Archives of Sexual Behaviour* 30, no. 4 (2001): 423–37.

31. Jane P. Sheldon, Clara A. Pfeffer, Toby E. Jayaratne, Merle Feldbaum, and Elizabeth M. Petty, "Beliefs about the Etiology of Homosexuality and about the Ramifications of Discovering Its Possible Genetic Origin," *Journal of Homosexuality* 52, no. 3–4 (2007): 111–50.

32. Tom W. Smith, "Cross-National Differences in Attitudes towards Homosexuality," *GSS Cross-national Report* 31 (2011).

33. Matthew Waites, "Analysing Sexualities in the Shadow of War: Islam in Iran, the West and the Work of Reimagining Human Rights," *Sexualities* 11, no. 1–2 (2008): 64–73.

34. BBC News, "Cameron Threat to Dock Some UK Aid to Anti-Gay Nations," October 30, 2011, http://www.bbc.co.uk/news/uk-15511081.

35. Joanna Jolly, "Africa's Lesbians Demand Change," BBC News, February 27, 2008, http://news.bbc.co.uk/2/hi/africa/7266646.stm.

36. World Bank, *World Development Report 2011* (Washington, DC: World Bank, 2011).

37. Keyan Keihani, "Beyond Bounds: A Brief History of Male Homosexuality in Islamic Culture," *Iranian Archives* (2005), http://iranian.com/Opinion/2005/December/Homosexuality/index.html.

38. World Bank, *World Development Report 2011* (Washington, DC: World Bank, 2011).

39. A.Š. Rimac, "Determinants of Homonegativity in Europe," *Journal of Sex Research* (2009): 24–32; J. Gerhards, "Non-discrimination towards Homosexuality: The European Union's Policy and Citizens' Attitudes towards Homosexuality in 27 European Countries," *International Sociology* 25, no. 1 (2010): 5–28.

40. IMF, *World Economic Outlook April 2011* (Washington, DC: IMF, 2011); "Any male person who, in public or private, commits, or abets the commission of, or procures or attempts to procure the commission by any male person of, any act of gross indecency with another male person, shall be punished with imprisonment for a term which may extend to 2 years" (Penal Code of Singapore, Section 377A).

41. Robin Mathy, "Suicidality and Sexual Orientation in Five Continents: Asia, Australia, Europe, North America, and South America," *International Journal of Sexuality and Gender Studies* 7 (2002): 215–25.

42. See, for example, R.C. Friedman, "Homosexuality, Psychopathology, and Suicidality," *Archives of General Psychiatry* 56, no. 10 (1999): 887–88.

43. Mathy, "Suicidality and Sexual Orientation," 223.

44. K. Corsaro, "Remembering 'White Night'—San Francisco's Gay Riot," *Bay Times*, May 18, 2006.

45. J. Novick, "Dan White and His America," *Threepenny Review* 28 (1987): 15–16.

46. Ibid.

47. C. Pogash, "Myth of the 'Twinkie Defense,'" *San Francisco Chronicle*, November 3, 2003.

48. G.M. Herek, "Heterosexuals' Attitudes toward Bisexual Men and Women in the United States," *Journal of Sex Research* 39, no. 4 (2002): 264–74.

49. *Huffington Post*, "Westboro Baptist Church to Picket Funerals of Arizona Shooting Victims," January 9, 2011.

50. J. Gettleman, "Americans' Role Seen in Uganda Anti-gay Push," *New York Times*, January 3, 2010.

51. J. Loftus, "America's Liberalization in Attitudes toward Homosexuality," *American Sociological Review* 66, no. 5 (2001): 762–82.

52. M. Smith, "Social Movements and Judicial Empowerment," *Courts, Public Policy, and Lesbian and Gay Organizing in Canada* 33, no. 2 (2005): 327–53.

53. Ibid.

54. G. Filax, "Producing Homophobia in Alberta, Canada in the 1990s," *Journal of Historical Sociology* 17, no. 1 (2004): 87–120.

55. United Nations, *Human Development Report 2010* (New York: United Nations, 2010).

56. Gerhards, "Non-discrimination towards Homosexuality"; Rimac, "Determinants of Homonegativity in Europe."

57. United Nations, *Human Development Report 2010*.

58. H.O. Gert Hekma, "Leftist Sexual Politics and Homosexuality: A Historical Overview," *Journal of Homosexuality* 29, no. 2–3 (1999): 1–40.

59. United Nations, *Human Development Report 2010*.

60. Gerhards, "Non-discrimination towards Homosexuality"; Rimac, "Determinants of Homonegativity in Europe."

61. United Nations, *Human Development Report 2010*.

62. M.L. Eva Jaspers, "'Horros of Holland': Explaining Attitude Change towards Euthnasia and Homosexuals in the Netherlands, 1970–1988," *International Journal of Public Opinion Research* 19, no. 4 (2007): 451–73.

63. Gerhards, "Non-discrimination towards Homosexuality"; Rimac, "Determinants of Homonegativity in Europe."

64. Frank Newport, "Mississippi Is Most Religious U.S. State; Vermont and New Hampshire Are the Least Religious States," Gallup, March 27, 2012, http://www.gallup.com/poll/153479/Mississippi-Religious-State.aspx.

65. Ibid.

66. G.M. Herek, "Heterosexuals' Attitudes toward Bisexual Men and Women in the United States," *Journal of Sex Research* 39, no. 4 (2002): 264–74.

67. Frederick Solt, Philip Habel, and J. Tobin Grant, "Economic Inequality, Relative Power, and Religiosity," *Social Science Quarterly* 92, no. 2 (2011): 447–65.

68. Ibid.

69. A German saying that describes a principle of law in the Middle Ages that allowed escaped serfs freedom after a year and a day in the city.

70. Statistics Canada, "Gay Pride . . . by the Numbers."

71. Stephen O. Murray, *American Gay* (Chicago: University of Chicago Press, 1996).

72. John D'Emilio, *Sexual Politics, Sexual Communities: The Making of a Homosexual Minority in the United States* (Chicago: University of Chicago Press, 1983).

73. Richard Florida, "The Rise of the Creative Class," *Washington Monthly* 34, no. 5 (2002): 15–25.

Chapter 6

1. Emile Durkheim, *Suicide: A Study in Sociology*, trans. J.A. Spaulding and G. Simpson (Glencoe, IL: Free Press, 1951).

2. Adam Wagstaff and Eddy van Doorslaer, "Income Inequality and Health: What Does the Literature Tell Us?" *Annual Review of Public Health* 21 (2000): 543–67.

3. Ibid., 543.

4. Ulf-G. Gerdtham and Magnus Johannesson, "Absolute Income, Relative Income, Income Inequality, and Morality," *Journal of Human Resources* 39, no. 1 (2004): 228.

5. Ibid.

6. John Asafu-Adjaye, "Income Inequality and Health: A Multi-Country Analysis," *International Journal of Social Economics* 31, no. 1–2 (2004): 195.

7. Eric Backlund, Geoff Rowe, John Lynch, Michael C. Wolfson, George A. Kaplan, and Paul D. Sorlie, "Income Inequality and Mortality: A Multilevel Prospective Study of 521,248 Individuals in 50 US States," *International Journal of Epidemiology* 36 (2007): 590.

8. Martin Karlsson, Therese Nilsson, Carl H. Lyttkens, and George Leeson, "Income Inequality and Health: Importance of a Cross-Country Perspective," *Social Science and Medicine* 70 (2010): 875.

9. M.G. Marmot, S. Stansfeld, C. Patel, F. North, J. Head, I. White, E. Brunner, A. Feeney, G.D. Smith, "Health Inequalities among British Civil Servants: The Whitehall II Study," *The Lancet* 337 (1991): 1387–93.

10. Sabine R. Kunz-Ebrecht, Clemens Kirschbaum, Michael Marmot, and Andrew Steptoe, "Differences in Cortisol Awakening Response on Work Days and Weekends in Women and Men from the Whitehall II Cohort," *Psychoneuroendocrinology* 29, no. 4 (2004): 516–28.

11. Marmot et. al, "Health Inequalities."

12. Victor R. Fuchs, "Reflections on the Socio-Economic Correlates of Health," *Journal of Health Economics* 23, no. 4 (2004): 653–61.

13. Ibid.

14. T. Theorell, R.A. Karasek, and P. Eneroth, "Job Strain Variations in Relation to Plasma Testosterone Fluctuations in Working Men—A Longitudinal Study," *Journal of Internal Medicine* 227 (1990): 31–36.

15. G. Veenstra, "Income Inequality and Health. Coastal Communities in British Columbia, Canada," *Canadian Journal of Public Health* 93, no. 5 (2002): 374–79.

16. Ana Diez-Roux, Bruce G. Link, and Mary E. Northridge, "A Multilevel Analysis of Income Inequality and Cardiovascular Disease Risk Factors," *Social Science and Medicine* 50, no. 5 (2000): 673–87.

17. S.V. Subramanian and I. Kawachi, "Income Inequality and Health: What Have We Learned So Far?" *Epidemiologic Review* 26 (2004): 78–91.

18. I. Kawachi and B.P. Kennedy, "Income Inequality and Health: Pathways and Mechanisms," *Health Services Research* 34 (1999): 215–27.

19. Centers for Disease Control and Prevention, US Department for Health and Human Services, "CDC Health Disparities and Inequalities Report – United States, 2011," *Morbidity and Mortality Weekly Report* 60, http://www.cdc.gov/mmwr/pdf/other/su6001.pdf.

20. N. Kondo, G. Sembajwe, I. Kawachi, R.M. van Dam, S.V. Subramanian, and Z. Yamagata, "Income Inequality, Mortality, and Self Rated Health: Meta-Analysis of Multilevel Studies," *British Medical Journal* 339 (2009): 4471.

21. Ibid.

22. Kawachi and Kennedy, "Income Inequality and Health."

23. Nadine R. Nowatzki, "Wealth Inequality and Health: A Political Economy Perspective," *International Journal of Health Services* 42, no. 3 (2012): 403–24.

24. Ana Diez-Roux, Bruce G. Link, and Mary E. Northridge, "A Multilevel Analysis of Income Inequality and Cardiovascular Disease Risk Factors," *Social Science and Medicine* 50, no. 5 (2000): 673–87.

25. Enrico Materia, Laura Cacciani, Giulio Bugarini, Giulia Cesaroni, Marina Davoli, Maria Paola Mirale, Loredana Vergine, Giovanni Baglio, Giuseppe Simeone, and Carlo A. Perucci, "Income Inequality and Mortality in Italy," *European Journal of Public Health* 15, no. 4 (2005): 411–17.

26. Nadine R. Nowatzki, "Wealth Inequality and Health: A Political Economy Perspective," *International Journal of Health Services* 42, no. 3 (2012): 403–24.

27. Graham Scambler, "Health Inequalities," *Sociology of Health and Illness* 34, no. 1 (2012): 130–46.

28. Bruce G. Link, Jo C. Phelan, Richard Miech, and Emily L. Westin, "The Resources that Matter: Fundamental Social Causes of Health Disparities and the Challenge of Intelligence," *Journal of Health and Social Behaviour* 49 (2008): 72–91.

29. Ibid.

30. Scambler, "Health Inequalities."

31. George D. Smith, David Blane, and Mel Bartley, "Explanations for Socio-Economic Differentials in Mortality: Evidence from Britain and Elsewhere," *European Journal of Public Health* 4 (1994): 131–44.

32. Link, Phelan, Miech, and Westin, "Resources that Matter."

33. Scambler, "Health Inequalities."

34. J. Lynch, P. Due, C. Muntaner, and G.D. Smith, "Social Capital: Is It a Good Investment Strategy for Public Health?" *Journal of Epidemiology and Community Health* 54, no. 6 (2000): 404–8.

35. Kawachi and Kennedy, "Income Inequality and Health."

36. N.M. Rimashevskaia and O.A. Kislitsyna, "Income Inequality and Health," *Russian Social Science Review* 47, no. 4 (2006): 4–23.

37. T. Fujiwara and I. Kawachi, "Social Capital and Health: A Study of Adult Twins in the U.S," *American Journal of Preventive Medicine* 35 (2008): 139–44.

38. Rimashevskaia and Kislitsyna, "Income Inequality and Health."

39. Andrew Leigh and Christopher Jencks, "Inequality and Mortality: Long-Run Evidence from a Panel of Countries," *Journal of Health Economics* 26 (2007): 1–24.

40. Nicholas Bakalar, "Researchers Link Deaths to Social Ills," *New York Times*, July 4, 2011, http://www.nytimes.com/2011/07/05/health/05social.html?_r=0.

41. Alison Bing, *Venice and The Veneto: City Guide*, 6th ed. (London: Lonely Planet Publication, 2010).

42. Public Health Agency of Canada, *A Report on Mental Illness in Canada* (Ottawa: Public Health Agency of Canada, 2012), http://www.phac-aspc.gc.ca/publicat/miic-mmac/chap_1-eng.php.

43. American Psychiatric Association, *Diagnostic and Statistical Manual of Mental Disorders: DSM-IV-TR*, 4th ed., text revision (Washington, DC: American Psychiatric Association, 2000).

44. Centre for Addiction and Mental Health, *Mental Health and Addiction Statistics: Prevalence and Incidence* (Toronto: CAMH, 2012), http://www.camh.ca/en/hospital/about_camh/newsroom/for_reporters/Pages/addictionmentalhealthstatistics.aspx.

45. Ibid.

46. Philip S. Wang, Michael Lane, Mark Olfson, Harold A. Pincus, Kenneth B. Wells, and Ronald C. Kessler, "Twelve-Month Use of Mental Health Services in the United States: Results from the National Comorbidity Survey Replication," *Archives of General Psychiatry* 62, no. 6 (2005): 629–40.

47. Andrew Scull, *The Most Solitary of Afflictions: Madness and Society in Britain, 1700–1900* (New Haven: Yale University Press, 1993), 217.

48. Erving Goffman, *Stigma: Notes on the Management of Spoiled Identity* (Englewood Cliffs, NJ: Prentice-Hall, 1963).

49. Jamie Wiebe, Phil Mun, and Nadine Kauffman, *Gambling and Problem Gambling in Ontario 2005* (Guelph, ON: Ontario Problem Gambling Research Centre, 2006), http://www.gamblingresearch.org/content/research.php?appid=1043.

50. Mood Disorders Society of Canada, *Problem Gambling* (Guelph, ON: Mood Disorders Society of Canada, 2010), http://www.mooddisorderscanada.ca/documents/Consumer%20and%20Family%20Support/Problem%20Gambling%20Edited%2020Dec2010.pdf.

51. The Conference Board of Canada, *Health Report Card: How Canada Performs* (Ottawa: The Conference Board of Canada, 2012), http://www.conferenceboard.ca/hcp/details/health.aspx.

52. Organization for Economic Co-operation and Development, *Your Better Life Index* (Paris: OECD, 2012), http://www.oecdbetterlifeindex.org/#/11111111111.

53. The Conference Board of Canada, *Health Report Card*.

54. OECD, *Your Better Life Index*.

55. Ibid.

56. Ibid.

57. Ibid.

58. Organization for Economic Co-operation and Development, *Better Life Index, Canada* (Paris: OECD, 2012), http://www.oecdbetterlifeindex.org/topics/community.

59. Ibid.

60. OECD, *Your Better Life Index*.

61. Ibid.

62. Ibid.

63. Ibid.

64. Ibid.

65. Richard Wilkinson and Kate Pickett, *The Spirit Level: Why Equality Is Better for Everyone* (New York: Penguin Books, 2010).

66. Ibid.

67. The Equality Trust, "Teenage Births," 2012, http://www.equalitytrust.org.uk/research/teenage-births.

68. Lori M. Hunter, "U.S. Teen Birth Rate Correlates with State Income Inequality," Population Reference Bureau, April 2012, http://www.prb.org/Articles/2012/us-teen-birthrate-income.aspx.

69. Equality Trust, "Teenage Births."

70. Ibid.

71. The Equality Trust, "Obesity," 2012, http://www.equalitytrust.org.uk/research/obesity.

72. Ibid.

73. The Equality Trust, "Mental Health," 2012, http://www.equalitytrust.org.uk/research/mental-health.

74. Ibid.

75. The Equality Trust, "Drug Abuse," 2012, http://www.equalitytrust.org.uk/research/drug-abuse.

76. Ibid.

77. Ibid.

78. Cathy Schoen, Robin Osborn, David Squires, Michelle M. Doty, Roz Pierson, and Sandra Applebaum, "How Health Insurance Design Affects Access to Care and Costs, by Income, in Eleven Countries," *Health Affairs* 29, no. 12 (2010): 2323–34.

79. Claudia Sanmartin, Christian Houle, Stephane Tremblay, and Jean-Marie Berthelot, "Changes in Unmet Health Care Needs," *Statistics Canada* 13, no. 3 (2002): 15–21.

Chapter 7

1. National Institute on Alcohol Abuse and Alcoholism, US Department of Health and Human Services, "Alcohol, Violence, and Aggression," *Alcohol Alert* 38 (1997), http://pubs.niaaa.nih.gov/publications/aa38.htm.

2. R.J. Stevenson and L.M.V. Forsythe, *Stolen Goods Market in New South Wales: An Interview Study With Imprisoned Burglars* (Sydney: New South Wales Bureau of Crime Statistics and Research, 1998).

3. Canadian Mental Health Association, *Mental Illness and Substance Abuse Disorders* (Ottawa: Canadian Mental Health Association, 2005), http://www.cmha.bc.ca/files/7-mi_substance_use.pdf.

4. Michael Menaster, "Psychiatric Disorders Associated with Criminal Behaviour," *Medscape*, April 12, 2012, http://emedicine.medscape.com/article/294626-overview.

5. Carol Brandford, Diana J. English, and Cathy Widom, *Childhood Victimization and Delinquency, Adult Criminality, and Violent Criminal Behavior* (Washington, DC: US Department of Justice, 2002).

6. Alister Lamont, *Effects of Child Abuse and Neglect for Adult Survivors* (Melbourne: Australian Institute of Family Studies, 2010), http://www.aifs.gov.au/nch/pubs/sheets/rs20/rs20.html.

7. Edwin H. Sutherland, *Principles of Criminology*, 4th ed (Philadelphia: J.B. Lippincott, 1947).

8. Mark Warr, *Companions in Crime: The Social Aspects of Criminal Conduct* (Cambridge, UK: Cambridge University Press, 2002).

9. James C. Howell, "The Impact of Gangs on Community," *National Youth Gang Center Bulletin* 2 (August 2006), http://www.nationalgangcenter.gov/Content/Documents/Impact-of-Gangs-on-Communities.pdf.

10. Dana Mitra, *Pennsylvania's Best Investment: The Social and Economic Benefits of Public Education* (Philadelphia, PA: Education Law Center, n.d.), http://www.elc-pa.org/BestInvestment_Full_Report_6.27.11.pdf.

11. K. McMullen and Jason Gilmore, "A Note on High School Graduation and School Attendance, by Age and Province, 2009/2010," *Education Matters: Insights on Education, Learning and Training in Canada* 7, no. 4 (2010). Statistics Canada catalogue no. 81-004-X, http://www.statcan.gc.ca/pub/81-004-x/2010004/article/11360-eng.htm.

12. A. Himebauch, Matt Kuhls, Lindette Thornton, and Joanna French, "Sociological and Environmental Factors of Criminal Behaviour," University of Delaware, 2000, http://www.udel.edu/chem/C465/senior/fall00/GeneticTesting/enviro.htm.

13. Don C. Gibbons, "Crime and Punishment: A Study in Social Attitudes," *Social Forces* 47, no. 4 (1969), http://www.jstor.org/stable/2574527.

14. Alfred Blumstein, Jacquiline Cohen, Daniel Cork, John Engberg, and George Tita, *Diffusion Processes in Homicide* (Washington, DC: US Department of Justice, 2002), https://www.ncjrs.gov/pdffiles1/nij/grants/193425.pdf.

15. Bruce D. Bartholow, Brad J. Bushman, and Marc A. Sestir, "Chronic Violent Video Game Exposure and Desensitization to Violence: Behavioural and Event-Related Brain Potential Data," *Journal of Experimental Social Psychology* 42, no. 4 (2006): 532–39.

16. Paul Duncum, "Attractions to Violence and the Limits of Education," *Journal of Aesthetic Education* 40, no. 4 (2006), http://muse.jhu.edu/journals/jae/summary/v040/40.4duncum.html.

17. Neckerman and Torche highlight some of these issues in their brief literature review on the links between inequality and crime. Kathryn M. Neckerman and Florencia Torche, "Inequality: Causes and Consequences," *Annual Review of Sociology* 33 (August 2007).

18. Muzafar Shah Habibullah, "Crime and Income Inequality: The Case of Malaysia," *Journal of Politics and Law* 2, no. 1 (2009): 55.

19. Matz Dahlberg and Magnus Gustavsson, "Inequality and Crime: Separating the Effects of Permanent and Transitory Income," *Oxford Bulletin of Economics and Statistics* 70, no. 2 (2008): 129–53.

20. Joanne M. Doyle, Ehsan Ahmed, and Robert N. Horn, "The Effects of Labor Markets and Income Inequality on Crime: Evidence from Panel Data," *Southern Economic Journal* 65, no. 4: 717–38.

21. John Gibson and Bonggeun Kim, "The Effect of Reporting Errors on the Cross-Country Relationship between Inequality and Crime," *Journal of Development Economics* 87 (2008): 247–54.

22. Eric Neumayer, "Inequality and Violent Crime: Evidence from Data on Robbery and Violent Theft," *Journal of Peace Research* 42, no. 1 (2005): 101–12.

23. Lisa Stolzenberg, David Eitle, and Steward J. D'Alessio, "Race, Economic Inequality, and Violent Crime," *Journal of Criminal Justice* 34 (2006): 303.

24. Sener Uludag, Mark Colvin, David Hussey, and Abbey L. Eng, "Democracy, Inequality, Modernization, Routine Activities, and International Variations in Personal Crime Victimization," *International Criminal Justice Review* 19, no. 3 (2009): 265–86.

25. Sully C. Calderon-Martinez and Jorge Noel Valero-Gil, "About the Relation of Inequality and Poverty with Crime in Mexico," *Journal of International Business and Economics* 12, no. 1 (2012): 72–76.

26. Joseph Deutsch, Uriel Spiegel, and Joseph Templeman, "Crime and Income Inequality: An Economic Approach," *Atlantic Economic Journal* 20, no. 4 (1992): 46–54.

27. Stefan Dietrich Josten, "Inequality, Crime and Economic Growth: A Classical Argument for Distributional Equality," *International Tax and Public Finance* 10 (2003): 435–52.

28. Marvin D. Krohn, "Inequality, Unemployment and Crime: A Cross-National Analysis," *Sociological Quarterly* 17, no. 3 (1976): 303–13.

29. Adam Whitworth, "Inequality and Crime across England: A Multilevel Modelling Approach," *Social Policy and Society* 11, no. 1 (2011): 27–40.

30. Martin Daly, Margo Wilson, and Shawn Vasdev, "Income Inequality and Homicide Rates in Canada and the United States," *Canadian Journal of Criminology* 43, no. 2 (2001): 219–36.

31. Francois Bourguignon, Jairo Nunez, and Fabio Sanchez, "A Structural Model of Crime and Inequality in Colombia," *Journal of the European Economic Association* 1, no. 2 (2003): 440–49.

32. Dongxu Wu and Zhongmin Wu, "Crime, Inequality and Unemployment in England and Wales," *Applied Economics* 44 (2012): 3765–75.

33. Gabriel Demombynes and Berk Ozler, "Crime and Local Inequality in South Africa," *Journal of Development Economics* 76 (2005): 265–92.

34. Marg Hooghe, Bram Vanhoutte, Wim Haardyns, and Tuba Bircan, "Unemployment, Inequality, Poverty and Crime," *British Journal of Criminology* 51 (2011): 1–20.

35. Jongmook Choe, "Income Inequality and Crime in the United States," *Economic Letters* 101 (2008): 31–33.

36. Hooghe, Vanhoutte, Haardyns, and Bircan, "Unemployment."

37. W. Henry Chiu and Paul Madden, "Burglary and Income Inequality," *Journal of Public Economics* 69 (1998): 123–41.

38. Fahui Wang and Martin T. Arnold, "Localized Income Inequality, Concentrated Disadvantage and Homicide," *Applied Geography* 28 (2008): 259–70.

39. Ibid., 259.

40. Pablo Fajnzylber, Daniel Lederman, and Norman Loayza, "Inequality and Violent Crime," *Journal of Law and Economics* 45, no. 1 (2002): 1.

41. Bruce P. Kennedy, Ichiro Kawachi, Deborah Prothrow-Stith, Kimberly Lochner, and Vanita Gupta, "Social Capital, Income Inequality, and Firearm Violent Crime," *Social Science & Medicine* 47, no. 1 (1998): 7–17.

42. Christopher Jencks, "Does Inequality Matter?" *Daedalus* 131, no. 1 (2002): 49–65.

43. T. Wing Lo and Guoping Jiang, "Inequality, Crime and the Floating Population in China," *Asian Criminology* 1 (2006): 103–18.

44. Susanne Karstedt, "Legacies of a Culture of Inequality: The Janus Face of Crime in Post-Communist Countries," *Crime, Law and Social Change* 40, no. 2 (2003): 295–320.

45. Ibid., 295.

46. David Halpern, "Moral Values, Social Trust and Inequality," *British Journal of Criminology* 41 (2001): 236–51.

47. Ibid., 236.

48. Stephen Cernkovich, review of *The Many Colors of Crime: Inequalities of Race, Ethnicity, and Crime in America*, edited by Ruth D. Peterson, Lauren J. Krivo, and John Hagan, *American Journal of Sociology* 114, no. 1 (2008): 248.

49. Karen Parker, *Unequal Crime Decline: Theorizing Race, Urban Inequality, and Criminal Violence* (New York: New York University Press, 2008).

50. Lesley Williams Reid, "Unequal Crime Decline: Theorizing Race, Urban Inequality, and Criminal Violence," *Contemporary Sociology* 38, no. 5: 424–25; Lisa Stolzenberg, David Eitle, and Stewart J. D'Alessio, "Race, Economic Inequality, and Violent Crime," *Journal of Criminal Justice* 34: 303–16.

51. Bruce Western and Becky Pettit, "Beyond Crime and Punishment: Prisons and Inequality," *Contexts* 1, no. 3 (2002): 37–43; Bruce Western, "Mass Imprisonment and Economic Inequality," *Social Research* 74, no. 2 (2007): 509–33.

52. Western and Pettit, "Beyond Crime."

53. John Hagan, "Beyond the Classics: Reform and Renewal in the Study of Crime and Inequality," *Journal of Research in Crime and Delinquency* 30, no. 4 (1993).

54. Ibid., 485–86.

55. Ibid., 487.

56. J.R. Blau and P.M. Blau, "The Cost of Inequality: Metropolitan Structure and Violent Crime," *American Sociological Review* 47 (1982): 45–62.

57. Hagan, "Beyond the Classics," 487.

58. Ibid., 486.

59. Ibid., 490.

60. Edwin H. Sutherland, *White Collar Crime* (New Haven: Yale University Press, 1983).

61. Ibid., 88.

62. Ibid., 234.

63. Jessica Klein, "Cultural Capital and High School Bullies: How Social Inequality Impacts School Violence," *Men and Masculinities* 9 (2006): 53–75.

64. Ibid.

65. Ibid.

66. Ibid.

67. J.S. Hong, H. Cho, P. Allen-Meares, and D.L. Espelage, "The Social Ecology of the Columbine High School Shootings," *Children and Youth Services Review* 33 (2011): 863.

68. Klein, "Cultural Capital," 64.

69. Ibid., 66.

70. Ibid., 60.

71. Hong, Cho, Allen-Meares, and Espelage, "Social Ecology," 863.

72. Jessica Klein, "Sexuality and School Shootings: What Role Does Teasing Play in School Massacres?" *Journal of Homosexuality* 51 (2006): 39–62.

73. Ibid., 43.

74. Hong, Cho, Allen-Meares, and Espelage, "Social Ecology," 863.

75. Glenn W. Muschert, "Research in School Shootings," *Sociology Compass* 1 (2007): 68.

76. Klein, "Cultural Capital," 61.

77. Ibid., 66.

78. Russ Schanlaub, "School Shootings," *Law & Order* 57 (2009): 56–60.

79. N. Gibbs, T. Roche, A. Goldstein, M. Harrington, and R. Woodbury, "The Columbine Tapes," *Time International* (1999): 154.

80. Muschert, "Research in School Shootings," 63.

81. Klein, "Sexuality and School Shootings," 49.

82. Muschert, "Research in School Shootings," 63.

83. Hong, Cho, Allen-Meares, and Espelage, "Social Ecology," 863.

84. Ronald C. Kramer, "Poverty, Inequality, and Youth Violence," *Annals of the American Academy of Political and Social Science* 567 (2000): 127.

85. Ibid.

86. Hong, Cho, Allen-Meares, and Espelage, "Social Ecology," 864.

87. Kramer, "Poverty, Inequality, and Youth Violence," 129.

88. Ibid., 131.

89. Michael Foucault, *Discipline and Punish: The Birth of the Prison* (New York: Vintage Books, 1995).

90. Erving Goffman, *Asylums: Essays on the Social Situation of Mental Patients and Other Inmates* (Chicago: Aldine Publishing Co., 1962).

91. Donald Clemmer, *The Prison Community* (New York: Holt, Rinehart and Winston, 1965).

92. Samuel Perreault, "The Incarceration of Aboriginal People in Adult Correctional Services," *Juristat* 29, no. 3 (2009): 5. Statistics Canada catalogue no. 85-002-X.

93. Ibid.

94. Ibid., 9.

95. Ibid., 15.

96. Shannon Brennan, "Police-Reported Crime Statistics in Canada, 2011," *Juristat* (2012): 6. Statistics Canada catatlogue no. 85-002-X.

97. Bruce Western, "Mass Imprisonment and Economic Inequality," *Social Research* 74, no. 2 (2007): 509–33.

98. Ibid.

99. Cheryl Marie Webster and Anthony N. Doob, "Punitive Trends and Stable Imprisonment Rates in Canada," *Crime and Justice* 36 (2007).

Chapter 8

1. Konrad Lorenz, *Studies in Animal and Human Behaviour* (Cambridge, MA: Harvard University Press, 1971).

2. Sigmund Freud, *Civilization and Its Discontents* (London: Penguin, 2002); see also the Einstein-Freud correspondence on war at http://www.zionism-israel.com/Albert_Einstein/Einstein_Freud_Why_War.htm.

3. George Stroumboulopoulos, *Love, Hate, and Propaganda, Part II: 1939/1940: Selling War* (Toronto: CBC, 2009), http://www.cbc.ca/documentaries/lovehatepropaganda/episode-guide.html.

4. Thomas Malthus, *An Essay on the Principle of Population* (London: 1798).

5. Leila Austin, "The Politics of Youth Bulge: From Islamic Activism to Democratic Reform in the Middle East and North Africa," *The SAIS Review of International Affairs* 31, no. 2 (2011): 81–96.

6. Robert Macculloch, "Income Inequality and the Taste for Revolution," *Journal of Law and Economics* 48, no. 1 (2005): 93–123.

7. Ibid., 93.

8. Walter L. Goldfrank, "Inequality and Revolution in Rural Mexico," *Social and Economic Studies* 25, no. 4 (1976): 397–410.

9. Ibid., 407–8.

10. Melinda Mills, "Globalization and Inequality," *European Sociological Review* 25, no. 1 (2009): 1–8.

11. E. Wayne Nafziger and Juha Auvinen, "Economic Development, Inequality, War, and State Violence," *World Development* 30, no. 2 (2002): 153.

12. "Globalisation, Inequality and Violence," *Whitehall Papers* 70, no. 1 (2008): 40.

13. Christopher Cramer, "Does Inequality Cause Conflict?" *Journal of International Development* 15 (2003): 397–412.

14. Ibid.

15. Hari Bapugi and Suhaib Riaz, "Economic Inequality and Management," *Human Relations* 65 (2012).

16. Samuel Bowles and Arjun Jayadev, "Guard Labor," *Journal of Development Economics* 79, no. 2 (2006): 328–48.

17. Giacomo De Luca and Petros G. Sekeris, "Land Inequality and Conflict Intensity," *Public Choice* 150 (2012): 119–35.

18. Carrie L. Yodanis, "Gender Inequality, Violence against Women, and Fear: A Cross-National Test of the Feminist Theory of Violence against Women," *Journal of Interpersonal Violence* 19, no. 6 (2004): 655–75.

19. Carla M. Machain, T. Clifton Morgan, and Patrick M. Regan, "Deterring Rebellion," *Foreign Policy Analysis* 7, no. 3 (2011): 295–316.

20. Juan F. Vargas, "Rebellion, Repression and Welfare," *Defense and Peace Economics* 22, no. 5 (2011): 563.

21. Richard Wilkinson, "Why Is Violence More Common Where Inequality Is Greater?" *Annals New York Academy of Sciences*: 1 (2004).

22. Ibid., 1.

23. James A. Robinson, "Social Identity, Inequality, and Conflict," *Economics of Governance* 2 (1999): 85–99.

24. Marie L. Besancon, "Relative Resources: Inequality in Ethnic Wars, Revolutions, and Genocides," *Journal of Peace Research* 42, no. 4 (2005): 393–415.

25. Ibid.

26. Gudrun Ostby, "Polarization, Horizontal Inequalities and Violent Civil Conflict," *Journal of Peace Research* 45, no. 2 (2008): 143–62.

27. Graham K. Brown and Arnim Langer, "Horizontal Inequalities and Conflict: A Critical Review and Research Agenda," *Conflict, Security and Development* 10, no. 1: 27–55.

28. Ibid.

29. Lars-Erik Cederman, Nils B. Weidmann, and Kristian Skrede Gleditsch, "Horizontal Inequalities and Ethnonationalist Civil War: A Global Comparison," *American Political Science Review* 105, no. 3 (2011): 478–95.

30. Rachael Diprose, "Decentralization, Horizontal Inequalities and Conflict Management in Indonesia," *Ethnopolitics* 8, no. 1 (2009): 107–34.

31. Ibid., 107.

32. Joshua R. Gubler and Joel Sawat Selway, "Horizontal Inequality, Crosscutting Cleavages, and Civil War," *Journal of Conflict Resolution* 56, no. 2 (2012): 206–32.

33. Ibid.

34. Ostby, "Polarization."

35. Gudrun Ostby, Henrik Urdal, Mohammad Zulfan Tadjoeddin, S. Mansoob Murshed, and Havard Strand, "Population Pressure, Horizontal Inequality and Political Violence: A Disaggregated Study of Indonesian Provinces, 1990–2003," *Journal of Development Studies* 47, no. 3 (2011): 377–98.

36. Ibid., 377.

37. Pauline E. Peters, "Inequality and Social Conflict over Land in Africa," *Journal of Agrarian Change* 4, no. 3 (2004): 269.

38. Gjermund Saether, "Inequality, Security and Violence," *European Journal of Development Research* 13, no. 1 (2001): 193–212.

39. Ibid., 210.

40. Frances Stewart, *War and Underdevelopment* (New York: Oxford University Press, 2001).

41. Frances Stewart, "Inequalities and Conflict: Choosing Policies for Peace," IFPRI Policy Seminar, February 23, 2010, http://www.youtube.com/watch?v=A1wNwjZqEgM.

42. Francis Stewart, "Root Causes of Violent Conflict in Developing Countries," *British Medical Journal* 324 (February 9, 2002): 344.

43. Ibid.

44. Paul Collier and Anke Hoeffler, "Greed and Grievance in Civil War," *Oxford Economic Papers* 56, no. 4 (2004): 563–95; James D. Fearon and David D. Laitin, "Ethnicity, Insurgency, and Civil War," *American Political Science Review* 97, no. 1

(2003): 75–90; Havard Hegre, Ranveig Gissinger, and Nils Petter Gleditsch, "Globalization and Internal Conflict," in *Globalization and Armed Conflict*, eds. Gerald Schneider, Katherine Barbieri, Nils Petter Gleditsch, 251–76 (Oxford: Rowman & Littlefield, 2003).

45. Jean-Yves Duclos, Joan Esteban, and Debraj Ray, "Polarization: Concepts, Measurement, Estimation," *Econometrica* 72, no. 6 (2004): 1737–72.

46. Ted R. Gurr, *Peoples versus States: Minorities at Risk in the New Century* (Washington, DC: United States Institute of Peace Press, 2000); Frances Stewart, "Crisis Prevention: Tackling Horizontal Inequalities," *Oxford Development Studies* 28, no. 3 (2000): 245–62.

47. Collier and Hoeffler, "Greed and Grievance in Civil War."

48. Gurr, *Peoples versus States*; Charles Tilly, *From Mobilization to Revolution* (Reading, MA: Addison-Wesley, 1978); Joan-Maria Esteban and Debraj Ray, "On the Measurement of Polarization," *Econometrica* 62, no. 4 (1994): 819–51.

49. Esteban and Ray, "Measurement of Polarization."

50. Gurr, *Peoples versus States*.

51. Gudrun Ostby, "Polarization, Horizontal Inequalities and Violent Civil Conflict," *Journal of Peace Research* 45, no. 2 (2008): 143–62.

52. Ibid.

53. Such studies include Collier and Hoeffler, "Greed and Grievance in Civil War"; James D. Fearon and David D. Laitin, "Ethnicity, Insurgency, and Civil War," *American Political Science Review* 97, no. 1 (2003): 75–90; Havard Hegre, Ranveig Gissinger, and Nils Petter Gleditsch, "Globalization and Internal Conflict," in *Globalization and Armed Conflict*, eds. Gerald Schneider, Katherine Barbieri, and Nils Petter Gleditsch, 251–76 (Oxford: Rowman & Littlefield, 2003).

54. Yodanis, "Gender Inequality, Violence against Women, and Fear," R.B. Whiley, "The Paradoxical Relationship between Gender Inequality and Rape: Toward a Refined Theory," *Gender & Society* 15 (2001): 531–55; Kersti Yllö, "The Status of Women, Marital Equality, and Violence against Wives," *Journal of Family Issues* 5 (1984): 307–20.

55. Yodanis, "Gender Inequality, Violence against Women, and Fear."

56. Johan Galtung, *Peace: Research, Education, Action. Essays in Peace Research*, vol. 1 (Bucuresti, Romania: CIPEXIM, 1975); Johan Galtung, "Cultural Violence," *Journal of Peace Research* 27, no. 3 (1990): 291–305.

57. Elizabeth M. Brumfield, "Origins of Social Inequity," in *Research Frontiers in Anthropology*, eds. Carol R. Ember and Melvin Ember (Englewood Cliffs, NJ: Prentice Hall, 1994); Gerald M. Erchak and Richard Rosenfeld, "Societal Isolations, Violent Norms, and Gender Relations: A Re-examination and Extension of Levinson's Model of Wife Beating," *Cross-Cultural Research* 28, no. 2 (1994): 11–133.

58. Mary Caprioli, "Gender Equality and State Aggression: The Impact of Domestic Gender Equality on State First Use of Force," *International Interactions* 29, no. 3 (2003): 195–214.

59. Mary Caprioli, "Primed for Violence: The Role of Gender Inequality in Predicting Internal Conflict," *International Studies Quarterly* 49 (2005): 161–78.

60. J. Huber, "Macro-Micro Links in Gender Stratification," in *Macro–Micro Linkages*, 11–25 (Newbury Park, CA: Sage Publications. 1991).

61. R.L. Blumberg, *Making the Case for the Gender Variable: Women and the Wealth and Well-Being of Nations* (Washington, DC: Agency for International Development: Office of Women in Development, 1989).

62. Erik Melander, "Gender Equality and Intrastate Armed Conflict," *International Studies Quarterly* 49 (2005): 695–714.

63. Caprioli, "Primed for Violence."

64. Mary Caprioli, "Gendered Conflict," *Journal of Peace Research* 37, no. 1 (January 2000): 51–58.

65. C. Bunch and R. Carrillo, "Global Violence against Women: The Challenge to Human Rights and Development," in *World Security*, eds. M.T. Klare and Y. Chandrani, 229–48 (New York: St. Martins Press, 1998); S. Rowbotham, *Dreams and Dilemmas* (London: Virago Press, 1983).

66. United Nations Population Fund, "Ending Widespread Violence against Women," 2003, http://www.unfpa.org/gender/violence.htm.

67. J.A. Tickner, *Gendering World Politics* (New York: Columbia University Press, 2001).

68. L.D. Kaplan, "Woman as Caretaker: An Archetype that Supports Patriarchal Militarism," *Hypatia* (1994): 123–34.

69. Joshua S. Goldstein, *War and Gender: How Gender Shapes the War System and Vice Versa* (New York: Cambridge University Press, 2001).

70. Caprioli, "Gendered Conflict," 61.

71. J. Mostov, "Sexing the Nation/Desexing the Body: Politics of National Identity in the Former Yugoslavia," in *Gender Ironies of Nationalism: Sexing the Nation*, ed. T. Mayer, 41–59 (London: Routledge, 2000).

72. K. Jayawardena, *Feminism and Nationalism in the Third World* (London: Zed Books, 1986).

73. David Fite, Marc Genest, and Clyde Wilcox, "Gender Differences in Foreign Policy Attitudes," *American Political Quarterly* 18 (1990): 492–513; Lise Togeby, "The Gender Gap in Foreign Policy Attitudes," *Journal of Peace Research* 31, no. 4 (1994): 375–92.

74. Mary Caprioli and Mark A. Boyer, "Gender, Violence, and International Crisis," *Journal of Conflict Resolution* 45 (2001): 503–18.

75. J.J. Pettman, *Women, Nationalism and the State: Towards an International Feminist Perspective*, Occasional Paper 4 (Bangkok: Gender and Development Studies Unit, Asian Institute of Technology, 1992).

76. Caprioli, "Primed for Violence."

77. C. Tilly, *From Mobilization to Revolution* (New York: Random House, 1978).

78. J.C. Davies, "Toward a Theory of Revolution," *American Sociological Review* 27 (1962): 5–19.

79. Ted R. Gurr and Barbara Harff, *Ethnic Conflict in World Politics* (Boulder: Westview Press, 1994).

80. Tilly, *From Mobilization to Revolution*.

81. S.M. Murshed, "Civil War, Conflict and Underdevelopment," *Journal of Peace Research* 39, no. 4 (2002): 389; Davies, "Toward a Theory of Revolution."

82. Galtung, *Peace*.

83. C. Pateman, *Participation and Democratic Theory* (Cambridge, UK: Cambridge University Press, 1970).

84. T. Sideris, "Rape in War and Peace: Social Context, Gender, Power and Identity," in *The Aftermath: Women in Post-Conflict Transformation*, eds. S. Meintjes, A. Pillay, and M. Tursher, 142–58 (London, UK: Zed Books Ltd., 2001).

85. Galtung, *Peace*.

86. S.M. Murshed and Scott Gates, "Spatial-Horizontal Inequality and the Maoist Insurgency in Nepal," *Review of Development Economics* 9, no. 1 (2005): 121–34; Stewart, "Crisis Prevention."

87. Nicholas Sambanis, "Do Ethnic and Nonethnic Civil Wars Have the Same Causes? A Theoretical and Empirical Inquiry (Part I)," *Journal of Conflict Resolution* 45, no. 3 (2001): 259–82.

88. James D. Fearon and David D. Laitin, "Ethnicity, Insurgency, and Civil War," *American Political Science Review* 97, no. 1 (2003): 75–90.

89. Jose G. Montalvo and Marta Reynal-Querol, "Ethnic Diversity and Economic Development," *Journal of Development Economics* 76, no. 2 (2005): 293–323.

90. Minority Rights Group International, "War: The Impact on Minority and Indigenous Children," 1997, http://www.minorityrights.org/10111/reports/war-the -impact-on-minority-and-indigenous-children.html.

91. Gurr, *Peoples versus States*.

92. Anthony D. Smith, *The Ethnic Origins of Nations* (Oxford, UK: Blackwell, 1986).

93. Karoly Takacs, "Effects of Network Segregation in Intergroup Conflict: An Experimental Analysis," *Connections* 27, no. 2 (2007): 59–76.

94. Macartan Humphreys and Jeremy M. Weinstein, "Who Fights? The Determinants of Participation in Civil War," *American Political Science Review* 52, no. 2 (2008): 436–55.

95. Martin Lipset and Stein Rokkan, "Cleavage Structures, Party Systems, and Voter Alignments: An Introduction," in *Party Systems and Voter Alignments: Cross-National Perspectives*, eds. S.M. Lipset and S. Rokkan, 1–64 (London: Free Press, 1967).

96. Ibid.

97. Seymour-Martin Lipset, *Political Man* (Baltimore: Johns Hopkins University Press, 1960).

98. Joshua R. Gubler and Joel S. Selway, "Horizontal Inequality, Crosscutting Cleavages, and Civil War," *Journal of Conflict Resolution* 56, no. 2 (2012): 206–32.

99. Gubler and Selway, "Horizontal Inequality"; Donald L. Horowitz, *Ethnic Groups in Conflict* (Berkeley: University of California Press, 1985); Lipset, *Political Man*; Douglas W. Rae and Michael Taylor, *The Analysis of Political Cleavages* (New Haven, CT: Yale University Press, 1970).

100. Gubler and Selway, "Horizontal Inequality."

Chapter 9

1. The Conference Board of Canada, "Income Inequality," January 2013, http://www.conferenceboard.ca/hcp/details/society/income-inequality.aspx.

2. Jeffrey Simpson, "Do We Care that Canada Is an Unequal Society?" *Globe and Mail*, July 20, 2011, http://www.theglobeandmail.com/commentary/do-we-care-that-canada-is-an-unequal-society/article587510.

3. Ibid.

4. Catherine Cozzarelli, Anna V. Wilkinson, and Michael J. Tagler, "Attitudes toward the Poor and Attributions for Poverty," *Journal of Social Issues* 57, no. 2 (2001): 207–27.

5. Dorota Lepianka, Wim V. Oorschot, and John Gelissen, "Popular Explanations of Poverty: A Critical Discussion of Empirical Research," *Journal of Social Policy* 38, no. 3 (2009): 421–38.

6. Cozzarelli, Wilkinson, and Tagler, "Attitudes toward the Poor."

7. Linda I. Reutter, Gerry Veenstra, Miriam J. Stewart, Dennis Raphael, Rhonda Love, Edward Makwarimba, and Susan McMurray, "Public Attributions for Poverty in Canada," *Canadian Review of Sociology and Anthropology* 43, no. 1 (2006).

8. Ibid.

9. Robert D. Crutchfield and David Pettinicchio, "'Cultures of Inequality': Ethnicity, Immigration, Social Welfare, and Imprisonment," *Annals of the American Academy of Political and Social Science* 623 (2009): 134–47.

10. *Income, Poverty and Health Insurance in the United States: 2011—Highlights* (Washington, DC: Social, Economic, and Housing Statistics Division, US Census Bureau, 2012), http://www.census.gov/hhes/www/poverty/data/incpovhlth/2011/highlights.html.

11. Chantal Collin and Hilary Jensen, *A Statistical Profile of Poverty in Canada* (Ottawa: Parliamentary Information and Research Service, Library of Parliament, 2009), http://canadianroots.ca/data/uploads/resources/prb0917-e.pdf.

12. Linda I. Reutter, Gerry Veenstra, Miriam J. Stewart, Dennis Raphael, Rhonda Love, Edward Makwarimba, and Susan McMurray, "Public Attributions for Poverty in Canada," *Canadian Review of Sociology and Anthropology* 43, no. 1 (2006).

13. Marina Bastounis, David Leiser, and Christine Roland-Levy, "Psychosocial Variables Involved in the Construction of Lay Thinking about the Economy: Results of a Cross-National Survey," *Journal of Economic Psychology* 25 (2004): 263–78; Chris L. Coryn, "Antecedents of Attitudes towards the Poor," *Indiana Univserity South Bend Undergraduate Research Journal* (2002).

14. Bastounis, Leiser, and Roland-Levy, "Psychosocial Variables"; Cozzarelli, Wilkinson, and Tagler, "Attitudes toward the Poor."

15. Robert E. Lane, "Self-Reliance and Empathy: The Enemies of Poverty—and of the Poor," *Political Psychology* 22, no. 3 (2001): 473–92.

16. Bill O'Grady, Stephen Gaetz, and Kristy Buccieri, *Can I See Your ID? The Policing of Youth Homelessness in Toronto* (Toronto: Justice for Children and Youth and Homeless Hub Press, 2011), http://www.homelesshub.ca/ResourceFiles/CanISeeYourID_nov9.pdf.

17. Dorota Lepianka, Wim V. Oorschot, and John Gelissen, "Popular Explanations of Poverty: A Critical Discussion of Empirical Research," *Journal of Social Policy* 38, no. 3 (2009): 421–38.

18. Clarke E. Cochran, Lawrence C. Mayer, T.R. Carr, N. Joseph Cayer, Mark J. McKenzie, and Laura R. Peck, *American Public Policy: An Introduction*, 10th ed. (Boston, MA: Wadsworth Cengage Learning, 2012); Joseph M. Bessette, John L. Pitney Jr., Lyle C. Brown, Joyce A. Langenegger, Sonia R. Garcia, Ted A. Lewis, and Robert E. Biles, *American Government and Politics: Deliberation, Democracy, and Citizenship* (Boston, MA: Wadsworth, Cengage Learning, 2012).

19. Organization for Economic Co-operation and Development, "Revenue Statistics—Comparative Tables," *OECD StatExtracts*, http://stats.oecd.org/Index .aspx?QueryId=21699.

20. Ibid.

21. Luiz de Mello and Erwin R. Tiongson, "Income Inequality and Redistributive Government Spending," *Public Finance Review* 34, no. 3 (2006): 282–305.

22. Inter-Parliamentary Union, "Women in National Parliaments," February 1, 2013, http://www.ipu.org/wmn-e/classif.htm.

23. Nuray Sakalh-Uğurlu and Peter Glick, "Sexism and Attitudes toward Women who Engage in Premarital Sex in Turkey," *Journal of Sex Research* 40, no. 3 (2003): 296–302; Margaret De Judicibus and Marita P. McCabe, "Blaming the Target of Sexual Harassment: Impact of Gender Role, Sexist Attitudes, and Work Role," *Sex Roles* 44, no. 7–8 (2001): 401–17.

24. Shelley Phipps, *The Impact of Poverty on Health: A Scan of Research Literature* (Toronto: Canadian Institute for Health Information, 2003); Dennis Raphael, Toba Bryant, and Ann Curry-Stevens, "Toronto Charter Outlines Future Health

Policy Directions for Canada and Elsewhere," *Health Promotion International* 19, no. 2 (2004): 269–73.

25. Lyle Scruggs, "The Generosity of Social Insurance, 1971–2002," *Oxford Review of Economic Policy* 22, no. 3 (2006): 349–64.

26. Meredith Minkler and Pamela Fadem, "'Successful Aging': A Disability Perspective," *Journal of Disability Policy Studies* 12, no. 4 (2002): 229–35.

27. Ibid.

28. Laurent Begue and Marina Bastounis, "Two Spheres of Belief in Justice: Extensive Support for the Bidimensional Model of Belief in a Just World," *Journal of Personality* 71, no. 3 (2003): 435–63; Robbie M. Sutton and Karen M. Douglas, "Justice for All, or Just for Me? More Evidence of the Importance of the Self-Other Distinction in Just-World Beliefs," *Personality and Individual Differences* 39, no. 3 (2005): 637–45.

29. Laurent Begue and Marina Bastounis, "Two Spheres of Belief in Justice: Extensive Support for the Bidimensional Model of Belief in a Just World," *Journal of Personality* 71, no. 3 (2003): 435–63.

30. J. Dzuka and C. Dalbert, "The Belief in a Just World and Subjective Well-Being in Old Age," *Aging and Mental Health* 10, no. 5 (2006): 439–44.

31. Ramzi Nasser, Jacqueline Doumit, and James Carifio, "Well-Being and Belief in a Just World Among Rest Home Residents," *Social Behavior and Personality: An International Journal* 39, no. 5 (2011): 655–70.

32. Anna Duner and Monica Nordstrom, "Intentions and Strategies among Elderly People: Coping in Everyday Life," *Journal of Aging Studies* 19 (2005): 437–51.

33. Alison L. Chasteen and Scott F. Madey, "Belief in a Just World and the Perceived Injustice of Dying Young or Old," *Journal of Death and Dying* 47, no. 4 (2003): 313–26.

34. Mia Dauvergne, "Crime Statistics in Canada, 2007," *Juristat* 28, no. 7 (2007). Statistics Canada catalogue no. 85-002-X, http://www.statcan.gc.ca/pub/85-002-x/85-002-x2008007-eng.pdf.

35. *White Paper on Crime Discussion Document No. 4 "The Community and the Criminal Justice System"* (Washington, DC: Department of Justice and Equality, 2011), http://www.justice.ie/en/JELR/Pages/WPOC_Discussion_Doc_4.

36. Daniel W. Brickman, "The Implications of Essentialist Beliefs for Prejudice" (doctoral dissertation, The University of Michigan, 2009); Jane P. Sheldon, Carla A. Pfeffer, Toby E. Jayaratne, Merle Feldbaum, and Elizabeth M. Petty, "Beliefs about the Etiology of Homosexuality and about the Ramifications of Discovering Its Possible Genetic Origin," *Journal of Homosexuality* 52, no. 3–4 (2007): 111–50; Peter B. Wood and John P. Bartkowski, "Attribution Style and Public Policy Attitudes toward Gay Rights," *Social Science Quarterly* 85, no. 1 (2004): 58–74.

37. Amie C. Braman and Alan J. Lambert, "Punishing Individuals for Their Infirmities: Effects of Personal Responsibility, Just-World Beliefs, and In-Group/Out-Group Status," *Journal of Applied Social Psychology* 31, no. 5 (2001): 1096–1109;

Nita Mawar, Seema Sahay, Apoorvaa Pandit, and Uma Mahajan, "The Third Phase of HIV Pandemic: Social Consequences of HIV/AIDS Stigma and Discrimination and Future Needs," *Indian Journal of Medical Research* 122, no. 6 (2005): 471–84; S. Surlis and A. Hyde, "HIV-Positive Patients' Experiences of Stigma During Hospitlization," *Journal of Association of Nurses in AIDS Care* 12, no. 6 (2001): 68–77.

38. Wood and Bartkowski "Attribution Style and Public Policy."

39. Melanie A. Morrison, Todd G. Morrison, and Randall Franklin, "Modern and Old-Fashioned Homonegativity among Samples of Canadian and American University Students," *Journal of Cross-Cultural Psychology* 40, no. 4 (2009): 523–42.

40. A. Furnham, "Just World Beliefs in Twelve Societies," *Journal of Social Psychology* 133 (1991), 317–29.

41. A.J. Lambert, T. Burroughs, and T. Nguyen, "Perceptions of Risk and the Buffering Hypothesis: The Role of Just World Beliefs and Right Wing Authoritarianism," *Personality and Social Psychology Bulletin* 25, no. 6 (1999), 643–56.

42. Daniel Bar-Tal, "Collective Memory of Physical Violence: Its Contribution to the Culture of Violence," in *The Role of Memory in Ethnic Conflict*, eds. E. Cairns and M.D. Roe, 77–93 (Houndmills, England: Palgrave Macmillan, 2003).

43. Ibid.

44. Cheryl R. Kaiser, S. Brooke Vick, and Brenda Major, "A Prospective Investigation of the Relationship between Just-World Beliefs and the Desire for Revenge after September 11, 2001," *Psychological Science* 15, no. 7 (2004): 503–6.

45. Elizabeth J. Krumrei, Annette Mahoney, and Kenneth I. Pargament, "Demonization of Divorce: Prevalence Rates and Links to Postdivorce Adjustment," *Family Relations* 60, no. 1 (2011): 90–103.

46. Richard Sennett and Jonathan Cobb, *The Hidden Injuries of Class* (London: Cambridge University Press, 1972).

47. Jeffrey Simpson, "Do We Care that Canada Is an Unequal Society?" *Globe and Mail*, July 20, 2011, http://www.theglobeandmail.com/commentary/do-we-care-that-canada-is-an-unequal-society/article587510.

48. Ibid.

49. Gosta Esping-Andersen, *Social Class, Social Democracy and State Policy: Party Policy and Party Decomposition in Denmark and Sweden* (Copenhagen: Nyt fra Samfundsvidensbaberne, 1980).

Index